KENTUCKY:
DECADES OF DISCORD
1865-1900

KENTUCKY: DECADES OF DISCORD 1865-1900

Hambleton Tapp
James C. Klotter

THE KENTUCKY HISTORICAL SOCIETY
FRANKFORT, KENTUCKY

ISBN-10: 0-916968-05-7 (cloth)
ISBN-13: 978-0-916968-05-2 (cloth)
ISBN-13: 978-0-916968-36-6 (paper)

Library of Congress Catalog Card Number: 75-30400

Printed in the United States of America

To Holman Hamilton

CONTENTS

ILLUSTRATIONS

PREFACE

In early 1973, the editorial staff of the Kentucky Historical Society projected a four volume history of Kentucky and reported the proposal to the Executive Committee, which endorsed it. The first of the four volumes, *Kentucky: Settlement and Statehood, 1750-1800* by George Morgan Chinn, recently came off the press. This book is the second volume to be published. Two others, covering the 1900-1975 period, and the 1800-1865 era, are in preparation. Two of the purposes of the project are (1) to treat these four periods of Kentucky history in greater depth than has been to date and (2) to compose the material in a manner that will attract the general reading public, as well as historians.

Why was this volume written? The simplest answer is that such a contribution was greatly needed. Little is known about this important period, perhaps because no in-depth history of it has appeared. The general histories of the Commonwealth treat the post-Civil War period rather cursorily. One of the most used histories, Collins' two volume work, ends in 1874. Survey histories, including Thomas D. Clark's excellent one, are too limited in space to investigate in depth. The able Zachariah Frederick Smith in his 1895 revised edition devoted but 78 out of 858 pages to the period; Nathaniel Southgate Shaler's 1884 work allowed only 16 out of 408 pages; and William E. Connelley and E. Merton Coulter's more recent two volume work covers the era in less than 100 of their 1200 pages. Almost every consideration leads to the conclusion that a full treatment of the 1865-1900 period has been long overdue. This volume attempts to fill that historical void.

The authors were under few illusions regarding the complexity of the period. Commercial, political, cultural, sectional, and agricultural rivalries abound throughout. Generalizations remain difficult and dangerous, but must be made.

Kentucky society was one of contradictions; it was in change but unchanging, educated but illiterate, genteel and cultured but violent and crude, urbanized and industrialized but rural and agricultural, complex and diverse but simple and stereotyped. The society produced a James Lane Allen and a Frank Duveneck and at the same time a "Devil Anse" Hatfield. It gave the nation such leaders as Henry Watterson and John G. Carlisle but also such men as "Boss" Whallen. It furnished great orators, but also demagogues; dedicated statesmen, but also crass politicians; strong leaders but also weak followers; active reformers, but also repressive reactionaries. The Commonwealth felt the divisive effects of Civil War, the despair of depression, the shame of scandal, and the shock of assassination. At a time when America was being transformed and was leaving behind one way of life, Kentucky often fought that transformation and met change reluctantly. It is that society, that era, that this work examines.

ACKNOWLEDGEMENTS

As usual, space does not permit the authors to thank each person who has given assistance. First and foremost, however, recognition must be given the Kentucky Historical Society Executive Committee, who approved the project, the director, William R. Buster, who supported it at every turn, and the various staff members of the Society, each one who aided in his or her special way. The library staff, composed of Anne McDonnell, Linda Anderson, Rose Lawrence, Doris Nave, and others also deserve special recognition. Dianne Wells assisted in the typing and retyping of the manuscript. Elizabeth Perkins, Nathan Prichard, Martha Blazer and Mary Hamel have aided in the gathering of illustrations. Mary Lou Madigan read and commented on the manuscript, typed much of the final draft, and helped proof the finished project.

In Lexington, the staff of the Margaret I. King Library, University of Kentucky, has given full support. Many of the newspapers used were read in the library's microfilm area and Mary A. Sullivan and her staff are complimented for the fine collection of newspapers they have assembled. In Special Collections, Jacqueline Bull shared her profound knowledge of the period, pointed out items of interest and suggested applicable manuscript sources. Anyone who has worked with her knows her professionalism, kindness and warmth. Charles Atcher, Charles C. Hay III and virtually the entire Special Collections staff were significantly helpful. James R. Bentley and Nelson L. Dawson of The Filson Club as usual provided meaningful assistance and direction in locating useful materials

ACKNOWLEDGEMENTS

in their extensive collection. Some items were examined in the Lexington Public Library, the University of Louisville Library, the Louisville Free Public Library, the Kentucky Library at Western Kentucky University, the Eastern Kentucky Library and the Manuscript Division, Library of Congress. All their staffs aided. J. Winston Coleman, Jr., George M. Chinn, Lowell H. Harrison and other historians have supported and encouraged the project almost from its inception. David F. Burg, himself the author of a volume recently published by the University Press of Kentucky, read the entire manuscript and offered suggestions that improved the work. Material was quoted with permission from Francis Butler Simkins and Charles P. Roland, *A History of the South,* © 1972 by Alfred A. Knopf, Inc.

The authors recognize the value of indirect aid as well. Dr. Tapp's wife Zerelda, his children and grandchildren, and Dr. Klotter's wife Freda, and his children, have, in their own way, contributed significantly toward whatever success this work may achieve.

I

A BACKWARD LOOK

The end of the Civil War found Kentucky in a deplorable condition. During the conflict the state had sustained heavy human and economic losses, and the internecine strife had left violent antipathies. The people were in a mood to hate, retaliate, and destroy. It seemed that a black cloud hung over the "dark and bloody ground"; there was little joy in the land.

Throughout most of the struggle the Commonwealth had been under military control and guarded by Union troops. Military rule had at times been harsh, oppressive, and highly partisan, contributing to political and social bitterness, as well as to economic disruption.[1] Many battles and skirmishes had been fought in the state, causing property destruction and depletion. Particularly crippling and costly had been the lightninglike cavalry incursions of Brigadier General John Hunt Morgan, celebrated Confederate raider. His frequent expeditions had wrought the destruction of railroad and telegraph lines, the seizure of horses and food supplies, the burning of warehouses, and the devastation of much property generally. Morgan's raids had frightened people and kept them in constant anxiety, and the marching and countermarching of opposing armies over the state further weakened their morale. In addition Union troops had sometimes become reckless, unlawfully appropriating and destroying property and insulting citizens; and the "Home Guard," some of whose provost marshals were notorious for stupidity and treachery, had frequently and groundlessly accused citizens of southern sympathy apparently as excuse

1

to confiscate their property, and thrown them into jail.[2]

Enhancing the misery was the dastardly and deadly work of the guerrillas—gangs of lawless desperados who preyed most effectively upon the weak and defenseless. This despicable jetsam of the war specialized in depravity. Tools of this depravity were intimidation, whipping, plundering, burning, robbing, raping, and murdering. Guerrilla bands roved over every section of the state throughout most of the war and for several years following.[3]

By the end of the conflict, Kentucky had suffered dangerous depletions of livestock, agricultural supplies, most foodstuffs, and good money was scarce. During the war, Union officials had commandeered supplies at will and in return had given vouchers to loyal citizens who were tardily, if ever, paid. So gross had been the abuses that even loyal Union citizens protested. Furthermore, the slaves, believing freedom near, had become restive and little inclined to work. In fact hundreds had fled from the farms even during the war. Added to such economic and social problems was widespread political confusion.[4]

Political Disaffection

The reasons for political confusion and dissatisfaction were numerous. Not least of these was the continuance of federal military rule and martial law for many months following surrender of the Confederate armies. Then too, decided bitterness resulted from the "high-handed" rule of the state's federal commander, Major General John Marshall Palmer, who used his office to free the slaves.[5] Particularly disconcerting and irritating to a majority of the people was the Thirteenth Amendment, submitted to the Kentucky General Assembly by Governor Thomas E. Bramlette on February 7, 1865. Assemblymen generally reasoned that ratifying the proposed amendment would be "legalizing a wrong" and would violate Lincoln's "solemn promise" that the "rights of the slave-holding states" not in rebellion "would be maintained." Nor did the Commonwealth's lawmakers fail to point out and deplore frequent violations of the Constitution by federal authorities, and they could scarcely find language sufficiently strong to express disapproval of Negro enlistments in the federal armies. They also played upon the theme that adoption would in effect set up political and social equality for Negroes.

A few practical minded men in the state government, realizing that slavery in the United States was doomed, had favored ratification upon the basis of federal compensation, first to the extent of $36,000,000, then to $100,000,000. Governor Bramlette had advocated this practical stand. But at the time, few of the lawmakers seemed desirous of being practical. Bitterness and hatred appeared to control their actions. Nor was the Congress inclined to make antiadministration Kentucky an enormous financial present.

In the end the Thirteenth Amendment was soundly beaten: in the senate the vote stood 23 to 10; and in the house, 56 to 28.[6] In refusing to ratify, the Kentucky General Assembly further aroused the anger of the congressional majority. Regardless, slavery was dead, even in Kentucky, as Bramlette had recognized as early as April 1865, when he declared, "Our whole labor system is broken up and utterly demoralized." Hastening the demise of the "peculiar institution," before adoption of the Thirteenth Amendment, had been the Kentucky-born General Palmer's lavish distribution of railroad passes to slaves. This had practically effected the coup de grâce of the moribund institution in the state.[7]

The fight over adoption of the Thirteenth Amendment had tended to solidify Kentucky political alignments. During the war, political alignments had been more or less fluid and indefinite, although by the beginning of the year 1862, a majority of the state's people opposed secession and believed that the Union should be saved. A majority of these were Union Democrats, generally conservative. There were two smaller groups—namely, a southern-sympathizing group (Regular Democrats), not necessarily secessionists, and a pronorthern, emancipationist group, which had, with some reservations, accepted the Republicans' Congressional program. In the state, members of the Republican party

3

("Radicals") during the war had enjoyed a degree of power dispro-
portionate to the party's small membership, both because of the
ability of its leaders and its close association with the Lincoln
government. Socially, Kentuckians had a good deal in common
with Upper South southerners.

As the war progressed Union officials steadily became more
oppressive in the Commonwealth. They were responding in part to
pro-Confederate declarations and activities, including aiding and
abetting pro-Confederate guerrillas. In the wholesale repressions,
many loyal Union citizens suffered. These were not slow in re-
proaching the Lincoln government, particularly Union civilian and
military officials in the state.

Even high Union Democrat leaders, including Governor Bram-
lette, a former colonel in the Union Army, and some powerful
Union editors gradually cooled toward national Republican rule.
During 1864 they had returned to the Democratic party and, that
year, supported General George B. McClellan for president. Union
Democrats had early opposed the Emancipation Proclamation
(January 1863), were incensed by suspension of the writ of *habeas
corpus* and federal interference in state elections, and regarded the
Thirteenth Amendment as the "last straw" in a long line of
"insults, usurpations and deceptions."

By the end of the conflict numerous Union men believed that
the "heroes in grey" should be quickly restored to their former
social, economic, and political position in the state. Their support
was a great boon to the southern-sympathizing party, as well as to
the ex-Confederates, who steadily gained prestige and preferment,
while the "Radicals" steadily lost ground.[8] Most of those who left
the "Radicals" joined the conservative Republicans or the Democrats, who by reason of numbers controlled Kentucky politically
by the summer of 1865.

Many other reasons may be advanced for Kentucky's switch
from acquiescence in wartime Union and Union Democrat leadership to anti-Republican thought and action. Not the least general
reason was the innate and indigenous conservatism of Ken-

tuckians. Conservative thought, with some exceptions, had more or less prevailed in Kentucky since the beginning of statehood in 1792. Generally speaking, conservative proslavery men had written the state's three Constitutions (1792, 1799, 1849). In the presidential election of 1860 Kentucky had cast its vote for the conservative Constitution Union candidates, Bell and Everett, thereby repudiating the extremist views of both proslavery and antislavery men. It was rather natural therefore for Kentuckians, the war ended, to revert to their old conservatism. Most of them perhaps would have been content to return to the status quo as of 1860, slavery and all. Thus Kentucky not only turned antinorthern but also oscillated all the way to an active prosouthern view, minus secession.[9] Many interpreted this shift as a repudiation of reforms and industrialism, and as an alliance with an agrarian, states' rights past.

Seeds Of Violence

Lawlessness and violence abounded in Kentucky society during the decades immediately following the war. The seeds had been sown during the conflict itself. In addition to the sectional divisions, strife in the state had been internecine, which enhanced bitter animosities. Since most of the people who had been involved continued to live in Kentucky after the war, often side by side, bad feeling, often resulting in violence, continued to the turn of the century and even beyond.

Continuing guerrilla operations in the state were a significant factor in postbellum discord. Among the dreaded bands were Confederate soldiers out of touch with their commands and having no means of livelihood other than brigandage. In fact, stragglers, deserters, and draft-jumpers from both armies had in many cases joined lawless criminal elements to swell the guerrilla menace. In the caldron of violence was a unique band known as "Partisan Rangers," authorized during the war by the Confederate command to operate behind Union lines. Completely out of touch with authority, many of this band became marauders. In time they became so incorrigible and lawless that several Confederate leaders referred to them as "guerrillas." General Thomas L. Rosser, in a letter to General Robert E. Lee, declared that they were "without discipline, order, or organization," that they swarmed "broadcast over the country, a band of thieves, stealing, pillaging, plundering, and doing every manner of mischief and crime."[10]

The fighting men gone and normal processes interrupted, it was perhaps natural for criminally inclined men, especially deserters, to form mounted bands and to prey upon defenseless persons in poorly protected communities. Lawless bands could swoop down on isolated farms, villages and towns to terrorize and intimidate their inhabitants. They plundered, robbed, whipped, shot, hanged, and destroyed with apparent impunity.

Even deserters from Union armies formed guerrilla companies. Well mounted on stolen horses and well armed, these companies terrorized, plundered and murdered in the same manner as other notorious outlaw bands, including those of Quantrill and Sue Mundy (Jerome Clarke). Conditions became so deplorable in the state that after Appomattox even returning Confederate soldiers often joined state and federal troops in running down these bandits.

Another to gain notoriety was the Union Home Guard, established by the Union controlled General Assembly in May, 1861, to suppress any and all pro-Confederate activities in the counties. Ages of the Home Guard ranged from sixteen to sixty-five. It was organized ostensibly to take the place of the State Guard, largely pro-Confederate. The Home Guard acquired many duties and privileges after the departure of the State Guard. Nevertheless, though authorized by the state, it was not a state militia; the men were county volunteers and received no pay. The organization was, however, armed by the state. Its arms were to be those turned back by the disbanded State Guard. But it is unlikely that many rifles were turned back. As "armed police," without necessary military restraints, these quasi-soldiers assumed the task of regulating their communities to suit their own purposes. They preyed especially upon southern sympathizers, real and imaginary, and in many instances they perpetrated acts of violence and gross injustices, which caused bitterness lasting for a generation. Members of the Home Guard were themselves sometimes little better than guerrillas.[11]

Even so, as the depredations of guerrillas were committed more frequently upon Union-sympathizing families than Confederate, Union military authorities in the state, particularly Major General Stephen G. Burbridge, federal military head, authorized retaliation against southern-sympathizing families through confiscation of property and hostages.[12] Grave injustices were inflicted on many innocent people. The most extreme acts had been the executions of Confederate prisoners in 1864, as reprisals for guerrilla crimes.

Another source of violence had been the "bushwhackers," who operated principally in the Kentucky highlands. These "undercover" men, hiding behind trees, rocks or cliffs, began early in the war to ambush troops of either army, depending upon their loyalties, but mostly Confederates. Many Confederate men were consequently killed while passing through eastern Kentucky enroute to southern camps, while some Union men moving up and down the valleys met like fates. Though most Kentucky mountaineers stuck with the Union, many, especially in Floyd, Morgan, Breathitt, and Knott counties, were Confederate in sympathy. Contributing to the people's afflictions were the so-called "Regulators," self-appointed men in affected communities. Local vigilantes in effect, they organized to put down violence and took the law into their own hands.

Yet another cause of violence arose to plague the harassed populace. It emanated from some of the freedmen. Following the Emancipation Proclamation, slaves in Kentucky were encouraged in many ways by Union officers to leave their masters and seek freedom. Slightly more than 20,000 enlisted in the Union Army, an act strongly opposed by a majority of Kentuckians. By federal law, wives and children of enlisted Negro soldiers were given their freedom. Free railway passes and the Thirteenth Amendment followed.

Many of the freed Negroes, some of whom had served as teamsters and construction workers in the Union Army, settled in separate communities near towns or cities where they ran their own affairs. Pressed for subsistence, some resorted to stealing. Farmers' chickens and pigs fell prey to their thievery; losses became notable. Exasperated farmers welcomed relief in most any form. In due time, small groups of bold men in certain communities rose to punish these blacks. Stimulus was added to their vigorous actions by Negroes' efforts to participate in political and civil affairs. These bands of whites followed the practices of the Ku Klux Klan. They intimidated, whipped numerous Negroes, burned houses, and occasionally hanged blacks.[13]

The list of lawless organizations should not omit the Loyal League, a patriotic sounding designation whose bent seems to have been violent partisanism. This order operated chiefly in Republican-dominated eastern Kentucky. Though pleased to give attention to suspected Klansmen and overzealous pro-Confederates, its main object may have been to keep Democrats and ex-Confederates out of county political power. In Harlan County, for instance, persons were beaten for voting Democratic. Under whatever name, the devastating and bloody attacks and reprisals in some of the mountain counties were horrible.

Examples of violence and lawlessness are too numerous to list all the incidents individually, but the following events of the four year period 1870-1873 indicate the extra-legality of the times. In December 1870, fifty men took a Negro from a Cynthiana jail and hanged him; in June 1871, sixteen ex-laborers of the Red River Iron Works attacked a boarding house in Estill County in an attempt to punish Negroes for moving into their jobs there; in August the state militia was called out in Frankfort because of various shooting incidents which resulted in the deaths of two whites and wounding of two others, and the hanging of two blacks and wounding of four others; in October 1872 a Shelby County

Negro was killed after he refused to leave his farm as ordered by a lawless group; in November three Negroes were dragged from their homes in Jessamine County by a mob and killed; later in the month, a lynch mob of seventy-five people failed in its murderous design when two Negroes were spirited from the jail, but later recommitted and legally executed. Perhaps it should be pointed out that six years later a band of assassins set fire to some homes near Frankfort, shot the Negro occupants as they ran out, and threw their bodies into the flames to be reduced to ashes.[14]

The legacy of war violence was further enhanced by yet another development. Governor Bramlette had, toward the close of his administration, issued numerous pardons to persons convicted of crimes; many received them even before reaching the penitentiary. The governor maintained that "war fever" had caused many good men to break the law—men who would, he contended, be good citizens in normal times. He therefore pardoned many upon the belief that peace would restore normal conditions. Unfortunately, many of those pardoned were actually confirmed criminals and a menace to their communities.

It was frequently the case that in localities where heinous crimes and atrocious injustices had been perpetrated, posses of outraged citizens formed, routed out of bed suspected persons, innocent or guilty—including Negroes, guerrillas, and pardoned men—and hanged them to nearby trees. Champ Clark wrote that "so many men were lynched in Kentucky in two or three years that a person traveling through the woods instinctively would pick out an eligible limb on which to hang somebody."[15]

Some of the lawlessness, as indicated, had political associations. There seems to be little doubt that some southern-sympathizing Democrats felt kindly toward certain lawless forces, whether called Regulators, guerrillas, or Ku Klux, while many of the "Radicals" (or Republicans) were friendly toward other lawless groups. In some Democratic counties, local officials were inclined to wink at Ku Klux activities, while in some counties under Republican control, officials were friendly toward Regulators and

9

Loyal Leaguers. Generally speaking, local officials throughout the state, demoralized by the violence, bloodshed and destruction caused by the war, made little effort to apprehend criminals and bring them to justice.[16]

Political Readjustments

By 1859 the Democratic party had gained political domination in Kentucky. The national crisis in 1860 had, however, brought schism in its ranks and caused two distinct factions to develop. The more numerous faction was known as Union Democrat. This powerful group was instrumental in preventing Kentucky's seceding, although the most effective leadership in the early days had been given by former Whigs.

A minority contingent of the Democratic party was known as the Southern Rights wing. Many of its adherents believed in secession, at least in the abstract, and some favored armed support of the Confederacy. Covertly this faction aided the southern cause in many ways throughout the war. After the elections of 1861 it bided its time politically for a more favorable day.

The Republicans of Kentucky, dubbed "Radicals" during the war, had evolved partly from the prewar Whig, Know-Nothing and Opposition parties. They constituted a small minority in the state. The name "Radical" came from the activities of the Radical Republicans in Congress. The Lincoln administration favored those who had voted for it, and the Kentucky "Radical" leaders therefore, as indicated, enjoyed prestige and power with the federal government that were quite out of proportion to their party's numerical strength.

As the more numerous Union Democrats gradually cooled toward federal policies, the "Radicals" hewed more closely to the national Republican party line and sought to strengthen their organization. Though federal support and patronage helped greatly, they never controlled the state. The wartime governors, James F. Robinson (1862-1863) and Bramlette (1863-1867), owed their elections to the support of the Union Democrats. In time, many of the Union Democrats, dissatisfied with the national administration, styled themselves "Conservatives," as opposed to "Radicals." They did not become disloyal to the Union, although as federal rule became more unpopular, they grew somewhat more friendly to the Southern Rights faction, which called itself the Regular Democratic party. Both the Union and the Regular Democrats sent delegations to the Democratic National Convention, held in Chicago on August 8, 1864. There the two wings fused and the amalgamated "host" supported McClellan for president.

Following the Civil War the prosouthern wing of the Kentucky Democratic party exercised more and more control over the party, until at length its dominance was complete. Coalition of persons who had fought to save the Union with those who had fought to split it appeared most unlikely, and some Union Democrats refused to succumb to the leadership of ex-Confederates. Yet coalition actually occurred. High among the reasons for the strange marriage were Union officials' abuses, real and imagined, and the national administration's policies. There was an understandable sympathy for a defeated, humiliated, and suffering southern people, and many bold returned Confederates, extremely ambitious for political office and aware of the political climate, expelled a tremendous amount of effective propaganda. Furthermore, of some importance was the fact that the "Radicals" had either made little effort or had failed miserably to do a good public relations job in the state.

Long before the end of the conflict, Union prestige in Kentucky had shrunk. Considering the fact that more than 90,000 Kentuckians were enlisted in the Union service as compared to not more than 35,000 Kentuckians in the Confederate Army, the situation appears bizarre indeed. The Democrats easily won the August elections of 1864. A district race for election of an Appellate Court judge constituted the principal contest.[17] In that race the Democrats had been seriously handicapped. On the day before the election the name of their candidate, Appellate Court Judge

Alvin Duval of Georgetown had to be withdrawn because of pressure from General Burbridge. Nevertheless, their leaders promptly telegraphed the name of the venerable and popular Judge George Robertson ("Old Buster") to the voting places with instructions to write it in on the ballots. Thus that picturesque old jurist was elected over the "Radical" candidate (actually an able and dedicated Union man), Mortimer Murray Benton of Covington, by a majority of 442 votes.

The November presidential election of 1864 was held in an atmosphere fraught with bitterness and violence throughout the Commonwealth. General Burbridge made strenuous efforts in Lincoln's behalf. He employed military force, intimidation, promises of financial gain, and even arrest and banishment of some high state officials. Yet, conservative Union men, led by Governor Bramlette and most Union and Southern Rights Democrats, had been quite determined to keep the election free. By means of the press and the stump, they whipped up considerable feeling against federal usurpation. Bramlette and his supporters charged that the military was interfering in state elections; that former owners of federally appropriated property were neutralized by the promise of being paid for "your horses, niggers and corn, and your hogs," if they voted for Lincoln. The Bramlette campaigners charged too that multifarious tyrannies and outrages were committed in the trade regulations and in the arrests of officials, as well as of private citizens. They excoriated the declarations and working of martial law, intimidation, and extreme measures generally. They declared that the "Radicals" were trying to "break the just pride and subdue the free spirit of the people, which would only have fitted them for enslavement." Union Colonel Frank L. Wolford had actually begun raising troops to prevent Burbridge from interfering with the Democrats' suffrage. Regardless, the election results indicated a signal victory for the McClellan ticket.[18]

The August 7, 1865 election was another triumph of Democrats over Republicans. The victorious party that year secured control of both branches of the General Assembly, though by only a few votes. Democrats captured five of nine congressional seats and also elected a state treasurer by a majority of 105 votes—in a total of 84,269.[20]

The principal issues of the campaign had been the Thirteenth Amendment and the effort of returned Confederate soldiers to regain civil and political rights. The conservative Union man, George D. Prentice, editor of the powerful and influential *Louisville Journal*, believed because slavery was actually dead that the amendment should be ratified by Kentucky, as did Governor Bramlette. Even a majority of the Union men, perhaps, abhorred the federal abuses, the record of General Burbridge and the high-handed policy of his successor, General Palmer.[20] Policy-wise, nonetheless, neither a federal policy of permissiveness nor repression would have been entirely satisfactory.

The Conservatives (mostly Democrats) finally came around to advocating restoration of political and civil rights to the returning Confederate soldiers. They thus espoused a popular cause. Disillusioned with "Radicalism," perhaps a majority of the people reached the point of full sympathy for the lean and destitute boys in grey. Moreover, Democratic party leaders were quick to realize the strength which these ex-Confederates, their families (many of whom were prominent and powerful), and friends could add to the party. Consequently, courting the returned "heroes" became a settled policy, although obviously not all of the former Union Democrats went along. By contrast, little was done in Kentucky, other than by joyous loved ones, for returning Union soldiers who had offered their lives to save the Union.

The people having spoken in the August election of 1865, the legislature proceeded to repeal all the 1862 wartime measures which deprived Confederates and their sympathizers of political and civil rights. Even Governor Bramlette, as well as several other popular ex-Union officials, came to favor a pro-Confederate program, and ex-Union Colonel Wolford, as legislator from Casey County, led the fight to repeal the expatriation acts.[21] Repeal of these measures left the popular ex-Confederates free to participate in Kentucky politics. Ironically enough, the pendulum swung so far prosouthern that ex-Union soldiers were in danger of being persecuted for legitimate wartime activities in the state. The procedure left the Republicans, as one reported, "bewildered and amazed." Such "ingratitude and sheer affrontery," wrote an astonished Union man, "are unbelievable."

Not yet whipped, however, the Republicans ("Radicals") pondered ways and means of preventing the Democrats from making further gains. Many, aware of Kentuckians' conservatism, began to advocate policies more in accord with Kentucky feelings, "or ruin stared them in the face."[22] The Republicans sought therefore to advance President Andrew Johnson, already preempted by the Conservatives, as their leader, holding that this gesture would signify their conservatism.

A Republican caucus during the legislative session of 1865-1866 adopted such conservative resolutions as endorsement of Johnson's policy, condemnation of Negro suffrage, restoration of the writ of *habeas corpus*, and removal of federal troops and the Freedmen's Bureau from the state. Some Republicans regarded the resolutions as hypocritical, weak and defeatist. In the long run this retreat, though appearing sagacious, gained the party nothing.

It had been soon evident to the Conservatives that the alert and daring ex-Confederate soldiers could mean the difference between defeat and victory. None recognized it more clearly than the "rebels" themselves, who took full advantage of their propitious position. As Professor Coulter put it, "Instead of simply picking up the crumbs that fell from the official table, the Confederates were resolved to seize the whole banquet."[23] Many prominent ex-Confederate leaders hastened to groom themselves for public office. Nor was their task very difficult. One of Morgan's cavalrymen wrote: "Indeed the feeling is so strong where I have been with all *true* Democrats, that a large majority of them, or at least of those I have heard talk, say that they will not vote for any man, for the future, if they can help it, who has not seen service in the Confederate army."[24]

14

Another test of party and prosouthern strength came in 1866, in the race for clerk of the Court of Appeals. The preceding Democratic convention was controlled by prosoutherners, among whom were Charles A. Wickliffe (candidate for governor in 1863) and ex-Governor John L. Helm. Delegates retreated from the extreme position that only ex-Confederates be selected. Duvall, who was only mildly prosouthern (but who in running for the same office in 1864 had been forced by Burbridge to flee the state) was named to run for clerk of the Court.[25]

The convention adopted the following resolutions, often repeated in the years ahead:

(1) That the Federal Government is one of limited and restricted powers. (2) That the exercise of any power by the Federal Government not delegated to it by the Constitution is a usurpation to deprive the people of their liberties. (3) That Congress has no right to deprive any state of representation in Congress. (4) That the Federal Government has not the right to try civilians by military commissions and drumhead courts-martial. . . . (6) That the question of suffrage belongs exclusively to the states. (7) That we recognize the abolition of slavery as an accomplished fact, but earnestly assert that Kentucky has the right to regulate the political status of the negroes within her territory. (8) That the writ of habeas corpus *should have been fully restored as soon as the war was ended.*

Calling for economy in federal spending and prosecution of those in the federal service guilty of fraud and corruption, and demanding the disbanding of the large federal armies, the convention sounded a note of high praise for President Johnson for his vetoes of the Freedman's Bureau and the Civil Rights bills. At the same time Kentucky's congressional delegation was commended for opposing the congressional reconstruction program. This convention marked the real beginning of the postwar Democratic party in Kentucky.[26]

Fearful of the new ex-Confederate domination of the Democratic party, some Conservatives (Union Democrats) and moderate "Radicals" (Republicans) sought to fuse their forces in order to check the ascendant ex-Confederates. Among the active leaders were General Thomas L. Crittenden, Governor Bramlette, Colonel John Marshall Harlan, John H. Harney, editor of *The Louisville Democrat*, and Richard R. Bolling. The members formed a rather uneasy and artificial combination and adopted an old party label, Conservative. General Edward H. Hobson, of Greensburg, one of the captors of General Morgan, became this amalgamated organization's candidate for clerk of the Court, after Bolling declined the nomination.

People increasingly favored the Democratic party as the campaign progressed. They eschewed "Radicalism" as connoting tyranny, anti-constitutionalism, and violence. Soon Conservatives began deserting Hobson. Even Harney, becoming disgusted with the trend of events, carried his *Louisville Democrat* to the support of the Democrats, while candidates everywhere were disclaiming connection with "Radicalism."[27]

Great excitement and much violence prevailed around the polls on election day. No less than twenty men were killed. The voting, however, went as expected. The Democratic party gained a thumping victory. Many counties, erstwhile safely Republican, elected Democratic judges, sheriffs and other officers. Judge Duvall won decisively by a vote of 95,979 to Hobson's 58,035.

One prominent newspaper reporter interpreted the results "as a straight cut rebel victory."[28] This statement was not quite accurate. The vote represented the strength of a reunited Democratic party, the party to which a majority of the voters normally adhered. Moreover, that party during the campaign had enjoyed the support of most of the state's newspapers, including the *Louisville Courier*, the *Louisville Democrat*, and the Lexington *Observer and Reporter*. The Negro question doubtless played a part. The outstanding leaders of the Democratic campaign were ex-Confederates, who proved resourceful, bold and clever. Victory gave them control of the party.

The Commercial Bank
of Grayson

RECEIPT

Checks and other items are received for
deposit subject to the terms and conditions
of this Bank's collection agreement.

#28 07/25/11 12:08:13 PM CR07/25/11.
133 COMMERCIAL BANK OF GRAYSON 2 JUL I
LNS ACCT/NOTE #: ****1875-*0620
PAYMENT AMT: $183.58
Sign Up Now for Free E-Statement

With ex-Confederates in control, the Conservative party (mostly Union Democrats) rapidly declined. The struggle in the future would be between the ex-Union controlled Republican party and the ex-Confederate controlled Democratic party. The Republicans had learned a costly lesson and they resolved never again to show any disposition "for compromise and coalition at the sacrifice of principle."[29] Tough and resilient, they soon forgot the defeat and were quickly raised in spirit and ready for another combat. After a time their party was able to eliminate the uncomplimentary name "Radical" and that of Republican came into general use.

On January 10, 1867 the General Assembly rejected the Fourteenth Amendment by overwhelming pluralities. Aside from the fact that perhaps a majority of the Kentucky leaders believed the amendment unconstitutional, the Assembly refused to support a measure which it believed was designed to disenfranchise whites and to enfranchise Negroes. It held that the state and not Congress possessed the right to determine suffrage qualifications.[30]

Although the 1866 attempt of certain leaders to split the Democratic party and to weaken the ex-Confederates' grip had been unsuccessful, opposition to "rebel" control was far from dead. After all, a majority of that party's adherents had been Union Democrats. Many were convinced that, as a matter of justice, ex-Confederates should not control party machinery and also hold the elective offices. Consequently, another interparty fight developed in the election of a United States senator in the spring of 1867.

The old southern wing put forward former Governor Lazarus W. Powell while the old Union Democrats supported the incumbent Garrett Davis, who, though a staunch Union man, was one of the most relentless enemies of Thaddeus Stevens and his Radical Republican colleagues in Congress. During a long period of voting, Republicans in the state's General Assembly supported various men, including William H. Randall, John A. Prall, James Speed, and Benjamin Helm Bristow. Though Powell always commanded a plurality, he was never able to secure a majority. After twenty unsuccessful ballots, the two factions agreed to elect Davis, who on the next ballot received seventy-eight votes and a clear majority.[31] To some observers, Davis' election represented a Union victory, and it was thought that harmony had been restored in the Democratic party.

II

THE BEGINNINGS OF
EX-CONFEDERATE
DOMINATION

Harmony in the Democratic party had not been restored, however, as the political events of that important year, 1867, soon revealed. Looking to the campaigns for the General Assembly and for Congress, the Democratic committee called a convention to meet in Frankfort on February 22 of that year. Aggressive pro-Confederate leaders, many of them prominent before the war, quickly gained complete control of the convention, named the candidates, and wrote the platform.[1] John L. Helm (Elizabethtown), father of the late Confederate Brigadier General Ben Hardin Helm, was nominated for governor, and John W. Stevenson (Covington), for lieutenant governor. Among the other nominees were: John Rodman (Frankfort) for attorney general; D. Howard Smith (Georgetown) for auditor; James W. Tate (Frankfort) for treasurer; James A. Dawson (Munfordville), incumbent and former Union officer, was renominated for register of the land office; Zachariah F. Smith (Henry County) for superintendent of public instruction.

After professing loyalty to the Union, demanding constitutional government, and praising President Johnson for his courageous vetoes of "Radical" reconstruction legislation, the convention platform then boldly declared that "the attempt now being made by Congress to reduce ten States in this Union to mere territorial dependencies, and to hold them as subjected provinces under the iron heel of military despotism, is not only the greatest political outrage that was ever attempted in this country, but a malicious and flagrant violation of the Constitution and in direct conflict with the decision of the Supreme Court of the United States." In addition, it called upon the President to issue a proclamation "granting pardon and general amnesty to all who were engaged in the late rebellion."

The Union Democrat leaders, Governor Bramlette, Lieutenant Governor Richard Taylor Jacobs (Oldham County), and others, angered by the "theft of all the offices by the rebels," spearheaded a revolt. Calling themselves Conservatives, they announced a convention of Union Democrats for April 11. That convention nominated candidates for state offices, with William B. Kinkead (Lexington) for governor, and adopted a platform. In calling this convention, the Conservatives issued an address to the people. It asserted that Union Democrats had opposed secession and fought to save the Union, and that at the end of the conflict they had shown compassion, kindness, and magnanimity to the destitute Confederates. The address further declared that the returned "rebels," instead of showing gratitude, had selfishly seized leadership of the party, greedily grabbed all the offices and were now striving to make the names of these kindly Union men anathema throughout the entire state. It declared that Unionists were proscribed and ostracized from party leadership, principally because they had fought to save the Union.[2]

One plank in the Conservative party platform reveals clearly their basic thinking. It asserted:

> *that the National Government possesses the moral, legal and constitutional right and power to use "men and money" to put down and suppress rebellion and civil war; that it is the duty of the Government to do it, and that it is essential for the future peace and prosperity of our whole country that this principle should be recognized by all the people as one of the fundamental and practical principles of the Government; and that the brave men, who in the Army and Navy, upheld the honor of the flag and fought for the Union and the*

Constitution, deserve the gratitude of the nation and should be honored for it.

The "Radical" (Republican) convention had met at Frankfort on February 26, only four days after the Democratic conclave. At that time its delegates probably were not aware of what the Union Democrats would do. It would seem that the time had come for the Republicans and Union Democrats to make another effort at fusion and collaboration. However, in view of past unpleasant experiences, the former remained obdurate, and perhaps threw away an opportunity to win. They nominated a full state ticket, with Colonel Sidney M. Barnes (Irvine) for governor, Richard Tarvin Baker (Alexandria) for lieutenant governor, and Colonel John Mason Brown (Louisville) for attorney general. Their platform declared in part:

We believe in the right of the local people of the States, through their representatives in both Houses of Congress, to settle the terms on which the disturbed relations of the rebellious States to the Union may be restored, and that, in common with the Union men of the whole country, we insist on such terms as will make a speedy restoration of the States, lately in rebellion, to their former positions in the Union, compatible with the continued safety of the Republic, and the protection of life, liberty, and property to all men.[3]

Had the Republicans seen fit to yield a bit, the two Union parties might have united. Unfortunately for both politically, the people at the time were greatly agitated over the Fourteenth Amendment, which was extremely unpopular in the state. While the Republicans championed this amendment, both the Union and Confederate Democrats vigorously opposed it. The ex-Confederates, who controlled the Democratic party, had the advantage throughout in popular appeal. Many steadily invoked prejudice and profusely waved the "bloody shirt."

Prior to the 1867 general election, a special congressional contest was decided on May 4. The Democrats won a complete victory, taking every district. Wrote one disgusted Republican, "Kentucky is today as effectually in the hands of rebels as if they had every town and city garrisoned by their troops. With a rebel Governor, rebel Congressmen, rebel Statehouse and Senate, rebel Judges, rebel Mayors, rebel municipal officers, rebel policemen and constables, what is to become of the poor blacks and loyal white men God only knows." Elected to Congress at that time were several men who came to be well known—among them John Young Brown (Henderson), the Second Congressional District; J. Proctor Knott (Lebanon), Fourth District; and James B. Beck (Lexington), Seventh District.

In the August election for state officers the Union men suffered an even greater defeat than in May. Helm, the regular Democratic candidate, received 90,225 votes; Kinkead, the Union Democrat, 13,167; and Barnes, the Republican candidate, 33,939. Helm received a majority of 56,286 over Barnes, and 77,058 over Kinkead.[4] An anguished Union editor cried: "Kentucky failed to secede in 1861. By a strange conjunction of circumstances what the rebels failed to do that year, they freely realized in the year 1867." Talk of congressional reconstruction of Kentucky was often heard. Even Charles Sumner, United States Senator from Massachusetts, declared in a letter to Brigadier General James S. Brisbin in Lexington: "Nothing can be more certain than that Kentucky at this time is without a republican form of government."[5]

At this critical juncture on September 3 the aged Helm, veteran political and industrial leader, was inaugurated governor. Too ill to travel to Frankfort, he took the oath of office at his home in Elizabethtown. Five days later he died, and on September 13 John W. Stevenson succeeded him.

At that time Kentuckians were avidly interested in the sensational case of General Burbridge, whom the General Assembly sought to bring to trial for his war acts in 1863 and 1864. Though the lawmakers failed to have him appear before a committee for a

Governor and Senator John W. Stevenson

Collection of the Kentucky Historical Society

Governor Thomas E. Bramlette

Courtesy of The Filson Club, Louisville

hearing, so bitter was public feeling against him that he was hounded from place to place and depicted as a blood-thirsty fiend. Of him Coulter wrote: "They [the people of Kentucky] relentlessly pursued him, the most bitterly hated of all Kentuckians, and so untiring were their efforts, that it finally came to the point where he had not a friend left in the state who would raise his voice to defend him." In fact, public hatred of the luckless Burbridge reached such proportions that politicians sought to ruin their opponents by charging them with friendship or association with him.[6]

On February 10, 1868, James Guthrie resigned his seat in the United States Senate, because of physical disabilities, and the legislature, then in session, quickly elected Thomas C. McCreery, a prominent Owensboro Democrat, to succeed him.[7]

The election of state officials in 1868 aroused considerable public interest. For many months prior to their state convention, the Democrats had made overtures to the few remaining Union Democrats (Conservatives) to return to the old fold, inviting them back as men interested in defending American freedom and the Constitution against tyranny and usurpation. In reply Richard Jacob, lieutenant governor under Bramlette and a colonel in the Union army, set the price of fusion as division of the party offices, surcease of the "unjust warfare" against Union men, admission that secession was settled permanently, and a card of thanks to Union soldiers and sailors for their work in saving the Union.[8] Though seeming reasonable, these demands were not met—an indication of the influence pro-southern Democratic leaders enjoyed with the people. They judged correctly that the public in general was now prosouthern.[9] In the end they won anyway; most of the Union Democrats returned, no concessions granted.

Those who refused to return, men who had fought for the Union, could find no logic in supporting for office men who had striven to destroy the Union. Among these, John Marshall Harlan of Louisville decided definitely to throw in his lot completely with the Republican party. He found congenial spirits in a few other leaders, including James and Joshua Speed and Judge Bland Ballard of Louisville, Colonel William H. Wadworth of Maysville, Milwards of Lexington and Burnams and Capertons of Richmond. Such prominent conservative men coming to the fore would further erase "Radical" from the Republican party name in the state.

Because of the death of Governor Helm in 1867, a special election was called for 1868. In their state convention held at Frankfort, February 22, 1868, the Democrats nominated Stevenson for governor, together with a ticket friendly to the South, and adopted a platform favoring general amnesty and "Constitutional government."

On February 27, the Republican convention in Frankfort nominated R. Tarvin Baker for governor, and endorsed U.S. Grant for president and James Speed for vice-president. Their platform revealed an inclination "to embrace wholly the program of the national party and in no wise to cater to any sectional whims of any weak-hearted Kentuckians."

The canvass proved drab indeed. Stevenson was not an effective campaigner. In fact, he did little speaking. The Republicans, however, were too weak and uncertain to effect strong local organizations. They did, however, make a belated effort to enlist Union Democrats to their cause, a ruse which failed miserably. Considering the wretchedness of the southern states, the excesses of reconstruction, the persecution of President Johnson by the "Radicals" nationally, together with the resurrected Burbridge atrocities, the local Republicans were at a disadvantage. In the August election, the Democrats gained a landslide. Stevenson received 115,560 votes to Baker's 26,605. The majority was said to have been the largest for any candidate in the state's history to that time.

A presidential election was due in November, and the only ray of hope held by dejected Kentucky Republicans was the announcement that a sufficient number of states had ratified the Fourteenth Amendment to make it a part of the Constitution. They thought that this amendment would disqualify many Democratic officials and guarantee Negro suffrage.

The national results of the November election greatly buoyed the depressed Republicans. In the state, however, the Democrats retained something approximating the unprecedented August vote. The total stood at over 115,000. The Republicans, having gained more than 12,000 recruits since the last election, posted a vote of 39,605 for Grant and Colfax.[10] And, though a full delegation of nine Kentucky Democrats was elected to Congress, the Democratic party was overwhelmingly defeated nationwide. Horatio Seymour, wartime governor of New York, carried only eight states. The local Republicans could therefore find some reason to rejoice and celebrate, in spite of their poor showing in Kentucky. It was clear that many changes would be necessary before their party could win a state election. As indicated, however, more conservative leaders were already advancing toward leadership of the party. They were soon chartering a new program. John M. Harlan came to the fore as the new and strong leader of Kentucky Republicans. President Grant also appointed an abler group of men to federal offices in the state.

The reorganization of the Kentucky Republican party did not, however, have immediate influence upon the state's electorate. Ex-Confederates continued to be elected by overwhelming majorities to state offices. Whereas, the General Assembly of 1868 was termed "scarcely more than the meeting of a Confederate regiment," that of 1869 was even more top-heavy with ex-Confederates and their sympathizers. Democrats that year secured 128 of the 138 legislative seats, and Tate was easily reelected state treasurer.[11]

The General Assembly of 1869, after a stinging indictment of the Fifteenth Amendment by Governor Stevenson, promptly and decisively rejected that measure. Thereafter the lawmakers spent considerable time fruitlessly seeking means to prevent Negro voting, against the advice of Henry Watterson, who challenged them to accept the Fifteenth Amendment in good faith as a part of the Constitution. Watterson's view apparently had the support of the most progressive Democrats. Meanwhile the Republicans assiduously courted Negroes, believing that the black vote would give their party 100,000 votes and thereby bring victory in the next local election, August, 1870.

In that contest Negroes were generally allowed to vote. A few Democratic officials, however, intimidated and prevented some from casting their ballots. But there was only a modicum of violence. Indeed, it was very small considering the magnitude of the "revolution" of Negro voting. The result was the old story of a Democratic victory. Two reasons advanced for the triumph were the reluctance on the part of many Republicans to support black suffrage and the all-out effort by the Democrats to win.[12]

Immediately preceding the advent of Negro voting in the state, an election was held to choose a United States senator. This was done in a joint session of the two houses of the General Assembly, December 14, 15 and 16, 1869. The event brought out considerable bitterness, as it resurrected the old Burbridge controversy. The three leading Democratic contenders were Governor Stevenson, Senator McCreery, and Congressman Thomas Lauren Jones of Newport. Stevenson had previously accused McCreery of having recommended Burbridge for a federal appointment in the revenue service. McCreery indignantly denied the charge. During the course of several months of heated controversy Jones challenged Stevenson to fight a duel. The governor declined the invitation on grounds of his position and his being a believer in the Christian religion. However, long before the challenge was issued, the election had been concluded. Stevenson was elected on the fifth ballot. The one Republican candidate, Hugh F. Finley of Whitley County, had received ten votes on each ballot. Stevenson resigned as governor on February 13, 1871, and Preston H. Leslie, president of the state senate, became acting governor.

Prior to the United States senatorial contest, the August, 1870 congressional elections occurred, and the Democrats again won all nine of the congressional seats. The returns, as compared with the vote in the congressional elections of 1868, reveal a sizable increase in the number of votes cast, a total of 147,700. This increase was especially reflected in the larger Republican vote—57,249 as compared with 35,816 in 1868. Nevertheless, the Democrats had received a safe majority of 33,102.[13]

Perhaps the most significant fact associated with the political history of Kentucky during the readjustment period immediately following the Civil War was that ex-Confederates gained control of the Democratic party and promoted it to a position of complete political domination in the state. Their success may be partly accounted for by the probable desire of the people to return to an antebellum social, political and cultural status. Conversely, the state's Union men failed to convert their hard-won victories on the field of battle into postwar political control. It is strange indeed that the vanquished ruled the victors. Equally surprising was the failure of the more numerous and prominent Union men to develop a strong party capable of winning elections. Important also was the sympathetic feeling of Kentuckians generally toward the South and the prevalent bitterness on the part of most people toward the North.

III
BOURBONISM AND THE NEW DEPARTURE

A new factionalism developed after a time in the all-powerful Democratic party in Kentucky. But it did not cause a real split; nor was there any appreciable leaving of the party. Using a general and none too accurate expression, it was the old story of liberals and progressives arrayed against conservatives and reactionaries. (The terms are used relatively.) Actually, many of the former were in some respects neither very liberal nor very progressive, except in the desire for industrial progress. The conservatives were dubbed "Bourbons," their opponents "New Departure" Democrats.[1] The former, being the more numerous and powerful, controlled the party machinery and state conventions. Perhaps the first indication of a sharp difference of opinion came in connection with accepting or rejecting the Fourteenth and Fifteenth amendments.

The leader of the "New Departure" was Henry Watterson, powerful editor of the state's biggest newspaper, the Louisville *Courier-Journal.* Watterson, a realist, was eager for industrial progress, as well as desirous of unity and harmony in the Democracy throughout the nation. He came out strongly in favor of accepting the amendments. In his advocacy, Watterson, southerner and ex-Confederate though he was, reasoned that the Democratic party of Kentucky stood a better chance of advancing the best interests of Kentucky by alliance with both the northern and southern wings of the party. Moreover, he was realistic enough to realize that national ratification of the amendments was inevitable. Why should not Kentucky move along with the progressive majority?

29

What could it possibly hope to gain by tearfully, sentimentally and stubbornly embracing and clinging to a dead cause? In an editorial of August 16, 1871, he declared:

> As we have accepted confiscation in the Thirteenth Amendment, we propose to accept the other two [amendments] as its logical consequences; to let the whole Negro question go by default; to take the Negro where he stands as a free man, citizen, and voter, and try to improve and utilize him; and by this liberal and progressive policy, to regain possession of the Government and check aggression upon the States without disturbing any of those individual investments, whose dislocation would involve us in more agitation and perhaps additional wars.

Carrying the subject further, Watterson wrote:

> The war destroyed slavery, and with destruction of slavery, it removed the element of cohesion from the Southern States. Ties of association are always strong and the memory of old association must warm the heart of Southern men for many years. But when we come to consider practical affairs, we at once see that that which is exclusively Southern is essentially weak, for, though it may attract us, it repels those whose cooperation is indispensable to all our political enterprises. We must form new alliances, based on the altered conditions of our life. Those alliances cannot be constructed upon by-gone issues and obsolete interests, and still less will they respond to sympathies which are confined to our own bosoms. They must be liberal and provincial, and he is the best friend of the South, as also the country at large, who teaches this lesson with greatest persistence and earnestness.[2]

Summing up somewhat, the able editor declared: "The only difference that exists in the Democratic Party can be stated in a single sentence. Shall we accept or shall we reject the Fourteenth and Fifteenth amendments?" Colonel Isaac Caldwell and Judge

George Washington Craddock, "representing," as Watterson caustically remarked, "the ecumenical council at Frankfort . . . trying to establish a close corporation in Kentucky outside of the National Democracy . . . declare for rejecting them [the amendments] as nullities. The National Democracy as represented in all the State conventions which have yet assembled and by all the prominent leaders who have yet spoken declare for accepting them." Preston H. Leslie and J. Proctor Knott (whose ability Watterson greatly admired) opposed the amendments and thereby leaned to the "Bourbon" side.[3]

Watterson sought increased industrial advancement in the state. Intelligent, tremendously vital, well-traveled, a keen observer, an avid reader, he had readily discerned the rapid advancement of the states north of the Ohio River. At the same time he did not fail to note the apparent stagnation and povery in the South. He attributed the North's rapid rise to its industrial development (especially manufacturing), the rapid increase in immigrant population, acceptance of Negroes as citizens, and increasing support of public education. He noted also that the people of the North were rapidly forgetting the War and eagerly looking to the future for greater progress, wealth and happiness.

Greatly impressed with this progress, Watterson hoped that Kentucky would adopt some of the policies succeeding north of the Ohio River. To this end he formulated and advocated a thorough housecleaning politically in Kentucky and the "installation of new furniture." He could find no intelligent reasoning in the doctrine that service in the Confederate Army, *per se*, entitled one to public office. He thought the time had arrived when members of his party in the state should realize that the war was over and that its issues were dead. Nor could he find any rationale for keeping alive the bitter hatreds which the unfortunate struggle had engendered. The vigorous editor maintained that winning votes through rousing the bitter passions and hatreds of a departed past was poor strategy. He felt that all the Kentucky Democrats should not only strive to adjust themselves to the new order of things,

New Departure Democratic leader Henry Watterson

Courtesy of The Filson Club, Louisville

including Negro testimony in the courts, but should boldly stand for progress generally. "Marse Henry" (as he was later called) begged the leaders of his party to crusade for natural resource development, the building of railroads and turnpikes, the improvement of navigation, the building of factories, the encouragement of immigration, the putting down of violence and lawlessness, and the fostering of public education in order that prevailing illiteracy, ignorance, intolerance, and crime might be eliminated.[4]

Louisville, the state's largest city and business metropolis, was quite naturally the center of "New Departure" thinking. A good portion of its population, being industrially minded, was prepared to welcome increased factories, railroads, capital, and population. Many of the prominent citizens were impressed by the industrial expansion and rapid increase in wealth north of the Ohio River.

The center of the Bourbon Democracy was the rich Bluegrass region, with its landed aristocrats and many ex-Confederate lawyers, editors, and planters. The principal journalistic organ of "Bourbonism" was the *Kentucky Yeoman*, edited by Colonel Josiah Stoddard Johnston, an ex-Confederate officer of General John C. Breckinridge's staff who enjoyed considerable power, not only in speaking for the conservatives, but in shaping party policy and controlling the organization machinery. Colonel Johnston was for many years chairman of the party's powerful state central committee.[5] The *Yeoman* enjoyed the patronage of much of the state's county Democratic press, which appeared glad enough to follow its lead and reflect its opinions.

The Bourbons maintained a sort of catechism of principles which was followed rather rigidly. The cornerstone (unwritten of course), almost a *sine qua non*, was that ex-Confederates should maintain control of the Democratic party and that service in the Confederate army or navy should be the basic test for candidacy and for nomination by the party for public office.

By and large, the "Bourbons" refused to accept the decision of Appomattox, eschewed a possible new order, perhaps looked backward more than forward, made a fetish of the "Lost Cause." The

33

Bourbon Democratic leader J. Stoddard Johnston

Bourbons regarded agriculture as the basic and best industry and occupation, and many saw evils in industrialization. Some still leaned to the prewar plantation and slavery system and resented the freed Negro. They exploded at mention of the Thirteenth, Fourteenth, and Fifteenth amendments to the federal Constitution. Many of them (comparable to aristocratic antebellum southern plantation owners) believed only "persons of quality" were capable of running political affairs. Often uninterested in public education, they guffawed at the thought of education for Negroes.

Bourbons, who were lacking in neither intelligence nor attractiveness, viewed reform measures with suspicion. They seemed to worship at the shrine of the dead past. To many the "Lost Cause" appeared as real and dear as a loved one passed on. They abhorred the Freedmen's Bureau, (which had struggled for the Negroes' civil rights, including education) and the "bizarre" idea of Negro testimony in the courts. Recalling that the people generally had deplored Republican rule, so-called, in the state during the war, they took wartime "Black Republican" misrule, tyranny and oppression as part of their propaganda. In addition, they "waved the bloody shirt" long and vigorously, extolled and apotheosized the "soldier in grey," rehashed the touching scenes of the war, found new laurels for the South and new crimes for the "Yankees." The tales of Republican misrule in the South during Reconstruction were a most fertile and favorite field for exploitation. Bourbon orators pictured their Kentucky under Democratic rule as the only "simon-pure" free state in the Union, the only effective guardian of the federal Constitution, and the only vital champion of the southern states suffering under northern tyranny.

These Kentucky Bourbons differed somewhat from their southern neighbors. Though given the same designation by contemporaries, their programs varied widely. In the South generally Bourbonism featured retrenchment, reduced taxation, rejection of the agrarian ideal, white supremacy, financial frugality, oligarchical rule, encouragement of industrialization, aversion to federal power, and ex-Confederate political domination.[6] As noted, while the group called Bourbons in Kentucky stood for many of these tenets, they did not—like their southern brethren—depart from a worship of the agrarian, prewar ways. And while some of the Bourbons supported railroads in their region, in general, Kentucky's conservative faction at this time looked with disdain at the industrialization of the state.

It was instead their factional enemy, the New Departure Democrats led by Watterson and William Campbell Preston Breckinridge of Lexington, who gave railroads and industry the strongest support. But this group in turn fought reduced taxation and accepted black voting. Chiefly united only in their desire to keep the Republicans out of power and Democrats in, neither of the two factions represented in all aspects the Bourbon leadership and programs prevalent in other southern states. In many ways, then, Kentucky presented a political picture unique in the region.

The State Political Conventions of 1871

The Democratic delegates assembled at Frankfort, May 3, in the hall of the House of Representatives (Old State House). Judge Craddock, Chairman of the State Central Committee, called the meeting to order. The small auditorium early became so crowded and the air so stale that the meeting moved to the green in front of the Capitol. Craddock explained that the issue was "whether all powers shall concentrate in the General Government, or remain distributed as heretofore." The "revolutionary Republicans," the leader of the Bourbon branch suggested, sought "despotism and black equality."

The gathering proved to be far from orderly. At one point the permanent chairman, General Lucius Desha of Harrison County, shouted that he was "presiding over a mob" and threatened to quit. The speeches bristled with castigations of "Radical" outrages, usurpations, and tyrannies. As twilight settled down, the group became so disorderly and the proceedings so confused

36

partly because of darkness, that few could be certain as to what was happening.

During the course of the convention a spirited race developed for the nomination for governor. The names of Governor Leslie, John Y. Brown, John Quincy Adams King of McCracken County, Judge John T. Bunch of Jefferson County, Thomas L. Jones, Elijah C. Phister of Mason County, the venerable Judge Richard Hawes of Bourbon County, and J. Proctor Knott were eventually presented. The contest at first was between Leslie, who enjoyed the advantage of encumbency, and Brown. It became clear, however, that Brown could not beat Leslie. Leslie soon received 638 votes, a majority. Knott reached a high of 432.

Leslie was not especially popular, even with his own party. He was said to have a colorless personality.[7] Since as an orphan he had worked his way up from poverty in that section of Wayne County which is now a part of Clinton, he had enjoyed little opportunity for education. He began the practice of law in Monroe County. His pro-Confederate proclivities, together with the geographical location of his residence and his willingness to accept the Bourbon philosophy, contributed to his political advancement.[8] John G. Carlisle of Covington received the nomination for lieutenant governor. He was declared by one commentator to be "by odds the ablest man on the ticket." However, the ex-Whig Leslie was sober, conservative, and safe. Watterson commented, "We did not get, we may as well confess, very happy in Governor Leslie." Another editor wrote: "Whilst it is true local interests were ignored to some extent in nominating our candidate for Governor, and a man selected who does not seem to have even a germ of progress or improvement in his entire being, nevertheless this should not create lukewarmness. . . ."[9]

Because Leslie as state senator had opposed passage of the Southern Railroad Bill, many Democrats in central, northern, and southern Kentucky were antagonistic to him. Moreover, in Louisville he was regarded as an enemy of the "New Departure." But it could not be denied that he had aided and abetted the Confederacy, a fact sufficient to extenuate many shortcomings. In his favor too were the indispensable party machinery, a "Bourbon" leaning, the L & N Railroad, the Louisville ward bosses, and the tobacco interests. "No one (not even McCreery)," thought one editor, "could have beaten Leslie."

Among the nominees for other offices were D. Howard Smith for auditor (incumbent); John W. Rodman of Franklin County, who had been obliged during war to flee to Canada because of Confederate sympathy, for attorney general; James W. Tate, incumbent, known far and wide for affability and desire to be accommodating, for treasurer; and Howard Andrew Millett (H. A. M.) Henderson, Fayette County, for superintendent of public instruction. Each of them had had a prosouthern association. One of the most popular men at the convention was the young Lexington lawyer and editor, Colonel W. C. P. Breckinridge, another of Morgan's trusty officers, already known as "the silver-tongued orator." The throng early called upon him for a speech, and he obliged graciously and mellifluously.[10] Henry Watterson, though not extravagant in his praise, thought the nominees "good Democrats, deserving well of their party and their country."

As the time for Negro voting was imminent, much talk was devoted to the subject—most of it was adverse. The sentiment of many at the convention was probably expressed by Captain D. T. Toles of Green County. A reporter on the spot recorded the essence of Toles' remarks in these words: "He had run for county clerk, and announced that he wanted no nigger votes, and that is the principle on which he wanted the Democrats of Kentucky to stand (appluase). If he was a nigger he would be a Radical, and, as he was a white man, he was a Democrat; that was the best way he could explain the difference between the two parties (Laughter)."[11]

The platform adopted by the convention declared for general amnesty, decried graft and corruption by Republicans in high office, deplored the inequalities brought about by the Republican national administration in collection and distribution of taxes,

Governor Preston Leslie

Collection of the Kentucky Historical Society

insisted that the preservation of constitutional liberty was possible "only through the States," inveighed against federal usurpation and tyranny in connection with reconstruction, and viewed with alarm the "un-constitutional encroachments" by the federal government upon the rights of the states. Another plank declared against violence and lawlessness. It promised that the Democratic party would pass needed legislation to punish the lawless and to "secure to every person ample protection of life, liberty, and property, under laws enacted by our own legislature, and administered by our own courts."

Though not failing to stir feeling by references to an unpleasant past, the platform clearly omitted as much as it included. It made no reference, for instance, to the development of natural resources, industrial expansion, improving labor conditions, aiding the unfortunate, or needed educational advancement.[12]

On May 17, the Republican delegates assembled at Frankfort. Without fanfare and in a businesslike manner, they named candidates for the state offices and adopted a platform. For governor John M. Harlan of Frankfort and Louisville, an ex-Whig aristocrat, former attorney general and colonel in the Union army, who had recently left the Conservative party and joined the Republicans, was nominated by acclamation; for lieutenant governor, George M. Thomas, Lewis County; for attorney general, William Brown, Jessamine County; for auditor, William Krippenstapel, Louisville; for treasurer, General Speed S. Fry, Boyle County; for state superintendent of public instruction, W. E. Moberly; and for register of the land office, Joseph K. McClarty of Rockcastle County.

With the exception of Harlan and the colorful General Fry, the nominees were not generally known over the state. It was calculated, however, that Harlan, Fry, and Krippenstapel, editor of the Louisville *Volksblatt*, would run well. One Bluegrass editor asserted that the Republican convention was "a cut and dried affair, made up largely of Federal office-holders, mostly self-appointed delegates." He was of the opinion that Colonel Harlan

Republican gubernatorial candidate and Supreme
Court Justice John M. Harlan

Collection of the Kentucky Historical Society

would have great difficulty in reconciling his past and present, averring that the candidate at different times had been proslavery, anti-Negro suffrage, anti-Lincoln, pro-McClellan, and "anti-Radical."[13] The "New Departure" leader Watterson and the Bourbon leader Johnston, on the other hand, were under no delusions about Harlan's ability. "He [Harlan] immediately commended himself to the reasoning portion of the old Radicals," wrote Professor Coulter, "and commanded the respect of intelligent Democrats."[14]

Harlan, in his acceptance speech at the convention, was aggressive, yet restrained to a degree unknown to the old Radicals. He charged that the General Assembly had "stubbornly refused to pass laws to repress lawlessness," that the "Democratic Party have, by their total policy, turned away from our borders the immigration that we want to improve and foster our material interests and make us prosperous. . . . Such men," he declared, "will not come to our State until they are assured of protection to life, liberty, and to property."

Proceeding, he declared, "I want such legislation and such a policy as will cause works of internal improvements to spring up in the state." Echoing the New Departure Democrats he stated, "I want railroads all over the State. The great principle of equality should prevail, and railroad facilities should be granted." To Harlan, industrialization meant progress. Upon the Negro question he declared, "The Legislature has refused to allow the colored man the right to testify in the courts," a policy not adopted by returned Confederate soliders, but by "stay at homes." Concerning those who "wave the bloody shirt," he said, "It will be my duty to arraign the conduct of those who, by their rancor and bitterness, have created trouble. This class of men have pandered to prejudice and the passions of the times and have increased much of the lawlessness which but for them had passed away."

Harlan declared that "there are men here who are ashamed that they were in the Union Army, but I am not one of these." In closing, he reiterated his determination to stand by the Fourteenth and Fifteenth Amendments, thus putting the Republican party of the state in line with the national party's policy. It was clear, however, that he wished the campaign to be waged on state and not national issues.[15] Harlan likely believed that in national affairs the Republican party might justly be assailed. The Democrats were confident of it.

The platform adopted by the convention was one reflecting Harlan's views on industrial, political, and educational advancement. It asked for the calling of a convention to revise the state constitution,[16] favored inviting immigrants to Kentucky to help develop her natural resources, and excoriated the Democratic General Assembly for both its action and nonaction. It charged that the legislature refused to legislate against the Ku Klux, which prevailed in many parts of the state, "intimidating and murdering peaceful citizens, defying the officers of the law, overawing the courts, and boldly invading the capitol while the legislature was in session." It denounced that body's refusal to pass a law permitting Negro testimony in the courts as "unchristian" and "unworty of the age in which we live." The platform vigorously took to task the Democratic party in power for "largely increasing the public debt," shaping legislation so as to turn immigrants away from the state, and so "pandering to the passions incident to the late Civil War as to keep alive a spirit of sectionalism and place the people of Kentucky in an attitude of hostility to the inevitable results of the war." With black voters in mind, the Republicans reiterated their stand against the Democratic policy of "discrimination against the colored population," and chided the Democratic party for failing "to perform the high and solemn duty of a government in not making adequate provision for the education of all children in the State." They indicted the Democratic party for attempting to "prevent the enforcement . . . of the Thirteenth, Fourteenth, and Fifteenth Amendments." The platform, moreover, stood for "complete amnesty to all of our fellow citizens, of every State, who are laboring under disabilities by reason of their participation in the late rebellion"; it also held out the olive branch to the southern states, hoping for them all the "blessings and prosperity to be enjoyed under a republican form of government."[17]

The platform may have been designed in part to appeal to the New Departure Democrats who were advocating some of the same things. However, partisanship was too strong and wartime memories were too close to permit many voters to go over to another party.

Although Henry Watterson was not converted, he was somewhat impressed by the reformed Republican program. He wrote:

> *The proceedings of the Republican convention at Frankfort realized all that we anticipated. The nomination of General Harlan; the conciliatory tone of the resolutions and speeches; the respectability and moderation of the gathering bore out our preconception of a minority seeking converts. The succeeding canvass is not likely to vary these somewhat commonplace features. There is little room for the Republicans to make headway in Kentucky. . . .*

Watterson had definitely decided to stick with the Democratic party—to work for reform in and through it.[18] Nevertheless, Harlan came nearer standing for the things "Marse Henry" advocated than did the "Bourbons" and the Democratic platform.

The ensuing canvass, characterized by joint debates between Leslie and Harlan and other candidates, was hard fought throughout. The Republican standard-bearer was a singularly striking figure—large, fine looking, college educated, cultured, and impressive. Champ Clark, the able Democratic leader of later years, had as a boy heard Harlan speak in 1863. At that time young Harlan appeared on the platform with Governor Bramlette. "The first really great man I ever saw," declared Clark later, "was Col. John Marshall Harlan." Clark wrote that Harlan was as "magnificent a specimen of a physical man as one would have found in a month's journey—standing six feet three in his stockings, weighing two hundred avoirdupois without an ounce of surplus flesh, red-headed, blond as a lily, graceful as a panther, he was the typical

Kentuckian in his best estate." Describing Harlan's mental and educational equipment as "superb," Clark, in further describing the occasion, declared that "Governor Bramlette was a large, handsome man and made a good speech, but Harlan easily over-topped him mentally, physically, and oratorically. Mere chunk of a boy as I was, I could see that Harlan was the greater man."[19]

On the other hand, Leslie was unprepossessing in appearance, a poor speaker, and a colorless candidate. Yet, in spite of the vast personal differences between the two candidates, Harlan was at a disadvantage. His changing stand on various issues in the past was decidedly hurtful to him. Regardless, the facts that he was a Republican and had served in the Union army would most likely have caused his defeat. In the canvass, the shrewd Democratic leaders knew what would appeal to the voters, and made the most of it. They charged Harlan with being a "political weathercock" and hounded him with excerpts from old speeches against the Radicals. Leslie took comfort, during the joint debates, in con-fronting him with past declarations. In one speech Leslie reported Harlan's having told the public a few years past that the Repub-lican's policy was "revolutionary, and if carried out would result in the destruction of our free government. . . ." "That," Leslie declared, "was a correct view of it. . . ."

Declaring that he would rather be right than consistent, Harlan, though regretting his 1859 proslavery sentiments, pleaded with Kentuckians to acquiesce in the results of the war and to cease supporting the "suicidal" Democratic policy of "opposition and obstruction." He begged them to look to the future and forget the dead past.[20]

Moreover, the Republican candidate was charged by Democratic stumpers as being an advocate of social equality between the two races. Though vigorously denying this charge, he was injured by the damaging propaganda. Many were quick to believe and to spread the charge.

In return, Harlan took the Democratic administration to task for failure to break up the "lawless bands" and the Ku Klux. But he made some bitter enemies when he accused the powerful Louisville and Nashville Railroad of being a railroad monopoly, "absorbing the capital of the state and controlling its politics." He supported the building of the Cincinnati-Southern line, for one reason to relieve the state from the clutches of the L. & N. He chided the Democrats for opposing a system of taxation based upon ability to pay (the income tax) and bitterly assailed the newly enacted and unpopular rate-bill system of raising money for common school support. This system placed the burden of support upon many of the people least able to pay. He was perhaps most eloquent in pleading for the industrialization of the state, the development of its natural resources, and the improvement of the public school system.

During the campaign, Leslie, perhaps because of Watterson's behavior, swung a bit closer to the New Departure. He was rather successful in focusing the people's attention on national affairs, particularly upon Republican wrongdoing and wastefulness. Meanwhile, fellow orators invoked the past to remind the people of the "horrors" of "Republican rule" in Kentucky during the war. General Harlan was at a decided disadvantage in trying to justify the Grant administration which was odious in the eyes of most Kentuckians. Yet he attracted many able conservatives, including Richard T. Jacob, James F. Robinson, and Leslie Combs, to his program for the state.[21] But the Democratic Party was too strong.

The vote, August 7, was 126,455 for Leslie; 89,299 for Harlan. The greatest majority was piled up by H. A. M. Henderson, who enjoyed a lead of 43,598 over his nearest opponent, the Reverend William M. Pratt of Lexington. The total figures represented the largest vote ever cast in the state by either party. The new General Assembly would have 35 Democrats and 3 Republicans in the upper house, and 82 Democrats and 18 Republicans in the lower. Of the 116 counties, the Republicans carried 25. In addition to carrying many of the eastern Kentucky counties, among them Carter, Clay, Jackson, Bell, Knox, Laurel, Lee, Magoffin, Monroe, Owsley, Pulaski, Russell, Wayne, and Whitley, Harlan carried three central Kentucky counties—Fayette, Garrard, and Jessamine. He barely missed Woodford and Boyle. He also carried Christian with its large Negro population. His strongest support had come from the Union-minded mountaineers and from the counties with sizeable Negro populations. Perhaps the most impressive item of the results was the fact that Harlan received better than 60,000 more votes than the "Radical" candidate for governor, R. T. Baker, had polled in 1868, while Leslie gained less than 11,000 over Stevenson's 1868 vote.[22] It was clear that the Republican party enjoyed most of the Negroes' suffrage.

Far from discouraged, the defeated Republicans actually were jubilant. The pleased editor of the *Cincinnati Gazette* declared that the election of the Republican ticket in "almost any other state in the Union would have been no greater victory than was won in Kentucky." Watterson admitted that Harlan was "a man of ability and made a good race for Governor." Another delighted Ohio editor, grooming the defeated Republican candidate for vice president, declared: "Mr. Harlan needs no other introduction to the American people than by the canvass he has made of his State. It was distinguished for spirit, pluck and fact, and was sustained by admirable physical powers and a popular style of public speaking."[23]

The Democrats, noting their comfortable margin of victory, were not worried. They were conscious of Republican gains but not frightened. It was convenient for the Bourbon press, led by the *Kentucky Yeoman* and the *Lexington Press*, to blame Watterson and the *Courier-Journal* for not having enthusiastically supported Leslie, who "failed to catch the vision of economic and social progress" and talked of Congressional tyranny and "vengeful autocracy."

Watterson, however, remained unperturbed. He extolled his party and did some interesting analyzing: "Why is it that, with an acceptable and eloquent nominee for Governor, with the perfect organization of a hopeful minority, with an apparent schism in the ranks of their adversaries, the Republicans have been able to make such scanty headway against the square and substantial majority which they sought to reduce and break down?" He declared that "notwithstanding Leslie's blunder . . . and his lack of personal magnetism, he walks over the track, and with the entire Democratic ticket."

"It means," Watterson concluded, that "it is a silent and outstanding protest against years of wrong, the memory of which survives. It is an active and live assertion of popular freedom against the insidious workings of the Central power. It is a declaration on the part of Kentucky that gives the country to understand that such is our dread of Radicalism that we prefer all else to the bare possibility of a political domination inspired from Washington."[24]

Preston H. Leslie was inaugurated governor at Frankfort, September 5, 1871, amid an impressive crowd of officeseekers and well-wishers. The occasion was made solemn by the appearance of the venerable Chief Justice George Robertson who, though paralyzed and unable to rise from his portable chair, administered the oath of office to Leslie in a firm voice and then sank back exhausted on his pillow. When he fell back, all thought him dead. Yet he raised his head and smiled feebly, at the same time tendering his resignation as chief justice to the governor.[25]

Leslie's brief message filled the people with hope. He frankly committed the administration to a New Departure program of "school reform, universal education, internal improvement throughout the State and law and order." He was frequently interrupted by prolonged applause.

All now looked to the meeting of the General Assembly to convene toward the last of December, a legislature to be made up largely of Democrats. In the house were gathered a few prominent men and men soon to be prominent. Among these were Cassius M. Clay, Jr., of Bourbon County, future gubernatorial hopeful; Richmond's James Bennet McCreary, future governor; future United States Senator Joseph Clay Stiles Blackburn from Woodford County; William Cassius Goodloe, nephew of Cassius Marcellus

Clay and Republican leader from Lexington. In the main, however, the lawmakers were "men of the soil." Half of the members of the house were listed as farmers, practically all of whom were Democrats. Attorneys made up a quarter of the membership. In the senate, however, 22 of the 38 members were lawyers. Relative youth characterized the personnel of that chamber. Fully half of the senators were less than forty years of age.[26]

Foremost of all the pressing problems for that body to act upon was the matter of suppressing lawlessness. Upon this point Watterson declared, "All of us know the Ku Klux do exist . . . in sufficient measures to disturb our peace. . . ." The Louisville editor stated that there was "not a newspaper in Kentucky . . . which has not published cases of outlawry and denounced the Ku Klux. . . . It is our business to suppress violence . . . The people must begin to legislate for the peace of society in a liberal spirit."

Governor Leslie devoted a sizeable portion of his message to the legislature on December 6, 1871 to the subject of lawlessness, which had in some instances, he declared, "assumed an organized form, executing its violence and perpetrating its acts under cover of the night, by bodies of men too powerful to be resisted by the citizens, and so disguised that they cannot be recognized and brought to trial for their misdeeds; and thus are enabled to defy both the law and its officers." He believed, however, that failure to bring criminals to justice resulted more from the shortcomings of local officials in doing their duty than from lack of laws. Be this as it may, he nevertheless recommended that the legislature "pass such additional laws as shall be necessary to more certainly reach the various forms of crime as it crops out at the hands of organizations and other evil-disposed persons, so much to the terror and shame of the people." And he suggested that "some law imposing more stringent and severe penalties upon public officers for their failure and neglect to look after and enforce the penal and criminal laws" might be given consideration, as well as the enactment of additional legislation for the "capture and bringing to trial of offenders."[27]

Leslie's suggestions, strengthened by favorable public opinion, caused the General Assembly to pass a law against organized violence. This statute declared: (1) The writing or posting of theatening notices would be a crime punishable by a fine of $1 to $100 and not less than three months in jail. (2) The conspiring of any two or more persons to intimidate or alarm any person or to commit felonies would make the perpetrators liable to penitentiary imprisonment of from six to twelve months or a fine of from $100 to $500 and three months in jail. (3) Any two or more persons who should band together and "go forth armed and disguised" would be subject to the same penalties.[28] This legislation, together with public opinion, went far toward retarding organized violence in the form of Ku Klux or Regulators; however, general lawlessness for some time to come would show little indication of abatement.

Governor Leslie had, in spite of noisy opposition, recommended the passage of legislation permitting Negro testimony in the courts in cases involving persons of the white race. Consequently, in January the General Assembly enacted a law declaring that "No one shall be incompetent as a witness because of his or her race or color." A few days later Bland Ballard, federal judge at Louisville, refused to take further Negro cases which could be tried under state law, giving as his reason passage of the statute admitting Negro testimony.[29] Thus was ended a problem which for several years had been a source of bitter conflict.

True to his promise, Leslie, calling attention to the report of Superintendent of Public Instruction Henderson, recommended to the General Assembly the passage of laws designed to improve the state's public school system, particularly laws making possible increased funds, improvement of school buildings, and the development of a better system of Negro education.

There is no subject upon which you are called to legislate of more importance to the public welfare, and which should excite a more earnest interest in all who love their country and their kind. The stability of our free institutions, and the good order of society, rest upon the virtue and intelligence of the people, to the promotion of which nothing except religion . . . can more efficiently contribute than a wise and thorough system of popular education. [30]

In an able report Henderson had set forth his plan for improving Kentucky's public school system. The report included what was designated as the "Great Desiderata," the essentials to a "well furnished School System." Among these desiderata were recommendations for (a) a general statute allowing school districts to tax themselves "without the necessity of special legislation," (b) a law providing for the building of good schoolhouses upon a uniform plan, (c) a normal school for the professional training of teachers, and (d) a general law allowing cities and towns to tax themselves for the purpose of establishing graded schools.

In spite of Governor Leslie's hopeful phrases in education's favor and Henderson's forward-looking program, the General Assembly did practically nothing to better a system which, according to educators, was "really wretched."[31] Two reasons for failure to enact legislation were lack of genuine interest on the part of the lawmakers and the long drawn out debate over passage of the Cincinnati Southern Railroad bill.

The governor reported at some length upon the state's financial condition. At the close of the fiscal year, October 10, 1871, the state deficit was a little over one million dollars, while the resources of the Sinking Fund were almost two and a half million.[32] Deducting the total outstanding indebtedness from the Sinking Fund total (leaving a balance of $1,366,448.89), a reader is impressed with the sound financial condition of the state treasury. But the impression is not accurate. During the fiscal year the state spent more than it was receiving. Actually, a deficit of nearly four hundred thousand dollars had been left. The governor had estimated that a deficit of more than $286,000 would occur. He pointed to the greatly increased demands upon the state government since 1865, giving as one reason the fact that the cost of handling of lunatics alone had risen from $104,000 to $243,000. Stating that other increases were in like proportion, he asked the General Assembly to make provision for eliminating the annual deficits. Leslie also suggested issuance of state bonds in the amount of $500,000, bearing interest at 8 percent per annum.[33] The General Assembly responded by passing such a measure on January 18, 1872. With an eye to public sentiment, the chief magistrate expressed opposition to the passage of additional tax measures. However, he did ask that body to pass legislation pointing to equalizing the assessments in the counties. He declared that only in a few counties was property assessed at full 100 percent value, that in most districts assessments did not exceed 50 percent of actual value.

One of the governor's other recommendations was the enactment of legislation providing for a geological survey. "I am satisfied," he stated, "that accurate and generally diffused information, such as science is able to give us, concerning the vast natural resources of our state, will form the starting point of a new era in the industrial progress and prosperity of the Commonwealth." He pointed out that a "complete and detailed geological survey" would ascertain the correct geography, make possible an accurate topographical map, and bring out the various geological formations of the state; it would as well indicate locations of good coal and distinguish the different beds of iron ore. It would lead, he predicted, to soil analyzations and also reveal the varieties and quality of building stones, other minerals and mineral springs, and valuable timbers. He thought that revelation to the world of Kentucky's vast undeveloped natural wealth would, should the state government encourage it, cause "streams of capital and immigrants to flow into the commonwealth." The governor deplored the fact that Kentucky had been buying minerals and timbers from states not nearly as richly endowed with these resources and pointed to the fact that many states much younger than Kentucky had long since begun to develop their resources, thereby attracting capital and immigrants. He declared that these had already far outstripped the Bluegrass State. Pursuant to Leslie's recommendations, bills were introduced in the General Assembly providing for a geological survey and for an immigrants' bureau.[34] While neither of these measures obtained sufficient votes for passage at that session, it was evident that the governor was moving closer to the Watterson wing.

The Cincinnati Southern Railroad Controversy

Soon after Appomattox, industrially minded leaders in Kentucky became intensely interested in the development of better transportation facilities. They stressed particularly rapid development of turnpikes, waterways, and railroads, not only to improve the state but to make profits. The impetus for transportation facilities throughout the nation came from those cities which were interested in tapping areas with rich resources for commercial purposes.

By 1870 railroad stock companies were being formed by the score in Kentucky, and the legislature was grinding out charters with reckless abandon.[35] Counties and cities floated millions in bonds to build railways. The movement took on the proportions of frenzy; everyone, it seemed, wanted to "get in" on the good thing. Investors conjured up visions of millions in profits. Even prior to 1870, the citizens of Lexington and Fayette County, perhaps jealous of Louisville, had voted $450,000 to construct the Lexington and Big Sandy Railroad, to tap the rich mineral and timber resources of undeveloped eastern Kentucky. Woodford County citizens had voted $400,000 in bonds for the project. Tremendous speculation accompanied many rail projects. Many of the roads planned were never built. Money was handled recklessly and soon many counties and cities found themselves with huge obligations on their hands and little tangible evidence of much having been accomplished. By 1871, almost $14,000,000 had been voted for railroads in the state. Ambitious projects would begin, hundreds of thousands would be spent, money would run out with destinations far away. As funds were exhausted, many of the pseudotycoons found the termini of their roads in the wilds completely out of touch with a town or city.

Partisans of several roads in Kentucky had made an effort in 1869 to induce the General Assembly to provide for the issuance of $10,000,000 in bonds to aid railroad development in the state. A powerful Louisville and Nashville Railroad lobby, however, had been able to exert enough influence to kill the proposed legislation. Nevertheless, 143 miles of road were built in Kentucky in 1872. By the end of the next year 1,266 miles of railroad were in actual use in the state. So notable had been the progress that Governor Leslie devoted considerable space in his message to the 1871-1872 legislature concerning strides recently made in transportation and to flattering prospects for greater achievement in the immediate future.[36]

The establishment of the Cincinnati Southern Railroad, a line projected from Cincinnati through Covington and central Kentucky to either Knoxville or Chattanooga in 1868, brought on one of the most heated political and commercial controversies in Kentucky history.[37] The principal opposition to building the road came from Louisville, particularly from the Louisville and Nashville Railroad. Louisville was a bitter commercial rival of the Queen City; and the Louisville and Nashville Company feared that a railway from Cincinnati through the heart of the Bluegrass state would deprive it of central and eastern Kentucky business and make Cincinnati, instead of Louisville, the commercial mecca of the Commonwealth. Moreover, Louisville and Cincinnati were militant rivals for the business of the South.[38]

Businessmen of Cincinnati, finding trade to the South largely barred via Louisville, had determined upon building a road of their own through central Kentucky. Under the guidance of a prominent leader, Edward A. Ferguson, they were able to persuade the citizens of their city to vote favorably upon a municipal bond issue of $10,000,000 to be used in constructing the road; were able also to circumvent a section of the Ohio constitution prohibiting cities' permitting their citizens to vote their credit or money in aid of a company or corporation.[39] The people of central Kentucky were jubilant. In fact the entire South, especially east of the Mississippi, was eager for the success of the project.

Louisville and the Louisville and Nashville Company, becoming alarmed, began to take measures designed to prevent the Southern road's being built. First, they began dealing more gently with central Kentucky. Then they projected a counter line to Chattanooga from Louisville, expecting an alliance with the Ohio and Cumberland Railway. Leading Louisville and Louisville and Nashville spokesmen were General Basil W. Duke, Colonel Isaac Caldwell and Henry Watterson, who defined the Cincinnati Southern Railroad as a "monstrous humbug."[40]

Louisville strategists, realizing that the real test would come in the state's General Assembly in connection with rights-of-way, set the stage for a propaganda campaign designed to inflame Kentuckians against Cincinnati. The Queen City was northern, they reminded, had fought for the Union, advocated abolition of slavery, was located out of Kentucky, and was in the habit of going Republican. Louisville and Nashville orators, making the most of the opportunities, encountered little difficulty in enlisting the almost solid support of all of western and a sizeable scattering in eastern Kentucky. Ironically enough, the Bourbons, because of geographical location, strongly supported the Southern Railroad bill. The Cincinnati partisans secured the services of lionized General John C. Breckinridge, who had recently returned from self-imposed exile. The principal argument favoring the bill was centered upon the economic development and growth of the state which the road would make possible.[41]

Opponents of the bill in the legislature concentrated upon the question of constitutionality, contending that a road through Kentucky with a charter drawn by Cincinnati was indeed a bizarre and exotic thing in legal circles. The idea of Cincinnati's buying Kentucky and the touchy matters of state sovereignty and state honor were broadcast widely. Debates were long and heated. Preston Leslie, at that time still in the state senate, apparently felt obligated to the Louisville and Nashville Company. He seemed to forsake his Bourbon brethren for the Louisville partisans, at least at that time.

On March 1, 1870, the senate voted 22 to 13 against the bill to authorize the "extension and construction" of the road within the state. Three days later the house voted 49 to 43 to table the measure, and the following day a motion to reconsider was rejected by 46 to 31. A message from the Tennessee legislature expressed regret at the Kentucky Assembly's action.

The following year in January, 1871, the General Assembly again rejected the measure, even after the governor of Georgia had sent a commission to urge its enactment. The people of central Kentucky, indignant and angry, protested vociferously. Public meetings at Lexington, Covington, Danville, Harrodsburg, and other places denounced the legislature, which had spent most of its time debating the issue, and appealed to Congress to grant the charter. Moreover, Bluegrass towns began boycotting Louisville.[42]

Following the second defeat, a bill was introduced in Congress, February 9, 1871, by Senator John Sherman of Ohio, to promote construction of the Cincinnati Southern road. This action was warmly approved generally in central Kentucky but, taking the state as a whole, the action was generally disapproved. The bill was characterized as "an open act of Congressional interference in state matters." Even many erstwhile legislative friends of the bill now expressed decided opposition to the road's being built under congressional charter. A joint resolution offered in the General Assembly on February 11 set forth that body's principal points of opposition, the burden of the argument being along the line of the old question of invasion of state rights by the federal government. The final resolution instructed the United States senators from Kentucky to vote against the congressional measure. During this time, members of the Congress from Kentucky were deluged with memorials and petitions from central Kentucky town meetings, all urging the harassed solons to support the "Ferguson Bill."[43]

In Congress, two Kentuckians, James B. Beck in the lower house and Garrett Davis in the Senate, waged a determined battle to delay action. Their tactics were apparently successful, because one regular and a special session closed without passage of the measure. Meanwhile, interest shifted back to Kentucky.

The central Kentucky Democrats now threatened to play their trump card. They would indicate to the obdurate politicians their intention of deserting the party through the summer campaign and election unless the Southern Railroad bill was passed. Real threats were made through the *Woodford Weekly* and other Bluegrass papers.

In spite of this ominous warning, however, the Democratic convention, meeting in May, had nominated Leslie, an enemy of the bill. Carlisle, an outstanding proponent of the measure, had been chosen to run for lieutenant governor. The platform was silent on the Cincinnati Southern Railroad. On the other hand, the Republican platform endorsed the Southern bill, and Harlan spoke for it during the summer campaign.[44]

At the beginning of the legislative session in December, the proponents of the legislation gained a signal victory in the election of James B. McCreary of Madison County, a staunch friend of the measure, as speaker of the house. Another circumstance favorable to passage was the decision of the Southern's trustees to keep Cincinnati lobbyists away from Frankfort. Moreover, proponents also seemed agreeable to certain amendments designed to confer a measure of control to the state's General Assembly and jurisdiction to Kentucky courts.[45] Although torrid debates continued in both chambers, the "acrimony" of the last two sessions, a reporter noted, had now disappeared. The bill's victory in the house, 59-38, "was received very quietly, it having been a foregone conclusion." The few Republicans generally, regardless of geography, supported the bill. In the senate, supporters of the bill warned Louisville not to oppose them too hard or else they would pull down their oppressor, the L & N Railroad. A senator demanded that the question be put: "We the people of Central Kentucky want the road, and if we are willing to bear the enormities charged upon this bill, in God's name let us test the results of our own judgement and convictions." On January 28, with the chamber crowded to overflowing, the senators voted, after a debate that included Civil War appeals to both sides. A 19-19 tie resulted. President pro tempore Carlisle of Covington cast his vote for the road. Apparently Governor Leslie was not disposed to oppose enactment of the measure into law now that the people had spoken through their representatives.[46]

Great was the rejoicing throughout central Kentucky, with mass meetings and firing of cannon in Lexington, Danville, and other towns. The struggle had been unique in the annals of Kentucky. It resulted in the breakup of one of the most complete monopolies (that of the city of Louisville and the Louisville and Nashville Railroad) ever enjoyed by an American city.

Legislators did not spend all their time at their work. The governor had his levees, and the Capital Hotel, where almost half of them stayed, had a "hop" (the Assembly Ball) every Friday night. On occasion the faithful were rewarded: Senator-elect McCreery gave a banquet to honor those who selected him during the session. The menu included sea turtle soup, oysters, venison, grouse, duck, partridge, squirrels, buffalo, rabbit, quail on toast, sardines, lobsters, beef tongue and other, more common, meats. The lawmakers partook of "the leberal [sic] flow of splendid, sparkling champaigne wine."

With such nighttime activities, it is little wonder that reporters noted a listlessness, a "kind of apathy" in the sessions during the day. As the General Assembly neared its end the two houses "accomplished little or nothing" toward clearing their calendars.[47]

The legislative session, 1871-1872, ended March 25. It was not one notable for reformative enactments. Although it passed 1,015 acts and 41 joint resolutions, most of them were of a private nature, purely local and largely selfish in interest. Most of the measures were for the benefit of individuals, particularly for the "benefit of the late sheriff" of such and such a county. Numerous measures were to help turnpike companies. Some of the acts were to permit localities to vote upon prohibiting the sale of spiritous liquors; many were to authorize taxing for schools in single towns.

Most of the measures most needed were not passed. All-important education and taxation reform measures had little, if any, chance of passage. During the session, much discussion had been devoted to the state's eleemosynary institutions, particularly to the questions of mounting expense costs and rapidly increasing numbers leading to overcrowding. A measure, reflecting conditions in the states was passed to provide for appointment of persons to take charge of pauper lunatics who could not be taken to the asylums because of overcrowded conditions. Such persons were to be paid $200 per year by the Commonwealth for each lunatic they cared for.

Of tremendous interest to the politicians, and a labor upon which considerable time was spent, was the provision for redistricting the state into ten congressional divisions. Living up to their previous high standards in the art of gerrymandering, the lawmakers realigned the political map in such a way as to make it difficult to send a single Republican candidate to Congress. Another purely partisan bill pressed through the two houses was a measure designed to retain in office the incumbent council of the city of Lexington for four additional years, beginning in March of 1873. The legislation had been intended to prevent new Negro voters from exerting influence in the Lexington city elections. However, the purposes of the bill were so blatantly apparent that Leslie vetoed it, writing, "We can never truly and effectually remedy a political evil by exceptional laws."[48]

It was stated that, by and large, the state suffered no loss when the solons decided to disband.

IV

THE PEOPLE

Various efforts were made to discover and to stereotype the typical Kentuckian. Some writers and cartoonists living out of the state presented the mountaineer as the typical Kentuckian; others preferred the central Kentucky gentleman.

Those favoring the mountaineer depicted him as barefooted, denim clad, black slouch-hatted, shaggy bearded, swarthy, rifle-toting, moonshine-drinking, shiftless, and feud-inclined. Those selecting the Kentucky gentleman revealed him as a suave, attractive julep-drinking figure with goatee, long black coat, fine Stetson hat, and southern drawl—a courtly and gallant man knowledgeable in horseflesh, games of chance, and feminine elegance.

These stereotypes failed to include numerous small farmers, tenants, urban dwellers of Louisville or Covington, small business-men, professional people, Negroes, or any number of other groups. Actually there was no typical Kentuckian. The sons and daughters of the Commonwealth prided themselves on being an extremely individualistic people, and different.

The census reports did not recognize the individuality; cold statistics reported the state's population at 1,321,011 in 1870 and 2,147,174 thirty years later. This overall growth was offset by the fact that the state was falling from eighth largest in population among the states to twelfth in that thirty year period. After a half-century of expansion her growth rate trailed the national average: Kentucky's population growth of almost 25 percent between 1870-1880 fell below the nation's rate of 30 percent; a

13 percent increase from 1880-1890 was only half the country's rate of 25 percent; and the 15.5 percent in the last decade of the century still fell short of America's 21 percent.[1]

Gradually, alert citizens became aware of other changes. The antebellum fears of black domination lessened somewhat as the percentage of Negroes in Kentucky's population dropped steadily from nearly 17 per cent in 1870 to a little over 13 percent—almost the national average—by the century's end. To many white Kentuckians this was a desirable decrease; others feared a possible labor shortage. As a result, in 1870 the Lexington *Observer and Reporter* predicted the South and Kentucky would employ Chinese laborers due to the "demoralized state of African labor." Emigration to Kansas and elsewhere by Negroes throughout the South also affected Kentucky. Notices of Negro migration occasionally appeared in Kentucky newspapers.[2] The advocacy of effective means of attracting white immigrants was notable even in political platforms.

Kentucky in fact had few immigrants. Less than 5 percent of the population was foreign-born in 1870, and by and large the postwar foreign born concentrated in the urban areas along the upper Ohio River. Interior cities, including Lexington, had few immigrants and local efforts to attract them failed to gain more than negligible results. A Swiss and five German colonies in Laurel County and single German colonies in Lincoln, Rockcastle, Boyle, Lyon, Edmonson, and Christian counties remained as exceptions. The new wave of immigration from eastern Europe in the late nineteenth century so effectively by-passed Kentucky that in 1900 the state had fewer foreign-born (50,000) than thirty years earlier. The mountain counties of Johnson, Owsley, and Perry with a combined population of over 28,000 had a total of three foreign-born. German and Irish immigrants still predominated in 1900 as in 1870. Nathaniel Southgate Shaler in his *Kentucky: A Pioneer Commonwealth* argued that the Commonwealth had been "relatively dormant" since the end of the war because of its "natural torpor" and failure to attract immigrants. "The quickest form of profit," he maintained, "is gained by the immigration of well-trained and laborious people."[3] To Shaler and others, this lack of immigration reflected a failure. If new ideas, different lifestyles and cultural patterns occurred in Kentucky, they would have to come basically from a native, white, Anglo-Saxon citizenry.

Even few native-born Americans immigrated to Kentucky. In 1900 nine of every ten citizens living in the state were native born. Surrounding states provided most of the immigrants to Kentucky, and most of her own emigrants settled in those same states, not far from the old Commonwealth. But few in Kentucky desired, or perhaps could afford, to leave the state; eight of every ten born in the state never settled elsewhere. With few immigrants entering, few Kentuckians leaving, and a decrease in the overall Negro population, Kentucky's population remained remarkably tight and homogeneous, and became increasingly so during each decade to 1900. While still strongly individualistic, Kentuckians paradoxically were becoming characterized by more conformity.

Urban Life

Urban areas presented a major exception to this pattern. Negroes left the farms after the war for cities, especially Lexington and Louisville. Thus while Negroes constituted only 13 percent of Kentucky's total population in 1900, they were one-fifth of Louisville's, nearly 40 per cent of Lexington's, and more than half of Winchester's populations. While few Negroes lived in Newport and Covington, both cities did have large German and Irish immigrant populations, as did Louisville. Overall, 10 percent of Kentucky's urban population was foreign-born, as compared to only 1 percent in rural Kentucky.[4]

Like the rest of the nation, Kentucky became more urbanized. Louisville doubled in population from 100,000 in 1870 to over 200,000 by 1900, making the city the nation's eighteenth largest. By century's end, the Commonwealth's most populous cities were Louisville, Covington with 43,000, Newport with 28,000 and

THE PEOPLE

Lexington with 26,000. Almost one-fifth of all Kentuckians dwelled in urban areas. Comparatively, Kentucky's cities at best were either holding their rank or declining. This one-fifth was far less than the national average of urban population—more than 37 percent in 1900.[5] The key to Kentucky's development was not urban influence. The cities were, however, the commercial centers of the state.

In the late nineteenth century, the cities evolved characteristics more resembling those of the early twentieth century than those of the antebellum era. Lexington, for instance, with a population of over 16,000 in 1880 boasted 7 banks, 8 newspapers, 22 churches, 30 doctors, 45 lawyers, 47 manufacturing firms, and 153 retail grocers. Two years later the first telephone service was inaugurated, a few electric lights were set up along Main Street, and a mule-drawn street car ran over nine miles of track. By 1890 an electric street car replaced the mule drawn one on an eighteen mile service.[6]

A visitor described Louisville in 1880s as a city of broad, well-paved, well-shaded avenues whose somewhat uniform houses gave "an air of comfort, occasionally of elegance and solid good taste. The city has an exceedingly open, friendly, cheerful appearance." A prosperous city, Louisville appropriated over $100,000 for its fire department and the police department had a budget of over $150,000. By 1890 electric cars with nearly forty miles of track made mass public transportation available to most areas of that city, changing housing patterns so that early suburbs resulted. In 1879 Louisville opened a telephone exchange and four years later had electric lights in regular operation.[7] Even some smaller cities, including Hopkinsville, Paducah, and Maysville, had electric lights, cars, and telephones by the early 1890s.[8]

For a time it seemed that fire and flood would be the major threats to urban growth. In Lexington two blocks of houses were destroyed in an 1872 fire, several buildings in an 1875 one, the Phoenix Hotel four years later, the Opera House in 1886, and the courthouse in 1897.[9] Other towns suffered similar fates. The Paris

63

courthouse burned in 1872; Hopkinsville suffered $250,000 damage in 1882 and Harrodsburg $200,000. The most damaging fire of the entire period ended a boom city's rapid expansion when a Middlesboro fire in 1890 left 2,000 homeless after destroying or heavily damaging thirty-eight buildings at a loss of $350,000.[10] The threat of fire and the absence of effective firefighting equipment diminished the attractiveness of urban communities. The destructive Louisville flood of 1883 and tornado of 1890 added to that city's woes.

But despite detractions of fire, flood, disease, and other dangers, the city continued to be a commercial center for surrounding areas. More and more people from rural areas responded to the glamor and promise of city life. They did not see—or chose to ignore—the slums, the work houses, the sweatshops, the filth, the crime. A variety of shops, more doctors and specialists, an opportunity for advancement, good educational systems, and better cultural events—all this and more was offered to young men or women fresh from what they perceived as a dull, drab rural life. While many disillusioned and disappointed emigrants returned to their home communities, others stayed, and some prospered.

Life in the city could be leisurely and attractive, especially for those in the upper class. Laura Clay, daughter of Cassius, the emancipationist, revealed her day-to-day activities in her 1878 diary. What she experienced and did, while not always typical, exemplifies the life of many urban young women of her class. She rose between six and seven most mornings, invariably cleaned the lamps, then usually sewed until dinner. Typical afternoon fare included a long reading session, in which she favored *The Woman's Journal* and the classic English authors. Then came perhaps some shopping. Visits to and from friends and relatives varied the routine somewhat. As a member of the literary club she attended its functions, and enjoyed the parks and open air concerts.[11]

Village Life

For the majority of Kentuckians, however, a city was merely an exciting place to visit, a place in which to trade or perhaps to indulge in a few little sins. It was not their home. Still predominately rural throughout the nineteenth century, Kentucky depended on farming as its largest single occupation. Newspapers described the farmer as the bone and sinew of the country. Nathaniel Shaler told an Englishman that although the people were "absurdly conservative yet they present the highest type of rural life which the country affords, the only region which would remind you of the best parts of your own island." James Lane Allen believed that being a farmer at this time implied "no social inferiority, no rusticity, no boorishness," as was true elsewhere. Even the small towns, he noted, still bore the "pastoral stamp."[12] The urban ethos would not win out until the twentieth century.

The rural Kentuckian, far from the railway, hampered by extremely poor or nonexistent roads in many sections, had a limited and provincial background. His sources of information were often oral ones, spread by traveling salesmen, peddlers, or strangers passing through, or else a local newspaper with its report of crop conditions, accidents, sicknesses, social events, marriages, or just about anything else a resourceful editor could include. The rural mail carrier was often an eager purveyor of news, as well as the compulsive gossipers, who could not be resisted by news-hungry farmers, their wives, sons and daughters. There were too few schools, fewer libraries, and illiteracy was high.

For many Kentuckians their universe centered on a small hamlet where they received mail and purchased supplies. Hundreds of these small places, hardly villages, following the same pattern: Most had a general store, a mill of some sort, perhaps a blacksmith, and often a preacher, doctor or lawyer. Bradford's Store in Knox County, for example, had a population of fifty people, including a lawyer, two blacksmiths, three Baptist ministers (one of whom was also listed as a dentist), one shoemaker, one distiller (though one suspects some extralegal ones were around), and two operators of country stores. The postmaster of the village of Drip Rock, with its 150 people in Jackson County, also owned a farm and drugstore in the community. That community included general stores (one of whose owners was listed as a physician), two Baptist ministers, and one saw mill operator. Small villages with unique names abounded throughout Kentucky, and many Kentuckians knew places similar to Bee Lick (Lincoln County), Dog Creek (Hart County), and Head of Grassy (Lewis County) as their only commercial centers.

The slightly larger incorporated towns offered their residents and the surrounding farmers a more varied selection. For example, a town known as Commercial Point (sometimes called Buffalo Town) in Union County afforded its two hundred residents a flour mill, a saw mill, a tobacco factory, a drygoods store, a general store, two millinery shops, two saloons, a small jail, and a frame schoolhouse.[13]

A boyhood resident of one of those small towns later recalled the evolution of rural Kentucky as he knew it:

Old Fidelity was poor but proud. It had never been other than a small village, but, like so many of us, it had seen better days. As long as the railroad kept away from the county seat, that is, until 1891, Fidelity remained much as it had been in pioneer days, a self-sufficient village. Then came the railroad, and gradually the village began to show signs of deteriorating. Proud yet, in spite of being off the railroad, it was lacking in any importance except locally. Some of the citizens moved to the county seat or on to even more remote places.[14]

In all the small towns, hamlets, and villages, life usually centered on one building. The general store was "market place, banking and credit source, recreational center, public forum, and news exchange." There rural Kentuckians in isolated communities sat perhaps with their feet on a pot-bellied stove in winter or on a dusty porch in the summer and discussed religion, crops, weather, politics, and life in general. Here the proprietor dispensed smiles, local news, reminiscences, the mail, and everything from hay-racks to headache pills; from postage stamps to patent medicines; from pencils to peppermints; from cedar-posts to shoes: from pistols to coffins. Here the shopper received credit for his tobacco crop and bought a few "extras" for his family. Here voters cast their ballots for their favorite local politicians. Here they listened as the events of the distant county court were repeated almost verbatim by those in attendance, complete with a mimicking of the judges, lawyers and defendants. Here the owner of the store frequently read a letter to an illiterate farmer, wrote replies for him, advised him on possible courses of action, loaned him money if necessary—at a suitable interest rate—and kept him informed on the latest gossip. The pervasive influence of the country store affected many rural communities.[15]

G. C. Swetman's store at Wilbur in Lawrence County probably typifies the small country store of the time. but not all belonged to a Mutual Protective Society, as did Swetman, who found protection necessary in the violence-plagued area. Swetman's ledgers reveal that one Kentuckian purchased $13.64 worth of "goods," plus $.25 of calico, 1 pair of shoes, 1 bucket, 1 cup, 1 iron, 1 lid, 1 clock, 2 books, 13 horseshoes, 7½ pounds of coffee, 10 pounds of salt, 6 crackers ($.05), $.10 of "shugar," and $.05 of spice. In addition to these items, by October the purchaser paid off all his debts and purchased goods he had been unable to afford up to that point. Returning home that evening he brought 3 "pr. drawers," 2 pair of boots, 1 shirt, 1 hat, 1 handkerchief, 1 brush, "10 hair oil," and $.20 worth of candy.[16] The buying spree was over. For the next twelve months he would return to small weekly purchases, hoping that his credit would last until his crop came in. Throughout Kentucky the picture was usually similar: Farmers would buy on credit depending on the sale of their tobacco crop, or some other commodity, to pay off their debts.

Country stores, like their counterparts in the cities, served the shopper's clothing needs. Women lived in the age of the hourglass ideal. If the figure did not confrom to the ideal, it would be made to conform. It was unusual indeed for well dressed women to appear without a "retaining wall of jeans, steel, whalebone, and bamboo stays." If the upper body was not what was expected a crescent-shaped corset of woven wire was available. If the lower body exceeded requirements a tightfitting, laced corset could control both bulge and breathing. In the 1870s women were imprisoned in "wasp-like" waists, and their long trailing skirts brought *Harper's Bazaar* to call this the "street-cleaning-department style." The next decade began the vogue of a pannier, an overskirt draped back at the hips or back by a bustle; each season the pannier expanded. The decline of one style brought the 1890s and their full sleeves, sometimes called the "leg-o-mutton sleeve" because of the balloonlike appearance. High top shoes, with slender, oval toes and low heels, predominated. Stockings were warm, modest, and purely utilitarian, for ideally they were not to be exposed by ladies or seen by gentlemen. Protests arose against the unhealthy, heavy, long skirts, the tight shoes, the mass of steel in the form of corsets, but generally to no avail.[17] By the end of the period slit skirts were coming into style because of bicycles, but they were protested by those who attacked this surrender to modernism, this sinful apparel. Most women who purchased their clothes at the general store did so at what was known as the piece-goods counter. A few plaids, and the more colorful calicoes, were often lost in the more numerous bolts of drab material. Lace trim and a stove-ribbed sunbonnet added some variety to an outfit.

If possible, men's fashions were even less colorful than women's. Male southerners after the Civil War, "lived in an age of jeans." Formless and wrinkled in the legs, made of a coarse cloth lined with unbleached domestic, Kentucky jeans were known throughout the South. The basic outfit for men consisted of jeans, red flannels underneath, a formless jean coat, and calico, homespun, and hickory striped shirt. Not until after 1900 did the blue denim overall replace jeans. Workshoes, until the nineties formless brogans, usually sold for $1.25-$2.25 a pair. Not until well after 1880 did workmen have the problem of finding a left to match the right shoe in a barrel of brogans; no division existed until that

A well-dressed woman at the turn of the century

Collection of the Kentucky Historical Society

time. Made of hard leather, fastened with hardwood pegs, and having meager padding, shoes caused many a person to prefer bare feet.

"Sunday clothes" significantly differed. The cheap button shoe replaced the brogan. Pants, possibly supplied by the Mayfield Pants Company, replaced jeans. Tailors made most of the suits. Dressing for church, a man struggled with a shirt body, a set of starched cuffs, a detachable front, a high collar, collar buttons, and cuff links. One man recalled the suffering he endured:

> *Thin summer underwear had not been invented, so that when one was bundled up in his Sunday best, he was about the most wretched of mortals. As if this were not enough misery, there was the very stiff and very high collar, starched to the stiffness of a plowshare, that is, until the intense heat of the sufferer wilted the collar and allowed the starch to ooze delightfully down one's back. To drive across several miles of dusty road on Sunday morning to get one's girl, then several more miles to church, sit in public view and fan the girl with an open-and-shut fan until you got as hot as you did when cutting tobacco, my, what endurance we had! If the weather were intense, you had no time to stop fanning the girl to wipe your own steaming face and head off a river of sweat making for the freshly laundered collar. When services were through, so were you, a bedraggled thing, with a collar that looked like a poorly-wrung-out dishrag. And all the rest of the day, with dinner on the ground, you had to wear that abomination, which lost more and more of its respectable appearance. By the time the wet collar had gathered the dust of the miles back home, it looked more like a scrub rag than an ordinary dishrag.*[18]

Religious Life

Churches continued to be the centers of life in many rural communities. While Kentuckians traditionally thought themselves a religious people, statistics did not reflect that. The

600,000 church members in 1890 represented only a little over one-third of the population, not significantly different than that of surrounding states. Baptists (230,000 members), Methodists (140,000), Catholics (90,000), Disciples of Christ (75,000 — second largest in the nation), and Presbyterians (40,000) predominated.

Bible reading was a commonplace occurrence in homes of non-members, and large numbers of them went to church. The uncertain schedule of a poorly paid circuit-riding preacher plus the scarcity of church buildings in remote areas made membership in a certain sect meaningless to many. These people often attended whatever service was offered them in their isolated sites.[19]

Camp meetings had lost some of their popularity by the 1890s. But the spirit of the meetings remained. Revivalists toured the countryside with their messages and drew large crowds. The heavyset, coarse-speaking Dwight Moody preached at Louisville in 1885 and people fought to get seats, with one woman fainting and another suffering a broken arm. A Parks Hill camp meeting in 1890 featuring the "pulpit demagogry" of Sam Jones of Georgia drew an estimated ten thousand people, and this nationally known preacher continued periodically to tour the state. What two historians have remarked about southern camp meetings generally was true of Kentucky specifically: "They were, in fact, social clubs, news exchanges, and marriage marts, centers of rest and recreation, and a certain amount of merrymaking that did not have the approval of the church."[20]

Many Kentuckians were not impressed with either the religious spirit of the people or the education of the ministers. The Reverend William Moody Pratt of Lexington visited the mountain town of Beattyville in Lee County, found "a great many drunken men," and recorded in his diary that "the preachers are ignorant." Greenup County churches, he wrote, were "all feeble" and the ministers "ignorant men." The father of John

A baptism in the 1890s
Collection of the Kentucky Historical Society

Fox, Jr. wrote in his diary that a preacher in Bourbon County, "failed worse than any one I ever saw in the pulpit," while another diarist noted that unheated churches hindered attendance in the winter and warm weather brought other attractions.[21] Poorly educated ministers, scattered congregations, irregular services, inadequate facilities—all hurt churches in rural Kentucky. The "Social Gospel" movement largely swept by Kentucky, which remained generally fundamentalist, with an emphasis on other-worldliness. In Kentucky, as in the South, this religious conservatism, according to historians Frances B. Simkins and Charles P. Roland, "generated the puritanism that sought to curb the spontaneous hedonism of the Southern population. It bolstered the Southern belief in states' rights and local autonomy. It emphasized the family as the fundamental unit of society, and thus helped to preserve the strong sense of kinship which marked Southern thinking. It prevented Southerners from being utopian, from accepting a faith in the earthly perfectibility of man. . . . It reinforced the color line . . . through the role of churches, white and black alike, as conservators of social custom."[22]

Temperance

One area where churchmen supported change was in the temperance movement. Here the churches led the fight. Whiskey production in Kentucky increased from almost six million gallons in 1871 to over thirty million a decade later, and the temperance movement sought to end this trend. Governor Preston Leslie's order against using liquor at state functions was a symbolic beginning and an 1871 law forbade minors and inebriates from buying from liquor dealers. Three years later a petition with a reported 147,000 signatures was presented to the legislature, asking for a bill regulating whiskey sales. The first local option legislation resulted.[23]

"Temperance is epidemic in Western Kentucky now," the Hickman *Courier* proclaimed, as the editor blamed the bad brand of whiskey there for the disturbing trend. But whatever the reason, he was correct about the trend, and it was not confined to the western part of the state. The Order of Good Templars, organized in Lexington in 1867, spread throughout the state and together with the Women's Christian Temperance Union (W. C. T. U.), organized in the 1880s, enlisted many to the cause of prohibition. Local clubs sprang up and one, the secret Guardian Angel Society of New Castle, ruled that each young lady "will report the name of the young gentleman who she knows was intoxicated."[24] In many localities, allies of temperance attended picnics with typical programs like one with a one o'clock dinner, then recitations on "The Rum Maniac" and "The Drunken Child." Chautauquas were also useful in disseminating temperance arguments through lectures and as meeting places for local W. C. T. U. groups.[25]

The efforts met with some success and by the 1890s over fifty Kentucky counties were completely "dry" while over a score of others had one or more "dry" towns. In 1893, for example, Bowling Green, amid an all day prayer meeting and ringing of church bells, went dry by twenty-eight votes. Yet not all efforts were successful. The problem was clearly presented when the village of Temperance changed its name to Gold City. Worldly pleasures still attracted. An excursion down the Ohio River by a convention of Kentucky newspaper editors brought a Hopkinsville paper's report that "few templars were on board, and the amount of champagne drunk was amazing. Bottle after bottle was emptied and flung into the surging waves of the Ohio until some of the boys began to get, O! higher than the river. . . . Fun was the order of the day." In the mountains of Kentucky the storied "moonshine" was usually available and the London *Mountain Echo* openly described the changing situation: On March 1881, "moonshine is rather scarce now." Two weeks later the "meddlesome" revenue officers had "stampeded" the moonshiners. But within a month the paper reported that "Shooting matches and moonshine whiskey are as common as corn-bread."[26] The efforts toward prohibition would eventually win out in Kentucky, but the state continued to maintain its reputation as the home of good—and bad—liquor in the nineteenth century.

Rural Life and Work

On a typical day, the small farmer rose early, fed and watered the animals, and cast a wary eye to the still dark sky in an effort to determine the day's weather. He returned to the house, barely lit by a kerosene lamp perhaps, for a hearty breakfast. The usual fare of fried shoulder, or ham with red-eye gravy, or sausage, or bacon, with eggs, biscuits or cornbread, would serve him until the noonday meal. In his clumsy, formless brogans, jeans, perhaps with a hat to shield him from the sun, the farmer went out for a morning's work.[27] Such farmers used wooden beamed plow stocks, crude iron plow shapes, hand hoes, and other tools that indicated their dependence on earlier methods. Narrow profit margins made them hesitate to introduce newer, less tried methods, even if they wished to.

Larger farms used some of the increasingly mechanized and improved farm tools. The first modern plow—the chilled iron plow of James Oliver of Indiana—became available by the late 1870s. While most southerners stuck to the one-mule plow and the eight inch bottom, by the early 1870s some used sulky plows with more than one share. Spring-tooth disc harrows, patented by David L. Garver of Michigan, had the advantage of not catching on roots and rocks.

Farmers did not adopt the numerous drills and other machines for sowing or planting seeds until after the Civil War. Even then an expert hand broadcaster could still seed a large area. Mowing machines improved throughout the period, from a two-wheeled, hinged cutting-bar model of 1865 to a side-delivery rake, better adapted for mechanical leaders in the 1890s. Harvesters (at first the Marsh brothers' variety, then after 1870 several others) had platforms where men rode and tied the bundles of grain as fast as they came from the reel. The problem of binding the grain by hand was not solved until the 1880s when the self-binder enjoyed its success. In a day two men and a team of horses then could harvest twenty acres of small grain. Shucking and fodder-shedding machines and a corn binder had been patented by the 1890s.

Many Kentucky farmers, particularly the smaller ones, did not feel these advancements to any large degree. Hay, for example, was cut by a crude two horse-drawn mowing machine, then raked by a one horse-drawn rake, which dumped at intervals to form windrows. Using three-pronged pitch forks, workers pitched the hay into shocks. They then led horses or mules to the shocks, backing the animal closer and closer. The farm hands attached a chain, already attached to the hame, around the bottom of the shock. The other end of the chain would then be hooked to the other side of the hame. The horse or mule pulled the shock to the place where the large hay stack was to go up. There hay stackers with forks pitched the hay and formed the stack, tapered to a point. At the top a cap would be put on to turn rain and keep the hay from quickly rotting. Pitching up hay was hard, hot, sweaty work; it was not for boys. Some hay would simply be hauled to the barn and pitched up to the loft for winter feed. The stacks furnished winter hay as well. Similarly, tobacco especially and other crops generally were not greatly affected by the machine age in the nineteenth century.[28]

Work on the farm was hard, with long hours, changing weather and uncertain crop prices. Producing crops of tobacco, corn, wheat, hemp, hay, rye, cotton (in Fulton, Hickman, and Graves counties), and grasses involved a great deal of work, and tending livestock took its toll as well. Even the garden and orchard, if operated for more than family consumption, required careful attention. A long day began as the small-plot farmer settled behind his favorite mule, perhaps dust rising in choking clouds above his head, and began to plow.

A Knox County cabin in 1884

Courtesy of The Filson Club, Louisville

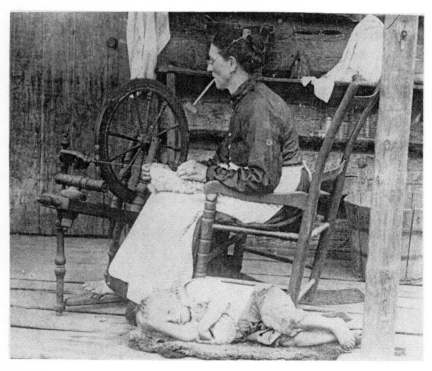

Spinning in the mountains

Collection of the Kentucky Historical Society

Back in the house his wife and daughters washed the clothes, cleaned and did other domestic work. They worked the garden and tended the fowls and tamer livestock. Then the woman and girls began preparation of the noon meal over a fireplace or new kitchen stove. In more isolated areas, and among the poorer families, the meal centered on abundant pork meat in the form of hams, bacon, shoulders, and sausage, with yellow trimmings—corn, hominy, and cornbread. To some of these homes milk and eggs remained luxuries, beef a rarity, green vegetables uncertain winter fare, and juices almost an unknown commodity. But even the tables of the poorer homes on those special occasions would fairly "groan" with food, even if it was not always the most nutritious.

More prosperous, better situated landowners had a more varied diet available. Numerous chickens produced fresh eggs daily and milk cows provided milk, butter, buttermilk, and cheese for the table. Mutton and beef—especially if "beef companies" were formed—gave relief from pork meat. Fruit from the orchard and fresh vegetables could be dried or canned for winter consumption. Rural families produced their own kraut, cider and vinegar. Wives exchanged at stores or with hucksters such items as eggs, meat, butter and vegetables for coffee, sugar, tea, cloth, buttons, and thread. If the wife found unexpected free moments she might sew or darn, work the new sewing machine or the family loom; spin linen from cotton, hemp, or wool; or perhaps prepare some lye soap.

The children, probably barefoot in summer, helped as well. They began working at an early age. First came smaller chores such as bringing in wood, making fires, feeding and watering the livestock, running errands, and milking. Mothers taught their daughters early to help them in sweeping, cooking, cleaning, and sewing. Fathers initiated the boys to work in the barn and in the fields. At hog-killing time they often helped grind sausage and performed other such tasks. Since rural schools did not operate long enough during the year to keep farm children from their work, the work-year of boys and girls was a long one.

Work combined with play at times. Many of the old frontier customs still survived, and some special events, including corn-huskings, remained much as they had almost a century before. A wedding brought forth wild celebrations. Newlyweds received their serenade and the custom of the "shivaree" still prevailed. A group would meet at a prearranged place, then march around the bride and bridegroom's house making as much noise as possible. A ride on a rail sometimes followed.

While square dancing in some locales was perceived "as the most immoral thing in the world," this did not hold true throughout all the state. In some areas certain dances received approval; in other areas different dances sufficed. Almost any occasion was an excuse for a picnic and men discussed politics, religion, crops, the weather, while the women prepared the table and had their own discussion. Children played in the forest, organized games, climbed trees, or perhaps went wading. Though swimming was often considered wicked "because it was purely for enjoyment," this did not make it any less enjoyable.

Neighbors' visits, friendly trading back and forth, socials, church attendance, conversation, and gossip tied an area's families closer together. Boys and girls met despite the distances and isolated farms. They courted and wed. Now and then a bit of scandal occurred. Human nature had its way of working. Mothers taught their daughters the importance of marrying early—and of being hard-working, child-bearing wives. Boys were told to strive for self-discipline and to be good husbands and providers for their families. The old puritan ethic of hard work became almost a religion to rural Kentucky.

The day to day routine of farm work ruled rural life. The farmer's world was dictated by daylight and by farm animals. Many found the work hard and seldom lucrative. With nightfall nearing came another meal. For tenants and small farmers their one to three-room house, frequently in need of repair, had to meet their needs. Some of their crude, homemade furniture set before the fireplace in the evening and the heavy dishes, tin cups, and wooden-handled eating utensils put away, the parents—if literate—perhaps read a weekly newspaper or the Bible, while children played with their homemade toys. Clocks were in many cases not possessed. Nightfall usually signaled the end of the day. Stirring the precious fire (matches remained a luxury), the weary group went to their cord beds with rope supports.

An occasional hunt, a weekly trip to the general store, an infrequent visit to a circus or fair, a journey to town on court day—these were the variations in a typical day. They came rarely.

Regional Life

In the latter part of the nineteenth century one of the heretofore most ignored areas of Kentucky came into sudden prominence. Settled by English and Scotch-Irish yeomen who scattered throughout much of Kentucky,[29] the eastern mountain region now came under new scrutiny. As feuds became news events, writers and reporters ventured into the area. Industry began to discover the almost untapped mineral wealth there. As a result the mountains became perhaps Kentucky's best-described region in 1890s. It was fashionable for young society men and women to tour portions of the mountains by the turn of the century.

Authors and other observers left detailed descriptions of the lifestyles of the region. John Fox, Jr., whose novels captured some of the spirit of the people, observed that the mountain dweller lived apart from the world: "the present is past when it reaches him." Isolation and strong individualism made unity of action difficult. This often led to a "primitive" righting of a supposed wrong. Fox saw the people as a "remnant of colonial times," a people forgotten by time. Log-rollings, house-raisings, corn-shuckings, quilting, wrestling, lifting barrels, savage fights—these were the heritages of the past that still remained. The pioneer's belief in signs and omens and even witchcraft still had its place in the life of the mountain farmer. Inhabitants continued the custom of holding annual funeral services for the dead several years after their death.

Compared to other southerners of this class, the mountaineer, Fox argued, was more clannish, prouder, more hospitable, fiercer, "more loyal as a friend, more bitter as an enemy."

James Lane Allen departed from his more familiar Bluegrass writing to study the mountain people as well. The mountain farmer, he wrote, supplemented his crops of corn, potatoes, tobacco, and flax with money "crops" of moonshine and ginseng ("sang"). The women in the area suffered most; they were old by thirty. Allen found that they had luxuriant hair but few teeth once past their mid-thirties. Those mothers with whom he conversed had an average of seven children.

A University of Chicago professor echoed similar sentiments. He found not a single wellmade wagon road in the area, and the roads that did exist were "rough to an almost incredible degree." As a stranger he had found a hospitable people but one whose diet seldom varied from hog and hominy, with salt bacon fare. Poor schools existed and the only regular social gatherings came at churches and at funerals. The writer found a shy, sensitive people.[30]

Fox, Allen, and the Chicago professor had not grown up in the region. A man who did presented a more favorable view. He, too, noted that conditions "now obsolete in other parts of the country," still existed in the mountains. Travel in the rainy season was impossible, he admitted: "The onward march of civilization has been checked by rocks and hills." Dancing had passed from the scene as something sinful but music at a bean stringing or an apple peeling was still approved. The mountaineer seldom overcame his isolation but a church quarterly helped. There young couples sat in buggies under shady trees whispering to each other, while some of the men sat around the church steps, swapping horses and other items. This picture of the mountains had few somber hues.

The story one man told of his life growing up in the area gives one example of the forces at work. As a youth he wore jeans, hickory shirt and no shoes. His sisters "hired out" to nearby farmers for $.25 to $1.00 a week. Later he married at nineteen to an eighteen-year-old who would bear him seven children. They cleared some land, built a log house, and raised five acres of crops the first year, losing $25 overall. Within five years his acreage had increased to 35 and the savings had grown to $250. Still later he purchased a 100 acre plot at $10 per acre, $250 down, the rest payable over six years. During his lifetime one brother had been killed in ambush, two sisters died of typhoid fever, and his father was shot in an election "row." On the latter occasion, he and two brothers returned to the town the next day, armed: "Our only retaliation to speak of is the muzzle of our guns; when all else fails us we at least have that left us." When he wrote those words he had served as a sheriff's deputy and a constable.[31]

More than anything else, these writers all agreed that the mountain inhabitants were isolated—from education, from new ideas, from good transportation, from the law, and from each other. While a few railroads inched tracks into the sparsely settled region, not until well into the next century would the barriers of isolation begin to fall. Many of the same traits that attracted novelists and journalists would continue.

Life and Death

Kentucky communities in 1870 had the largest families in the United States, averaging 5.7 persons. Family size declined in each following decade, to 4.9 to 1900, only slightly above the national average. Kentucky's birth rate was still higher than the American average and was again rising in 1900.[32]

Already large families were expanded by relatives who visited for long periods of time or simply lived with the family. Journalist Arthur Krock remembered his childhood days in Glasgow as ones exemplified by large family patters—usually "more than a dozen" in a family. Letters and diaries of the entire period are literally filled with visits to and from Aunt Mary or Counsin Billy or some other relative, bringing one observer to remark that, "In Kentucky all who are not related to each other are in love with one another." A relative's visit often interrupted dating habits, and frustrated youths more than once grumbled about a cousin's intrusion on their outings. Something of a clannish loyalty existed and this explained the sheltering of an aunt or uncle or distant cousin. A typical letter of the period underscores these observations:

> *My Dear Mother, . . . Lexington was covered for three days this week with Morgan's men who had a grand reunion. Bob Tyler came up to the reunion and is still with us. Eliza is very much pleased with Bob. Aunt Mary Tyler is also with us, she came up with Bob to visit Jennie Worley and Eliza invited her to stay part of the time with her. Henry and Cladwell are having a very hot canvass, which I suppose you see by the* Courier-Journal. *Everyone seems to think Harry is right in making it an aggressive canvass and says that he will be elected unless his opponents spend a great deal of money—We all went to Paris to attend poor cousin Henry's funeral, but it was not a sad affair at all, after the funeral was over most of us went to Mr. Brent's until time to return to Lexington and there had quite a reunion of the family. Brent, Talbott and I talking, laughing and enjoying ourselves generally, even to card playing.*[33]

Valued family ties were important not just in social affairs, but in political life as well.

High mortality rates in Kentucky made the existence of these large families even more remarkable. Drinking polluted river water, evading vaccinations in many cases, families seldom avoided typhoid or other diseases. Figures are not reliable or even available for all of Kentucky, but four cities—Louisville, Newport, Covington, and Paducah—did keep health statistics. All four had a higher death rate than the average for 346 of the nation's cities that recorded such figures. For whites, only Louisville matched or fell below the national average; for blacks both Covington and Louisville were healthier than the overall average; for foreign-born, all cities had significantly higher death rates than the average for other cities.

Particularly unhealthy, Paducah exceeded the national average by 50 percent with a death rate of nearly 28 per 1,000. Partly responsible for the high mortality rate were whooping cough (four times the national average), influenza, diarrheal diseases, consumption (tuberculosis), pneumonia, and measles. Typhoid fever and malarial fever remained the principal killers, however. While the rest of the nation's cities had a typhoid rate of almost 37 per 1,000, Paducah's rate was nearly 160, second highest of all the cities listed. Her malaria rate stood third highest in the nation.

The Commonwealth's largest city had a much lower mortality rate but nearly one-third of the deaths in Louisville in 1877 were of children under the age of one. Two decades of better medical care reduced that figure by half. Great epidemics still swept almost uncontrolled and an 1873 smallpox epidemic left nearly a hundred dead in Louisville.

Cholera swept the entire state that same year with a reported 49 deaths in Marion County, 47 in Simpson County, 33 in the town of Lancaster, and 22 in Adair County; Paducah and McCracken County reported 180 deaths, Bowling Green 66 dead, Louisville and Elizabethtown over 20 deaths each, and 11 fatalities were reported in Maysville. Still later in the century, the flux was believed to have caused over 300 deaths in Magoffin County, and 400 in Lee County.[34] The prevalence of death made it seem ever-present and added yet another uncertainty to the people's lives.

A doctor spent his life fighting death and disease. It was not an easy life. Robert B. Pusey, a doctor in Elizabethtown, left a physician's record in letters to his son. A dollar for an office call, ten dollars for childbirth, and up to one hundred dollars for surgery, earned the doctor an average of $5,200 a year, "a little above the average." Charging the high price of a dollar for the first mile and fifty cents for each subsequent mile on house calls, Dr.

Pusey often used a railroad tricycle to go far distances. He wrote on one winter day, "Yesterday I made two visits that made an aggregate of eighty miles—fifty by rail and thirty by buggy." It was not an unusual case. Writing to his son in November, 1888, he noted, "I went to bed at 2 o'clock last night and got up at 7 o'clock and started a six mile ride in the buggy. Made the drive in two and a half hours and then made a five mile ride in two hours. Made two calls in town, several trips to the drug store, then went to Sonora on train and rode horseback ten miles out and back, and made a trip to Claysville since. It is now 10 o'clock and I don't see that I am especially tired." He died the next year at the age of fifty-four.

Many advancements in medicine during the period caused the doctor's and his patients' lives to be easier. The State Board of Health—begun in 1878—soon discovered that of some five thousand physicians in the state, one thousand "doctors" had never attended medical schools. That figure dropped rapidly. Laws regulating dentistry and pharmacy were enacted and the medical schools in Louisville gradually gained a good reputation nationally. In 1887 a training school for nurses was established.[35]

Newspapers continued to advertise nostrums, and people continued to purchase unscientific remedies. Before the days of the Pure Food and Drug Act, and before federal laws regulated narcotic sales, the patent medicine business flourished in Kentucky. Advertisements, testimonials, and booklets proclaimed cures for almost all diseases, and occasionally manufactured new ones. Tonics, pills, ointments and drugs of all shapes and sizes were made available for the suffering soul, and if most tonics were heavily alcoholic and most ointments little more than petroleum jelly and perfume, many swore by their curative properties. Turpentine was "the universal medicine" of the South, and, along with castor oil, was found on the shelves of most rural homes. Most country stores offered opium, morphine, and other deleterious drugs, and advertised them often as opium gum balls at $3.10 an ounce. Inadequately trained country doctors frequently prescribed them when they could find no other remedy for some mysterious disease. In 1872 the legislature ordered to the insane asylum any person who "by the habitual or excessive use of opium, arsonic, hasheesh, or any drug, has become incompetent to manage themselves or estate with ordinary prudence and discretion." "Addicts were numerous," according to one historian.

Women had their "peculiar ailments" and men their own special diseases, and "doctors" offered "cures" for both sexes. One paper advertised a remedy for "errors of youth" while another presented what was said to be a clergyman's cure for "early decay" brought about by "baneful and vicious habits." Dr. Culverwell proclaimed his "celebrated cure" as a remedy for "spermatorhea," constipation, epilepsy, fits, and "all diseases induced by sexual extravagence etc." A ponderous "electric belt," advertised as being undetectable when worn, was said by its producer to be a cure for "lost manhood . . . exhaustion, impotency." While the age may have proclaimed the Victorian moral standards, various advertisements suggest that not all Kentuckians lived up to that moral code.

Many found it hard to avoid sampling a medicine proclaimed as miraculous in testimonials. After all, who could resist such products when presented in sentimental verse:

If your wife is weak and ailing
And has trouble with her liver,
And you want to make her happy
What's the best thing you can give her?
You might give her a nice new bonnet,
But her profit would be much greater
If you give her a bottle or two
Of Simmons Liver Regulator.[36]

Forgotten Kentuckians: Women

Some unhappy wives required more than Liver Regulator, for the issue of women's rights aroused bitter feelings among Kentuckians. A Frankfort newspaper suggested that the "wisdom of

the highest civilization and her own unerring instructive tastes"
assign women to the "sacred, hallowed sphere" of the home—but
not to the political sphere. If women voted, "Vaunting Amazons"
would replace the "poetry of creation" that men now knew. The
old slavery emancipationist, Cassius M. Clay, condemned the woman suffrage movement as one that led to atheism, paganism, and
"communism of the sexes." Writing under the pen name of
"Icarus," he argued that the "sciences" of phrenology and crani-
ology proved women more sentimental and emotional than his
sex. The younger, but no less critical, Henry Watterson also found
little to please him and called the Suffragettes "Silly Sallies and
crazy Janes." Dr. Stuart Robinson, a Louisville Presbyterian minister, attacked the new movement's leaders as "notorious as the
leaders of a fiery partisan infidel assault upon, not only our
common Christianity, but our social order."[37]

Women who evoked such words included Carrie Chapman Catt
and Susan B. Anthony, who spoke throughout the state with
mixed success. An 1879 tour covered many areas of Kentucky,
but newspaper accounts of the lectures often contained a comment similar to the one in a western Kentucky paper. After
Anthony had given her talk the reporter said that women "have no
business with the ballot. . . . God forbid that day will ever come
when our mothers, sisters, wives, and daughters will be found in
the profane and vulgar rabble around the polls. . . . We believe that
woman was intended to occupy the sphere of mother and wife."[38]

Most Kentucky women still occupied and accepted these roles;
some did not. The first suffrage organization in the state was
founded in Hardin County in 1867 but found little support and
died out. Five years later two out of state women spoke to
legislators on the subject but they too found few adherents. Such
efforts brought a Kentucky state senator's appeal: "Give me a wife
that can love, honor and look up to me as her lord and master, or
give me separation and death."

During the 1880s, a fledgling organization emerged to restrict
his options. After the national meeting of the American Woman

Suffrage Association met in Louisville in 1881, a group of Kentucky women organized the Kentucky Woman Suffrage Association, the first in the South.

Cassius Clay's own daughters led that early fight. The separation and divorce of their mother and father in 1878 was, according to one historian, "the trauma which awakened all the Clay women to the issue of woman's rights." Anne, Sally, Mary, and Laura Clay were prominent in the early efforts. Laura revealed her feelings in her 1874 diary: "To do what I can to help in the great cause of Woman's Rights seems to me that sphere of activity in His service to which God has called me both through my feelings which call me that way, and the education of life. . . . Born of anti-slavery parents, my birth, perhaps, and certainly my early education has taught me to hate oppression and injustice, . . . not a jealousy of men but a desire to see women awake to the higher life which God . . . has opened to them."[39] She served as president of the Kentucky Equal Rights Association from 1888-1912 and with Mrs. Josephine K. Henry and Mrs. Eliza Calvert Obenchain led the nineteenth century fight.

The cause met obstacles, not the least of which was a lack of interest from the women themselves. A Paducah writer in 1888 reported that, with the exception of herself, "I know of no woman in Paducah in favor of Woman Suffrage." As late as 1895 the Kentucky Equal Rights Association numbered only four hundred members. But sympathy with their aims grew; the 1890 petition presented to the legislature bore ten thousand signatures.

A student of the subject found that Kentucky laws regarding women were "among the most backward in the county." Women reformers would have agreed. Kentucky allowed divorce for adultery only when women were the offenders. Wives' wages went to their husbands, and a wife could make no will without her husband's consent. At one time Kentucky had led the nation in 1838 by allowing certain widows and spinsters to vote on school issues, but it had regressed since then. Finally in 1894, Governor John Young Brown signed one bill which allowed wives complete con-

Woman's rights leader Laura Clay
Courtesy of the University of Kentucky Archives

trol over their own personal property and enabled them to carry on business independent of their husbands, and another bill which gave all women in second class cities the right to vote on local educational matters (this was rescinded in 1902). Lexington's mayor had already named a woman to the school board in 1893 and the 1895 elections brought in four elected women representatives on the board. Acceptance of Sophonisba Breckinridge as the first woman lawyer in the state was made easier by her father's prominence. Even that did not help Bessie White Hager, who had to bring suit before being accepted as a pharmacist.

In higher education the cause progressed as well. Since 1880 the Agricultural and Mechanical College in Lexington had been co-educational, but it stood alone among Kentucky colleges in this respect. The Fayette Equal Rights Association pressured—and got—Transylvania to open its doors to women in 1889. Within four years, Georgetown College, Wesleyan College in Winchester, and Central University in Richmond had followed the trend. By 1899 Transylvania had appointed a woman professor of civil history and two women professors taught at State College.[40]

Yet while women made advancements, the goals of suffrage and legal equality remained only goals. Kentucky still believed in preserving the images of the southern lady, still stressed domesticity as woman's role, still voiced the chivalric code. If images conflicted with reality, if double standards existed, Kentuckians, by and large, only slowly agreed to change the images and set new standards.

Forgotten Kentuckians: Negroes

Double standards existed for another group as well. The latter years of the nineteenth century saw the maturing of racial segregation in Kentucky, and Negroes searched for their niche in Kentucky life. When Negroes were first allowed to ride Louisville streetcars in 1871 fights and several shootings occurred. Within a month a Negro brought suit because a conductor had ordered him to sit at the back of the car. Legal segregation was evident in an 1874 Louisville ordinance that required members of the fire department to be white citizens. The law was changed by 1888, so that if "able-bodied and of sober and moral habits," Negroes could fill the fireman's role. An 1876 act also forbade keeping black and white patients in the same buildings in the Lunatic Asylums. Legal segregation in Kentucky reached its nineteenth century peak with the enactment of the 1891 Separate Coach Bill, which provided that each compartment of a railroad car was deemed separate if divided by "a good and substantial wooden partition."[41] It was only the culmination of earlier acts, a continuation of a trend, not a sudden new development.

Informal segregation was apparent as well. Local jailors racially separated prisoners whenever possible and the Kentucky Penitentiary conducted separate prayer services every Sunday. A decade before the Separate Coach Bill became law, a mass meeting of blacks at the Lexington Court House raised a collection to aid a woman who was bringing suit against the railroad that refused her entry into the ladies' car. At the theater segregation also existed, and there were even separate bicycle races for blacks, who were forbidden to compete against whites. "Colored Fairs" were a partial result of pressures against blacks, and these fairs thrived in some locales. In September 1893, the Lexington Colored Fair reported its greatest attendance ever—some twelve thousand people.[42]

A case study of black life in Lexington reveals the urbanization process at work. Between the end of the war and 1870 the black population of the city nearly tripled in size, reducing the black-white ratio to almost one to one. While the few free Negro settlements prior to the war had been in racially mixed neighborhoods, the mass emigration in the 1860s destroyed that pattern. More houses and new communities were needed and by 1880 separate areas, including Brucetown, Pralltown, and Davis Bottom, resulted. The first two of these communities were 92 and 86 percent black, for example. This was not planned segregation but, as one historian concluded, "developed . . . largely as the accidental result of a combination of impersonal forces: the limitation of space in central Lexington, the availability of land within the outer circle, and the poverty of the Negro market for land."

Newcomers to the city found jobs as unskilled laborers; three of every four Negroes worked as servant, laundress, cook, laborer, farm hand, and factory worker. Only 11 percent of the black population in 1870 owned property valued at one hundred dollars or more. By the end of the next decade, Negroes made up 45 percent of Lexington's population but possessed only 6 percent of Lexington's wealth—partially due to the rural background of many Negroes, as well as the limited urban opportunities. The successful black businessman, together with the black leaders, had been free Negroes before the war. Most Lexington Negroes in 1880 worked at menial jobs, owned little property, and lived in segregated neighborhoods.[43]

Few white Kentuckians questioned social segregation. Those who had been imbued with the idea that slavery was a positive good and Negroes were an inferior race found it very difficult to treat them as social equals. Those who had grown up since the end of chattel slavery had nevertheless heard or read very little that did not picture the Negro as a subordinate race which must be uplifted by white efforts. Very few Kentuckians, or, for that matter, Americans, perceived the black man as their equal. Even men who fought for legal equality between the races—for example, William O'Connell Bradley and W. C. P. Breckinridge—did not often break the bonds of paternalism and stress social equality. James Lane Allen in an essay on Kentucky Negroes spoke for the past and not the future when he characterized the "African" as a superstitious, indolent, singing, happy-go-lucky, impressionable person who depended on whites for "enlightenment, training and happiness." Stressing the fight and the fiddle, Allen concluded that Kentucky Negroes remained "content with their inferiority." Even Methodist minister John J. Dickey, while rejoicing in "the elevation of the black race," could not bring himself to accept social equality.[44] If the educated in society accepted the notion of black inferiority and informal separation, the uneducated were even less enlightened. Violence against blacks often resulted from such feelings.

Despite severe barriers, including violence, Negroes did make some advancements. By 1871 Negroes were admitted to the bar. And in the heavily black-populated Christian county in western Kentucky in 1895 citizens elected a Negro to the city council and reelected him over the next twelve years. By 1898 Negroes held offices of county coroner, deputy jailer, constable of Hopkinsville, pension examiner, and county physician. But Christian was the exception where advancement resulted primarily from the strength of Negroes in the controlling Republican party in the county. Harassment and frequent fraud marked Negro voting efforts. A black candidate attempting to run for the Paducah city council was violently beaten. A Cincinnati paper reported that Negroes in Louisville in 1871 were forced to submit to voting tests, something not required of whites.[45] Negroes did continue to vote, however, in large numbers during the late nineteenth century.

The situation by the end of the century is reflected in journalist Arthur Krock's memories of his childhood in Glasgow. "The Kingdom," was a separate section where black houses were located, was not a slum, and houses there were usually not inferior to white homes. Raised by a black "mammy," he remembered that his most enjoyable companions were "the very ones whom their mothers would not permit to sit with me at the table." By high school this companionship ended according to "the accepted customs of the society." As a youth he noticed things that gave him "a strong sense of discomfort." Negroes would wave flies away from the table at meal time and the servant who served the food was recognized as a childhood friend. While whites were friendly to blacks, friendship stopped at social intermingling. Public transportation was segregated, in public assemblies blacks sat apart from whites, and whites never addressed blacks as "Mr." or

"Mrs."[46] Negroes belonged to a different caste and were treated accordingly.

The Kentuckians

What then was this Kentuckian—white or black, man or woman—like? Through the years historians and literary figures had tried to define the Kentucky character. On one point they agreed—Kentuckians were different. A writer in 1900 called him "a marked man . . . different from his fellowmen of other parts of the world." He explained this by the enthusiasm, freedom of speech, independence of action and "superlatively flamboyant conduct" of the Kentuckian. The homogeneity of the people also made them distinctive, he believed, and gave them a "love of personal liberty which amounts to a passion."

The Englishman James Bryce, after visiting Kentucky, wrote that it was one of the two southern states which possessed "the most marked individuality, or idiosyncrasies." The state's differences were so great, he felt, that he described it as "a sort of nation within the great nation." Other writers, including Shaler and Allen, compared the state to Bryce's England and found remarkable similarities. Shaler found in Kentucky "the last remnant of the 'Elizabethan spirit' in the South."[47]

For whatever the reason, Americans spoke of "the Kentuckian" and the words projected an image of their own, quite unlike any images brought to mind by the terms "Northerner" or "Southerner." Both the nation and the Commonwealth agreed that Kentucky citizens were distinctive.

V

SOCIETY AND ITS DIVERSIONS

"Social position," John Fox, Jr., observed " . . . is a question one rarely hears discussed: one either has it unquestioned, or one has it not at all." In the Bluegrass people talked about that area's own "Four Hundred" as the social elite. Their social base was the Bluegrass farmer whose ideal, James Lane Allen noted, was "neither vast wealth nor personal distinction, but solid comfort in material conditions."[1] Other towns and cities each had their own elite. In Elizabethtown, for example, social position was controlled, according to one observer, by "people of intelligence and refinement, of good breeding and with family traditions." While not all were intelligent or refined, an accepted elite did exist.

A successful businessman, one of the *nouveaux riches*, could enter the ranks, but he would have to assume "the trappings of aristocracy"—a country estate, prominent ancestors (often nonexistent), or most often, marriage into an old Kentucky family. While technically an open society, it opened only on its own terms. As one commentator observed of Lexington: "The simplicity of the society is perhaps due, in great part, to the fact that the controlling element consists of those who were born here of parents who were born here. . . . This hereditary adherence to the city causes hereditary friendships . . . and creates a simple, unaffected, unostentatious hospitality."[2] Though perhaps overstating the simplicity of the society, the writer was correct in pointing out the importance of old family ties to advancement in "society."

"Balls, soirees, marriages, etc. have been the order of the day," a western Kentucky editor wrote in 1871. He listed parties and balls as the most prominent aspect of social life in Kentucky. A Lexingtonian wrote that though the winter of 1890 was not as gay as the previous one, one girl still had "been to enough parties to break her down. She is really prostrated."[3] Card games, including whist, hearts, and the new fad of tiddly-winks, could not supplant the dance as the most popular party entertainment.

Dances, "hops," balls—whatever they were called—filled the social columns of Kentucky newspapers. No section was immune, and even small towns boasted of their "hops."[4] In Louisville one dance society had strict rules: two dollar dues, five "Germans" (dances) a winter, a girl must bring her escort's name on a slip of paper, dancing was to begin at nine o'clock and end by one o'clock, and "needless talking" would bring the offender a five cent fine. In Hopkinsville an overexuberant editor described a "social" there as an "elysium on Earth" with the garden lighted by Chinese lanterns and candles in the window panes, "which made them look like checkered groups of stars twinkling and scintillating and shedding their soft mellow light upon all around." On a similar occasion he wrote that "the Utopian paradise at last was found. . . . All, all, was happiness and pleasure."[5]

The extravagant banquets and balls of the larger cities perhaps overshadowed the social affairs of the towns. In the summer of 1890 Lexington welcomed a group of New England merchants as guests of the city with lavish decorations and entertainment. An example was the achievement accomplished by the famous Phoenix Hotel. The dining room windows of the hotel were covered with dogwood, while in the center of the room, "circumscribed by . . . four pillars and banked around with mosses, ferns and dainty grasses was a miniature lake, otherwise a mirrow." Two pyramids of a hundred lobsters each dominated the "lordly Bluegrass spread," which was impressive but a bit pretentious.[6]

While dancing at homes or at private parties was probably the most approved form of entertainment, the theater was not ignored. Most large towns and cities had an opera house where a few famous but mostly unknown actors appeared. After watching *Pinafore* and then the play *Lady Jane Gray* one woman thought them "grand, the acting was the best I ever saw and the dresses were very elegant." When Louisville dedicated a new auditorium in 1889, Edwin Booth performed in *The Merchant of Venice* before an audience attired in evening dress. All the "beauty and chivalry of the city" attended, according to a newspaper reporter, and "everyone had on their jewels" and new dresses. General and Mrs. Basil Duke, Henry Watterson, the Haldemans, the Belknaps, the Thruston Ballards—"everyone in society was there," the reporter concluded.[7] Macauley's theater opened in 1873 in Louisville and became a stopping place for many of the best plays and actors. Native daughter Mary Anderson made her debut there in *Romeo and Juliet* and soon moved to national fame. Lecturers in Louisville in the 1870s and 1880s included Robert Ingersoll, George Washington Cable, and Mark Twain.

However, the better, more refined dramas often did not attract large audiences. The Kentucky theater public preferred the less classical forms of entertainment. A Hopkinsville theater reflected popular taste when *As You Like It* attracted only half as large a crowd as the New Orleans Minstrels with their "side-splitting jokes and witticisms." After an Oscar Wilde lecture in Louisville the *Courier-Journal* reported that "Louisville society gave him the cold shoulder." At almost the same time the "Gen. Tom Thumb Troupe" was highly successful.[8] Popular shows—melodramas, comedies, minstrels, and burlesques—gained the theaters the patronage they sought. Even small villages often booked the traveling troops of players for short two to five-night stands. Most towns had their own version of an opera house where young children saw matinee performers while their elders applauded the actors' efforts at nights. While the quality of the fare varied, occasionally an accomplished troop on the way to another stand might stop and give a short performance. In such ways the theater came to rural Kentucky.

A Lexington paper advertised "Kate Reynolds in the great burlesque of Robinson Crusoe, supported by the Great Star Opera Company . . . Singing and Dancing! Shoo Fly! Shoo Fly! and other novelties," and this was typical fare. Other shows in 1870 included a man doing comic faces, another doing bugle calls, a woman satirizing the women's rights movement, a visit by the "Genuine Chinese Giant, Chang," plus the ever-present minstrel shows. When Madame Rentz's minstrels performed in Lexington in 1881 the police stopped the show and revoked their license. The mayor explained that a handbill advertising the show was immoral and "designed to awaken a prurient curiosity in the minds of men and youths. Its language was extremely filthy in its suggestiveness." The play itself was not indecent, according to a reporter who concluded, "Lexington is not a Sunday School exactly but there are some things she will not permit."[9]

John Whallen in Louisville played on the less than refined tastes when he took over the Grand Opera House, renamed it the Buckingham—"The Buck"—and turned it into a burlesque theater. Here men would stop to drink beer, smoke cigars, eat tasty food, and gaze at the scantily-clad show girls who danced, told ribald jokes, and "entertained." Family men and even church deacons were scandalously reported as visitors, as were businessmen from towns as far away as Paducah and Owensboro. The guests found relaxation with the racy girls at "The Buck"—a name which well-bred ladies in the Gay Nineties would breathe only in whispers.

Various tent shows competed with the theater for audiences. Besides minstrel shows and carnivals, the circuses drew large crowds. Both small and large towns attracted these circuses; in Maysville in 1876 a "Real Racing Hippodrome" with its Roman Chariot races, menagerie, circus, aquarium, museum, aviary, and "universal fair" offered the citizens everything—what it delivered is something else. Similar to the circuses in some ways, the Wild West shows toured Kentucky

An 1886 Macauley's Theater program

Courtesy of the R. G. Potter Collection,
University of Louisville

periodically. In 1890 one advertised two hundred Sioux Indians, "Custers Last Rally," and "the splendid triple Circus. The terrific gladiatorial combat. The marvelous trained elephants. The peerless Roman hippodrome . . . daring and unparalleled 40-horse act," plus somersaulting dogs, a tight rope walking horse, "Bugle Bill's cowboy band," and finally a stage coach, driven by "Round-up Bob."[10]

County Fairs and Other Attractions

More regular than these travelling shows were the annual county fairs held in summer or fall. In Lexington the fair association purchased a sixty acre plot near Broadway, laid out a race course and held its first annual fair in 1876. By the 1890s attendance numbered as high as twenty thousand. This story, with variations, was characteristic statewide. While the directors prohibited liquor on the grounds, the races and "skill" games of chance still remained. Strolling through the grounds one would notice an increase in women's exhibits each year, only to be distracted from his observation by the laughter from a puppet show or the sad melody of a blind singer of ballads. A medicine man and fortune teller might seek attention on the midway, while overhead an "aeronaut" in a balloon would rise to heights greater than one thousand feet. The aroma of a picnic lunch reminded one that fairs were social events where, above all, people met. Contests abounded, whether a horse, bicycle, mule, or even sack race, or pie-eating contest, tug-of-war, or exhibition drill.[11] At day's end, if still able, one could usually find a dance to attend, then hurry to bed, ready to begin again in the morning.

A colorful and unique fair opened in August 1883 in Louisville and continued for one hundred days. The celebrated Southern Exposition—organized as a corporation—had 1,732 stock subscribers who raised over $258,000 to help defray expenses. A central building covering thirteen acres and costing

The Southern Exposition Building
Reprinted from *The City of Louisville and a Glimpse of Kentucky* (1887)

three hundred thousand dollars was erected to house the 1,500 agricultural and mineralogical exhibits. Premiums that amounted to $6,750 were distributed for displays of corn, tobacco, cotton, and other products. All this attracted over 700,000 paid admissions. Bands and orators offered daily entertainment to the huge crowds and many celebrities, including President Chester A. Arthur, attended the Exposition, which proved to be one of the most effective means of advertising the resources, hospitality, and charm of Kentuckians to that time.[12]

The popular ring tournaments, often connected with the smaller fairs, attracted crowds as well. "Knights" on horseback would try to secure metal rings with their lances, usually for some prize. John Fox, Jr. made these affairs even more famous with his tale of the eastern mountains, *A Knight of the Cumberland*. Hickman sponsored one such tournament in 1871 and it typified others throughout the period. A fifty dollar prize (in greenbacks) and the right to crown "the queen of love" were the prizes. The judges ruled that lances must be eight feet long and riders would be given twelve seconds riding time. Steamboats offered half-fare from nearby river communities so all could cheer their local champions and observe the "chivalry, gallantry and beauty" involved. At nine o'clock the affair began with young men dressed in the style of the knights and squires of twelfth and thirteenth century England, lances held high ready to spear the rings. After the usual flowery speech by a politician, the "jousting" began. The winner in this instance speared twenty-eight rings in his three twelve-second rides and thus chose his favorite damsel as the queen. The five hundred spectators followed the champion to "the Pagoda" to crown the queen and begin dancing.[13] The pageantry ended, the entertainment had just begun.

The popular "hunts" at race tracks lacked the flourishes of a ring tournament but frequently were connected with fairs. At a charity exposition in 1891, a crowd that included Governor

John Y. Brown, ex-governor Wade Hampton of South Carolina, ex-Union General Don Carlos Buell, Senator J. C. S. Blackburn, and Congressman W. C. P. Breckinridge watched as five hundred dogs chased three foxes around the track. One fox returned safely to his den. The ever-popular band music entertained the enthusiastic crowd as they watched similar chases involving some deer and then a wolf.[14]

But people reserved their real enthusiasm for the horse. County fairs featured horseshows where steeds in fancy harness brought their owners prizes and purses or dejection. Three, four, and five gaited saddle rings, roadster rings, pony rings and the like attracted much attention at each gathering.

While some southern states had difficulty reconciling piety with pleasure, and thus limited the Sport of Kings, Kentucky had no such difficulty in the nineteenth century. Only slowly recovering from the wartime seizures of some of the best horses, racing improved and thrived.[15] In 1870 a *Harper's Monthly* story told how the state "at this time takes the lead as the 'blood horse region' of America." Louisville held its first Kentucky Derby in 1875 and within the decade the event attracted national attention. Racecourses, James Lane Allen believed, now had less drinking and fighting than before the War, for the thoroughbred received more attention than previously.[16]

A writer for *Harper's Magazine* in 1883 noted that the modern Kentucky Trotting-Horse Breeders' Association track in Lexington accommodated 10,000 people. He found horse-talk "the one subject always in order" in the town. After describing a typical farm, the reporter observed that while the stables were "clean and wholesome" they did not have the "fantastic elegance of adornment such as are now growing in favor among ourselves in Northern cities." The owners of the steeds resembed English country gentlemen and were "of a sober-minded, even religious cast"—certainly not the swash--buckling, hard-drinking men he expected to find.[17] Other

A ring tournament in the mountains
Reprinted from John Fox, Jr., *A Knight of the Cumberland* (1906)

tracks opened to challenge Louisville and Lexington, among them one at Latonia in 1883. Throughout Kentucky interest in racing continued and expanded in the late nineteenth century.

Many of the same group that frequented the tracks continued to gather at the springs. While they never recovered their prewar vitality, Kentucky's watering places remained popular resorts. One woman wrote in 1877 that "It has been dull in Lex.—as many persons are at Crab Orchard, which is the most fashionable resort at present."[18] Ten miles east of Stanford in Lincoln County, the resort was run by Isaac Shelby, Jr., grandson of the Governor, and he had recently built a $150,000 three story brick building. For $18.00 a week or $75.00 a month, one could indulge in "amusements of all kinds—music, ball-room dancing etc." plus the less publicized roulette, poker and cock-fighting.

J. Winston Coleman, Jr. interviewed a man who had visited Crab Orchard Springs in the nineties and remembered it as a place with a handsomely furnished house, "commodious parlor," and "heavily upholstered lounging chairs and settees" where one could doze or converse as one wished. After the noon meal and usual siesta the day began in earnest: "the ladies . . . would appear again, garbed in stones and bustles, silks, satins and fine raiment, adorned with all the frills and fine bows necessary for a perfect ensemble, together with diamonds, pearls, and jewelry of great value." They would then ride on horses or in carriages or perhaps go the lake where "bathers splashed around the raft at all hours." The blast of a horn brought a notice of the evening meal, followed by the ever-present dancing in the ball-room. "Turkey in the Straw" opened the evening and "when the oldsters began to retire," the polka was danced, until the late hours brought a waltz and "Good Night Ladies."

Other springs sought patronage as well. Rockcastle Springs in Pulaski County advertised fishing, boating, bands, balls, a "ten-pen alley," croquet lawns, fresh vegetables, skilled waiters,

The Churchill Downs Grandstand
Courtesy of the R. G. Potter Collection,
University of Louisville

The Fayette County Association track
Reprinted from W. H. Perrin and others,
Kentucky: A History of the State (8th ed., 1888)

Crab Orchard Springs resort
Reprinted from *The City of Louisville and a
Glimpse of Kentucky* (1887)

and, of course, the waters. Newspapers described the resort as "a veritable Eden for children, a sanatorium for the invalid, a paradise for lovers, and a haven of rest for the tired." Sebree Springs in western Kentucky was a place where "sociable, friendly and whole-souled" people attended, its advertisements said, while eight hundred guests could be lodged at Paroquet Springs in Bullitt County. Many other resorts, including Cerulean Springs in Trigg County, sought patrons in much the same manner.

But after a revival of prosperity in the nineties, the springs continued to decline, never to regain their former prominence. The rise of the Virginia resorts now made more accessible by railroads, patent medicines with their own "cures," and other social events like chautauquas, were all factors in the decline.[19]

The chautauquas rose to prominence by the late nineteenth century. The Bluegrass Chautauqua in 1888 at Lexington's Woodland Park lasted two weeks. For forty cents admission—or three dollars a "season"—the visitor could enter the grounds. Many of the most respectable families would "camp" there throughout the season. Inside they saw a hundred tents (12 feet by 16 feet) which rented for six dollars a season (eight dollars with a floor). Chairs, tables, washbowls, sheets, pillows and cots were available for rent as well. Perhaps attracted by the band music at the auditorium, the visitor would turn to the lectures featuring speakers of various promise. Music lessons, memory lessons, Bible study, teacher training, and temperance meetings were all available, as were lectures covering almost every conceivable topic. One attending an 1897 session might audit addresses on "Abraham Lincoln" by Henry Watterson, "The Last Days of the Confederacy" by ex-General John B. Gordon, "The Work of the Spirit of God," "The Ravages of Rum," "Our Mountain Work and Its Needs," "The Church and Labor Unions," "Evolution of the Republic," or "The Evils of Socialism." There might appear also Harry S. Riggs and his "marvelous birdlike whistling." "Stereopticon views" supplemented lectures or visitors might enjoy supper in their tent as they listened to band music. A reporter promoted the chautauqua when he noted that "nothing is sweeter and more enjoyable than the twilight and evening hours upon these beautiful grounds where one can be with friends or sit in silent meditation and rest and watch the interesting passers by."[20] Educational lectures were not the main attraction of the chautauqua; it afforded the opportunity to meet friends and to be thrilled by the gathering together, with all its possibilities.

Holidays, including the Fourth of July, Christmas, and Confederate Memorial Day were celebrated throughout Kentucky. While the Fourth of July was, for a time, mostly a Negro holiday in the South, in Kentucky whites and blacks alike celebrated it. But all in all, Kentuckians, generally a gregarious, outgoing, fun-loving, hospitable people, did not need the excuse of a formal occasion to celebrate. Barbecues, picnics, and political gatherings continued to be popular throughout this period. A Democratic barbecue in 1884 for the party's candidates had a menu of one hundred fifty sheep, a hundred hams, ten beef cattle, and a thousand gallons of burgoo. A barbecue for the Grand Army of the Republic members attending their national convention in Louisville in 1895 reportedly drew nearly a hundred thousand people.[21]

Kentuckians celebrated their Confederate ties more often, however, than Union partisans did their organization. There were several Confederate associations, including the United Daughters of the Confederacy, Confederate Monument Association, Morgan Men, and the Confederate Veteran Association. The latter organization was designed to cultivate social relations and "to see that no worthy member shall ever become an object of public charity." A five dollar initiation fee and four dollars a year dues helped defray expenses. On occasion the various groups entertained the members, and in an 1889 affair the Monument Association held a dance for over six hundred veterans at Louisville's Armory. The hall was draped with

Confederate colors and the waitresses dressed in gray. The hostesses represented such prominent families as Helm, Buckner, Castleman, Breckinridge, Haldeman, Watterson and Wickliffe. Of the 232 former members of the Orphan Brigade in attendance, a reporter noted the next day, over one-third held some political office.[22] To be a Confederate veteran in Kentucky did not hurt one politically or socially.

Court Day

But of all the gatherings, County Court Day still affected the most people. Even small isolated communities that would never see a circus or fair had their court day. James Lane Allen believed that the Kentuckian was not fond of lectures and did not spend much money on theaters, but loved his county court day. He wrote that while the judge sat quietly on the bench inside, "the people fought quietly on the streets outside, and the day of the month set apart for the conservation of the peace became the approved day for individual war." A stranger to the event might question whether the fights were quiet and wonder how anyone got anything accomplished. Tooth doctors, patent medicine men, a band of minstrels, and many others all sought a wary farmer's attention—and money—while sound of sheep, cattle, and horses almost drowned out all other noise. The stranger would notice a predominance of men, for it was not quite proper yet for women to mingle in the crowded thoroughfares and hear the harsh language or see the frequent fights. Merchants draped their windows in their gaudiest colors and tried to "work off" old goods at high prices. They knew that men shoppers would spend little time quibbling over items that interested their wives. Too much was occurring out on the street to remain long inside a store.

By foot, carriage, buggy, spring-wagon, rockaway, or horseback, people crowded into the county seat to swap horses or other animals, to sell hams and other products, or just simply to gawk and talk. As the sun started to set, the exodus back to the small rural homesteads began. By nighttime the small town would once again regain its sleepy status, with the only hint of what had happened being a letter from an irritated citizen protesting the "filth" left behind by the cattle, "which the city authorities make no attempt to remove."[23]

Sports

Kentuckians discovered new diversions and interest in sports blossomed. Baseball originated in the North in the 1850s, but the South accepted it after the war. In Lexington in April 1867, a group of amateurs led by A. K. Wooley organized the Ashland Baseball Club, and the local nine began to play other nearby teams. By 1870, games between the Cincinnati Junior Reds, the Lexington Orions, the Frankfort Valleys and the Louisville Eagles were reported. Kentuckians generally lost to the Ohioans. There were such scores as 25-13 and 27-19. One man suffered a broken nose but such incidents did little to hinder the sport's growth. A reporter in 1875 noted that "there seems to have been a sort of sporting revival in regard to base ball and the amateur clubs are all engaging professional players."[24]

Professionalism had hit the local clubs, but not enough professionals were on the field for Lexington when the visiting Cincinnati Red Stockings defeated the home team 13-2 before a large crowd who had paid twenty-five cents admission apiece. In Frankfort the White Stockings beat the Capitals 17-3, while the "Bostons" beat the Ludlow team 8-4 the same year. The status of baseball in Kentucky was further revealed when the St. Louis Brown Stockings defeated Lexington 17-5; to make it more embarrassing the Bluegrass team had been so poorly prepared that the St. Louis Club "loaned" them two players. That helped them little, for the Browns' pitcher threw a baffling pitch, "englished to an unusual degree." The amateur and semiprofessional teams soon avoided the professional teams and left Louisville's entry in the professional league to take on the Cincinnati club regularly.[25]

Women played the sport, but without a great deal of male encouragement. Under the headline of "Female Bat-Slingers" the Lexington *Leader* of May 25, 1890 described a game between the Lexington team and the visiting female Black Stockings. A totally masculine crowd watched the "fair willow wielders . . . neatly but not profusely attired in short red and black-striped dresses which came barely to the knee." Sarcastically, the reporter noted a "slight drawback" for the females when they stopped to arrange their hair or "adjust their slipping hose." Since they did not slide into bases, they were further handicapped. Their pitcher "could knock out a hen's eye . . . at four paces" but it "did not take the boys long to get on to her curves." Lexington won the ball game 10-2 and the reporter concluded, "but then a woman is a woman."

The first intercollegiate football game was played in New Jersey in 1869. Within a little more than a decade the American version of rugby reached Kentucky. As early as 1880 Kentucky University (Transylvania) met Centre College at the Lexington City Park and the papers reported: "Kentucky University defeated Centre College 13 3/4 to 0. . . . A large crowd of ladies and gentlemen, estimated at 500, witnessed the game. The game lasted two hours. . . .One of the Danville boys had his hand cut badly by falling on a piece of glass." The next year Kentucky University played State College (University of Kentucky) and was defeated 7¼-1; but it got revenge a week later, winning 2-1. Few games were reported between 1882-1890, but from 1891-1894, Centre College recorded three consecutive unbeatin sessions. By 1892 certain rules were used: five points for a touchdown, two for a "kick for goal," a forty-five minute half with a fifteen minute rest, no forward pass, three downs to gain five yards and goals 330 feet apart. A season for State College in 1893 began successfully with an 80-0 win over

Georgetown, then a 56-0 victory over Tennessee at Knoxville before four thousand fans, but when they met Central University of Richmond they lost 48-36. Immediately a protest was lodged that one Central player—"the human plow"—had played for Kentucky University before and was a professional. While baseball divided along professional-amateur lines, the division was less clear-cut in football.[26]

Professionalism hurt collegiate football, but more serious was the continuing debate over the sport itself. An injury in the very first game in Kentucky set the pattern, for lack of protective equipment, makeshift playing fields, poor coaching in technique, all made for possible injuries. A Maysville ordinance in 1877 made it unlawful for any "person or persons to play at football, or any other game of a character calculated to disturb the quiet of the people." An attack on the game in 1893 brought a defense of it as "a scientific game . . . played on scientific principles" whose players made better grades and had better control of their tempers. Critics did not agree. State College nearly abolished football in 1896. However, formal faculty controls enabled it to remain and fifty dollars was appropriated for the sport. The results were gratifying to its backers; two years later in 1898 the "Immortals" at A & M won seven games without a loss and outscored their opponents 181-0.[27] Modern organized sports had a firm foothold in Kentucky.

Besides team sports, Kentuckians enjoyed other forms of recreation. The bicycling craze came in the latter part of the century and in 1881 the Lexington Bicycle Club was organized and ordered five English bikes. Four years later Hopkinsville repealed, at the request of ten bike owners, a city ordinance prohibiting the riding of bicycles on the streets. By the nineties the "safety" bicycles made cycling safer and notices of bicycle races appeared more frequently in newspapers. A Labor Day race in 1896, covering a hundred miles from Lexington to Covington, was won in the time of six hours and seven

A & M College's football "immortals" of 1898
Reprinted from *Pictorial Art Souvenir 1901 of
the Kentucky State College (1901)*

One of Centre College's unbeaten teams of the 1890s
Reprinted from Frederick A. Wallis and
Hambleton Tapp, *A Sesqui-Centennial History
of Kentucky (1945), Vol. I*

minutes.[28] Some feared that horse-racing's popularity was threatened.

Tennis and croquet were played mostly by the "fashionable set." Large but select crowds watched tennis tournaments on grass courts at homes of the wealthy. But at least one Grange had such equipment for the farmers. However, the games were probably not as popular among farm people as glass ball shooting. Certain groups enjoyed cock fighting.[29]

Hunting as a sport appealed to all classes. Hunting clubs, including the Iroquois Hunt and Riding Club of the Bluegrass, were popular. John Fox, Jr. described a rabbit hunt by members of the Iroquois Club as an event where no special dress was prescribed but where ladies usually wore fashionable outfits. A "spirit of recklessness" pervaded the chase, whether rabbit or fox. But even the poorest in the land possessed a gun and someone could always furnish hounds· the "music of the dogs" could be heard far into the night and the darkness did not distinguish between the Bluegrass aristocrat or the poor white. Fox wrote that nowhere in the South was coon-hunting "more popular than in Kentucky—with mountaineers, negroes, and people of the Bluegrass."[30] This popular sport of "old" Kentucky continued into the new century.

Social Life in Microcosm

What was life like, then, for a young man or woman growing up in the 1890s? A Louisville girl nostalgically remembered it as a time "when family counted, and money was important, but . . . backing and the personality of the girl were what carried the day." Social life there included visits to Cave Hill Cemetery, "a favorite courting place" with its lakes and parkland, moonlight excursions on the river, picnics at Fern Grove Island, night trolley rides, sleigh rides "with oyster stew and crackers and hot chocolate and doughnuts at some boy's house afterward," ice-skating, summer fire-works, and Macauley's theater, which was expensive, because a "hack," flowers, and five-dollar tickets all added up for a gentleman and his date.[31]

A more extensive recording of social life and dating patterns is found in one young man's diary. On January 1, 1890 he began keeping a record of "my monotonous life." Sixteen years old, almost six feet tall, weighing only 120 pounds, he began shaving in September, two weeks before he left for college.[32]

Before departing, he made a difficult choice. In February of that year he had met a young girl who had "quite a fascination for me." Shy, reluctant and hesitant, he observed from afar for a time, waiting at the drug store for a glimpse of her. Finally by June he gathered the courage to call on her at her home and by the end of July the two were going together to watermelon parties, card parties, and church socials. As the time approached for him to leave for Harvard and her for a Staunton, Virginia, school, the two were going on carriage rides along the reservoir with "little negro Tom" as an escort. In the middle of the month the student decided upon the University of Virginia for his schooling.

Disillusionment with Virginia or with his "Miss Anna," or both, soon set in and he transferred to Yale. After returning to read law in his father's office in northern Kentucky, he was no longer the introverted, shy beau. He now listed in his diary some ninety-one "Lady Acquaintances in this vicinity," complete with a coding system. His varied activities in 1897 included such sample entries as:

August 9—We all went up the Creek tonight—fifteen of us—and took supper at the Elm Tree Spring, drifting back by moon-light and passing the hours with music and singing.

August 13—Clara and I enjoyed a bicycle ride.

September 2—Island Canoe Club Camp, where the afternoon we spent rowing, canoeing, eating.

October 23—Bicycle ride out to Milldale this afternoon. Saw part of the football game.[33]

Much of what he recorded is almost timeless and could have occurred in 1790, 1890 or the present. Some of his activities were firmly tied to ante-bellum days and would die out, while still others would grow and thrive in the twentieth century.

Kentuckians slowly moved from one world into another, the world of the 1900s. In 1900 they were but three years away from the first transcontinental automobile trip and the first plane flight. By 1901, Marconi could send signals across the Atlantic, and two years later the first commercially successfully movie was produced. Yet, though near, that was the future. In 1900, Kentucky stood between two worlds.

VI
TRIALS OF THE NEW DEPARTURE

Midway in his administration, Governor Leslie became noticeably more interested in enactment of laws designed to make the state more progressive and modern. Prior to that time, though mildly concerned, he had been content to go along generally with the Bourbons, had even been accused of permitting ultra-conservatives to dictate policies. Two years as chief executive, however, had not only acquainted him with the routine of government but had caused him to realize the need for legislative reform. He devoted the latter part of his term as governor to the advocacy of New Departure proposals. The tide of conservatism, however, would be too strong to stem, and he would retire from office a disappointed man.

The Liberal Republican Movement

Long before the end of General Grant's first administration, thousands of reformers, disappointed with the Republican regime because of its corruption, high tariff, and "oppression" of the South, sought to prevent his reelection. Conscious of the fact that the "Grant crowd" controlled the machinery of the Republican party, some of the leaders of the reform wing advocated the launching of a new party, a liberal Republican party. Foremost among these were Carl Schurz, Jacob D. Cox, Lyman Trumbull, Frank P. Blair Jr., and B. Gratz Brown, together with the prominent editors Horace Greeley, Horace White, Samuel Bowles,

Whitelaw Reid, and Murat B. Halstead. These reformers called a convention to meet in Cincinnati on the first Wednesday in May, 1872.

Conscious of the inability of his own party to win nationally, Henry Watterson threw in his lot with this group. He wished, above all, relief for the South in the form of removal of federal troops, destruction of carpetbag-scalawag rule, and return of home rule. He knew that the leaders of the liberal Republican movement felt as he did upon these matters. He realized too that they regarded the Civil War as over and that they accepted not only the results in good faith, but also the Thirteenth, Fourteenth and Fifteenth amendments as accomplished and irrevocable facts. Watterson believed that the combined liberals of the Republican party and the entire Democratic party could win the presidency, gain control of Congress, and overthrow Radical Republican rule and the abuses of the Grant administration. His thinking more closely resembled that of the liberal Republican leaders than that of the Bourbons who controlled his party in Kentucky.

At the Cincinnati convention Watterson was quickly accepted as one of the leaders. He even became one of the celebrated "Quadrilateral" (Bowles, Halstead, White, and Watterson), which determined upon the nomination of Charles Francis Adams for president.[1]

Unfortunately for the movement, Horace Greeley, instead of the more suited Adams, received the nomination, through the strategems and connivances of Whitelaw Reid and certain New York politicians, together with the Missourians, Blair and Brown.[2] The latter was able to secure the nomination for vice president. The platform, however, was liberal and included an invitation to the Democrats and the South to join the movement. Nevertheless, the nomination of Greeley, an eccentric though able editor, killed all chances of the Liberal Republicans' winning. Most of the blame was heaped upon Blair and Brown, who were acrimoniously and vehemently reproached by the pure reformers and idealists, the most disturbed of whom was Carl Schurz. The "Quadrilateral," though greatly shaken, decided to support Greeley with every ounce of editorial ability the members singly and as a group could muster.

Watterson's principal task was to persuade Democrats in Kentucky that their only hope nationally was to support the Liberal Republican ticket. He therefore devoted several powerful editorials to the problem. That of May 17, 1872, attempted to strike to the heart of the question. He wrote:

> *Should Horace Greeley be elected President of the United States by the cooperation of the Democracy, we shall have an honest and faithful administration. That will be a great gain alike to the Democratic party and the country. Nobody doubts Greeley's honesty, nobody believes that he would deliberately countenance or connive at official rascalities of any kind. With his inauguration nepotism would come to an end. He has no worthless relatives to place in fat offices, and, if he had a thousand, it would be all the same. In his appointments he would select men whom he believed qualified. . . . Under an administration with Horace Greeley at its head there would be no Leets and Stockings extorting money from the people months after the exposure of their crimes; no custom house vampires like Casey retained up to the very eve of another Presidential election; no notoriously infamous persons like Consul-General Butler suffered to go on unmolested, dishonoring and degrading the American name abroad. With Greeley as President—we should have a Chief Magistrate that would spend his summers at Washington instead of Long Branch, and whose attention would not be occupied, to the neglect of public business, with bull pups and fast horses, Partagas cigars and old Bourbon.*

And Watterson thought the South would profit by Greeley's election. "From the election of Greeley," he declared, "universal amnesty would result. . . .Will it be no gain if the nominee of the Cincinnati Convention, standing on the Cincinnati platform succeeds over Grant, with his proscription, his Ku Klux laws, his suspension of the writ of habeas corpus, and his carpetbag policy?" He explained the Cincinnati platform, stressing its strong stand for civil service reform, supremacy of the civil over military authority in time of peace, and "recognition of the principle that the power of the Federal government is limited by the Constitution and that the proper guarantee of local interests is found in state legislation. Would this be no gain for the Democratic Party?"

In a realistic vein, the young editor, trying to take what seemed the most practical course, wrote:

> Democrats would of course prefer a Democrat for the Presidency; but that, we regret to say, is wholly out of the question. . . .Shall we prefer a straight ticket that is sure to be beaten. . . ? If Greeley is successful, as must be the case . . . should he receive Democratic support, the Republican party will be in a helpless minority. . . . Even in the event of Greeley's defeat the position of the Democratic party would be greatly improved, for, then, our organization being still intact, the dissensions in the Republican party would be past reconciling.[3]

Watterson's cogent, plausible and frequent arguments readily bore fruit with the Kentucky Democracy. One prominent county editor declared:

> We now feel assured that the plain, manifest duty of our party, and all who love their country with patriotic fervor, is to give in our allegiance to the Liberal Party for the present . . . to battle for one great leading purpose, to wit: The overthrow of the Grant dynasty . . . and thus form a great national party . . . for . . . the perpetuity of free government, universal amnesty, states' rights, and a last peace.[4]

Although the Bourbons were cold to the idea of amalgamation, the terse, truculent writing of Watterson and the other "New Departure" editors, together with the idea's logical appeal, elicited favorable responses from the state's Democrats generally.

The principal issue facing the Democrats at their June 20 state convention in Frankfort was endorsement of the Cincinnati convention platform and nominees. Some of the leading Bourbons assembled favored an independent Democratic ticket. Pandemonium resulted when General Basil Duke introduced a resolution designed to require the Kentucky delegation to vote (at the National convention to be held in Baltimore) for Greeley and Brown as the Democratic nominees for president and vice president.

Fearing a hopeless split and walkout, the party organization leaders would not permit the Duke resolution to come to a vote.[5] As adopted, however, the general platform, which vigorously denounced the Grant administration for "failures and abuses," provided that the delegation vote as a unit. Care was taken by the managers to elect a majority of delegates known to be favorable to Greeley's nomination.[6]

Delegates to the Baltimore convention held at Ford's Theater, July 9 and 10, wasted little time in adopting the Cincinnati platform—670 delegates out of a 732 total; or in nominating Greeley with 686 votes in spite of the protests of Senator Thomas F. Bayard of Delaware and Jeremiah S. Black of Pennsylvania, attorney general and secretary of state under Buchanan. Perhaps most Democrats felt as a Kentucky editor did following the "tumult and the shouting." He wrote: "We do not think it necessary for Democrats to become enthusiastic over Greeley. He is not a Democrat, and we do not want to shout for him, but in desiring his election we are in dead earnest. There is no probability that we could elect a Democratic President, and in the present crises, as sensible men, we ought to acquiesce in the next best thing that can be done."[7]

The Republicans' state convention, having met at Louisville on March 14 with John M. Harlan as permanent chairman, endorsed Grant and Harlan for president and vice president and instructed the delegates to the national convention, to be held in June, to vote for the renomination of Grant. That meeting was attended by an uncommonly large number of Negroes who were loud in their demand for proportional representation on committees and in offices. They claimed to represent 42,000 members of the Republican party in the state. The white leaders, however, were not disposed to confer upon them positions of importance and power. But the Negroes were profusely showered with convention courtesies and flattery. The convention praised Grant and his administration, and it passed a resolution praising Harlan "for sacrifices and services in behalf of its country" and presenting his name for vice president.[8]

Kentucky, in spite of the fact that fifty-three of its newspapers supported Greeley and only five stood for Grant, failed to warm up greatly to the eccentric editor of the New York *Tribune*. The final vote in the state was 100,212 for Greeley and Brown to 88,816 for Grant and Henry Wilson and 2,374 for Charles O'Connor of New York (a famous lawyer and nominee of the Labor Reform party and of the Straight-out Democrats, whose convention was held in Louisville) and John Quincy Adams, Jr. The falling off in the Democratic vote from August 1871 was 23,473, while that of the Republicans was only 267. Actually Greeley narrowly carried Kentucky. Republican candidates for Congress made impressive proportionate gains, particularly young William O'Connell Bradley of Lancaster, who received in the heavily Democratic Eighth District 9,925 votes to 10,874 for his opponent, Milton Jameson Durham of Danville.[9]

In the nation Greeley suffered an overwhelming defeat, having carried only six of the thirty-seven states—Missouri, Texas, Georgia, Kentucky, Tennessee, and Maryland. He had gained not one electoral vote from a northern state. The anguished, disillusioned, heart-broken man survived the shock less than three weeks. Watterson had missed being prophetic by a wide margin.[10]

Leslie's Message to the Legislature, December, 1873

Although usually mild mannered and conciliatory, Governor

Leslie, in his "State of the Commonwealth Address" to the General Assembly, reported forthrightly to the lawmakers a state of affairs generally unsatisfactory, indeed in many instances deplorable. The message revealed a genuine desire for leadership and real humanitarian sympathies.

To Leslie's mind the most alarming problem was general lawlessness, which had continued unabated since the last session. He felt that the basic weakness lay in the citizens who were "reluctant, from fear or favor, . . . apathy or terror, to disclose what they know" and who looked more and more to the authorities at Frankfort, instead of to the local authorities, for the apprehension and punishment of organized violators of the law. He averred that, in some instances, "criminals have been purposely left to go at large until proclamations offering rewards for their apprehension could be secured." He was not only perturbed about the weakness, often venality, of county law enforcement officials, but about the "great number of escapes from jails through the state."

The chief executive asked the lawmakers to enact legislation giving the governor power to appoint a "Commissioner of Inquiry" with power to go into an area of prevalent lawlessness and proceed with "the same power and jurisdiction possessed by any court of inquiry in the state, and also with the inquisitorial powers of a grand jury." The commissioner, thought the governor, should be clothed with authority to have persons arrested and held for trial in the circuit court of a county.

Regarding money matters, Leslie, although maintaining the soundness of the state's financial position, indicated that expenditures of the state government for the fiscal year ending October 10, 1873, exceeded receipts by over half a million dollars and that the deficit had been made up by borrowing from the Sinking Fund. Again he appealed to the legislators to improve the revenue laws. He declared once more that in many counties much property was not listed for taxation at all, that in a greater number it was assessed at not more than half of its actual value, that in only a few counties was it listed at its real value. Moreoever, he pointed out that the total property valuation of the state in 1872, according to the auditor's report, was $22,653,959 less than for the previous year, and $372,181 less for 1873 than for 1872. Indicating that the county assessors were generally failing to discharge their duty, Leslie recommended legislation looking to a "Board of Equalization" for the state as well as one for each county, with power to act to increase or diminish assessments, thus establishing central agencies with legal power to bring about uniformity and justice in assessments throughout the state.

Upon the question of dishonest public officials, the chief magistrate spoke out boldly. He declared that delinquent, often dishonest, sheriffs were cheating the state out of a large amount of its revenues after collecting them. He asked that the General Assembly repeal the law giving extensions of time to sheriffs for settlement with the state, and requested that lawmakers cease passing bills giving individual sheriffs such extensions. The governor declared that to the year 1872 sheriffs owed the state $517,241.21, much of which seems simply to have been stolen, and that the embezzling sheriffs were immunized by special acts of the legislature. Thus venal legislators and dishonest sheriffs had developed a goodpaying "racket," one that might have wrung praise from the inimitable "Boss" Tweed, the members of the New York Custom House gang, or the infamous "Whiskey Ring." The result of the system prevailing in the state was that the treasury was often without funds. It is likely that had it not been for the Sinking Fund, which stood convenient for plundering, the Commonwealth would have defaulted. As matters stood, the poverty-ridden school teachers, miserably underpaid, were obliged often to wait six months or longer without one cent of pay whatsoever.[11] Worse still, in some counties school commissioners and trustees, catching teachers in desperate straits, would buy up the suffering pedagogues' claims at ruinously low sums, and thus return tidy profits.[12]

Governor Leslie also called attention to the fact that corporations, growing enormously rich from plundering the people's and the state's natural resources, were practically tax-exempt, made so by charters granted by the legislature. "Most of the banks," he declared, "pay practically no taxes." And the rates were not uniform. Some were taxed at the rate of fifty cents on each share of $100 of capital stock, while others paid at the rate of twenty-five cents. "Why should the bank," he asked, "or any other corporation organized for like purposes, be granted an exemption from burdens which other property has to bear?" He noted that "railroads enjoy similar exemptions," pointing out that much of the railroad mileage had been paid for by citizens of counties, cities, and towns through special taxes, and that the "stock so subscribed is virtually a mortgage upon such localities, and has been, or is being, paid dollar for dollar." He declared "the division of the surplus capital of the State to corporations enjoying such immunities must inevitably result in imposing an increased rate of taxation upon the real estate and producing classes, besides lodging a dangerous power in the hands of these privileged institutions." Stressing an agrarian theme, Leslie stated that "moneyed institutions are organized and operated in the interest of rings, and, instead of meeting the wants and relieving the necessities of the farmer and other producers, are ready to help the monopolist in his efforts to take advantage of the necessities of the producer, and control the market for purposes of richer speculation; while, at the same time, colossal railroad companies abuse their chartered power in exacting capricious, exorbitant, and oppressive rates of freight from those who are compelled to use their roads." The embattled governor appealed to the lawmakers to examine the charters of corporations in the state with the idea of "revisal by the legislature in the interests of the public."

Nor was Leslie's report on the state's income from its toll turnpike stock optimistic. Although pleased that the Commonwealth had invested nearly $3,000,000 in these roads, "thus greatly improving transportation," the governor stated that the investment brought, in 1872, a return of only $33,550,19. However, he was certain that "if a proper agency were employed to attend to the interest of the State in these corporations, and secure its equitable share of their earnings, the amount received from them by the public treasury would be greatly increased." He intimated that a good share of the state's return from its stock in these turnpike corporations was being stolen by company officials for the benefit of private stockholders. He insisted that the state should secure the "election of suitable directors in each [company] to introduce the proposed reforms." In fact he earnestly solicited the lawmakers to pass legislation for the "appointment of a Commissioner of Turnpike roads." Leslie rather fully depicted unsatisfactory conditions in the insane asylums and in the penitentiary. The state had since 1857 followed a policy of contracting or renting out prisoners to agents or companies. The work was done by the convicts in a factory at the penitentiary in Frankfort and all of the equipment was supplied by the state. The state's principal object was to earn money for the care of the convicts and upkeep of the prison. On the part of the manufacturer, the object was to make profits. Actually the state lost money in the transaction. The governor declared that since the year 1865 the annual charge "of the institution on the public treasury has reached the enormous amount of forty thousand dollars." Under the contract the lessor paid the state $8,000 per year for the hire of six hundred convicts—slightly over four cents per day per convict. The governor hinted that the unfortunate fellows were being brutally driven like slaves and barbarously punished for slight offenses. The state had been supplying three inspectors to look into the working conditions and treatment, an arrangement which had failed miserably. Leslie recommended the appointment of one inspector, competent and adequately paid, who should be in daily attendance at the penitentiary, and "whose duty it shall be to examine into all matters connected with the government, discipline, and police of the penitentiary, and make a report thereof every month to the Governor." He also requested provision for a physician and a chaplain. It seems clear that the fine, enlightened penitentiary legislation pressed through the General Assembly by John Breckinridge in 1798 had been discarded and forgotten.

Particularly vehement was Leslie's call for the passage of a law prohibiting the vending and giving of strong drink to voters on election days. He declared that "the greater part of the undue excitement, lawless violence, riots, and personal encounters, often ending in bloodshed, as well as the corruption of voters and fraud . . . is attributable to the free use of intoxicating drinks." It was ardent spirits, not "party zeal that collects those noisy, turbulent, and riotous crowds which surround the polls, and often by their violence prevent the peaceful, quiet citizen, from casting his vote; which makes the voting place an arena for the settlement of old feuds in bloody conflict and the occasion of new ones." Leslie pointed to the fact that many states had obtained good results from laws against selling alcoholic beverages at and near polling places on election days.[13]

The only bright spot in the governor's otherwise gloomy report to the General Assembly concerned the launching of the Geological Survey. He stated that Professor Nathaniel Southgate Shaler, a native of Campbell County and a distinguished scientist at Harvard University,[14] had been appointed as the Survey's head and that work was already being projected in the eastern coalfield. Assuming the correctness of Governor Leslie's report, Kentucky's government was desperately in need of reformation.

Despite his party's platform, Leslie had recommended further state centralization in his call for measures dealing with lawlessness and taxation. He had angered the Bourbon faction by stressing property tax reform, and had disagreed with the New Departure wing by noting the need for fairer taxation of corporations and railroads. Changes advocated by Leslie in the granting of sheriffs' extensions and in his call for reexamination of the turnpike situation alienated other groups. The Governor's stress on minor prison reform and limited prohibition would also attack certain vested interests. His reform program would require careful handling if it was to succeed.

Legislative Session, 1873-1874

In spite of Governor Leslie's forthright report and prudent recommendations, the General Assembly of 1873-1874 enacted very little important legislation. Of the 596 acts and 25 joint resolutions passed, nearly all were of a "private or local character and of no general interest." Many of the acts of a local nature were again for the relief of sheriffs desiring extensions of time before settling their financial obligations in the matter of tax collection due the state. One notable achievement was an act providing for submission to the voters at the next regular election the question of calling a constitutional convention to revise the outmoded document of 1849.

During the session a bill designed to regulate the sale of intoxicating liquors was passed. The measure, providing for local option, stated that on petition of twenty legal voters in any civil district, town, or city, or in any county, "the judge of the county court shall direct an election . . . on the question of whether spiritous liquors shall be sold therein, and, if a majority . . . vote against it, then it shall be unlawful for any person to sell . . . on penalty of a fine of not less than $25 nor more than $100." This act, though not all that organized prohibitionists had wanted, came only after widespread agitation and memorials from the Blue Grass Temperance Convention and the Grand Lodge of Good Templars bearing the signatures of 147,000 citizens. Acts were also passed providing for appointment by the governor of a state board of pharmacy and examinations and licensing of pharmacists, and for graduation by those wishing to become physicians from some chartered school of medicine and certification by boards of examiners before licenses could be issued to practice in the Commonwealth.

In addition to passage of a law to establish a system of education for Negroes, the General Assembly enacted legislation concerning the eleemosynary institutions. The division, formerly known as the House of Reform and subsequently converted into the Fourth Kentucky Lunatic Asylum, was declared to be the

Central Kentucky Lunatic Asylum, and $100,000 was appropriated to extend and improve it, one-third to be used in providing accommodations for Negro "lunatics." The Institution for the Education and Training of Feeble-minded Children, which had been converted into the Third Kentucky Lunatic Asylum, was reestablished for its original purpose, under charge of nine commissioners, to be appointed by the governor.[15]

Eleemosynary Institutions

The Commonwealth operated what were known as the Eastern Insane Asylum at Lexington, the Central at Anchorage, and the Western at Hopkinsville, plus the Institution for Deaf Mutes at Danville, the Institution for the Education and Training of Feeble-Minded Children at Frankfort, and the Institute for the Blind at Louisville.

Usually overcrowded, these institutions were always underfunded. Each legislature appropriated money in proportion to local strength in that session. The result was a sizeable, often vital, difference in the income an institution might expect. The Eastern Insane Asylum, for example, received $102,000 for 1872 but after various fluctuations, the figure dropped to only $68,000 ten years later. Within two years the figure had risen to over $100,000. The year 1882—particularly bad for the insane asylums—saw appropriations to Central and Western fall to their lowest point in the period from 1872-1885. On the other hand the "Deaf and Dumb Asylum," as it was called, received its highest appropriation of the period that same year. The decade from 1872-1882 brought only a very slight increase in funds to all the institutions. The effects of the 1873 depression and building additions, do not explain the completely inconsistent budgets that the legislators voted for the institutions. The answer must be found largely in the constant stress on financial conservatism by both parties and the seeming willingness to engage in "pork barrel" appropriations—all at the expense of patients and students.[16]

Conditions inside these institutions were far from ideal. Of the more than 1600 patients treated at the Anchorage Asylum in 1900, 164 died—over 1 in 10. Nearly one-third of the deaths were of people who had been confined less than one year. At the Lexington center 76 patients died the same year.

Several other public charitable establishments in a few of the state's cities provided other services. Louisville's House of Refuge had over 200 children under the age of sixteen in 1877 and kept them busy working in the laundry room, the sewing room, the shoe shop, the garden, or the willow shop—much in the manner of Dickens' *Oliver Twist*. The Almshouse in Louisville housed nearly 350 people that same year, including 30 children under the age of ten. There, too, mortality was high: 17 adults and 10 of the children died within the year.[17]

The Elections of 1874 and 1875

The only state election in 1874 was that of clerk of the Court of Appeals, which the Democrats won handsomely. The successful candidate, Thomas C. Jones, Owensboro, received 114,348 votes out of a total of 167,852 votes cast. In the congressional elections, the Democrats fared equally well, with the Republicans winning only in one district, the Ninth, in which John D. White, Manchester, won by a small majority of 629 votes.[18]

The Democratic state convention of 1875, whose duty it was to select candidates for state offices, met at Frankfort on May 6 and 7. It convened on the lawn of the State Capitol (Old State House). Describing the "immense crowds," an enthusiastic reporter wrote that the "solid banker and merchant, all resplendent in new broadcloth coats and silk hats, were there side by side with the horny-handed Patrons of Husbandry [Grangers]."

George Washington Craddock, chairman of the State Central Committee, called the convention to order at noon, and General Lucius Desha was elected temporary chairman over John Milton Elliott of Boyd County. A heated contest developed for the nomination for governor. Among the candidates were James B. McCreary, John Stuart Williams of Mount Sterling, J. Stoddard Johnston, and J. Q. A. King.

It was more or less a contest between ex-Confederate officers, with McCreary, one of John Hunt Morgan's officers, winning out on the fourth ballot over General "Cerro Gordo" Williams who was, prior to the convention, considered a sure winner in spite of attacks in local papers of western Kentucky on his private morals. The nominees for other offices included: John Cox Underwood, of Bowling Green, for lieutenant governor; Thomas Edward Moss, Paducah, for attorney general; D. Howard Smith, incumbent, for auditor; James W. ("Honest Dick") Tate, incumbent, for treasurer; H. A. M. Henderson, incumbent, for superintendent of public instruction; and Thomas D. Marcum, ex-Union officer from Louisa, for register of the land office.

The platform adopted contained one commendable quality — brevity; otherwise, its smooth verbiage was made up of the usual platitudes and current complaints apparently calculated to stir the wrath of the people toward the "wicked" Republican administration at Washington and to deflect their thinking from Kentucky's dire need for reform which, if begun, might necessitate additional taxes.

The document abounded in such statements as, "we hold it to be absolutely essential to the preservation of the liberties of the citizens that the several states shall be maintained in all their rights, dignity, and equality, as the most complete and reliable administration of their own domestic concerns, and the surest bulwarks against anti-Republican tendencies."[19] It made no promise of reform in state government; the platform writers chose not to mention state affairs at all. The leaders felt confident of their ability to switch the attention of the voters to the abuses and scandals of the Grant administration. They were in no position to boast of positive achievements in the state government.

Although Henry Watterson endorsed the ticket, he entertained some doubts about what its members, once in offices, would do

Governor James B. McCreary

Reprinted from *Biographical Encyclopaedia
of Kentucky (1878), Vol. I.*

for the well-being of the state. Where was "New Departure" or reform coming in? "The whole ticket is good," he wrote. "It is one on which the Democracy everywhere can rally, and to which those who have lost hope of any improvement under the present controlling influences of our national affairs may come and help swell the tide of opposition that is sweeping our whole country." Continuing, he urged, "It will be well for Colonel McCreary to take the earliest opportunity to sound the keynote of the campaign, and to open the canvass on a broad and liberal basis that will look not only to the advancement of the interest of the National Party, but to the improvement of commercial, industrial and political interests and methods of our own Commonwealth."[20]

On May 13, the Republican convention met in Louisville. Judge William Cassius Goodloe, Lexington, nephew of General Cassius Marcellus Clay, was elected both temporary and permanent chairman. He pushed the meeting along vigorously. Perhaps no other Republican was as eminently qualified for the gubernatorial nomination as John M. Harlan, who consented to accept the honor and try his fortunes once more on the hustings.[21] Robert Boyd, Laurel County, was nominated for lieutenant governor, and Judge Goodloe for attorney general. Rodolphus B. Ratliffe, Princeton, was nominated for auditor and Dr. William J. Berry, Hartford, for treasurer. The convention made no selection for superintendent of public instruction, stating that politics should not be considered in the choice of a school head. The inference was that Henderson, the Democratic incumbent and nominee, was satisfactory to the Republicans. Somewhat later, however, the Republicans named Gilroy Wells Griffin, lawyer, editor, and distinguished author, as their candidate, to the chagrin of the Democratic nominee. Reuben Patrick, Salyersville, was named as candidate for register of the land office.[22] With the exceptions of Harlan and Goodloe, the nominees were not generally politically known, although geographically they were well selected. Judge Goodloe, though known, was yet an uncompromising Radical; he was, however, strong in Fayette County.

Unlike the Democratic platform, that of the Republicans was unduly long and covered a variety of topics. The Republicans, greatly in the minority and out of office, could afford to promise a progressive program. The dilemma of whether to endorse the Grant administration faced them, and they decided in the affirmative. They found kind words for the Negroes and spoke of "equal and exact justice to all, of whatever nativity, race, color, or persuasion, religious or political." Nor did they flinch from standing in favor of the unpopular Resumption of Specie Payment Act, passed that year by a Republican Congress, declaring for resumption "at the earliest date consistent with the business interests of the country."[23] Quite clearly the Republican party in Kentucky was not controlled by debtor farmers.

The convention went out of its way to praise the fine work of Benjamin Helm Bristow of Elkton and Louisville, as secretary of the treasury in the Grant administration.[24] The platform also made a strong statement favoring extension of the public school system and increased opportunities for Negroes "in their separate schools until those opportunities are equal to those of white children." Again, it declared not only for a constitutional convention to revise the state's instrument of government but also for legislative action to set up agencies to attract immigrants to the state.

The platform-makers, like their rivals, intended the arraignment of the opposition party to be their strongest plank. "We arraign the Democratic Party of Kentucky," the platform declared, "for failure to pass laws for the encouragement of immigration, by failure of which we see immigrants passing our State into other States having fewer natural advantages than ours; for their dilitoriness in suppressing Ku Kluxism by which our State acquired a reputation which deters immigrants; for a long course of special legislation, creating monopolies and conferring valued privileges on favored individuals at the expense of the public; for its multiplication of offices and its disregard of constitutional restrictions; for failing to make sufficient provision for the prompt payment of

Republican leader and Secretary of the
Treasury Benjamin H. Bristow
Reprinted by permission from Ross A. Webb,
Benjamin Helm Bristow @ 1969 by the
University Press of Kentucky

teachers of the common schools; . . .for an extravagance of administration which has increased the annual expenditures of our State government to nearly three times what they were before the war."[25]

The campaign, in spite of General Harlan's wishes, was strenuous in the extreme. Both Harlan and McCreary, who had been officers on opposite sides in the Civil War, were inured to the rigors of the road, and McCreary did not shrink from joint debates, which were conducted throughout the canvass; McCreary, the younger man, was painstakingly careful. "What he lacks in brilliancy," stated the *Paducah News*, "he will make up in force of character."[26] Harlan was a finished orator. The Republican candidate centered his attack on the extravagance, the corruption, and the reaction of the Democratic state administrations since the Civil War, while McCreary leveled his guns against the Grant administrations, particularly indicting Republicans for the abuses of Carpet-bag-Scalawag administrations in the states of the South. This propaganda was still effective; some of it was doubtless true.

Practically all of the state's press was Democratic, and it supported McCreary. Harlan's principal newspaper support came from the *Louisville Commercial*. This thriving metropolitan paper attacked Leslie's pardon record and Democratic extravagance. The editor of the *Commercial* was Colonel Robert M. Kelly. He took to task the Democratic party in the state for reckless fiscal policies and overspending; he quoted the state auditor as saying that "taxes must be increased, or the State go in debt at the rate of $150,000 a year."

On the pardon question, the same editor wrote:

One who has examined the prison records states that 527 convicts have received pardon during Leslie's term of office, or 159 the first year, 121 the second year, 122 the third year, 125 the last eight months. . . .Startling, indeed, is this exposure of official clemency. That a governor with the reputed courage, nerve, and love of justice of Leslie . . . and whose administration plumed itself on its rigid adherence to the demands of law—should thus deal out pardons by wholesale, is astonishing beyond belief. If Leslie thus scattered the benefits of pardon so freely among the inmates of the penitentiary, who knows the length and breadth and height and depth of clemency he exercised toward accused and condemned criminals before they reached the limits of actual prison confinement? Five hundred convicts in four years! Is there no earthly way of stopping this terrible abuse of constitutional powers?[27]

Try as strenuously as they might, however, the Republicans were unable to convince the voters that the Democrats should be driven from power. The results of the August 2 election were a foregone conclusion. The entire Democratic ticket was elected. McCreary's vote was 126,976; Harlan's 90,795—a majority of 36,181 for the young Democratic standard-bearer. Henderson again received the largest majority of the Democratic candidates. Harlan, had he chosen, could have boasted of one distinction. He received more votes by 5,000 than any other candidate on the Republican ticket, while McCreary received the smallest Democratic majority. But Harlan was now weary and discouraged. He seemed to realize the "immensity of the social forces working against Republican success in post-war Kentucky." Harlan had gained 1,712 more votes than in 1871, while McCreary received only 521 more votes than had Leslie in 1871. The Republican standard-bearer carried Fayette County by a sizable margin and, in many of the Bluegrass counties McCreary won out by only narrow margins, which may be attributed to the Negro vote. Strangely enough, Harlan's vote in the mountain counties, which were sparsely inhabited, was not as impressive as in 1871. Again he carried populous Christian County in western Kentucky. For the General Assembly the Democrats were again remarkably successful: 32 to 6 Republicans in the Senate; 89 to 11 Republicans in the House.[28]

The call for a constitutional convention was voted down overwhelmingly. Of the 286,316 votes cast in the general election, the convention call received only 85,466. Under the constitution every vote not cast in favor of was in effect a vote against—that is, 202,850 against. Watterson, both discouraged and disgusted, declared: "The indifference of our people, as manifested in their indisposition to vote on the question of the call, has ever given color to the presumption that they are not averse to the creation of monopolies, the granting of unequal privileges, and all the special legislation that our new lawmakers, following in the footsteps of their predecessors, may choose to indulge in."[29] "Marse Henry" was perhaps crediting the voters with more civic righteousness than they possessed. With nearly one-third of the enfranchised totally illiterate and the large land owners suspicious, conservative, and reluctant to change, it was not surprising that reform measures were steadily voted down—or failed to be voted upon at all.

The weary Leslie left office on August 31, 1875.[30] That day McCreary was inaugurated governor amid a colorful military and civil display. He delivered a pleasing address, taking meticulous care, as was his custom, to say nothing that might offend.[31] However, he did hold out promise in declaring:

> My earnest effort shall be to adopt a policy that will promote alike the interest of all citizens, and add to the greatness both of the State and the Union. I desire especially to see popular thought and energy directed into channels of usefulness: To the establishment of manufactures in our midst; the improvement of our labor system; to the opening of mines; to the encouragement of immigration, whereby farmers, mechanics, artisans, and miners will come here, level our forests, develop our mineral regions, build railroads and cities, turn our vacant lands into fertile farms, and our hillsides into smiling vineyards, and thus benefit and beautify our State and augment our revenue.

"McCreary wishes to advance agriculture," ran a *Courier-*

Journal article, "relieve the individual of some of his tax burden, erect schoolhouses and churches, so that instruction will be as free as the air we breathe and thousands of children throughout the length and breadth of our State will annually give thanks to the great Rule of the Universe for that education. . . ." Waxing warmer upon the beauties and efficacies of education, McCreary invoked the poetic muse, as well as the Holy Scriptures, to express his hopes and expectation for Kentucky's advancement through public enlightenment. Then, too, the governor wished to see "the records of secession, coersion, and reconstruction filed away forever" and asked for "peace and reconciliation." Moreover, he promised really "to be governor."

The occasion was one of felicity and good feeling. Most every one could find something pleasing in the address, which really referred to good things rather than promised them. Even the Republican *Commercial* was, on the whole, inclined to praise the speech and to wish the governor well.[32] The dark night of strife, conflict, partisanism, and hatred seemed to be closing. The dawn of a new day of unity, amity, harmony, and reform appeared to be breaking. Whether it was merely illusion and mirage only time would tell.

VII
EX-CONFEDERATE
RULE AND PANIC
POLITICS

Under the disheartening circumstances of the Panic of 1873 and its aftermath farmers quite naturally sought not only persons and organizations as scapegoats, but also expendients—movements, laws, parties—which promised improvement of economic conditions. Capitalists and big business, particularly the railroads, came in for a large share of blame, as did the Republican party, known as the "sound money" party and understood to be the author of the "crime of 73" (an act discontinuing the coining of silver) and of the Resumption Act, 1875, which seemed to strike the death knell of cheap money by putting greenbacks on a par with specie. Debtor farmers desired inflated money, because they believed it would be easier to obtain. They wished to use it in discharging their debts and, desiring higher prices for their products, they knew that cheap money would cause a rise in prices. Furthermore, they wanted more money to be put in circulation. However, the acts of 1873 and 1875 tended in the opposite direction.

Economic stress usually causes criticism and a certain degree of boycotting of major political parties, especially the party in power. It also encourages growth of third parties promising relief. During the hard times which began in 1873 Kentucky was no exception to this rule. The Democratic party in the state was pressed to adopt resolutions favoring relief for the farmers. The Granger Movement, begun as an agrarian social organization, was encouraged to stand for economic and political reforms and to become a political party. Although the Grange did not become a

Kentucky political organization, its members did exert a strong influence upon the dominant Democratic party, causing the adoption of a few farm relief planks and the election of many Grange-minded men to office.

Farmers of the "black tobacco" belt in western Kentucky, suffering more severely from the Panic than any others, accused Democratic leaders of betraying the economic interests of the poor farmers and of "selling-out" to the "interests," particularly the railroads. Governor Leslie was charged with being a "special interest" man, particularly after his term as governor, when he was dubbed a railroad lobbyist.[1]

Rural newspapers over the state took up the cause of the farmers, blasted the "special interests," and demanded relief and reform. Even the *Yeoman*, somewhat of an administration organ, sympathized with the hard-pressed agrarians. It carried excerpts from the *Southern Agriculturalist*, a Grange partisan, and was particularly zealous in citing and quoting articles critical of the banks. The charge was that the "rich banks" were practically exempt from taxation, while the poor farmers paid "from 60 to 80 cents on every $100 worth of property." Poor men were being robbed while millionaires of Kentucky and the nation went virtually untaxed, according to critics.

As a result of Grange activities, the Democratic party in the state had taken increased interest in the agricultural problems. In 1873, a farm-relief man, Willis B. Machen of Lyon County, was appointed by the governor to the United States Senate to fill out the unexpired term of Garrett Davis.[2] The farmers' plight brought such vehement agitation from hard-hit western Kentucky that for the time being the Bluegrass Bourbons seemed on the verge of being driven from control of the Democratic party.

Agrarian interests mustered impressive strength in the General Assembly of 1876. The legislature was made up almost completely of new members, most of whom knew next to nothing about legislative procedure. The session got off to a bad start because of an impasse occasioned by a stubborn contest in the election of the speaker of the house. Nine candidates were nominated. On the twenty-second ballot, William J. Stone, like Machen from Lyon County, was elected 89-11 over the one remaining candidate, Republican John Feland, of Christian County. Whether or not Stone's victory was one for the hard-pressed and Granger-minded agrarians of western Kentucky, as suggested by some state historians, does not seem readily clear. It is true, however, that more farmers were members of the 1876 Assembly than in past years. In fact, Henry Watterson reported that 64 members of the lower house were affiliated with the Grange.[3]

Grange-tinged publications had brought about the expectation of relief through legislation. Numerous chapters of the Grange throughout the state had worked upon representatives in advance for favorable laws to alleviate the plight of the distressed farmers. However, the parsimonious Governor McCreary in his message to the legislature on January 3, 1876 not only did not mention relief for farmers, but failed to note agrarian depression. Contrariwise, he spoke of the bountiful harvest and the prosperous condition of the state, thanking the Deity for His manifold blessings.

The governor's message did not give promise of great reform. Delighted that a surplus of over $361,000 existed in the state treasury as of October 10, 1875, McCreary hoped that further reforms would be made toward equalizing assessments.[4] Among his recommendations were these: That the law be amended so that a board of examiners might be set up for the insane asylum with power to examine and send back to their families "harmless imbeciles," thereby making possible the relief of overcrowded conditions and causing a saving of money to the state; that a system be devised to propagate and protect fish; that the state's Agricultural and Mechanical College, which had declined in attendance from 300 students in 1870 to 80 in 1876, be removed from Kentucky University and made an independent institution; that, to relieve overcrowded conditions at the penitentiary, convicts be sent outside the enclosure to work; that the amount constituting grand larceny be raised, so that fewer persons be sent to the penitentiary, and that young first offenders not be put with hardened criminals;[5] that an appropriation be made for a monument to the memory of General John C. Breckinridge; that the report of the commissioners settling the boundary line (near Henderson) between Indiana and Kentucky be accepted; that the report of the commission which had revised the "Code of Practice" be accepted; that legislation be passed looking to the establishment of a bureau of agriculture and statistics; that the General Assembly finish its business within the 60 days allotted by the constitution, so that the rule of biennial session might be followed—a means of saving the state perhaps $100,000 each year; and that less legislation of a special, private nature be passed. He thought, furthermore, that the General Assembly should provide for the selection of "accomplished and eminent citizens as agents for the commonwealth in trying to attract immigrants to the state," and praised the work of Professor N. S. Shaler and the Geological Survey, recommending that it be continued.[6]

Governor McCreary expatiated on public education, making use of Washington's prophetic words in its behalf. He called attention to the fact that, during Z. F. Smith's incumbency as state superintendent of public instruction, the people had voted to impose a tax upon themselves for school purposes, "which with the then existing tax, and with other resources, yields nearly a million dollars annually," and he thought the time had come to correct defects in school legislation. He was delighted with the recent report of the popular Superintendent Henderson on public education and quoted freely from it. Following Henderson's argument, the chief executive advocated the establishment of normal schools by the state.

On the subject of Negro education, McCreary revealed a tinge of Bourbonism. He thought that Negroes had got off to a good start with their public school system. "It is hoped," he stated, "that the colored people will take hold of the system presented to them, and show that they appreciate it by earnest efforts to have their children attend school. . . .Persons who seek to make the colored people dissatisfied with the system that has been provided are doing them a great injury." He pointed with pride to the Negro education law passed by the last General Assembly, declaring that it had brought in during the past year $21,660.68! He pointed apparently also with pride, to other sources amounting to $12,996.60, making a total of $34,657.28![7]

Generally speaking, McCreary's message indicated an intention to let the legislature act as it saw fit. He neither strongly championed nor insisted upon anything, unless it was economy. On the other hand, if ever a General Assembly needed guidance and leadership, it was that of 1875-1876. Many of the members were easy target for demagogues and lobbyists. From the beginning substantive reform had little chance of passage, because of the general economy-mindedness and lack of leadership to frame and maneuver through a genuine reform program. Watterson, sensing the situation, warned that economy at the expense of needed reform was no economy at all.[8]

During the canvasses for election to that General Assembly candidates had castigated former lawmakers for extravagance, and they had succeeded in convincing numerous farmers that government spending had a good deal to do with the general scarcity of money, as well as with high taxes. Many of the newly elected representatives, feeling therefore that their mission was to save money, centered attention upon cutting the salaries of chaplains, clerks and small office-holders at the capital. As a result of the economy program much time was frittered away, only a few thousand dollars were saved, and incalculable damage was done the public service. McCreary, in spite of an ever-present cautiousness and conservatism, as well as a perennial penchant for economy, was not satisfied with a little patching here and there. However, this policy doubtless satisfied the Bourbons, who opposed most reform and abhorred and shuddered at the thought of higher taxing of their fertile lands. A small segment of the population, perhaps the extra 5,000 who had voted for Harlan and for Henderson, was possibly concerned. The rank and file made no outcry at the legislature's failure to pass needed reform measures.

During the legislative session, Democratic representative James B. Blue, of Union County, introduced a bill appropriating funds for locks and dams along the Kentucky River. Day after day he glowingly pictured the blessings the state would derive from such a project and predicted that the investment would be enormously profitable. But the plea fell upon deaf ears. His bill was defeated. This issue inspired a certain member of the house, amused at the proceedings, to compose a lengthy poem on Blue's tenacious effort. One stanza perhaps will suffice:

> To naught his mightiest efforts fell
> Before the host of hostile foes,
> That drove his schemes to death and hell
> By shouts, not ayes but noes.[9]

The bitterest fight of the session developed over efforts of agrarian legislators to reduce the legal rate of interest from 10 to 6 percent Quite naturally banks and capitalists generally were extraordinarily exercised. Much of the press, especially urban journals, under the influence of business and actuated by laissez-faire doctrines, opposed the change. Watterson, as an apostle of industrial and business development and enterprise as well as a disciple of Adam Smith and John Stuart Mill, argued heatedly that the natural workings of supply and demand should not be tampered with. He declared that the proposed usury law was the "consummation of folly, ignorance and narrow-mindedness." The *Commercial*, leaning decidedly toward business interests, also bitterly opposed the proposal. After the most strenuous effort the agrarians, goaded perhaps by their Grange constituents, rallied and passed an act reducing the interest rate from 10 to 8 percent.[10]

Far less difficulty was encountered in reducing the rate of taxation on $100 of property from 45 to 40 cents—a reduction of 12½ percent. Farm-oriented solons felt they were doing a real

146

service to the state and their constituents by enactment of this measure. Bills followed that made possible establishment of an agricultural, horticultural, and statistical bureau, again reflecting the lawmakers' Grange-mindedness. A piscatorial preservation and propagation measure, the need for which McCreary had dwelled upon eloquently and earnestly, passed without trouble.

Concerning eleemosynary institutions, the lawmakers passed acts designed to amend and reduce into one measure the several laws concerning the lunatic asylums, to appropriate $3,500 to have cells in the penitentiary better ventilated and $25,000 for construction of additional cells. After long and acrimonious debate, a measure to work convicts outside the prison walls passed the house, but failed in the senate. Saving of money being the great desideratum, however, the lawmakers, conscious of wretched, even horrible conditions in the overcrowded ancient penitentiary, enacted a law providing for time reduction of convicts' sentences for good behavior—five days on each month. They passed a measure increasing the amount of money involved in a felony—from $4 to $10—and this guaranteed sending relatively fewer persons to the penitentiary. The Geological Survey fortunately was given another two-year lease on life by the parsimonious legislators. A bill providing for registration of voters, was vetoed by the governor on the ground that it was unconstitutional. The legislature closed with some"rollicking" sessions. A reporter wrote of one that "paper wads and pamphlets flew on all sides until spectators and members felt there was little security save in flight."[11]

Although known as a "do-nothing" body, the General Assembly of 1875-1876 passed 1,037 acts and 54 joint resolutions. The great mass of the legislation, as usual, was of a special, or private, nature. The body received a full measure of criticism from the press. Even its apologist, the *Yeoman*, admitted "some first class demagogues" in the session and declared that it had never said "they were a body of Solomons." Henry Watterson thought this assembly a "less enlightened body than its predecessors."[12] The most outspoken critic, however, was the *Commercial*. Editor Kelly wrote of the legislative meeting as "a very unprofitable session"—one which passed lots of private bills that never should have been passed. The session "will serve to illustrate so plainly to the people," he declared, "that the dullest may understand the folly of believing that good intentions will answer as a full substitute for knowledge and experience." Kelly contended that the Democratic party was to blame, "and cannot put its shortcomings and misdeeds off on the Grangers." He wrote that very few Grangers were elected over Democrats, and "such as were belonged to the Democratic party, with few exceptions." The Louisville Republican editor asserted that there was little leadership in either house and declared that, had there been, something might have been accomplished. The "green" members would have been glad to follow a good leader, he thought. "Those few who knew any parliamentary laws," he wrote, "used it oftener in senseless filibustering to the destruction of their influence than in any other way." Kelly concluded by asserting that "the general sentiment of the State will be one of relief, that the session is over."[13]

So disappointing were the agrarian lawmakers that agriculturalism in Kentucky politics gradually subsided. This was certainly to the liking of Henry Watterson, who once more was skillful enough to play a major role in diverting public attention to the national scene. He was able temporarily to focus the wrath of local agrarians upon the "high" Republican tariff and national Republican "misrule" and to convince farmers that their economic ills would not be ameliorated until the Democrats were in power in Washington and a tariff for revenue only was adopted. Thus further schism in the Democracy was prevented.

Agitation reconcentrated against the Republican party in the nation. Watterson's statements pleased the farmers, who were ready enough to be convinced that the Republican tariff contributed greatly to their economic ills: "This is the monster that affrights the hardened soul of bounty-fed avarice," Watterson had written. "It is the dread specter that stands at the door of as wicked and as heartless a monopoly as ever wrung blood and tears from the needy and the weak, the widow and orphan."[14]

The Hayes-Tilden Election, 1876

The failures of the 1875-1876 General Assembly were not long remembered, even by editors. The all-important presidential election of 1876 was approaching, and Kentucky would play a prominent part.

The Republican state convention, meeting at Louisville in famed Liederkranz Hall on May 10, 1876 to choose delegates to the national convention in Cincinnati, drew up a platform calling for civil service reform, resumption of specie payment, adequate support of public education, and equal justice before the law regardless of color. The Republicans again highly praised the honest and efficient Benjamin H. Bristow for his distinguished service to the nation as secretary of the treasury and recommended him to the national convention as presidential timber. Some delegates wished the convention to declare for Oliver P. Morton of Indiana, whose representatives had done some preconvention work; however, most delegates enthusiastically supported and endorsed Bristow.[15]

The Democratic state convention met in Louisville on May 25 to select delegates to the national convention and to appoint candidates for electors. With General Lucius Desha again as permanent chairman, it adopted a platform calling for limitation of the growing powers of the federal government and the restoration of equal powers among the states. It charged that "corruption and partisanism" in the Grant administration were responsible for the "deplorable moral and business conditions." The platform stood for repeal of the Resumption Act of 1875, though declaring "for gold and silver as the true basis for a currency and for resumption of specie payments as soon as economically wise." This stand, somewhat ambiguous and misleading, was obviously taken to please both cheap and sound money men. On the tariff, the platform made a "revenue only" declaration. It also adopted the unit rule.[16]

Democrats waged a vigorous canvass in Kentucky because they believed that a national victory was in sight. They were well justified in this assumption, because the nation seemed enthusiastic for the highly respected, reform-minded Governor Samuel J. Tilden, a reformer who gained a national reputation for driving the notorious Tweed gang out of power in New York City. In all the country, perhaps the most zealous and fervid supporter of the "Sage of Gramercy Park" was Henry Watterson, who was regarded as Tilden's spokesman. Even prior to the St. Louis convention the Louisville editor had written, "We do not say that Governor Tilden is the only Democrat who can be elected; but we do say that he can best gather together the elements of success. . . . He is still governor of New York, still the favorite of the states upon which we must rely for success. . . ." At the convention Watterson was elected temporary chairman and with the help of J. Stoddard Johnston he read and declaimed a resounding keynote speech. During the campaign, Watterson penned some of the strongest editorials of his great newspaper career. People throughout the nation read them. The editorials carried a pungent, truculent, and a plausible reasoning that apparently appealed to millions.[17]

During the campaign in the state the Democrats centered their attack, as usual, upon the shortcomings of the Republican administration in the nation and they waved the "bloody shirt" profusely. On the other hand, the Republican speakers struck out at conditions in the South, particularly in Kentucky, and once more sounded the note of reform. One of their principal speakers was the reformist Bristow. At Hopkinsville, on October 28, he declared:

> *You know full well how the Southern politician has attempted to harrow the feelings and excite the prejudices and hates of the people of the South on this subject—Negro suffrage. Instead of accepting the necessary and inevitable*

*results of their own acts of 'madness, folly, and wickedness';
instead of taking the Negro by the hand and leading him in a
friendly way into the paths of virtue, intelligence, and material prosperity, they have appealed to the passions and pre-
judices of race against race, until they have excited the
ignorant and vicous deeds of violence and outrages which I
do not care to recount, and which cast a dark shadow over
the entire South.*

Bristow stated that Southern politicians were elected to office
by raising Civil War issues and by "croaking" over the "unhappy
condition" of the South "caused by Republicans." He averred that
southerners lived in the dead past. "Meanwhile," he declared, "the
world moves on. North, east and west of us thrift and prosperity
are seen on every hand, but the South 'drags its slow length along,'
neither prospers as its should, nor advances in civilization, as it
must." Touching upon the South's rich natural resources, Bristow
declared that "capital will not flow in rapidly until the South
accepts the new order and respects the rights of all." He made a
plea to southerners to throw off the "yoke" of present leadership
and educate the people generally, Negroes as well as whites.[18]

Early returns indicated that the nation had gone for Tilden. The
morning after the election, November 8, announcements indicated
that Tilden had 196 electoral votes, 11 more than a majority, and
that his popular vote was 4,300,316—a majority of 264,300.
Apparently all of the nationally important newspapers, except the
New York Times, conceded a Democratic victory. The *Times'*
hesitancy gave certain astute and seasoned Republican managers
an idea. They got busy. As is well known, an electoral commission
declared Hayes elected, but not until the question had been aired
in the halls of Congress and throughout the nation. It seemed for a
time that another civil war might occur.

During the critical time of the disputed election, Watterson, at
Tilden's request, consented to serve out an unexpired term in the
lower house of Congress "for the purpose of acting as the Demo-

cratic candidate's personal representative." From Washington, as Arthur Krock pointed out, the embattled Louisville editor sent "flaming editorial dispatches" to his newspaper.[19] "Marse Henry," convinced that Tilden had been honestly elected, felt certain that a determined "conspiracy" of "sinister, though prominent Republican leaders," backed by President Grant, "who controlled the army," was on foot to seat Hayes, even at the cost of bloodshed. He was disgusted with the Democratic leaders for hesitating day after day, week after week, to take positive action—hesitancy even in the face of incipient "conspiracy" to "count out" Tilden, the rightfully elected President as he believed, and to defraud the people. Moreover, the Louisville editor was infuriated at the complacency and apparent impotency of Democrats in Congress. Reaching the conclusion that only the insistency of the people under the right of petition could stir Congress to action, the indignant Watterson sent out a call for the people to swing into action. He proposed that a "peaceful army of 100,000 men" converge on Washington. The proposal, carried in a *Courier-Journal* editorial on January 8, 1877, further enjoined the Democrats of the state to "provide for the presence of at least ten thousand unarmed Kentuckians" in Washington. Though the editorial counseled peace, it was nevertheless bellicose, and, not only northern editors, but officials of the federal government itself were somewhat alarmed. Watterson's editorial was timed apparently to affect the Democratic convention scheduled to meet in Louisville on January 18th. "Marse Henry," in part, wrote:

> *If the convention wishes to do something, let it take ground firmly, not noisily, for the joint right of the two houses, fortified as it is by all precedent; and, having thus memorialized the Senate, let it provide for the presence of at least ten thousand unarmed Kentuckians in this city on the coming 14th of February.*[20]

As might well be surmised, Kentucky was thrown into such tremendous excitement that passions exceeded reason. On the eve of the convention all the Louisville hotels were overcrowded. Chief among the strategists were Governors Beriah Magoffin, Richard Hawes and James B. McCreary, and ex-Confederate generals William Preston and Lucius Desha, aided and abetted by the fire-eating Cassius M. Clay, who had broken with the Republicans.

One reporter wrote that "the spirit everywhere manifested is unmistakably belligerent. It may be fairly inferred from the general expression about the hotels tonight that the voice of the Kentucky Democracy is for war." The reporter, however, threw different light upon the subject when he observed that "these utterances mainly come from men whose span of life reaches beyond the limit of military service. Nevertheless," he concluded, "they undoubtedly represent a younger generation whose warlike disposition cannot be questioned."

The same correspondent thought the feeling at the Liederkranz Hall the next day—a meeting of 2,500 with only 2,000 seats—was an "unmistakably war feeling," though the gathering was characterized by unusual decorum, gravity, and thoughtfulness. Edward C. Marshall, a popular Versailles speaker, known far and wide for ready wit, regaled the concourse at some length with pleasing oratory. His position upon the serious question of the hour was that, while not liking war, he knew of "no other honorably way out." "Cash" Clay, "the Lion of Whitehall," denounced as "traitors, and deserving the death of traitors, all who factiously and unconstitutionally resisted the inauguration of Tilden and [Thomas A.] Hendricks. . . ." General Preston was vehement and Governor McCreary was, as usual, mild. General Basil Duke believed that Kentucky should be put "on a war footing at once."[21]

The convention adopted resolutions declaring that Tilden had won both the popular and electoral majority; asserted that an appeal to arms, "a last desperate remedy of a free people in danger of being enslaved," might be necessary, and called upon the National Committee to convoke a national convention, so that a few party leaders might be appointed on a commission with power to act at Washington, as action became necessary.

Though quite clear that Kentucky stood ready to back Watterson, Tilden and the Democratic congressional leaders seemed to shrink from decisive action. They simply were not prepared to go the limit. Apparently the Republican managers knew this. The best possible bargain therefore, Watterson thought, should be driven. A compromise was reached: Hayes was to be confirmed, all federal troops withdrawn from the South, and the South returned to southern leaders.[22]

Though he had played a prominent part and admirably served his idol, the "Sage of Gramercy Park," Watterson never quite forgot the Hayes-Tilden episode. As Krock remarked, "the controversy rested bitterly upon the soul of Mr. Tilden's chief apostle." Nor did the bitterness in Kentucky readily pass. "Never, except in 1861," wrote Krock, "was there so much likelihood as then that Americans would take up arms against one another."[23]

Kentucky River Navigation

The high pitch of passion, though leaving a decided feeling of bitterness on the part of numerous Kentuckians, did not long absorb the attention of the state's citizenry. Other developments soon gained their attention.

In February 1877 friends of internal improvement called a convention in Frankfort to discuss ways and means of enhancing Kentucky River navigation. The yeoman service of Representative Blue of Union County seems at long last to have borne fruit. Interest had developed to such an extent that the question of improving Kentucky River navigation had figured in the legislative canvasses in the summer of 1877. During that time the history of the river's navigation had been extensively explored. Kentuckians learned that from 1836 to 1871 the state had spent almost a million dollars in building five locks and dams on the Kentucky River. This expenditure, declared Governor McCreary, had brought manifold blessings. In his words:

*giving 95 miles of slack-water navigation, . . . not only greatly
benefited the counties of Carroll, Henry, Owen, Franklin,
Anderson and Woodford, by furnishing easy and convenient
transportation, and materially aiding the people of other
counties to get their products and minerals to market, but
increased the State revenue, and poured into the Treasury in
toll receipts as high as $49,638.77 in the year 1847.*[24]

The General Assembly, on February 24, 1869, however, had
leased these improvements to the Kentucky River Navigation
Company for fifty years, and had given the privilege to that
company of navigating the Kentucky River for that term, in
consideration of the sum of $1,500 per year for fifty years (to be
paid into the Sinking Fund), and of constructing nine new locks
and dams. Since the Kentucky River company failed to live up to
its obligations, the legislature of 1875-1876, by resolution, directed the attorney general to "proceed to repossess the locks and
dams and improvements, and to annul the contract and lease."
Suit was instituted and judgment rendered in favor of the state by
the Franklin Circuit Court, whose decision was later upheld by the
Appellate Court.

The Kentucky River Navigation Convention of 1877 adopted
resolutions calling upon the state to make improvements to the
extent that the river be utilized for satisfactory commercial transportation purposes. So popular was the cause that the governor,
becoming more animated in favoring, laid the entire matter before
the General Assembly of 1877-1878. He asked for an immediate
appropriation over $71,000 and submitted an estimate in amount
of a half million dollars for its consideration. This sum was to be
used in rebuilding numerous crib dams and foundations, as well as
in repairing locks and pier-heads. Temporarily abandoning his
financial conservatism, McCreary called for general improvement
of the navigation system of the entire state, naming numerous
counties that would be materially advanced and citing the fact
that "Kentucky has a greater water frontage than any other inland
state of the union."[25]

The time appeared propitious for real achievement in development of the state's inland waterways. Upon the subject Henry Watterson wrote:

If, with all the information and advice thus placed before it, the legislature cannot do something in the way of river and prison improvement the case is hopeless, or the present legislature is determined to aspire to a no more exalted destiny than the ignoble fate that has swallowed up several of its predecessors in the realm of nothingness.

The high hopes came to naught, however, when, as was charged, a fatuous and small-minded General Assembly, after wrangling throughout an entire session, passed (in the early hours of the morning of the last hectic day of the session) a weak bill nullifying and emasculating all the constructive suggestions of all the authorities upon the subject. The measure that finally got through provided that financial support for whatever improvement might be made on the Kentucky River, or any other state river, must come through special taxes voted by people in the magisterial districts along the rivers and by people in the towns and cities supposed to be most interested.[26] Preventing additional taxes was a magic phrase in Kentucky politics.

Legislative Bickering

The state election of August 6, 1877, failed to stimulate emotions. Only one state office, the treasury, was involved, and the races for the General Assembly attracted no unusual interest. As was expected, the Democratic incumbent, James W. ("Honest Dick") Tate rewon the finance post by a vote of 96,557 to 20,451 against his Republican opponent, Isaac H. Trabue.

The top-heavy Democratic legislature, convening December 31, jockeyed briefly to determine whether western or central and eastern Kentucky would be dominant. A United States senatorship was at stake,[27] and the vote on the speakership of the state house of representatives would reveal the comparative strength. On the tenth ballot Edward W. Turner of Madison County won out over John M. Bigger of McCracken County. The contest disclosed not only a preponderance of strength for eastern and central Kentucky, but also the probability that McCreary, should he desire, might be elected to the United States Senate. On January 8, 1878, four men were nominated for the coveted office, namely, John S. Williams, James B. McCreary, William Lindsay (Clinton) and Republican Robert Boyd of Laurel County; J. Proctor Knott was later presented. After much caucusing, the names of Knott, Lindsay and McCreary were withdrawn, and on January 17, Williams was elected.[28] In light of later developments suspicion of a "deal" seems reasonable.

On January 1, Governor McCreary had delivered his state of the commonwealth message to the joint houses. The tone of the report was optimistic, with the chief executive claiming that the state was prosperous. He stated that the treasury, on October 10, 1877, held a balance of $583,394.87, an indebtedness of only $183,394.00 and $1,368,142.20 in the Sinking Fund with which to liquidate the incumbrance. Only $9,394 of the debt was due prior to 1894. He reported receipts, from October 11, 1876 to October 10, 1877, of $1,484,000 and a balance outstanding from the federal government on the "Kentucky War Claim" of over $397,000. The governor expressed pride in the record of advancement in public education (both white and black) achieved under the leadership of H. A. M. Henderson. McCreary reported that money annually collected by state taxation for common schools amounted to nearly a million dollars, or approximately one-half of state funds, that a local tax had been voted in 873 districts, and that 700 independent schools, in addition to the 1,353 public schools were in session. The economy-minded McCreary declared that the promotion of education was simply prudent business because it was, "cheaper to build school houses and maintain schools, and thus reduce crime that always attends indolence and ignorance, than it was to build poorhouses and prisons and support paupers and criminals." He recommended that ample provision, in keeping with the actions in other states, be made for "the establishment of a Normal School."[29]

The governor strongly stressed adequate appropriation for the promotion of Kentucky River navigation. He also urged passage of legislation leading to a comprehensive program of prison reform, stating that even with the addition of 204 cells, the penitentiary, containing 744 cells, had 986 convicts crowded into it. Expressing alarm over an increase in crime, McCreary presented figures indicating that only 181 whites and 20 blacks were inmates in 1865, as compared with 453 whites and 533 blacks in 1878. The governor made three suggestions for alleviating conditions—namely, enlarging the penitentiary, building a branch prison, or "working the convicts, under State control, in coal mines and on railroads." He did not commit himself definitely in regard to the use of convicts in navigation improvement projects. He thought, however, that the lawmakers should explore the idea, but was careful to state that prisoners should not be permitted to come into competition with free labor.

McCreary was thoroughly committed to the idea of separating first offenders from habitual, hardened criminals, and pointed out the fact that many states had in operation houses of reform for juvenile delinquents, as well as separate prisons for criminals of different classifications. He thought, too, that the convict, his daily task completed, should be allowed by additional labor to earn money for "the benefit of his penniless, friendless, suffering wife and children at home." He referred to the forthcoming International Prison Congress at Stockholm and expressed the hope that delegates would be appointed to attend that conference.[30]

Unfortunately, the General Assembly, as usual, frittered away most of its time in passage of private bills and in petty wrangling about important ones, so that few measures of great import to the state were resolved into law. Early in the session the question of resubmitting for vote of the people the calling of a constitutional convention was introduced and passed in the affirmative. This time a new method of voting was adopted—namely, that

> it shall be the duty of the clerks or judges conducting the said election to propound distinctly to each voter the following interogatory: Do you vote for calling a convention or not? And if he answers in the affirmative, his name shall be recorded as having voted for calling a convention.

Nothing, however, was done to circumvent the mandate concerning percentage of the total number required for the call.

One act of considerable importance successfully passed was that provided for a state board of health, consisting of six members and a secretary appointed by the governor. The jurisdiction of the new commission was listed as public health, vital statistics and sanitary inspection, inquiries respecting the causes of diseases, death, epidemics, conditions, food, water, habits of people, health books for schools, and associated matters.

The legislature did pass three additional important bills, all meeting earlier Grange demands: (1) the legal interest rate was lowered from eight to six percent; (2) the Agricultural and Mechanical College was disassociated from Kentucky University and granted power to become an independent college, (3) property of railroad companies was to be assessed at the same rate, for taxation purposes, as other real estate, and power to appoint a board of equalization was conferred upon the governor.[31] Previously the law had fixed total valuation of state property at $20,000,000, which reduced by half or more the actual value, thus depriving the state of a great amount of tax moneys.

The session squandered time in debating a bill to reestablish the "whipping post." That measure was introduced to alleviate deplorable and overcrowded conditions in the penitentiary. Actually overcrowding was so acute that many convicts had to be kept in county jails, at considerable added expense to the state. In 1877 Kentucky paid out to the counties for this service $120,000 in jailors' fees. Heated debates fully developed the question of the expense of keeping convicts in county jails. A Simpson County case was reported, involving a thief who had stolen $7, for which offense he was confined in the county jail twelve months at a cost of $900 to the state. The "whipping post" bill passed the house but was killed in the senate. An act passed provided that contractors on public works might employ at their own expense 500 convicts, whose terms would expire within five years.[32]

Of the 1096 acts and 57 resolutions passed by the 1877-1878 legislature, less than 10 percent were public bills. Most of the measures were for the benefit of private individuals. Some of the assembly's members had been elected through the influence of prominent persons wishing personal favors, particularly sheriffs who desired to avoid financial settlement with the state. Some of these sheriffs had supported those candidates for the General Assembly who were agreeable to their bidding. The matter of economy was also a prominent factor. It was perhaps uppermost in the minds of farmers whose crops were at the time falling off in prices and whose lands were decreasing in value.

It is remarkable, however, that legislators, while refusing to appropriate money for desperately needed reform, showed no qualms in plundering the state out of large sums of money in padded mileage accounts, stationery that was never purchased, increases in salaries for legislative officials, and the like. Widespread dissatisfaction with the lawmakers resulted. One correspondent declared that the "whole thing was a bald-headed fraud." He thought the session "sickening, and I would be but too glad to bury the putrid mess. . . ." The indignant Watterson wrote that "the condition in which the late legislature left penitentiary affairs is simply disgraceful." He declared that the legislators had "wrangled for months" and "done nothing" and that "the prison matter will remain a standing indictment against the folly and incompetency of the body that passed a hundred days of this year at Frankfort doing nothing that might not have been done in onetenth of that time."

Another reporter described the wild scenes on the last hectic night of the session as disgraceful beyond compare. As the time of the legal session ran out, clocks in the house and senate were set back to allow hundreds of bills to be milled through. This correspondent captioned his article, "Closing Performance of the Farce which has had One Hundred Days Run." "All over the noisy house," the reporter stated, "excited men were gesticulating wildly" and "as the apparently interminable conflict continued, the gentle flow of drinks increased, until at least one member was scuttled, and others though not overflowing were full." He ended with the phrase "ludicrously disgraceful." At the closing minute, the frock-coated "statesmen," those who were in condition, poured out the strains of "Auld Lang Syne" and adjourned *sine die*.[33] Another chapter in the state's legislative history had ended.

The Election of 1879

The Republican state convention convened in Louisville, at the Masonic Hall on April 10. Though the chances of success were not promising, the apostles of the log cabin were undaunted. "They seemed to recognize" wrote one correspondent, "the fruitlessness of their undertaking; still, like Jason in search of the Golden Fleece and Ponce de Leon trying to discover the Fountain of Youth, they persist in their blind hope of one day securing the Governorship for one of their stalwarts."

At the convention William O'Connell Bradley was chosen temporary chairman.[34] He delivered a rousing keynote speech, which brought the convention to its feet. It was a stinging indictment of Democratic rule in the state, as well as a challenge to Republicans to hold fast to the party's principles. Indeed, his speech served as a basis for the platform adopted.

Apparently, candidates had not been picked prior to the convention, because, seemingly with unconscious spontaneity, several able men, including Judge William H. Randall of London, Curtis F. Burnam of Richmond, Dr. W. Godfrey Hunter of Albany, Hugh F.

Finley of Williamsburg, Eli Huston Murry of Hardinsburg, William Henry Wadsworth of Maysville, and Walter Evans of Hopkinsville and Louisville, were nominated for governor. Though most of these men had their names withdrawn, the race between Murray and Evans was close, with the latter winning out. The other persons nominated on the ticket were O. S. Deming of Robertson County for lieutenant governor; Bradley for attorney general; John A. Williamson of Newport for auditor; Richard P. Stoll of Lexington for treasurer; Malcolm McIntyre of Ohio County for superintendent of public instruction; and Matt O. Doherty of Louisville for register of the land office. Later A. H. Clark replaced Bradley, who did not want the nomination, and John H. Wilson, not O'Doherty, became the nominee for register of the land office.

The platform lauded the "achievements of the Republican Party in the nation" and expressed a willingness to defend all of the national Republican administrations. It again favored calling a constitutional convention and urged the people to vote for it. The document charged the Democratic party with encouraging lawlessness, and stated that "by continuous appeals to the lower passions of the people, and by the constant laudation and encouragement of that spirit of contempt for constituted authority," the people of the state had been educated into a disregard of law and order until the "good name of Kentucky has been blasted in the estimation of our sister states." It stood for educational reform, pointed to Democratic extravagance, encouraged immigration, declared for internal improvements, reform, and progress. The declaration closed with a strong expression in favor of "hard" money and an indorsement of General Grant's administrations.[35]

The Democratic state convention assembled in Louisville on May 2 with former United States Senator John W. Stevenson as permanent chairman. That assemblage, with the exception of the nomination of a candidate for state superintendent of public instruction, may be said to have been used mostly for the purpose of ratifying previously arranged nominations, and therefore, aside from occasional outbursts of oratorical eloquence, the proceedings transpired as planned.

Decisions reached in previously held county conventions were followed, so that it was well-known that Dr. Luke Pryor Blackburn from Versailles, then resident of Louisville, would be nominated by a big majority for governor. James E. Cantrill of Georgetown was nominated for lieutenant governor, Parker Watkins ("Polly Wolly") Hardin of Harrodsburg, for attorney general; Fayette Hewitt, perennial office-holder of Frankfort, for auditor; "Honest Dick" Tate for treasurer, and Ralph Sheldon of Nelson County (one who escaped with John Hunt Morgan from the Ohio State Penitentiary in November 1863), for register of the land office. All of the candidates were either ex-Confederates or Confederate sympathizers.

Blackburn Gains the Nomination

The nomination of Dr. Blackburn, who had little interest in politics, resulted from popular demand. Politicians were inclined to regard him as somewhat radical and feared that he would not be amenable to their wishes. The doctor had spent a good part of his life in heroic service in the relief of stricken people, especially in fighting the dreaded yellow fever and cholera. Much of his humanitarian service had been freely given in foreign countries. The services which had especially endeared him to Kentuckians were his herculean efforts to relieve the stricken people of Memphis in the yellow fever epidemic of 1873 and of Hickman, Kentucky during the yellow fever epidemic of 1878. Apparently oblivious to personal danger, Dr. Blackburn had ministered to suffering victims as long as the least hope for life remained. The man had become famous both at home and abroad, and the people of Kentucky felt that he should be given some public honor as a reward for his noble services. It was generally known that Blackburn was interested in bringing about state reforms which in 1879 were of some popular interest. Prior to the convention, Blackburn could boast of 935 pledged delegates, while his nearest opponent, Thomas L. Jones, could muster only 22.

The only fight in the convention concerned selecting the nominee for superintendent of public instruction. I. C. H. Vance of Danville declared that 1,500 people had assembled in Louisville just to nominate a state superintendent. This office, because a million or more dollars each year cleared through it, was regarded by many at that time as the most important in the state government. Eleven avowed candidates worked eagerly for the nomination. Even H. A. M. Henderson, though already having served eight years, sought another four-year term. He used his office vigorously to secure convention votes, a circumstance which contributed to his downfall. One correspondent declared: "Henderson's manner of conducting the canvass has been so disreputable, that the Democratic Party cannot afford to burden itself with such a load as he will prove to be, and his nomination is out of the question."[36]

While Henderson could muster more votes than any other candidate, he was unable to poll a majority. "Elder" Joseph Desha Pickett, professor and former acting president of the Agricultural and Mechanical College and once the beloved chaplain of John C. Breckinrdige's celebrated 'Orphan' Brigade, also desired the post. Politically powerful individuals, including Marshalls, Deshas, and Breckinridges, began lobbying for him. Then the "silver-tongued orator," Colonel W. C. P. Breckinridge spoke. A reporter made this comment:

The most eloquent speech of the many made during the session was that of W. C. P. Breckinridge, delivered after midnight in nominating 'the old white-haired Chaplain of Breckinridge's brigade' for the office of Superintendent of Public Instruction. It was the bugle call that consolidated the opposition and broke the 'mystic tie' upon which the present incumbent relied to tide him over the rough sea of popular discontent.[37]

The power of eloquence, plus a good bit of practical "politicing," secured the nomination for the thin-whiskered, bald, emaciated, serious-minded "Elder" Pickett.

The platform adopted by the convention was partly platitudinous and partly practical. After the usual deference to the Constitution and states' rights and the usual castigation of Republican usurpations, the document announced fairly strong approval of the call for a constitutional convention and, for the first time since the Civil War, took a stand for public education. It declared for "a general and efficient system of common school education" and pledged the Democratic party to take steps as to furnish every child in the state "the means of a fair English education." Regardless of these declarations, however, delegates were conscious of the fact that the Hayes-Tilden election was the best issue to bring before the people. The Democratic leaders knew too that the Republicans in their convention had strongly endorsed their party's administrations in the nation.

Democrats generally were pleased with the work of the convention. Watterson, busy blasting the Republican high tariff, took time out to say that the ticket was "good from end to end." He declared that "the 'Old Hero of Hickman' is put into the fight with a gallant staff, and one almost regrets that we have not an enemy better worth such a licking as they are going to get." He spoke of Blackburn as a "Kentuckian of the olden time—at once a hero and a gentleman—one who joins to a spotless manhood the self-sacrificing spirit of womanhood to whom Kentucky owes such sons. We shall win laurels in the contest for humane achievement and enlightened progress." Stoddard Johnston thought the entire ticket excellent; so pleased was he with prospects that he could even be charitable to Walter Evans, whom he declared was "an able speaker, a cunning debator, and decidedly one of the strongest men in his party."[38]

The summer's canvass, lively and colorful, brought out huge crowds. Old-fashioned barbeques, with plenty of food and whiskey, were very popular during the campaign. The state abounded with eloquent orators, all seemingly determined to be heard. Though Dr. Blackburn, because of poor health, was unable to take an active part, the Democrats, with a plethora of "spellbinders," had the edge over the Republicans, whose few "warhorses" were greatly overworked.

The Democracy's orators, with Boyd Winchester, Wat Hardin and Colonel Breckinrdige in the van, talked mostly upon national issues, firing broadsides at "Grantism," eastern money-changers, Republican favoritism of the capitalists against the farmers and workingmen, and the Carpetbag-Scalawag scandals. They leveled their heaviest artillery against Hayes' "fraudulent election" and conjured up and blasted the continued use of "bayonets at the polls."[39] As far as Kentucky voters were concerned, the Democrats were on the right track. Audiences were delighted with the smooth-flowing, entertaining oratory and wit. Democratic managers were convinced, even in June, that the entire ticket would sweep the state, so that, even in debate, they were never greatly perturbed. With the few Republican speakers matters were quite different. Many of their audiences were hostile, and in some places they needed the greatest fortitude to speak at all.

William O'Connell Bradley to the Forefront

Though Walter Evans spoke vigorously throughout the state, the Republicans' most powerful campaigner was Bradley, a rugged, hard-hitting champion, whose commanding presence, keen wit, and repartee, together with his forceful eloquence, compelled people to listen. His campaign speeches markedly fixed the pattern of Republican campaign speeches and policy in the state for the next two decades.

At the outset Bradley chided the Democrats for inconsistency in continuing to talk about the abuses and rascalities committed by "Carpetbaggers," who he reminded, "had long since been driven from power," whereas Democrats did not welcome an investigation of their own rule in Kentucky. He queried, "What has South Carolina or Louisiana to do with Kentucky?" Proceeding then to review the Bourbon record from 1865, he considered their fiscal affairs. The balance, he declared, in the state treasury, at the end of "Republican rule,"[40] October 10, 1865, allowing credits in Kentucky's favor against the United States government, was $3,199,493.54, after payment of all state indebtedness (including the money and securities in the Sinking Fund). In contrast, he stated that according to the *Auditor's Report*, the state had on October 10, 1878, an indebtedness of $1,067,993.87, including indebtedness to the Sinking Fund.[41] The total state expenditures, he declared, had increased from $251,722.70 in 1865 to $702,189.83 in 1878.[42]

Bradley continued with the statement that it cost more in Kentucky to convict and place a man in the penitentiary than in any other state in the nation. Moreover, he charged that "The Black Hole" of Calcutta "is a magnificient drawing-room in comparison to this disgrace to civilization [the state penitentiary] — this loathsome putrid pen, in which the novitiate in crime is thrown to die by the side of the hardened criminal."

Bradley turned his scorn upon Democratic gerrymandering in the state. In the presidential election of 1876 the Republicans, he stated, had cast 98,000 votes; the Democrats, 160,000; yet the Republicans had not a single member in Congress. Describing the Democratic talents in political map-making, he declared:

> *Districts of all shapes, from a cut ninepence to an elephant's snout, adorn the map of our state in the studied effort of the Democracy to stifle and deny fair representation to a people whom they at the same time are taxing to death to pay large salaries, extravagant rewards and felonious gold-grabs.*

Bradley bore down heavily upon Democratic policy on public education—for failure to provide and maintain an adequate system of public education. "If we would preserve this government for posterity, if we would consecrate this land to Freedom, we must encourage a liberal system of common schools," he admonished. It should be a system that would enable the "poorest child to contend for the grandest prizes that may be won in a Republic." He charged that "the Democratic Party has forgotten the minds of our children," that "we cannot help but feel a sense of mortification and shame," when "we look around and see how far behind in education Kentucky is."

He then enquired why "hardy and peaceful" immigrants turned with absolute fright from Kentucky. His answer was (1) violence and (2) poor educational opportunity. "The state," he declared, "boasts a record written in the blood of slaughtered men" and "denies to her children the means of procuring a common school education." Observing that "newer states fill up rapidly while Kentucky remains at a standstill," he called attention to the fact that only a few days before "a gang of cowardly assassins" near Frankfort had shot down innocent Negroes and consigned their bodies to ashes with the flames of their burning cabins. "Masked men," he continued, "repeatedly in the dead of night have whipped, shot down and hung in cold blood humble and unoffending citizens, until a mantle of blood has been thrown over our people."

Thus warmed up "Billy O. B." began his most vigorous indictment of the Democratic party: "It has been," he declared, "essentially and completely the party of hate"; it had persisted in waving the "bloody shirt" from "one end of the Commonwealth to the other." The expatriation law, he stated, had been repealed by the legislature through the work of Union men. After the repeal, the Democrats, he declared, had nominated a ticket composed almost entirely of the "secession element," and rugged, kindly old Union Colonel Frank Wolford, who had led the fight to repeal the laws, had been rudely cast aside in the convention to make room for ex-Confederates. This had occurred, he averred, in spite of the fact that from 1866 to 1879 the Union Democrats constituted more than two-thirds of the Democratic party in the state. His address closed with these words:

168

In the name of seventy thousand gallant men who sprang to the protection of the Union in its hour of peril; in the name of your own brave, generous manhood; in the name of soldiers dead and living; in the name of widows and helpless orphans; in the name of union and law; and in the name of freedom, justice and humanity, break the chains which bind you to the Democracy and rescue your state from everlasting ruin and destruction.[43]

Issues and the Election

A third party, known as the National, was in the field to try for farm and labor votes. The National party was the result of the joint meeting of the Greenback and the Labor Reform parties. It ascribed all the ills of society to the Resumption Act of 1875, the national banking act, the demonetization of silver, the retirement of the greenbacks and the payment of the public debt in gold. Its platform principles were, in the main, that all debts, public and private, should be paid with paper and that this paper need not be backed by anything. It strongly advocated the free issuance of greenbacks and public works at federal government expense.

Perhaps indicative of considerable dissatisfaction in Kentucky was the fact that the National party gained some followers. Its leaders had held a convention and nominated a ticket to run for state offices. The candidates were C. W. Cook for governor; D. B. Lewis for lieutenant governor; Isaac H. Trabue for attorney general; Henry Potter for auditor; W. T. Hardin for treasurer, and K. C. McBeath for register of the land office.[44]

Sometime during the canvass a "whispering campaign" against Dr. Blackburn developed, instigated apparently by the *Cincinnati Commercial*. The gist of the smear seems to have been that, some years previously, the *Chicago Tribune* had circulated a story to the effect that Blackburn, during the Civil War, had in Bermuda purchased clothing infected with smallpox and yellow fever and, through agents, had it sold in New York, Baltimore, Philadelphia, Washington, and Norfolk; and that Blackburn had not only not fought with the Confederate army but instead had taken refuge in Canada. The *Commercial* seemed pleased to run the story, particularly in 1879. On August 9 that paper quoted the *New York Nation* as stating that the *Cincinnati Gazette* repeated the story daily. Its story that day ended with the statement that yellow fever was Blackburn's "specialty"; that it seemed to "possess attractions to him which he cannot withstand, but is forced to pass his life either in fighting his enemies with it or in rescuing his friends from it."[45] Apparently Blackburn ignored the ridiculous charge, which obviously gained little credence in Kentucky.

The election returns gave Blackburn and the entire Democratic ticket a decisive victory: Blackburn, 125,799 votes; Evans, 81,882; Cook, the National candidate for governor, received 18,954 votes. Although the National showing was significant, especially in western Kentucky, it is clear that the mass of Grangers, Greenbackers, and the debtor-farmers voted the straight Democratic ticket. Edward F. Prichard, Jr., a political analyst, suggests that the Greenback showing of 8 percent came from the Democratic side, since their vote from 1876 declined 10 percent, while that of the Republicans remained the same. The Democrats also retained a commanding majority in the General Assembly. Once more the question of calling a constitutional convention to revise the instrument of 1849 had failed to gain the required number of votes.[46]

The retiring governor, James B. McCreary, speaking at great length at Blackburn's inaugural, gave a summary of his administration's achievements. He referred to the economic depression, "paralyzing business, crushing commerce, diminishing values and wrecking many fortunes," and declared that Kentucky had returned to "prosperity and abundance" as rapidly as any state.

McCreary spoke of the reduction of the tax on real estate, prior to the depression, from 45 cents to 40 cents on the $100, reminding that 20 cents of that was applied by law to support the common schools and 5 cents of it to the Sinking Fund. He said that the tax reduction, the depression, and preparation to resume specie payment had produced a shrinkage in the value of all kinds of property and a corresponding decrease in assessments. Besides, he declared, a law was passed to assess and tax railroads the same as other property, which, unfortunately, had reduced the amount received from railroads by half. He stated further that scarcity of money had interferred with collection of taxes by sheriffs, which, in turn, had caused such a shortage of money that the auditor was forced to decline paying ordinary claims against the treasury.

The governor, averring that he had adhered to a rule of strict frugality and economy, indicated that a big saving had been affected by limiting legislative sessions to the biennial limit during his encumbency as chief magistrate. Moreover, he pointed to the fact that by better management the state had been able to realize a larger return in dividends from its turnpike stock—an increase from $24,604.52 in 1874 to $32,649 in 1877.

McCreary, in his desire to justify his administration, congratulated his "fellow citizens" on the present reign of law in Kentucky, and cited Breathitt County, where bloody rule had been the order of the day, as one of the most peaceful counties in the Commonwealth. However, he made no effort to minimize deplorable conditions at the penitentiary, but rather blamed the legislature for failure to make adequate appropriations.

Perhaps the *Louisville Commercial*'s editorial estimate of McCreary as governor was sound: McCreary had been very attentive and industrious in the discharge of official duties; had been very cautious to avoid everything that would injure his record or bring criticism; had appointed none but Democrats to positions of "profit, trust or honor." The editor declared the McCreary's care "to avoid mistakes that would affect his prospects unfavorably has hindered him from accomplishing results in the way of reforming and improving our State administration that a bolder, more enterprising and less cautious man might have reached." But thought the editor, "as Governors go, he has been a good one, and is entitled to carry with him to private life the esteem and good will of his fellow citizens."[47]

VIII
A SHORT SEASON OF PROGRESS

The sixty-year old Dr. Luke P. Blackburn, prematurely old from a life of sacrifice to mankind, distinguished with citations from many states and nations and grateful for the affections of his fellow Kentuckians, took the oath of office as governor at noon on September 3, 1879. Having announced that he would seek no further political preferment following his term, he enjoyed the good wishes of the assembled politicians and friends. His inaugural address indicated little familiarity with political affairs. A sizeable portion of it, however, was devoted to a discussion of the silver money question, on which his views were favorable to free and unlimited coinage.[1] The subject of prison reform was perhaps closest to his heart, although he did not hold out hope for immediate progress.

At least one reporter predicted that Blackburn would make a good governor. This correspondent stated that the governor knew Kentucky needed reforms and, as he was neither "overcautious nor overtimorous," and desirous of "distinguishing his public career," he should make an outstanding chief executive. Moreover, Blackburn possessed a "suggestive and original mind." On the other hand, the same correspondent admitted that many were saying that the governor, being a philanthropist and humanitarian, would "throw open the prison doors and thereby encourage crime to run riot through the land." In fact, Blackburn had spoken feelingly about the deplorable conditions in the penitentiary. He abhorred the fact that tender youths were being thrown into narrow cells with hardened criminals. Though promising not to abuse the pardoning power, the governor stated that he would act according to what he thought the best interests of the state.[2] Time alone would tell.

Blackburn's frank New Year's Day message to the General Assembly in 1880 practically insisted upon the passage of certain reform measures. Strengthening his appeal was the fact that numerous prominent people were calling for even more reform, so that the lawmakers would probably be more inclined to go along, at least part of the way. The governor's address contained some of the points advanced by New Departure Democrats and by Republicans led by Bradley, although it was quite clear that he was doing his own thinking upon reform measures. The house, presided over by J. M. Bigger, of McCracken County, proved fairly receptive to Blackburn's program.

Fiscal Reform

The first matter for attention was the state's finances. The Democrat Blackburn seemed to echo Republican Bradley's contentions regarding the condition of the commonwealth's treasury. He openly admitted that the state for years had been living in a fool's paradise financially, even though several previous governors had sugar-coated reports concerning conditions, as Bradley had charged. Actually, the state government, for many years had been spending more than it had been receiving in revenue. Since February 7, 1867, the state treasury had received, and spent, $2,265,540.92, paid by the federal government in "war claims," and moneys had been milked from the Sinking Fund and spent, $913,371, as quoted by the governor. This represented a minimum total of $3,178,915 spent over and above revenue receipts. The "golden eggs" had been practically used up. Making financial matters more difficult were the facts that taxes had been reduced, the depression had shrunk values, and property was inadequately and unequally assessed. Moreover, the governor declared that

Governor Luke P. Blackburn
Collection of the Kentucky Historical Society

Kentucky's "state taxation" was less than that of "almost any State in the Union." It was 40 cents on the $100. Of this, 20 cents went to the school fund, and 5 cents to the Sinking Fund, leaving 15 cents on the $100 of property for state expenses. Matters had come to such a state that a deficit by October 10, 1880, of $679,912.35 was estimated.

The governor forcibly stated what should be done. The state should eliminate the "great frauds." He declared that frauds under the forms of law had robbed the treasury of tens of thousands of dollars. These frauds were in such seemingly innocuous items as witness claims, conveyance of prisoners from one county to another and to the penitentiary, trials at examining courts, and the summoning of unnecessary witnesses "for purposes of pay." He cited a case to indicate "what scandalous and villainous frauds are practiced." This case in Floyd County revealed that justices and constables were in the habit of starting certain prosecutions for felony in order to "manufacture claims against the State." According to Floyd County Judge J. E. Stewart:

> An officer will get two men to engage in a friendly fight, in which a rock or some weapon will be used so as to make a scratch, causing slight blood or a wound. The party doing the injury is then hired to go out of the county, but on the way he leaves word where the officer may find him. The officer then goes with a guard or two—generally two—, makes the arrest, and gets pay for transporting the prisoner from one county to another, and generally consumes some days on the trip.[3]

Blackburn recommended that no compensation be allowed to witnesses in any felony case before an examining court, or a court for final trial, except in cases where necessary witnesses were summoned from one county to another. He asked that no examining court be allowed more than two dollars in each case for its services. The commonwealth, the governor delcared, had been plundered out of so much money for conveying prisoners from one county to another that the legislature should allow only eight cents per mile for the officer in charge and six for the guard and prisoner.

The governor asked for a reduction in the number of circuit courts and courts of common pleas, criminal and chancery, adding even that all the latter should be abolished. He did state that reduction in expenses of lunatic asylums could not be made without detriment to the service. Importantly, he thought equal and uniform valuation of taxable property virtually a *sine qua non* to fiscal success, and insisted that the five cents on each one hundred dollars of taxable property should be restored. Mindful of the deficit, in order to get funds sufficient to run the government, he asked that $500,000 in six percent bonds be floated. Be it said in its favor, the General Assembly of 1879-1880 was responsive for the most part to the requests of the governor, a most unusual circumstance. Among reformatory acts passed pertaining to fiscal matters were: (1) authorization of the auditor to appoint agents to attend to revenue matters, "who shall see that persons who have failed to return their taxable property shall be summoned into court to give in their lists"; (2) that "sheriffs and collectors who have collected delinquent taxes and not accounted for them shall be prosecuted," and (3) "accounts of officers be investigated for possible overcharges or defalcations."

No provision, however, was made for either equal assessments or for raising them. However, in 1884, upon the insistence of Governor J. Proctor Knott, the General Assembly did pass an act to equalize assessments and to establish a board of equalizers. The 1879-1880 lawmakers also authorized the commissioners of the Sinking Fund to transfer the surplus in their account, and any surplus occuring later, to "Revenue Proper," and they did authorize the temporary loan of $500,000 in 6 percent bonds.[4] Many other recommendations were enacted by a legislature equally ready to cut costs and to reform the financial system.

In the judicial system certain changes were made also. The state was divided into eighteen circuit court districts. The new statute provided that "these circuit courts are to sit two terms in each county, except certain specified counties, in which a greater number of terms are to be held." The criminal, chancery and common pleas courts were abolished, except in certain counties, notably Jefferson. Moreover, concurrent jurisdiction with circuit courts was extended to quarterly courts involving sums not exceeding $200. A penalty was prescribed for soliciting service as a juror.

The law was amended providing that appeals could be taken to the Appellate Court for amounts involving as much as $100 and upward; from a magistrate to the quarterly court for from $10 to $25; and over $25 to either the quarterly or circuit court. An act fixed jurors' pay at $1.50 for each day of petit court and $1.25 to grand jurors.

Public executions, which had become highly sensational and heavily attended spectacles, were abolished and attendance limited to fifty or fewer persons. Witness fees in felony cases were fixed at $1 per diem, with four cents mileage for witnesses from outside the county limits, and officers speculating in witness claims were made subject to fines of $50. The title *Kentucky Reports* (decisions of the Appellate Court) was also adopted. The judicial reforms were calculated not only to cause great financial saving to the state, but also to improve the administration of justice. Making for a notable financial gain was the increase of the tax on real estate from 40 cents to 45 cents on the $100 of property.[5]

Prison Reform

More lengthy than any portion of the governor's report to the General Assembly was that devoted to the subject of conditions at the penitentiary. Declaring that he felt "the blush of shame" when contemplating the "accumulated horrors" to be witnessed at the prison, Blackburn begged the lawmakers to devise ways and means of alleviating the "present wretched and degrading penal system" and of establishing something in accordance with the "growing enlightenment of the age."

The chief executive had declared that 953 convicts were crowded into 780 cells. The cells, he stated, measured three feet nine and a half inches wide, six feet three and half inches high, and six feet eight inches long. Actually one cell was not large enough for one inmate. From January 1, 1878 to January 1, 1879, a total of seventy-four prisoners had died, which was a "fearful mortality." He cited the testimony of an eminent Frankfort physician, Dr. William Rodman, who had stated that though each prisoner should have in his cell 840 feet of air, two men in a cell received only 170 feet. Almost in the words of W. O. Bradley, the governor declared that the

> *Black Hole of Calcutta, so abhorred in history, was not much worse than this. Only think of it; two human beings crammed together in these dark unwholesome little dens. To what beastliness may it not lead; yet, to what beastliness has it not already led. . . . Shuddering delicacy will turn away and avert its head at the disgusting recital. The revelations would remind you of Sodom and Gomorrah. . . . Remember, our Constitution says, cruel punishments shall not be inflicted. If this is not cruel, the English language has lost all meaning.*

Blackburn stated that the object of all punishment should be the "prevention of crime and the reformation of the offender." However, Kentucky's system, he declared, "degrades and brutalizes," and "is a nursery of crime—it is the great college and university of crime." He asked again that "our present barbarous plan" be abolished, and "every vestige of the leasing system" be eradicated. "Cast off this mighty incubus and terrible evil," he pled.

Blackburn, a thorough student of penal reform, called for the erection of another penitentiary, the adoption of the warden system, the maintenance of a full time physician within the prison walls, a greater degree of sanitation, fresh air and space, religious instruction, humane treatment.

The governor thought that the system should be graduated, so that as a prisoner proved himself reliable, industrious and humane,

Prisoners returning from worship at the
penitentiary in the 1860s
Reprinted from *The Kentucky Penitentiary* (1911)

he might be allowed more and more freedom until he should be parolled. All the while a prisoner should be taught a useful trade and be made to feel that he was worth something to society. Blackburn believed too that, in cases of theft, not less than thirty-five dollars should constitute grand larceny. He supported the policy of committing lesser offenders to county jails, county workhouses, or some reformatory institution. In closing his remarks upon the subject of prison reform, he said: "Let us, therefore, abandon a policy which is based on abasement and cruelty, and whose only marks are degradation from the moment the wretched convict dons his striped zebra suit, until he emerges from the prison with hope forever crushed."[6]

Pending penal reform action by the legislature, Blackburn began issuing pardons on a scale larger than that of previous governors, who had not been niggardly in the matter. He especially favored discharging the incurably sick, so that they might go home to die, there surrounded by members of their families. The press voiced vigorous disapproval, the people generally frowned, and the Democratic politicians remembering Republican attacks and thinking of the next election, were highly indignant—apparently they never forgave Luke Blackburn.

In due time the General Assembly passed an act providing for a warden system. Under this law the warden was to be elected by joint ballot of the legislature and to be removable by the commissioners of the Sinking Fund, who were authorized to serve as the penitentiary commissioners (the personnel being the governor, secretary of state, auditor, attorney general and treasurer).

The warden's term of office was to be four years. His duties were to direct the prison and look after the diet, health, comfort, and discipline of the convicts. He was expected to keep at labor within the prison convicts not contracted for. In addition to the warden, a deputy warden, clerk, physician, and chaplain appointed by the commissioner were authorized. As to the question of convict labor, the commissioners were to hire out on contract the labor of 600 convicts. These were to be employed within the prison walls and to be let to the "highest and best bidder," the contract to run from one to four years, and the contractors were to defray the expense of keeping the prisoners, and to furnish those discharged with clothing and passage to their home counties. All convicts in excess of the 600 were subject to hire for work outside prison on such labor as the construction of railroads, canals, waterways, and levees. The United States government might also hire them for work on various public projects, including improvement of navigation. The warden system set up was supposed to eliminate the "terrible evils of the lessee system," which had "brutally wrecked" so many lives.[7] However, convict labor and an elected warden did little to better the lot of convicts.

The penal act further provided for commissioners to select a site for a new prison, to be known as the "Branch Penitentiary." Three commissioners, appointed by the governor, were authorized to receive plans and specifications for the proposed building, as well as to examine other prisons, to make a report, and to recommend a system of government for the proposed institution.[8] Unfortunately no provision was made for speedy action. Meanwhile, convicts died almost in droves in the foul pesthole at Frankfort. However, the governor, in spite of irritated politicians and editors, continued to build up an unprecedented pardoning record.

Blackburn appointed able men as commissioners of the proposed penitentiary: Circuit Judge Richard H. Stanton, Maysville, editor of the *Monitor*, Judge William M. Beckner, lawyer and editor of Winchester, and General Hylan B. Lyon, Eddyville. And he was as enthusiastic in regard to prison reform in 1882 as he had been in 1880. To the General Assembly of 1882 he made another stirring appeal and expressed the hope that the lawmakers would give "earnest attention" to the report of the commission on the Branch Penitentiary.[9]

Unfortunately the "solons" failed to give "earnest attention." They indicated little interest in spending money to make the lot of criminals more bearable. They chose only to appoint a committee to study the condition of the convicts leased to contractors—"to invesigate their treatment and management," and to ascertain whether or not they were "clothed and dieted, and given medical attention, guarded, housed, and worked as required by law."

The committee reported thus: "We unhesitatingly recommend an immediate repeal of the law establishing the leasing system; that the contracts with the lessees, violated in every particular, be immediately annulled, and the convicts withdrawn." They stated that 775 out of the 1,000 prisoners had been treated for scurvy in 1879. Deaths totalled 75 that year. One prisoner had been given 150 lashes as punishment. A sewer emptied near the window of the prison hospital. These conditions caused the committee to call for the removal of J. W. South, keeper of the penitentiary.[10] The recommendations, however, were not acted upon. The only alternative to the existing system was a new penitentiary, and legislators refused to spend money for that alternative.

Improvement of Rivers

Like his interest in penal reform, Governor Blackburn's interest in imporovement of navigation was keen. The "Hero of Hickman" took up where his predecessor had left off. Realizing that no help was forthcoming in appropriations from the General Assembly for such improvements, friends of navigation development had petitioned the Congress, through Kentucky representatives, to make appropriations. As a result, during the 1879 session the Congress had provided $100,000 for navigation improvements on the Kentucky River. Many Kentuckians, professing to be of the Jacksonian school, continued to express the belief that congressional appropriations for internal improvements were unconstitutional. Blackburn shouldered the task of persuading the lawmakers to accept the gift. Calling upon them to act as sensible men, he pointed out that Kentucky contributed from "seven to ten millions of dollars to the revenue of the General Government by taxes on our products." Was not the state due some return? In view of acute financial conditions in the state, he was inclined to feel that the Commonwealth could ill-afford refusal of such fortuitous money gifts. Moreover, the patient governor pointed out the appealing possibilities for the state in the development of vast untapped riches in timber, coal and iron which Kentucky navigation improvement might bring about.

The General Assembly responded by passing acts to accept appropriations by the federal government for improvement of Kentucky River navigation. In addition to accepting the 1879 congressional appropriation of $100,000 (the session of 1880 appropriated an additional $130,000), the Assembly also adopted a measure providing for transfer to the federal government of five Kentucky River locks and dams, constructed by the state.

Other special legislative acts ceded the right to acquire and condemn land and gave concurrent jurisdiction over the same to the United States government for the improvement of the Big Sandy and Licking Rivers, as well as for the construction of a canal around the falls of Cumberland River, and for other similar improvements. From time to time bills were passed to acquire land for the United States government for the purpose of building locks and dams and making other navigation improvements in the state. In 1881, the Congress appropriated $325,000 for improvement of Kentucky River navigation; $55,000 for the Big Sandy; $37,000 for that portion of Cumberland River flowing through Kentucky; $5,000 for the Tradewater, and a small sum for the Licking.[11] Thus the problem of river improvement was solved for the time being at no great cost to the Commonwealth.

The Superior Court

By 1880 the Appellate Court had fallen behind a year or more in its hearing schedule, and the number of cases continued to increase. The 1849 constitution limited neither the number of appellate court judges nor courts themselves, so that the establishment of a Court just under the court of Appeals became relatively simple.[12] The result in 1882 was the Superior Court.

Three popularly elected judges, paid $3,600 annually and selected from three districts for a four year term, would hear cases of $3,000 or less. To further relieve the higher court's docket, the Superior Court received appellate jurisdiction except in franchise, felony, probate, and statute cases. The Court of Appeals retained jurisdiction over the new court except in cases where less than $1,000 was involved or where there was no dissent by the Superior Court. However, even in these cases, if two judges declared that the question was "novel" and important, then further appeal could be made.

The new court, made up of able and conscientious judges, performed its duties well. James H. Bowden of Russellville, Adolphus Edward Richards of Louisville, and Richard Reid of Mt. Sterling won seats on the Frankfort court, with Bowden selected as Chief Justice by his fellow members. This court took approximately one-half of the cases formerly going to the Appellate Court. Soon the dockets of both tribunals cleared. Ironically enough, though, the new court was generally unpopular, not because it failed to accomplish the purpose for which it was chartered, but because its jurisdiction was limited to cases involving $3,000 or less. The jealous public charged that it was the "poor man's court" and that the poor man was barred from the Appellate Court, while moneyed people were free to use the higher tribunal.[13] The Superior Court could not outride this fatuous prejudice. In fact, this dissatisfaction caused its elimination by the constitutional convention of 1891. Actually, the establishment of the Superior Court constituted another of Blackburn's major reforms.

IX

EDUCATING THE PEOPLE

Kentucky's first code in the eighteenth century contained a law dealing with horses but none dealing with education. Almost a century later a Woodford countian bitterly complained that "the difficulty I meet in the work . . . is to get the people to understand that a Woodford County child is worth as much as a race horse and is entitled to as good a house."[1] On a scale of priorities Kentucky schools did not rank high. Despite a period in the 1840s and 1850s when the state stood in the forefront of southern education, by the 1860s the school system was woefully weak.

The condition of the common schools in 1867 when Superintendent of Public Instruction Zachariah Frederick Smith took office had been critical, because of the ravages of the war and lack of funds. The tax of five cents per $100 of property was producing only $185,000 annually. Smith insisted that the assessment should be increased to around $740,000 annually, an amount calculated as enough to keep the schools open for five months during the year. This would allow teachers from $19 to $25 per month in pay. It was estimated that the sum would mean an annual pupil expenditure of $2.37.

Somehow, "Zack" Smith succeeded—despite determined opposition from many legislators—in securing adoption of nearly all his educational program. His greatest achievement was the ratification by popular vote, in August, 1869, of a proposal to raise the state tax for school purposes from five to twenty cents. Within two

years Smith secured an increase in the amount of disbursement to
$968,000.

In 1871 white pupils reported in the census numbered 405,000,
a gain of 29,000 since December 1869, and school districts had
increased from 4,500 in 1869 to 5,000 in July, 1871. School
sessions now ran for five months, compared to only three months
in 1869. Improved teachers' salaries and moves toward uniform
textbook adoption also resulted. The school fund proper, on July
1, 1871, consisted of one state bond, bearing interest at six
percent for $1,327,000, and 735 shares of Bank of Kentucky
stock, valued at $73,500. The return from the fund was distrib-
uted, by constitutional mandate, on the pupil census per capita
basis.[2]

Much work remained to be done. Over one-fourth of all Kentuckians over the age of ten were illiterate in 1870—some
330,000 people. This figure declined throughout the decades, so
that by 1900 about 16.5 percent could not read and write.
Second best to Texas in the South, Kentucky's illiteracy rate
was still much higher than the national average of 10.7 percent.
Even more disturbing to enlightened Kentuckians was the fact
that almost one of every five eligible voters could neither read
nor write at the century's end. An educated citizenry had not
been achieved.

Superintendent Smith pleaded for aid in the fight for popular
education. His 1869 Report to the Governor argued:

Citizens Driven From Kentucky by Lack of Schools

*Already, many of our sturdy and industrious yeomanry
have turned their backs upon their old homes, and emigrated
among the strangers of a distant land; and we will plead in
vain for foreign supplies of labor to till our neglected farms,
while the agents of other States are able to hold out the
tempting bonus of one hundred dollars' worth of education
per annum against our meagerness and destitution. A man's
children are his hope, his pride, his all! For them he lives,*

labors and sacrifices. Open to the poor man the prospect of the advancement, culture and elevation of his children, and he will hazard all else for the attainment of these. Popular education would seem to be a necessity to a republican government. The people are the depository of sovereign power, and create its institutions and its officials by the exercise of their suffrage. If the character of the government depends upon the wisdom with which the suffrage of privilege is used, it is of paramount importance to the security of our lives, liberties, and property that the people should be enlightened and intelligent as sovereign electors; and to this end the government should provide ample means.[3]

Some writers blamed this educational situation on "the unfortunate pride of caste." Republican editor Robert M. Kelly believed that lack of progress in public education was due to "a prejudice against common schools, with many wealthy and influential people yielding them no support beyond their enforced payment of the State school tax." The editor stated that "wherever there is a feeling that common schools exist only for poor people it serves as a check against the best efforts of the workers in these schools for educating the masses." He was certain that the wealthiest and most influential people of many communities often took the lead against local taxes for school support, which discouraged "those less able" and helped to maintain a low standard of education in the local community.

The wealthy and educated usually sent their children to private academies instead. Most numerous in counties of high black concentration, academies functioned primarily as secondary schools but practically all had elementary departments. Most of the academies for girls were boarding schools as well. Chartered by the state, academies proliferated between 1860-1870 and declined slightly after that. They never educated large numbers of students; in 1870 they had only 15,000 pupils, compared to over 200,000 students in the public schools.[4]

Classrooms and Curriculum

The public school teacher facing his or her first school may have questioned choice of that profession, when confronting the deplorable school buildings. The Common School Report of 1871 described schoolhouses as "exceedingly rude and unsuitable" and noted that:

> *The observing traveler can mark the district school-houses by their desolate, lonely, uncared-for aspect. They are too frequently located on some barren and treeless hillside, where the hot suns of summer pelt down upon them, and the cold winds of winter have unbroken sweep; or on a narrow strip of land at the junction of highways, where the dust is sure to blow into the house from one or the other road; or by streets and railroads, in the neighborhood of factories, or the busiest portions of villages, where study will be interrupted and the persons and morals of the children endangered. Broken windows, swinging weather-boards, leaky roofs, are noticeable from without. Inside are filthy floors, smoked ceilings, and walls defaced with obscene images. The furniture is of the most primitive kind, and constructed with little or no reference to the comfort of those who are to use it. Appliances promotive of order and cleanliness are neglected. Hats and clothing are thrown on the floor or tossed over the benches. If there is a privy, it is a den of loathsomeness. Altogether, the common school seems to be a place which has few attractions, but much that is offensive and repulsive.* [5]

A few years later, Governor Preston Leslie gave a similar but perhaps exaggerated view of a typical schoolhouse, but one too nearly correct to dismiss:

> *A little square, squatty, unhewed log building, blazing in the sun, standing upon the dusty highway or some bleak and barren spot that has been robbed of every tree and blossom-*

ing shrub, without yard, fence, or other surroundings sugges-
tive of comfort to abate its bare, cold, hard, and hateful look,
is the fit representative of the district schoolhouses of the
Commonwealth. . . . The benches—slabs with legs in them so
long as to lift the little fellows' feet from the floor, and
without support for the back. The desks—slabs at angles, cut,
hacked, scratched, blotted, covered with geological stratas, or
luminated with knife carving overlaying the rude sculpturing
of previous years. Full of foul air and feculent odors. These
are the places in which a cruel parsimony condemns child-
hood to pass its bright young days. . . . A wayfaring man can
readily distinguish the school-house by its very unsightliness.
Its style challenges description, being too little for a stable,
too big for a sty or coop or kennel, too defective in the
elements of architectural proportion for a residence, and too
much dilipidated to create the idea that it belongs to any-
body's premises. . . . It seems to have been built simply for a
pen for prisoners, at the smallest outlay of money, labor or
skill; to call it economy would be making fun of language. It
stands an offense to justice, kindness, taste, without an
apology for its hideous blot upon the site. It invites no one to
its interior, and sends a shudder through the frame of the
pupil, daily, who approaches it.[6]

Given this environment, it was not surprising that schools did
not attract students; children of school age who attended scarcely
rose above 40 percent in the nineteenth century. A compulsory
attendance law—debated for years—finally passed in 1896, without
the governor's signature. It required children between seven and
fourteen to attend at least eight weeks of school, but the law was
generally ineffective.

For those children who did attend school, the elementary
course of study was the "3R's," geography, and American history.
The secondary courses included the "3R's," spelling, grammar,
composition, geography, American history, and "laws of health."
By 1888 physiology, hygiene, and civil government replaced "laws
of health"; and five years later Kentucky history was added to

the curriculum. Spelling bees, ciphering competitions, and other contests enlivened the school day.[7]

One of the popular series Kentucky school children used was the widely-known *McGuffey Readers*. Professor William Holmes McGuffey (1800-1873) compiled his series for Cincinnati publishers Truman and Smith (later the American Book Company), beginning with his first and second readers in 1836. By 1857 both the sixth reader and his *Eclectic Spelling Book* had been published. The series then went through edition after edition. The simple lessons, containing obvious, even explicit, moral lessons, sought at the same time to capture a student's interest. The wide popularity of the series indicates that it succeeded.

Kentucky schools also used a series published by the John P. Morton Company of Louisville. Authored by Samuel Griswold Goodrich and Noble Butler, the "American Standard School Series" was widely used throughout the South. Like McGuffey's books, these readers and spellers included moral lessons, godliness, jingles, and a little patriotism in their pages. Another volume in the series, P. A. Towne's *Mental Arithmetic* (1866) had such thought problems as: "A laborer agreed to work 50 days upon this condition; that for every day he worked he should receive $3, and for every day he was idle he should pay $1 for his board. At the expiration of the time he received $90. How many days did he work?" Selling for $2.00/dozen wholesale, a book such as this or *Goodrich's First Reader* found wide acceptance throughout Kentucky.[8]

Schools resembling Male High in Louisville followed a classical, traditional education in advanced programs. One of its 300 students in 1895 would take Latin, English, physiology, and algebra in his first year while his second year included German and physics. A third year scholar's course of study was Latin, Greek, German, English, chemistry and laboratory, and geometry; the fourth year offered political economy, surveying, psychology, logic, and astronomy to replace some subjects. Reading included Cicero, Virgil, Homer, Herodotus, Horace, Chaucer, and Shakespeare.

Few schools exceeded Male High School in size and few teachers were as well prepared as its faculty. Reports from various counties in 1881 noted the problem. The communication from Calloway County stated that "there is not a corps of efficient teachers," while the Carter County return observed, "Teachers are in great measure made up from failures from other occupations. No capable man will prepare himself for a profession that gives employment for only five months of the year at 'starvation prices.' " As one writer remarked, "Though the teacher was often underprepared, he usually was not overpaid."

Meager salaries were the school teachers' lot. In 1870 the typical school contained a single teacher with over forty pupils vying for attention. Since salaries were based on the number of pupils, the best teachers taught the largest classes.[9] They thus had the poorest opportunity to give individual attention, while poorer teachers who had less to give the student had the greatest chance. Salaries in the mid-1880s ranged from $9.33 to $28.00 a month in the public schools, for a school term of from three to six months that began in July or August. A farm laborer's yearly wage was higher. Even then, teachers' pay usually was received only after the completion of half the term. A few districts did vote a local tax to increase salaries, while some supplemented teachers' wages by giving them board. Louisville, with a tenth of the population of the state, expended $250,000 annually on her system—almost a third of the whole cost of education in the state. But aside from the better financed urban districts—Louisville paid from $350 to $700 a season—salaries remained very low.[10]

State superintendents of public instruction were by and large dedicated, though some lacked experience in the field of public education. County superintendents were generally unqualified, however. The law required them only to possess a "fair English education," be of good moral character, and over twenty-four years old. County superintendents presented other problems. Not until 1886 were they required also to have certificates from the state board of examiners. The 1870 salary of $100, plus 1 percent of the money disbursed by the superintendent, did not, of course, attract the best qualified men; in fact, it may have invited fraud. Twenty years later, the minimum salary rose to $250, but the position could still be filled by someone with no educational qualifications. Looked on as clerks by the community, superintendents also travelled poor roads and dealt with inexperienced teachers. The low prestige of the county superintendent hurt the entire system.

These were problems that superintendents of public instruction would face throughout the rest of the century. Dr. H. A. M. Henderson, state superintendent from 1871-1879, succeeded "Zack" Smith. In most respects an able superintendent, nevertheless he was at times irritable, somewhat given to conceit, and obviously ambitious to remain in office as long as possible. Unfortunately for him, at the end of his eight years in office, per capita funding had dropped to $1.60, due in part to the increase in pupils, the steady decrease in wealth during the 1870s, and the depreciation in the values of both personalty and realty.[11]

Henderson, a student of public education, particularly the best state and foreign systems, did succeed in bringing about many improvements. During his terms independent graded schools were organized in large numbers. Local district taxation (up to 25 cents) was made possible, teacher training institutes were vigorously pushed, and teacher certification was required. The single trustee to the district plan was inaugurated (superceding the three trustee system). Henderson set up a standard high school curriculum and a temporary normal school (to run for two summers), and he issued thousands of bulletins designed to improve teaching and to inform the public about school needs. He sought unsuccessfully to persuade the General Assembly to pass legislation providing for a permanent state normal school and for compulsory school attendance.

In view of the unfavorable economic conditions, it was practically certain that the people would strenuously oppose any general increase of taxes. Both Superintendent Joseph Desha Pickett (1879-1887) and Governor Luke P. Blackburn therefore pointed to local taxation for school purposes as the logical way to supplement state funds. Pickett also argued that local taxation was the best means of creating peoples' interest in local schools. He predicted that it would bring about, not only more money, but better buildings and facilities, better trained and abler teachers, and better attendance.[12] The idea of adequate local support of schools grew very slowly, however, because the people generally refused to tax themselves sufficiently to provide good schools. As local interest did slowly grow, the influence of the state office seemed to decrease. The end of the century found the state superintendent little more than a figurehead, although Pickett's successor, Ed Porter Thompson (1887-1895), fought vigorously for the cause of state education.

The General Assembly failed in 1880 to pass a comprehensive bill to reorganize the state's common school system. Many prominent friends of education consequently began to agitate the question to arouse public interest. A state central committee of prominent men was appointed to outline a program looking to legislative action. This nonpartisan group composed of Judge William M. Beckner (perhaps the most enthusiastic layman for educational reform of the period) General Don Carlos Buell, W. C. P. Breckinridge, Pickett, Wilbur F. Browder, George H. Cochran, William J. Davis and John Mason Brown met in Louisville, April 29, 1883, "to devise a plan for a complete educational organization throughout the state." The committe presented its report to Governor Knott, who in turn referred it to the General Assembly, which enacted a good portion of the recommendations into the Common School Law of May 10, 1884.[13]

The new law set up a general plan of school organization on the state, county, and district levels. It provided a uniform system. The measure defined the length of the school year, duties of state and county boards of education, and duties of the trustees. It forbade sectarianism in the public schools, outlined the duties and

Superintendent of Public Instruction,
H.A.M. Henderson
Reprinted from Barksdale Hamlett, *History of
Education in Kentucky* (1914)

Superintendent of Public Instruction,
Zachariah Smith
Reprinted from Barksdale Hamlett, *History of
Education in Kentucky* (1914)

Superintendent of Public Instruction,
Ed. Porter Thompson
Reprinted from Barksdale Hamlett, *History of
Education in Kentucky (1914)*

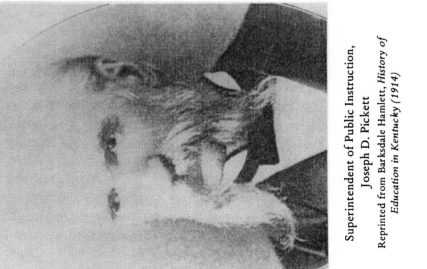

Superintendent of Public Instruction,
Joseph D. Pickett
Reprinted from Barksdale Hamlett, *History of
Education in Kentucky (1914)*

liabilities of examining boards, and explained the method of tax collection. The law also regulated the course of study, provided free textbooks for indigent children, and required local reports. It authorized for the first time a state teachers' association. The law discontinued the system of county commissioners and provided for popular county-wide election of county superintendents, as well as for a state board of education, consisting of the state superintendent of public instruction, the attorney general and the secretary of state, and two professional members elected by them. This board was given authority to make rules and by-laws, as well as powers in connection with course of study, textbooks, and health education. In an attempt to rectify poor conditions, the Common School Law set forth the process for condemnation and erection of school buildings, provided for better teacher examination, required county teacher institutes, authorized district school libraries, and defined teachers' authority.[14]

This was the most comprehensive school law passed in the state up to that time. But following its passage, localism in the state's educational system remained in the center stage. The state school fund, as constituted, could not support a reputable state public school system. Unless amended, this law meant that most of the money would have to come from local sources. Where the people were willing to tax themselves, good systems developed and the children of those locales became better educated. Such communities, however, were principally in heavily populated areas, of which Kentucky could boast only a few. On the state level, education throughout the remainder of the 1880s and through the 1890s seemed a drab, perfunctory affair indeed.

Overall, however, Kentuckians were not as poorly educated as some critics charged, for the Commonwealth ranked high among southern states. But, as usual, when viewed on the national level she and the South were far behind. A comparison of the state with two similarly populated neighbors confirms this:[15]

	Population	Property Value Per Capita	Total Expenditure for Education	Average Daily Attendance	Illiteracy Rate (General)	Average Salary Per Teacher Per Year
Kentucky	1,648,690	$547	$2,324,888	192,333	29.9	$133.10
Indiana	1,978,301	850	9,008,814	320,577	7.5	266.69
Tennessee	1,542,359	457	1,572,196	205,081	38.7	106.88

Individuals could still do much to help improve Kentucky education. The Reverend John J. Dickey, a Methodist minister, left central Kentucky in the early 1880s for Jackson in Breathitt County. Establishing a school, he led the fight for better education in that county: "I do not believe there is more devil in these people than there is in others. The difference is that here it is unrestrained and in other places it is restrained. . . . I believe they will be a mighty power for good." Yet he had much to overcome as he noted that "school houses are very indifferent and the teachers worse."

Dickey's optimism often gave way to pessimistic appraisals. "Breathitt countians," he wrote, "are indeed a primitive people in manners and customs. Their dress is very plain and their language homely." "Bloody Breathitt" deserved all her notoriety, he sadly observed, for "there are here the elements of a war as bloody as has ever reddened her soil. The trouble is the better class is cowed." In anguish, he wrote just before Christmas, 1883: "How long will Kentucky soil be drenched in blood? The murder mania seems to be on the increase." Three years later Dickey's diary contained the entry that "the devil seems to have made a fresh charge at Jackson."[16]

Dickey led a counterattack beginning with a revitalized school system. Earlier he had whipped a fourteen year old student for drawing a loaded pistol in class, but the real evil, Dickey believed, was that the "immorality of many teachers is greater than their ignorance." Reform them and a solution was near, he argued.

As a delegate to a political convention, the local county school superintendent, Dickey had heard, was so drunk he had to be helped home; he would be little help in the struggle. Dickey had more hope for a teachers' institute that would last a week in September, 1883 and bring together some sixty teachers for training. Topics discussed at the meeting included astronomy, decimal fractions, phonetics, teachers' pay, textbooks and school houses, plus other subjects. After it concluded, Dickey summed up his impression of some of the delegates. One teacher was "a common drunkard and uncontrollable thief and cannot write his name" while another was "a thief, a drunkard, a gambler without honor." A man sixty years old was rumored to be the father of over a score of bastards, while another teacher was at his thirty-third school because of his drunkenness. A woman teacher drew her pay but had no students: "She is so ignorant that the people will not send."

In the next thirteen years Dickey gathered funds for a new school building, which became the home of Jackson Academy, later Lee's Junior College, established the first newspaper—later bombed for its prohibition stand—and started a literary society. He revitalized Jackson's churches and aided in training better teachers. There were still poor teachers, and he had not transformed the county. But it was a start. Dickey felt God called him elsewhere, and in 1895 he moved to London to begin again: "The people must be reached."[17] Despite the individual efforts of men like him, Kentucky schools still did not serve enough people in the nineteenth century.

Higher Education

Higher education suffered from the war's effects, as the common schools had. Traditionally many of the state's brightest youths had entered schools outside the state—Princeton and Yale being examples. After the war this practice continued. Schools in the South were particularly popular, including the University of

Virginia and Washington and Lee, where 10 percent of the 1871 student body was from Kentucky.

Immediately following the war, few colleges thrived in Kentucky, and the once prosperous and prestigious Transylvania University lay in virtual ruins. But merged with and renamed as Kentucky University, it had nearly seven hundred students five years later. Part of the great student increase resulted from the presence of the new Agricultural and Mechanical College, a state institution.[18]

President John B. Bowman's dream was democratization of education: "Hitherto our Colleges and Universities have been accessible only to the few," he declared, "such are the expenses attending them. We therefore want a university with all the colleges attached, giving education of the highest order to all classes." Under his leadership, and then Dr. James K. Patterson's for the rest of the century, A & M College attempted to realize that dream.

But the path was neither easy nor smooth. Beset with internal dissention, fund shortages due to the 1873 depression, and then religious quarreling, A & M College and Kentucky University became involved in an acrimonious dispute. Enrollment dropped from 722 students in 1867 to 196 in 1878. The number of students at the A & M College, as part of Kentucky University, declined from 300 in 1869 to 66 in 1878. Governor McCreary advised the General Assembly in 1878 to create a commission to investigate affairs at the school.[19] Both the commission and the governor recommended that the connection between Kentucky University and the A & M College be dissolved, which was done.

Governor Blackburn then requested the General Assembly of 1879-1880 to launch the A & M College as an independent institution and echoed Bowman's thoughts when he declared: "We must make it emphatically, the *People's* College, a *representative* Institution in its highest and truest sense. It is our only State College, and should be worthy of our Commonwealth."

Responding to Blackburn's appeal, the legislature in 1880

passed a comprehensive law reorganizing the A & M College. The act provided that the managmenet of the institution be vested in a board of trustees, presided over by the governor, and composed of twelve members, nominated by him and ratified by the senate, for a term of six years. The students would be admitted through competitive examinations, but one pupil from each representative district was entitled to a free scholarship. The teachers and trustees of each common school were to select one pupil as a candidate for the scholarship, giving preference to young men of limited means, and the faculty was given the power to issue teachers' certificates.[20]

Lexington was selected as the location for the college, principally because that city outbid Bowling Green. City park was donated as the site and $30,000 in Lexington bonds were to be used to finance erection of buildings. Fayette County contributed $20,000 in bonds to purchase additional land. The new institution was to be supported by legislative appropriations, the remaining endowment,[21] and proceeds from a half-cent state property tax. The day of the dedication of the new Administration Building in 1882, the highlight of which was the eloquent address of Henry Watterson, was indeed propitious for Kentucky.

Commonly referred to as State College, the new school charged fifteen dollars tuition and a student could rent a room for less than five dollars a week. Under the "benevolent despot," President Patterson, students were tightly controlled. Demerits, which could lead to suspension, were given if a student was caught smoking or playing cards in his room, if he did not attend Sunday church service, if he left his room between taps at 10:00 P.M. and reveille at 5:30 A.M., if he left his room during the prescribed study hours, and if he moved from his assigned eating place at the dinner table. State College's cadet officers enforced these rules in the military school tradition.

A day in the typical student's life began at 5:30 in the morning. A half-hour later came inspection, followed by a 6:30 breakfast. After that meal a student was expected to resist the temptation to

A Kentucky school on a warm day
Reprinted from *The City of Louisville and a
Glimpse of Kentucky (1887)*

An A & M College classroom at the turn of the century
Courtesy of the University of Kentucky Archives

sleep by studying until 8:30. The steady knock of Patterson's wooden leg as he checked on his scholars would soon dispel any such thoughts of loafing, however. At 8:30 came chapel, then classes until the noon meal. After that, the schedule varied but usually included another study period from 1:00-4:00, followed by one hour of "military exercise." After supper, a three-hour study period lasted until 9:30 P.M. with no fraternizing between rooms allowed—supposedly. At ten o'clock, as the strains of "Taps" drifted across campus, all students were expected to be sleeping, readying themselves for another day.

Some students seemed to have ignored these strict rules. Pranks were common and few on campus quickly forgot the look on President Patterson's face when he saw a horse awaiting him in the second floor chapel one morning. A committee to investigate student misbehavior could not prove it, but while they examined the sleeping students, some of those same students secretly hurried out, removed the wheels from the committee's carriage and returned quietly to their rooms. College life was not entirely dull and regimented.

The first fraternity did not appear until 1893, rather late on the scene, and literary societies remained the focal point of extracurricular life until the early twentieth century. In debate young men impressed their young women and sought recognition, but more and more they were also turning to college sports.[22]

In the classroom, the curriculum was broadened from the old classical education and stressed more modern subjects and more technical courses. Teacher training became an important part of the curriculum; the first women students at State College studied in that area. By 1899 total enrollment had grown from its 1884 figure of 188 men and 43 women to 424 men and 126 women, while the faculty doubled in the same period from 15 men to 28 men and 2 women.[23]

Schools whose philosophy and curriculum differed from State College continued to attract students. Church-related institutions— Centre, Transylvania, Georgetown, Central University in Richmond, Kentucky Wesleyan in Winchester, and others—stressed a more classical curriculum than did State College. While not matching it in size, the other schools did not lack students. By the mid-1890s Centre College had 15 teachers and 184 male students. Wesleyan's 14 instructors taught some 380 pupils, while newly-founded (1890) Asbury College in Wilmore employed 10 professors to teach some 156 scholars. Union College, founded in 1879 and named by James D. Black, encountered some later financial problems, reopened in 1886, and by the 1890s had 6 teachers and 35 students. Georgetown numbered 20 teachers and 365 students (149 female), Central University (founded in 1873), some 859 pupils and 46 teachers. Virtually all the colleges had preparatory, collegiate, and professional departments. Numerous other institutions existed as academies, colleges, normal schools, high schools with collegiate departments, female institutes, and seminaries. While many offered sound instruction, others were no better than high schools, and some not as good. Tuition varied widely at the private institutions, but most were higher than State College's $20 per year: Asbury ($20), Union ($35), Georgetown ($45), Centre ($50), and Bethel ($55).

The grounds of Central University would later become the site of Eastern Kentucky University, while the Southern Normal School of Glasgow and then Bowling Green would be the basis for the later Western Kentucky University. Founded in 1875, the Southern Normal School later joined with Potter College (opened in 1889) and Ogden College (opened in 1877). Morehead Normal School, founded in 1887, followed a similar path to become Morehead State University.[24]

Professional schools continued their development, however halting. The legislative act of 1874 required all physicians to be medical school graduates. This resulted in the establishment of several schools that featured a weak curriculum and quick graduation. Other schools, however, maintained their standards. The Kentucky School of Medicine in Louisville had been founded in 1850 and reached its peak attendance in 1892 when its enrollment numbered 504. The Louisville Medical College, organized in 1869, included 30 faculty and 260 students in 1876, making it the largest in the South for that time. Central Unversity opened a medical department in 1874, while Kentucky University Medical Department in Louisville was established in 1898. Consolidation of many of the Louisville schools came about early in the next century. Not until 1890 did a four-year course become established. Quality medical training remained difficult under such circumstances.

While lawyers continued to receive their education in private law offices, some good law schools produced graduates. Lecturers at Centre included former governor and able lawyer Proctor Knott, Republican lawyer-politician John W. Yerkes and Democratic lawyer-politician Robert J. Breckinridge, Jr. The Louisville Law School, established in 1846, and among the first dozen degree-conferring schools in the Mississippi Valley, continued strong. Not until the early twentieth century, however, did these schools adopt the recommendations of the American Bar Association, founded in 1878.[25]

Negro Education

Prior to 1870 most schools for Negroes had been operated by the Freedmen's Bureau. Supported by funds from that body and by even more funds from the freedmen themselves, the schools received little or no local governmental aid. White Kentuckians gave them little popular support.

Kentucky, unfortunately, had the dubious reputation of being the leader among the border states in its violent opposition to the Freedmen's Bureau schools. In a two-year period to 1868 ten schools were burned and another blown up. Obstruction was so prevalent that it discouraged civic and religious freedmen's aid societies from sending agents into Kentucky; Tennessee received ten times as much money from these groups. By the fall of 1868 Bureau activities neared their end. But in the short period of its existence the Bureau had set up nearly 400 schools that served almost 19,000 students.[26] While most of these schools died with the Bureau, some remained, a reminder of Kentucky's duty.

In 1870 less than eight thousand Negroes attended the common schools. A year later Superintendent of Public Instruction Henderson, a Methodist minister who had fought for the Confederacy, turned to the problem of black education. With black voting now a fact, he argued, some form of education should be given the new citizens. He rejected integrated schools as "simply impossible in Kentucky," and instead proposed that money from Negro taxes be used to finance that race's schools. Henderson opposed a common fund because it would take money from white schools. Whether by design or not, his proposals if enacted would result in a large variance in funding for Negroes, who had not acquired much property. The auditors report showed total Negro tax receipts of only $2,232 in 1871 and $4,347 in the next year.[27]

In 1874 a separate school system for Negroes was organized under Henderson's guidance. Segregated by law and supported by black funds only, the schools had in particular one source of income not available to white schools—a poll tax. An act with more promise than power, the law provided for a school fund derived from the "present annual revenue tax of 25 cents, and 20 cents in addition, on each $100 in value of taxable property owned and held by colored persons," a capitation tax of one dollar on each black male above the age of 21, all taxes levied and collected on dogs owned or kept by Negroes, all state taxes on deeds, suits, or any license collected from Negroes, all "fines, penalties, and forfeitures," collected from Negroes, except the portion allowed to attorneys of the Commonwealth, a pro rata share of the proceeds from any public lands given by the United States, and all sums arising from any "donation, gift, grant, or devise, expressly designed to aid in the education of colored children." Funds were to be distributed by the state superintendent of public instruction.

Provision was made also for collection and distribution: The county school commissioner was required to divide the county into school districts, so that no district would contain more than 120 black children between 6 and 16 years of age. Three black trustees would be appointed in each district, and a teacher engaged for not less than three months each year, or two months if there were not more than 60 children in the district. Moreover, "no schoolhouse erected for a colored school shall be located nearer than one mile to a school erected for white children, except in cities and towns, where it shall not be nearer than six hundred feet." Negro school officers and teachers formed a state association and county institutes, and the state board of education prescribed a course of study and rules of government for black schools, following established school laws. Schools were organized in 452 districts in 93 counties in the first year of operation.[28]

Negro leaders found the system unsatisfactory. In convention at Lexington in November, 1875 they passed a series of resolutions designed "to procure such legislation, if possible, as will provide equal education advantages to every child in the State." Declaring that the new law failed to provide funds "sufficient to maintain free schools for the colored children in any portion of the State," the resolutions maintained that the funds for white children provided "almost nine times as much per scholar" as the funds for black children. Their figures were not totally correct but were near enough to the truth to make their point.[29]

Four years later in Louisville the leadership met and passed resolutions declaring the school fund wholly inadequate. In many districts school was not held at all, while in others the pro rata of the school fund was sufficient to hire none but the most incompetent teachers, they complained. The resolutions declared the average annual salary of the black teacher to be only fifty dollars— or, as they said, "about one-third of the average salary of . . . teachers in the other slave states." In conclusion the resolutions demanded an equal fund.

Under the leadership of Superintendent Pickett, also a minister and beloved chaplain of the Kentucky Confederate Orphan Brigade, two significant bills were enacted which aided black education. A proposed law in 1882 declared that "no such difference in the per capita due such white and colored pupil children should exist" and asked that all citizens vote on themselves an additional two cent tax to equalize the separate funds. Significantly, on August 6, 1882 the voters surprisingly gave the law nearly a seventeen thousand vote majority. While still segregated, the two separate systems now would be financed on an equal basis, according to the law. By the next year Negro schools received $1.30 per pupil, as compared to $.58 under the old system.

The second action by Pickett was his support for higher education for Negroes. Only at Berea College, the only integrated school in the South, could Negroes attend a Kentucky college, and the "mixing" of the races at Berea caused problems for that school until 1904. In 1873 it had nearly three hundred students, almost two-thirds of them Negroes. Such a situation did not appeal to white Kentuckians, and by 1886 a law was passed establishing Kentucky State Normal School for Colored Persons at Frankfort. Given a meager funding of three thousand dollars annually, the school opened with two teachers and fifty-five students. By 1900 enrollment had surpassed the two hundred mark, but it was still weak academically—as were many white colleges.[30] Yet a beginning had been made.

Negro educational needs still remained unfulfilled. In a Lexington mass meeting in 1886, black leaders called for better facilities, citing one case where ninety children and one teacher were crowded into a Lexington schoolroom twenty feet square. In Owensboro a Negro school building that measured thirty by forty feet had an average attendance of two hundred pupils. In that instance it was perhaps well that there was a high percentage of nonattendance. Poor educational facilities and poorly trained teachers haunted black educators as well as white.

Negro illiteracy stood higher than white but had declined from 55 percent in 1890 to 40 percent in 1900. When compared to whites, the percentage of blacks attending school did not differ significantly; it was the highest in the South, and was above the national average as well.[31] But black schools—usually inferior to white—were segregated and overcrowded, had second priority, and Negroes knew it. White schools, however, faced many of the same problems.

Kentucky's Schools

Whether black or white, the school child's education was less than ideal, especially in rural areas. There, perhaps in an isolated house along a creek hidden between two hills, the youngster arose from bed. After a standard, perhaps non-nutritional breakfast he journeyed out to the trace that served as a road. On rainy days chances of negotiating the mud path were almost nil. On sunny ones the trip to the school building was usually long. Some rode horses, others walked.

Finally after a long, dusty walk in summer or a cold bone-chilling trek in winter, the scholar reached what served as his school. In many cases the building presented a dull, dreary exterior that only reflected the interior. Poorly ventilated, ill-constructed, and virtually uncared for, the one-room schoolhouse served as much to hinder learning as to further it. But it was all many students had. Sitting on a slab bench, hoping to be near the fire on cold days, the sons and daughters of illiterate farmers saw before them a teacher whose education may have only recently escaped the illiterate level. The younger women teachers usually served only until they found a marriage partner, and the older teachers as a rule remained unmarried. Young men teachers generally performed the task temporarily to earn money for further education, or as a transient profession. Many of the older males—especially in rural areas—either could find no other work or else taught only as a sideline to their farming. With the salaries paid teachers, it was at best a poorly paying full-time job or a part-time one.

The student knew little of all this. He or she knew only that teachers arrived and were as quickly gone. Strict pedagogues responded to anyone's questioning their answers with a paddling; others were so lax that the children accepted their apathy and responded in kind. Somehow in this atmosphere, despite the conditions, the children learned. Their books sometimes were worn and torn, their seats hard, their schools dirty and cold, their teachers often ill-prepared and uneducated—but they learned. Some sons and daughters of illiterate farmers became literate fathers and mothers and their children in the next century might attend better schools, perhaps even colleges. The foundation for such progress—however halting and weak it was—came in the last quarter of the nineteenth century.

X

POLITICS OF THE
MAUVE ERA

The presidential election of 1880 in Kentucky brought neither innovation nor undue excitement. Some tumult ensued in the Democratic state convention, which met in Lexington at the Opera House on June 17, when Henry Watterson and other Tilden men attempted to have adopted the unit rule for the party's state delegation in the national nominating convention. Watterson's strategem was calculated to deliver the entire Kentucky vote to Tilden. Although most of the delegates to the state convention favored the selection of Tilden, some preferred former "Peace Democrat" United States Senator Allen Granberry Thurman of Ohio, called the "Old Roman," and a few wanted Horatio Seymour, former governor of New York and Democratic standard-bearer for the presidency in in 1868. The popular western Kentuckian, William Lindsay, especially championed the latter. Nevertheless, the resolution was inserted in the platform.

On the floor of the convention the entire platform, because it provided for the unit rule of voting, was voted down by a large majority. Seeing the temper of the delegates, Watterson moved reconsideration of the platform with the unit rule plank eliminated. This unexpected expedient apparently pleased everyone, so that immediately the low-tariff and anti-election-fraud platform was then overwhelmingly adopted. The Kentucky delegation rather solidly supported Tilden. Watterson, Lindsay, Stevenson, and William Preston were selected as delegates-at-large. The national convention, however, nominated General Winfield Scott Hancock for president and the wealthy and scholarly Hoosier, William H. English, as his running mate.

The results of the election in the state came as no surprise. Hancock and English received 148,718 votes. The Republican candidates, James A. Garfield and Chester A. Arthur, were given 105,761 votes. The Greenback party candidates, General James B. Weaver and B. J. Chambers, received 11,423, while the Prohibitionist Neal Dow could glean only 259.[1]

The year 1881 was dull in state politics. However, of passing notice was the fact that four Greenbackers were elected to the General Assembly and that James B. Beck was reelected to the United States Senate by an overwhelming majority in the joint meeting of the two houses of the legislature.[2]

In the congressional elections of 1882, the Democrats failed to make the usual "clean sweep." The First District returned an avowed Independent, Oscar Turner of Ballard County. A Republican, William Wirt Culbertson, of Ashland, won in the Ninth, while another "log cabin" candidate, John D. White, received a plurality in the Tenth. The Democrats captured the Second with James Franklin Clay of Henderson, the Third, John Edward Halsell of Bowling Green by a slender margin of 190 votes, the Fourth, Thomas Austin Robertson of Hodgenville, Fifth, Albert S. Willis of Jefferson County, Sixth, John G. Carlisle, Seventh, J. C. S. Blackburn, brother of the governor, Eighth, Phil B. Thompson, Jr. of Harrodsburg, and the Eleventh, Frank L. Wolford.

The Election of 1883

The Democratic leaders seemed delighted when the time arrived for electing a new governor. They were generally displeased with Governor Blackburn, who had little interest in party politics but great interest in helping humanity. Newspaper criticism of his unprecedented pardon record and of his fine and sentence commutation brought him into additional disfavor with the professional

Senator James B. Beck
Collection of the Kentucky Historical Society

politicians. The governor's independence in job appointments most infuriated policians. Blackburn seemed to be swayed by competency more than by party service, more even than by service in the Confederate Army.

The sentiment of the Democratic county conventions of 1883 called to elect delegates to the state convention, seemed to favor James Proctor Knott, "Old Duluth," of Lebanon, for the gubernatorial nomination, although Judge John S. Owsley of Stanford, General Simon Bolivar Buckner of Hart County, and Thomas L. Jones had scattered support. Some interest was also expressed for Louisville's sartorially elegant mayor, Charles D. Jacob. However, the "managers" were determined to prevent a split at the convention.[3]

Henry Watterson, prior to the meeting of the Democracy, issued several powerful editorials designed to guide the party in its platform making. He came out strongly for reform in public education, as well as for the development of natural resources and industry. And he evoked his favorite theme of tax and tariff revision, which he called the "Star-eyed Goddess of Reform."

The Democratic state convention of 1883, described as "bubbling over with enthusiasm, good cheer, and excitement," met in Louisville on May 16 at famous Liederkranz Hall. On the first ballot Jones received 205¼ votes, Knott 189½, Buckner 143¾, Owsley 110¼ and Jacob 90¼. For four ballots these men contested for the nomination. Then Jacob dropped out. On the sixth ballot Knott continued to gain strength and led with 232, followed by Jones 227 2/3, Buckner's 171¼ and Owsley's 104¾. Owsley withdrew the next day as the balloting began again. The race centered on Knott and Jones. When Owen County switched to Knott, others followed, Jones withdrew and Knott's nomination was made unanimous.

The gathering was marred by one rather disgraceful incident. Governor Blackburn rose to defend his administration. Cries that he sit down almost drowned out his speech. In the course of his remarks he made the statement that Kentucky has resources such

Governor J. Proctor Knott

Collection of the Kentucky Historical Society

as "no State in the Union has, and yet we find her lingering behind every other State in the Union." This was too much for the politicians to bear. They tried to shout him down, which caused the old reformer to lose his temper and shout back that he had the right to defend his administration. Blackburn declared that he had been unjustly abused for his pardon record, that he had expected to be criticized as an innovator, but that the man who charged corruption to his administration was a "liar—a base infamous liar." By that time the clamor was so deafening that he had to take his seat.[4]

Proctor Knott (1830-1911)[5] was a colorful figure. He was attractive, clever, witty, and keenly intelligent. His famous Duluth speech, delivered in Congress on January 27, 1871, against authorizing an extensive land grant to the St. Croix Railroad along the St. Croix River to Duluth, Minnesota, had placed him among the foremost orators of the day. Its masterly satire, ridicule, sarcasm, and humor have placed the oration in the realm of the classics.

Nominated as Knott's running mates were former Union Colonel James R. Hindman of Columbia for lieutenant governor; incumbent "Wat" Hardin for attorney general; incumbent Fayette Hewitt for auditor; incumbent "Honest Dick" Tate for treasurer; incumbent "Elder" Joseph Desha Pickett for superintendent of public instruction and J. G. Cecil for register of the land office.[6]

The Republican state convention met in Lexington, May 23, and nominated for governor Circuit Judge Thomas Zanzinger Morrow (Somerset), who had married Bradley's sister. Others on the ticket were General Speed S. Fry of Danville for lieutenant governor; Lewis C. Garrigus (who had served in the Confederate army from Logan County) for attorney general; Leroy R. Hawthorne of Campbell County for auditor; the Negro minister J. W. Asbury for register of the land office; Elder James P. Pinkerton of Carter County for superintendent of public instruction; and Edward Farley of Paducah for treasurer.

The Republican platform advocated educational reform, adjustment of the national tariff (a departure from the usual support for high protective tariff), the calling of a constitutional convention, encouragement of immigration, and repeal of the tobacco tax. It arraigned the Democratic state government for "practically nullifying the criminal and penal laws" and for bad conditions in the penitentiary and in charitable institutions. It commended the administration of President Arthur.[7]

The campaign opened on June 16 at Mt. Vernon, scene of a joint debate between Knott and Morrow. Although Judge Morrow was on home ground, he had no easy time with the clever, graceful Knott. Each contestant spoke an hour and a half. Morrow hammered at Democratic fiscal policy in the state government since 1867, charging that the admininstrations had been prodigal, wasteful, and had accomplished nothing. Perhaps taking cue from Bradley, he declared that in 1865 the state debt had stood at $6,000,000 with resources of the Sinking Fund totalling $9,000,000, and asserted that the Sinking Fund now (1883) had not a dollar, with the state in debt $400,000. He charged that Democratic administrations since 1865 had simply squandered the money.[8] The Republican candidate also inveighed against Blackburn's pardon record and came down hard on the governor's "remission of fines imposed in misdemeanor cases" on gamblers, persons running tippling houses, and carrying concealed deadly weapons, while quoting the Democratic Stanford *Interior Journal* at length. He hit "special legislation" abuse also. Morrow declared that the "political ostracism" of the Republicans had retarded the state's progress, and assailed Democratic orators for continuously "waving the bloody shirt."

Knott's speech, though containing considerable sophistry, was scintillating and effective. He denied that frauds had been committed by Democratic officials, declaring that the debt had been reduced from $6,000,000 to $174,000 and that the same proportionate disparity between the debt and the resources of the Sinking Fund existed in 1883 as in 1865. He stated that the state's tax burden under Democratic control had been kept low, while in other states, notably Iowa, Michigan, and Wisconsin, the taxes were nearly twice as high and debts far bigger. He agreed with Morrow that the assessment laws should be revised and favored calling a convention to rewrite the state's constitution. He bandied Blackburn's pardon record around at length and got a loud laugh from the audience when he read some petitions for pardons signed by Judge Morrow. This accomplished, he dealt at length upon the wickedness of the Republican high protective tariff. Both men were well received.[9]

The newspapers of the day were strictly partisan, with the Republicans, who had few publications, at a decided disadvantage. The work of Henry Watterson in one particular instance will serve to indicate the type of journalistic help given the Democratic candidates generally throughout the state. "Marse Henry," apparently feeling the party was vulnerable for handling of the state's money by Democratic officials, made strong efforts to boost orators defending the Democratic record. He especially commended perennial office-seeker P. Wat Hardin, a pleasing campaign speaker. The *Courier-Journal* carried Hardin's entire campaign speech, and Watterson vigorously praised it editorially. The editor labeled it a "fair and conclusive refutation of the false and misleading statements put forth by those who would slander their own kith and kindred for the sake of political power," and declared that Republican orators had "rehearsed these vile slanders from one end of the state to the other." He charged further that "irresponsible sheets have been found to retail them daily with a gusto indicative of delight at an opportunity to publish a falsehood." "Marse Henry" charged that these "shallow-brained slanders have made the Sinking Fund of the state the especial object of their attacks, attempting to prove that its resources have been misappropriated, wasted and illegally reduced." The Louisville editor stated that Hardin had disproved "each specific charge and accounted satisfactorily for every dollar of that fund," and that the attorney general had "handsomely turned the tables upon Republican critics by proving from official records that the most expensive circuit court district in the state is that one in which the

Judge, Commonwealth's Attorney and other officials, together with a majority of the voters, are members of the Republican party."

Watterson was especially critical of Bradley. "Mr. William O. Bradley," he wrote, "one of the shrewdest, and at the same time most reckless, of the Republican speakers in the present canvass everywhere on the stump assaulted the control of the state affairs by Democratic administration, heaping up charges with a disregard for the truth of history characteristic of the party he represents." "Marse Henry" stated that at last Hardin had met Bradley in debate and "utterly disproved the charges, and Bradley's guns thus spiked, the eloquent orator retired from the canvass." Watterson reiterated that the Republican charges were "unworthy a moment's consideration by the intelligent voters at the polls." He continued: "Attorney General Hardin has punctured the bubble. . . . Thinking men will hesitate long on Monday before casting a vote to take the State government out of the hands of the Democrats and place it in those of the Republicans."[10]

No particular reason, however, existed for Mr. Watterson's anxiety, because the entire Democratic ticket won without difficulty. Knott gained a majority of 44,434, having received 133,615 votes to 89,181 for Judge Morrow. The other candidates ran in like ratio, more or less, with the exception of the Negro, Asbury, who received only 71,677. On the Democratic slate, Pickett ran behind his colleagues by nearly two thousand votes. The Republicans as usual took their defeat philosophically. A leading editor thought that Morrow made a creditable race, stating that, practically unknown at the beginning of the canvass, he had made "many friends and gained great popularity."

The call for a constitutional convention lost once more. Of the 169,173 persons returned as entitled to vote for a convention, only 73,704 votes were cast favorably. During the forthcoming legislative session, the Democrats would be in complete control again, with thirty-three of their party to five Republicans in the senate and eighty-nine to eleven in the house.[11]

Knott's Inaugural

The inaugural, at Frankfort, September 4, was indeed a gala celebration. Citizens of the capital city made the occasion grand and impressive. "Frankfort," wrote one reporter, "has witnessed many inaugurations, has gathered many crowds and large ones, but this will be recorded in history as the most elaborate inaugural, in point of grand preparation and the crowd gathered to witness it, of any yet had."

The same correspondent, commenting upon the administration of Governor Blackburn, stated that the governor's term had been one "marked by a humaneness that has brought upon him the criticism of not a few as being wholesale in the exercise of the pardoning power. . . . If taken, the verdict of those who elected him would doubtless be that Governor Blackburn has, all things taken together, made a most excellent Chief Magistrate, and many people who are here today come to give him commendation, and meet him with friendship's warmest greetings as he comes back into the noble state of private citizenship." Blackburn was still popular with the multitude, particularly with those keenly interested in reform and those needing a helping hand.

Governor Knott was described as one not famed as a "philanthropist" but as one "active wherever intellect meets in the war of State interests, and where ready wit, quick perception and a will and ability to do, with a judgment and coolness, mark a man's place among his fellow-men." It was said that "his individuality was the magnate [sic] which drew to him his support" and made him the "people's choice."

The incoming chief magistrate's inaugural was disappointing to many in the audience who had expected the smooth-flowing oratory of which "Old Duluth" was capable, because a good portion of it was devoted to constitutional questions and to enforcement of the law. He made it clear that his chief interest was tax reform, particuarly improvement of the assessment system and he promised that the pardoning power would not be abused.

Knott had little to say about improving the system of public education.[12]

Reform Measures of Proctor Knott

Carrying his assessment reform idea to the General Assembly of 1884, Governor Knott declared that the principal reason for the deficit of $491,375 in the state treasury was in the "grossly defective system of assessment, rendered still more inefficient by the negligent and unsatisfactory manner in which it is administered." Noting that the state's last assessment placed property valuation at $374,500,000, the governor declared that "our real property alone is worth double that sum." He felt certain that equitable and full assessments not only would make possible a reduction of the state tax by twenty cents, but also rapid reduction of the deficit as well. Moreover, the chief magistrate declared that "much of our revenue is annually lost through exoneration, delinquent lists, and sales of land for taxes." Complaining that large amounts of property had been exempted by private acts of the legislature, he charged that various lottery companies plying their business in the state "pay not a doit into the Treasury." He recommended that the General Assembly completely revise and modernize the revenue laws, suggesting that, in order to provide time for adequate study of the problem, action not be taken until the session of 1886. At the same time, however, he called for a temporary addition of two and one-half cents on the hundred dollars in new taxes. This was designed to aid in liquidating the large deficit and to enable the state to meet its current obligations.[13]

Though failing to enact legislation looking to general revenue reform, the lawmakers did provide for a board of equalization and for a tax increase of five cents. Nevertheless, the deficit continued and Knott was obliged to confront the next General Assembly (1885-1886) with another plea. He pointed out by way of contrast that assessed values in Indiana for 1884 were

$804,291,273 as compared with Kentucky's $377,888,542 the same year and contended that the figures listing comparative aggregate wealth, $406 per capita in Indiana and $222 in Kentucky, were not actually correct. The governor declared that the real difference lay in the fact that property in Indiana was assessed at much nearer its actual value than in Kentucky. Again he called upon the Assembly to pass comprehensive reform legislation.

The legislature of 1885-1886, acting with unusual dispatch, referred the governor's recommendations to the committee on revenue and taxation (presided over by William L. Jackson, Jr., of Louisville), which was instructed to advise the ways and means committee (with B. A. Neale, of Graves County, as chairman).[14] The former, after long consideration, reported a bill, almost interminable in length, which was enacted into law on May 17, 1886. The measure made the tax rate 47 cents per $100 of real and personal property and established uniform assessments. It provided for a 75 cent tax on bank and corporation stock and fixed taxes on gas, telegraph, telephone, and express companies. Railroad property was reassessed and taxed at the regular property rate. Establishing taxation of turnpike stock dividends, the measure also required uniform tax books and set up penalties for falsifying tax returns. Various other provisions clarified vague or confusing parts of the old law.[15] Though the new law contained some obvious defects, it was the most comprehensive measure of its kind passed in Kentucky to that time.

The new law accomplished its main purpose giving the state government enough money on which to operate. Less than two years later, Governor Buckner declared that the measure had already made possible a surplus in the treasury. Whereas the revenue receipts for the fiscal year 1885-86 were $1,630,000 with a deficit of $293,000, those for the 1888 fiscal year reached $3,693,000.[16]

The increased revenues came in too late to benefit Knott's administration. Whatever plans for reform the affable governor may have entertained were largely nullified by scarcity of funds, which dogged him during the entire four-year period. Lack of money dampened whatever ardor he may have held for public school improvement. In his first message to the General Assembly, Knott had declared: "We may deprecate the evils of illiteracy, and descant upon the blessings of popular education as much as we will, but we will indulge the Utopian dream of a Golden Age, when every child in the state shall enjoy the benefits of good schools at public expense, a long time before it is realized with the meager pittance of $1.40 per annum, to the pupil, unless something shall be done to supplement it."

The governor had stated, however, that with two or three exceptions Kentucky was devoting a larger portion of its state funds to public education (more than 50 percent) than any other state in the Union. Two years later, Knott had reached the conclusion that the state had arrived at the limit of its ability to support the common schools from state revenues. He expressed the belief that if the system was to advance, it would have to do so through the support of some other financial expedient, such as other states had resorted to. He even hinted indirectly that the federal government might be able to supply the need, but failed to elaborate upon the suggestion.[17]

In the fall of 1884 metropolitan papers reported a pitiful tragedy in one of the contract convict labor camps. Superintendent W. B. Comer and Warden R. S. Perkins of the Comer Camp near Lexington were charged with the murder of two convicts. Evidence indicated that prisoners under their supervision were cowed from brutal treatment, that "sick men" were "whipped, beaten and kicked to death because physically unable to work." It indicated that John O'Brien, a sick prisoner unable to work, was handcuffed by Comer, whipped, knocked down and left in the broiling sun. A half hour later, according to reports, the luckless man was finally kicked into insensibility by the brutal Comer. The examining doctor testified that O'Brien's death was caused by beating and kicking. Further testimony revealed that the convicts in that camp were forced to work "from daylight till dark, without being permitted to sit down even for dinner"; that they were fed on fat meat and bread, receiving coffee only once a day; that at least four or five men in the camp were whipped each day. Testimony further indicated that the strap used was an instrument of extreme torture, being fourteen inches long, and the leather as "hard as wood."[18]

Finally under urging of the governor and public agitation caused by the abuses in the contract system, the General Assembly did act. Legislators introduced measures designed to prevent the hiring of convicts for labor outside the prison walls and passed an elaborate bill providing for the purchase of a suitable site at Eddyville for the Branch Penitentiary and an appropriation of $100,000 made for construction. The bill also provided for the appointment of commissioners with full authority to act, not only in matters pertaining to construction, but also in governing, treatment, sanitation, and religious and manual instruction.[19] With completion of the Branch Penitentiary, which was designed to be a reformatory for first offenders under thirty years of age, the prison situation improved somewhat, though the system was by no means a model.

To Governor Knott's administration must also be credited both the comprehensive public school law (though common school-minded laymen took the initiative) and the minute revenue bill, reforming assessment and collection. To it also goes credit for establishing monthly payments of teachers, continuation of the all-important Geological Survey, and establishment of a state normal school for Negroes at Frankfort.

Blaine-Cleveland Race

Kentucky Democratic leaders, sensing favorable possibilities of capturing the presidency in 1884, after a continuous "dry spell" since 1861, spurred themselves to unusual activity in the state. At the same time, the Republicans, perhaps fearful of losing federal patronage, put forth tremendous efforts to keep the Democratic majority at a minimum in the state. Throughout it was a campaign of abuse, villification, and slander, with Watterson of the *Courier-Journal* and Kelly of the *Commercial* issuing material designed for local editors, campaign "spellbinders," and the voting public.

Watterson, though well acquainted personally with James Gillespie Blaine, the Republican standard-bearer—and apparently fond of him—truculently assailed the candidate's character, particularly stressing the sensational "Mulligan Letters." "Marse Henry" declared that Blaine's guilt was so plain and damaging that "only a 'magnetic' statesman would dare ask the continued support even of a party so steeped in iniquity and so desperate as is the Republican organization. . . ." He continued by saying that "the Republican Party can afford to be defeated, but no party can afford to win with such a candidate." Watterson would usually follow these personal blasts with attacks on the "monstrous" Republican tariffs, leveling off with sweet phrases in behalf of his "Star-eyed Goddess" (tariff and revenue reform). So bellicose was Watterson against the protective tariff that the editor of the New York *World* (a Democratic paper) took sharp issue, branding him a "free trader."

In declaring that Blaine's was "as clear and unmistakable a record of crime perpetrated against the people as that which has made Burr infamous," Watterson reached a rather low level of abuse. He even pictured Blaine as a leading figure in a mining syndicate engaged in "starving miners and importing pauper laborers to take their places."[20]

Giant rallies, torch-light parades, and barbeques composed the highly sensational campaign. The Democracy staged a huge rally in Louisville at Liederkranz Hall, September 17, with Edward J. McDermott, Ben F. Robbins, and J. C. S. Blackburn, United States Senator elect, as principal speakers for the occasion. McDermott, a rising young lawyer, stated the issues as tariff reform, reduction of taxes, and making American commerce "as free as the air." He could not refrain from expressing "fear" of the "danger" of national degradation should a man "smirched as

Blaine is be elected to the highest office in the land." On the other hand, Grover Cleveland, the Democratic standard-bearer, he insisted, was comparable to Washington, Jefferson, and Jackson.

Robbins was introduced following McDermott's speech. He spoke at some length upon the "evils of Republicanism," stressing that the Republicans were undermining the American way of government. Robbins reiterated the Blaine scandals and depicted Cleveland as a statesman upon whose "private and public life" there was "no stain." He charged that the Republican tariff was robbing the laboring man to put money into the pockets of bloated plutocrats.

Jo Blackburn, the "real orator" of the occasion, opened his speech by remarking that the "Republican record and party should be in the criminal docket." He castigated the Republican party for "its sins" during the dark days of war and reconstruction. Artfully introducing his speech with a reproach upon those who would "dig up skeletons," he devoted a good part of his time to playing upon passions and hatreds engendered by the war and brought all his dramatic powers into action in describing the horrors of Reconstruction. He was prepared to defend the Confederate cause too. Of that cause and the punishment meted out to Kentucky Congressmen-elect in 1867, he said:

> And the loyal State of Kentucky that had never seceded from the Union, but who, thank God, amid all her loyalty, grew 47,000 of the finest disloyal sons upon whom the sun of God has ever fallen—the people of Kentucky sent their delegates there [to Washington] composed of men of spotless character, admitted ability, unquestioned patriotism and loyalty. They, too, were exiled from the council of your country. For nearly one year the Kentucky delegation wandered as outcasts about the streets of the capital of your country, and this grand old Commonwealth was voiceless by reason of Republican Expatriation.

The crowd responded uproariously.[21]

On the Republican side, Robert Kelly, of the *Commercial*, undertook to defend the protective tariff. He wrote that no class of American citizens profited more by its beneficences than the farmers, all of whose products were fully protected against foreign competition and 92 percent of whose products were consumed at home. He tried to defend Blaine by saying that the "Plumed Knight" had requested the newspapers of the nation to run the Mulligan Letters, stating that there was not a word in the letters which was not entirely consistent with the most scrupulous integrity and honor.

During the campaign, the Republican press freely circulated the story that Grover Cleveland had an illegitimate child by one Maria Halpin. This story was given wide currency throughout the nation. Cleveland's only comment had been, "Tell the truth," which forthrightness greatly heartened some of the editors, including Watterson, who saw manliness and nobility in it. In order to help Cleveland, certain papers began casting aspersions on the legitimacy of Blaine's marriage to Harriett B. Stanwood, and the good names of Mrs. Blaine and her children were dragged through the mire. Kelly declared that "the attack upon Mr. Blaine's family, upon his wife, and upon the sanctity of his home," was a disgrace to American politics.[22]

Never was there a time in Kentucky when orators were in grater demand than during the 1884 campaign. The speaker most in demand was W. C. P. Breckinridge, the "silver-tongued orator" of Lexington. From almost every county in the state, the call came for "Billy." Stoddard Johnston, chairman of the Democratic State Central Committee, urged him to speak in many counties, and Breckinridge tried to oblige. In addition, he took numerous out-of-state engagements. Wherever he went Colonel Breckinridge was lionized.[23]

The Kentucky Republicans held their grand rally at Liederkranz Hall in Louisville on the evening of October 18, with the old "war horse," Judge W. C. Goodloe, as principal speaker. It was a rousing partisan speech, which greatly pleased the vast audience. After fulsome praise of the Republican record, Goodloe went into the public record of the "Hangman of Buffalo," weighed it on Republican scales and found it sadly wanting, to the audible satisfaction of the crowd. He ridiculed the Democratic platform, accepting the *Cincinnati Weekly Times'* pronouncement that it "should have been slashed freely with a hatchet at both ends and in the middle," that it was "a mass of ambiguities." The popular orator "hit the road home" on the trail of Republican protection, and the concourse broke up in wild enthusiasm.[24]

The propitious omens of the August 4 election, which had carried a Republican, William Henry Holt of Mt. Sterling, to the Appellate Court, caused the "log cabin" followers to feel optimistic about the November election. As a matter of fact, they did quite well in the state. Cleveland carried it with 152,961 votes. Blaine received 118,122, while the Greenback candidate, Ben F. Butler, received 1,691 and the Prohibition candidate, John P. St. John, 3,139. In the congressional races, the Democrats elected ten candidates to one (in the Ninth) for the Republicans.

The following year, 1885, a state election was held on August 3 to choose a state treasurer. As usual, perennial office-holder "Honest Dick" Tate won overwhelmingly. He received 106,762 to 30,428 for his opponent. That year also, members of the state General Assembly were selected. Twenty-four Democrats and four Republicans were elected to the senate; eighty Democrats and twenty Republicans, to the house.[25] As usual the constitutional convention failed of passage, even though both parties again had endorsed it. So exasperated were the progressive editors of the *Covington Commonwealth*, the *Courier-Journal*, and the *Paducah News* that they advocated calling the convention without following the constitutional mandate.

The general election of August 2, 1886, failed to create much public interest. County officials were elected, as well as one Appellate Court judge, Caswell Bennett of Smithland, who was named from the First District without opposition. On November 2, Congressmen were chosen. Rather remarkable, as well as reflecting some restiveness on the part of the voters, was the fact that the Republicans returned three of the eleven.[26] Dissatisfaction with the Cleveland administration was a factor.

The Gubernatorial Election of 1887

The state Democratic convention of 1887 met at Liederkranz Hall in Louisville, May 4. The assembling of the delegates was given elaborate play by Henry Watterson in the *Courier-Journal*. The dazzling headlines read:

DEMOCRACY, THE HOST OF THE UNTERRIFIED, TAKES POSSESSION OF THE CITY. THE FINEST LOOK- ING BODY OF MEN EVER ASSEMBLED IN A CONVEN- TION, WITH LOYAL HEARTS AND EARNEST PURPOSE, THEY COME A POWERFUL HOST.

At the convention, it was a foregone conclusion that the pro- southern and perennial Bourbon officials—Hardin, Hewitt, Tate, and Pickett[27]—would be renominated, in spite of rather notable dissatisfaction over the state with the "Confederate Dynasty." Just as certain was it, too, that ex-Confederate General Simon Bolivar Buckner would head the ticket. Such was the talk of the party leaders around the bar of the still fashionable Louisville Hotel, Buckner headquarters, as the delegates slaked their thirst on good Kentucky bourbon. The money question was already giving the party potentates some worry, particularly western Kentucky Democrats. The farmers of their section, suffering from low prices and scarcity of money, were beginning to clamor once more for cheap money—free silver. However, the "sound money" men, in control of the party, were able to organize the convention. The convention was presided over by John G. Carlisle, sound money apostle and close personal friend of Watterson and Breckinridge, as well as Grover Cleveland.

The nominations went as expected, from Buckner on down. A good part of the convention's time thereafter was consumed by the diurnal "servants of the people," who expressed their gratitude to the delegates in florid and gallant rhetoric. Each promised to be even greater "statesman" and champion of the "peepulls' interest" than in the past. "Honest Dick" Tate, already having served as treasurer for sixteen years, indicated his intention of carrying on in the same faithful, honest manner as before, while that prince of electioneers and good fellows, P. "Wat" ("Polly Wolly") Hardin, regaled the delegates with mellifluous praise of the "gret" record of the Democracy.

The platform supported the Cleveland administration, civil service reform, "honest" money (meaning gold or money as good as gold), Irish "home rule," state's rights under the Constitution, tariff reform, betterment of labor's position; and it opposed importation of contract labor and child labor in mines and factories, as well as unfair competition of convict with free labor. It declared for development of natural resources, and economy in government; it also endorsed the administration of Proctor Knott, but said nothing about public education. Apparently the design of the platform makers was to stay away from state matters, especially fiscal, as far as possible. However, they probably had a suspicion that voters, at long last, were beginning to doubt the wisdom of keeping men in office for a generation simply because they had "worn the grey." For the first time some Democratic voters were showing some reluctance. Moreover, Cleveland and his policies were not popular with the "rank and file" of Kentuckians, and times were hard.[28]

The Republican convention assembled in the Masonic Temple at Louisville, May 11, with Curtis Field Burnam of Richmond as temporary chairman and Judge Thomas Z. Morrow as permanent chairman. While more militant than the Democrats, the Republicans in convention faced a similar dilemma: if they favored the policies of the national Republican administrations, a majority of the Kentucky electorate would be displeased; if they opposed those policies, they would lose national Republican patronage—a thing most distasteful. At the outset Judge Morrow stated that the

Governor Simon B. Buckner

Collection of the Kentucky Historical Society

members of the Republican party "have been ostracized, oppressed, downtrodden, socially and politically" in Kentucky, because of their political beliefs, and that "the Democrats have so districted the state that they thought they could win everywhere."

In like mood, John W. Yerkes of Danville, in presenting Colonel Bradley for the gubernatorial nomination, delcared, "To be a member of the Republican Party has ostracized men in this state." He said that Kentucky needed reform and spoke of the school system as being "as bad as it can be." The convention nominated "Billy O. B.," as Bradley was affectionately called, by acclamation with a great shout; then it selected a none too impressive ticket to go along with him.

The Republican platform called for "examination of the state's financial books," which "for nearly twenty years have been virtually sealed," condemned the wastage of the state's money, inveighed against convict labor in competition with free labor, favored encouragement of immigration to the state; endorsed federal aid for education (the Blair bill), stood for the protective tariff and development of natural resources, favored "home rule" for Ireland, condemned Cleveland's pension vetoes, and called for "justices" to labor.[29]

Bradley's acceptance speech, in striking contrast to that of the soldierly Buckner (affectionately called "Old Bolivar"), was both eloquent and lengthy. Every inch the "Plumed Knight," "Billy O. B." urged free discussion of the issues and pleaded with "Kentuckians to realize that the war is over" and to cease keeping alive the "smoldering embers." Again he reviewed the Democratic record of twenty years, particulary condemning it for failure in public education. He called earnestly for development of natural resources, declaring that, while having greater coal deposits than Pennsylvania, Kentucky bought half her coal from that state. He pointed also to similar conditions with lumber. Then he deplored the failure of the state to develop desirable navigation facilities. More seriously still, Bradley stressed the loss of able young Kentuckians to other states because of lack of opportunity at home. He ended with a clarion call for progress and reform:

The tender grace of a day that is gone will never return; the shadows that have faded into night will come no more. We are here to place upon Kentucky's queenly head the crown of progress and reform. We are here to improve her rivers, develop her minerals, utilize her forests, stimulate her farms, encourage her laborers, educate her children, and enforce her laws, until mountains and valleys shall be dotted with manufactories and happy homes; until her cities rise, and the music of the forge, the saw, the spindle, and the locomotive shall awaken the solitude of every forest and river within her borders.[30]

This speech was more or less his campaign speech—a canvass vigorously waged, with Buckner forensically at a decided disadvantage.

Two protest parties were also in the field: Prohibition, which ran Fontaine Talbot Fox of Bullitt County for governor. and Union Labor, with A. H. Cardin of Crittenden County for governor. Both groups nominated full tickets and waged active campaigns. The fact that a plank in the latter party's platform demanded a law providing for an investigation of all the state offices every ten years seems to indicate that people were thinking of inefficiency, wastefulness, and possible graft in the conduct of state offices.[31] The proposal to call a convention to revise the constitution was up for vote again that year, with all parties supporting the call.

The nature of Bradley's campaign speech readily threw Buckner on the defensive. He relied upon party strength and his own personal prestige. Bradley was able to draw him into only one debate. They met at Grayson. Bradley attacked the Democrats for creating "useless offices," including the Superior Court, the Railroad Commission, and the Bureau of Agriculture. He charged the party with extravagance in building a new penitentiary, rather

Governor W. O. Bradley

Collection of the Kentucky Historical Society

than remodeling the old one. Favoring the Blair bill and federal aid to education, he stressed those issues, then closed by defending Republican tariff policy.

Buckner rose and asked Bradley if he had stated in an earlier speech that Knott had written a speech delivered by Buckner. Bradley answered that he had, for this is what he had been told. The General resumed his talk, saying that for a man who would circulate this falsehood, "I can of course feel nothing but contempt." The "infamously false." charge now caused him, he added, to withdraw his invitation to joint debates. The Democratic candidate then launched an attack on protective tariffs, federal aid and "the privileged class."

Buckner and Bradley never met again in joint debate. Quite naturally Bradley did not discourage the suggestion that Buckner was afraid to meet him again, and perhaps he profited politically by the intimation. The Democratic campaign answered Republican attacks through slogans. Though Buckner's wife's name was not Betty, his followers praised the sixty-four year old general, his wife and their new-born child with the cry, "Hurrah for Bolivar, Betty and the Baby."[32]

As the canvass progressed, it was rather clear that the Democracy was not altogether harmonious. Prominent Democrats, including former congressman Milton J. Durham of Danville and state senator Albert Seaton Berry of Newport had criticized the Democratic state record before the convention and a prominent Democratic newspaper, the Henderson *Gleaner*, editorially had declared: "If the Democratic party in Kentucky can look on the present deformity of state affairs and then sleep well at night, it must have a tough old conscience. We should be ashamed of ourselves."

The Republicans were well united, had selected their ablest, most popular campaigner, and they knew that the people were suffering some misgivings about the efficiency and honesty of perennial Democratic officeholders. Bradley hammered relentlessly in favor of having the treasury examined—and he may have been on more solid ground than he realized. The Prohibition and Union-Labor parties too were calculated to take Democratic votes. One enthusiastic Republican declared that "the Prohibitionists and Knights of Labor vote will reach fifty thousand and at least fifty thousand Democrats who voted for Cleveland and Hendricks in 1884 will stay away from the polls."

Bradley's magnetic personality never showed to greater advantage. Although he lost, he was able to cut the normal Democratic margin of victory from approximately 40,000 to 16,197 votes. He had also the distinction of receiving 126,473 votes, unprecedented for the Republicans. Moreover, he made gains over the previous records of the party in 77 counties.[33]

Buckner received 143,270 votes; Fox 8,394; Cardin 4,434. Bradley ran 3,000 votes ahead of his ticket. Knott's plurality had been 44,434. Many counties formerly Democratic went Republican by small margins. In seven counties General Buckner's margin of victory was less than a hundred votes—eight in Bourbon and four in Todd. In Buckner's home county, Hart, the Democratic margin was small.

One editor who "scanned" these results declared that the Democratic party in Kentucky could become a power for good when it rid itself of "back-number statesmen and barnacles." He continued by stating that "Democrats, as well as Republicans, will watch the four years of Buckner's administration carefully. If it is a failure, the result of the contest in 1891 will pronounce a verdict upon it that can not be mistaken." The editor of the *Carrollton Democrat* wrote: "It did not require any more than ordinary common sense to foresee the result. Everybody ought to have known that it was inexpedient to nominate General Buckner. It might have been known that the many thousand old federal soldiers in Democratic ranks could not and would not vote for a Rebel general; it ought to have been known that the young Democracy, as well as the times, demanded a young and active and progressive man for Governor—which General Buckner is not."

The call for constitutional convention was, after sixteen years of struggle, voted favorably. Another favorable vote, however, was required to fulfill the constitutional mandate. This would be in 1889. The vote had been 162,337 for to 65,956 against.[34]

Buckner's Inauguration

The affable and popular Proctor Knott approached the end of his administration with perhaps as much a feeling of relief as of regret. Throughout the four year term, he had been hampered by shortage of funds. He had enjoyed some success in industrial development. The abuses of the wretched but passing system of convict contract labor had brought upon him much criticism, as had his rather free pardon record. Furthermore, his entire administration had been disturbed by lawlessness and violence, particularly in eastern Kentucky, which in the eyes of the nation gave new meaning to the ancient term "dark and bloody ground." The governor seemingly had been powerless to find a satisfactory solution to the problem, and it was left at incoming Governor Buckner's doorstep. Yet, in spite of transcendent difficulties, by and large the highly intelligent and charming "Old Duluth" may be said to have made a good governor.

Governor Knott's address upon retiring was magnanimous and graceful. It was, as one editor expressed it, "a fitting farewell to occupancy of the Gubernatorial chair that has gratified his constituents, and to a record whose reflection comes to honor the man who gave the people of Kentucky a clean administration, and draws closer to him the admiration of the state's people." Governor Knott's reference to ex-Governor Blackburn (then lying on his deathbed) was eloquent and deeply affecting. Waiving customary review of the achievements of his administration, the gallant Knott simply said: "I have nothing to say of my future conduct 'What is written is written.' My acts, whether important or trivial, have become a part of the inexorable, immutable history of the State." The same editor, who praised Knott, stated that Buckner's inauguration ceremonies were attended by "no great enthusiasm" and declared that the incoming chief magistrate's speech was a "piece of patchwork."[35]

Another prominent editor, commenting upon Knott's record, stated that the governor would carry with him in his retirement "the respect and confidence which his public life, his character, and conduct have always demanded."

At the time of Knott's nomination, Henry Watterson had written:

> *It is a nomination which commends itself alike to the heart and to the judgement of the people. It should mark a new era in the history of the state, an era of progress and of prosperity; an era of activity and enterprise, when Kentucky, imbued with new energies and inspired with new hope, will move forward to new conquests. . . . A man of strict personal integrity, a student and scholar, a statesman of experience and of courage in thought and action, the people of the state will place him in his high office with perfect confidence that what a governor can do, he will do to advance our material interest, to elevate our educational institutions, to amend and improve our political constitution, to maintain the laws and protect the lives and prosperity of the people.*

At the end of Knott's administration, "Marse Henry" wrote

> *What was promised at that time in his behalf, he has fulfilled. Only the most blind and most bigoted can deny the progress of the state during the past four years. On all sides have we seen the signs of activity and enterprise. Our cities have flourished, new roads have been constructed, the products of our mines and forests have been increased, wealth has accumulated, and today in all material matters, Kentucky is going more than at any previous period in her history.*

Though Knott had courteously refrained from "hogging" time belonging to the incoming governor at the inaugural, General Buckner spoke quite briefly, mostly to thank the people for having entrusted him with the high office. Watterson was able to state that the address was "clear, concise, and comprehensive."

Fortunately, the incoming governor enjoyed an interval of four months during which to acquaint himself with legislative needs and procedure. Of studious habits and uncommonly thorough, he set about diligently to learn, enjoying at the same time his mellowed old corncob pipe and his great dane. The sixty-four-year-old executive lately married to a charming Virginia lady of distinction, Delia Claiborne, derived his greatest pleasure out of things domestic—never the crowd, club, excitement, nor public function. Having a philosophical turn of mind, he had been happy enough to live since the war somewhat in semi-retirement, on his estate, "Glen Lily," in a secluded section of Hart County on Green River. There he had sat on the wide, cool veranda overlooking Green River, puffed his pipe, read and memorized Shakespeare, mused and philosophized hour after hour, day after day, apparently contented and happy.[36]

XI

"OLD BOLIVAR'S FIRST VICTORY"

Having little experience in governmental affairs and quite unfamiliar with the maneuvers of politicians and lobbyists, Buckner found his task as governor rather difficult. Political and business leaders did not expect him to be more successful as governor than he had been as military leader. Some doubtless mistook his frankness and sincerity for naiveté and concluded that he would be an "easy mark." His appearance and manner were "homespun," easygoing, and unassuming. On the other hand, many knew that he possessed granite-like honesty and would be determined to give the people an honest administration. That he had resolved at all costs to uphold the law inflexibly was perhaps not generally known by the politicians.

Legislative Meeting of 1887-1888

The first General Assembly of the new administration convened on December 30, 1887. With the election of Ben Johnson, rising lawyer of Bardstown, as speaker of the house, it may be said to have been well begun. Johnson won over the Republican candidate, General Speed S. Fry, of Boyle County, 70 to 28. Buckner's message to the joint houses, while lengthy as customary for the period, reviewed many matters of interest to the state and recommended legislation calculated to improve government, stimulate commerce and ameliorate social conditions.

Thanks to the labors of governors Blackburn and Knott, Buck-

239

ner assumed office with a surplus of $198,000 in the treasury, which was a great boon. However, he suggested some needed improvements in the new revenue law and recommended passage of legislation designed to curtail costs of criminal prosecutions. He recommended also passage of measures to punish local officials for failure to send to the state treasurer money collected in fines, to reduce costs of transporting prisoners, and to prevent exemption of private property from taxation.

The pardoning power, always a source of gubernatorial worry, brought from the chief executive a sensible, honest, and forward-looking statement. Though declaring that a large number of the pleas for clemency were devoid of merit and filled with gross misrepresentations, Buckner stated that an honest executive was obliged to study each minutely, even when being unable to obtain all the facts without great difficulty and expenditure of time. He advised enactment of a law making it the duty of the prosecuting attorney to furnish to the attorney general or the governor (when requested) a full statement of the facts established at the trial.

Railroad abuses perturbed the governor. He recommended equitable assessment of railroad properties, without impairing their efficiency, and increased powers for the railroad commission. He stated that 2,341 miles of roads were in operation in the state by December, 1887 and indicated that 244 miles had been constructed during that year. The total cost of these roads was listed at $76,513,000. Nevertheless, the assessed value of railroad properties was only $35,571,000, which was an increase over the previous assessment of $1,942,000.

Buckner reported that the 1886 gross earnings of the roads reflected an increase of more than 13 percent, with new earnings rising in about the same ratio. He stated that the commissioners had placed a value upon the property of $11,476,000 more than the sum at which the railroads had placed the assessment; pointed out that the difference, at the current rate of taxation, was equivalent to a tax of more than $54,000 in excess of what the roads would have imposed upon themselves. He felt that some equitable way of arriving at the real value of the railroads should be provided, and assessments made accordingly. Moreover, he recommended that the assessment of all railroads and bridges across the Ohio and of all street railways be assigned to the commissioners.

The office of the railroad commission should be in Frankfort, the governor thought, and one of the commissioners should be provided a salary sufficiently large to justify devoting full time to his duties, together with "an intelligent clerk to assist him as deputy." He believed that the commission not only should have power to assess equitably but that it should be enabled to require proper depot facilities, reasonable train service, maintenance of safety, just freight and passenger rates. And he asserted that the state's regulations should be harmonized with the Interstate Commerce Commission's regulations. However, he cautioned against enactment of laws which might be "harassing or injurious to the proper interests of our railways."

Governor Buckner reported at some length upon educational progress on the state level. Borrowing from Pickett's report, he listed the school population of the current year at 549,592 white and 107,144 black children. The apportionment of the school fund for white schools was listed at $1,044,224.80—an increase of $154,925.95 over the previous year—with $203,573.60 for Negro schools, an increase of $33,892.55. The per capita was $1.90. Regretting the failure of local districts to devote sufficient funds to aid in developing a satisfactory system of common schools, the governor expressed the belief that Kentucky's direct appropriations for school purposes ($1,247,798.40) was "greater than that of any other state, with one or two exceptions." He, like governors preceding him, was convinced that adequate financial assumption on the part of local districts was essential to a good system. He reported completion of the building at Frankfort for the Negro normal school.[1]

The James W. ("Honest Dick") Tate Defalcation Episode

So vehemently had Bradley demanded that the state treasurer's books be quickly and effectively examined and the findings publicized that a general sentiment crystalized. Many of the lawmakers urged passage of legislation early in the 1887-88 session for appointment of a commission to examine the books. However, Tate, long in office and trusted implicitly, was able to delay passage of the resolution for some weeks, giving as an excuse the need for time in which to get his books in order. Notwithstanding, one young legislator pressed the matter so perseveringly that the lawmakers finally acquiesced in a resolution for appointment of the commission to examine the books of the auditor and treasurer.

On March 20, 1888, the governor dispatched a message to the General Assembly announcing suspension of "Honest Dick" Tate. It was soon revealed that the treasurer had been missing from the capital for several days and that a shortage had been discovered in the treasury. "Such a flash of lightning, and a peal of thunder," wrote one authority, "as was never before seen or heard came out of a clear sky, and rocked the state as nothing had done since the war."

All sorts of wild rumors spread rapidly, and the legislature itself grew panicky. "The atmosphere about Frankfort," wrote Professor Stickles, "was such that almost everyone was under suspicion either as an accomplice of Tate or because of owing the treasury money, and those who had borrowed money from the treasury were numerous."[2] Fayette Hewitt, perennial office-holder and auditor, whose duty it was to examine the accounts of the state, came in for bitter censure for neglect of duty. However, no evidence of dishonesty on his part could be found. Hewitt, of course, shared the public's implicit faith in Tate's integrity and regarded his accounting as not needing examination. Tate, in office since 1868, having been re-elected regularly every two years by overwhelming votes, was immensely popular. A man with a genial, affable disposition, generous, kind, and always ready to accommodate, he had been affectionately given the title "Honest Dick" by a people confident of his moral strength.

Upon due consideration, Frankfort residents recalled that "Honest Dick's" family, though small, was extremely expensive and that a pretentious son-in-law, well established as a "scapegrace," mountebank, and swindler, had always seemed to have plenty of money. Moreover, friends and fellow officers appeared always able to obtain money from Tate simply by giving personal notes, or "I. O. U's."

As to recent happenings, Henry W. Murdock, a clerk in the auditor's office, stated that he had seen Tate on March 14 (the last day anyone had seen him in Frankfort) in the treasurer's office with a large roll of bills, and a coin purse which he pocketed, and that he detected in the treasurer's possession two tobacco sacks filled with gold and silver coin. Tate, it seems, had said something to Murdock about going to Louisville the following day. The auditor testified to having received a letter from Tate, written in Louisville March 15, stating that he would return to Frankfort the next day. "Honest Dick," failing to return, was impeached on four counts and expelled from office.

The legislative commissioners, John F. Hager and Ben C. Weaver, though working diligently, could not, because of the chaotic condition of the treasurer's records, quickly report the extent of Tate's defalcation, although they had, with little difficulty, established the peculations as having begun as early as 1872. They issued the statement, after a few days, that the embezzlement by 1882 amounted to $175,000. On April 21, Buckner reported to the legislature his belief that the entire defalcation would eventually be met by the sureties.

Tate's bond to the state was in the amount of $300,000 and his bondsmen included J. Stoddard Johnston, and others whose aggregate fortunes were estimated at $1,000,000. It was believed that other bondsmen, sureties in earlier years, could be added also. Tate's property was worth $50,000. Moreover, persons owing Tate (or the Treasury) were eager to pay. Meanwhile, Tate having been expelled, Buckner appointed Stephen G. Sharp, Lexington, to be state treasurer, and the General Assembly authorized $5,000 for the apprehension of the absconding Tate.[3]

Although it is difficult to deduct from the commissioners' tedious report the extent of the defalcations, it is possible to arrive at the conclusion that the total larceny reached $247,000. It was revealed that Tate had even befriended Governor Leslie with an advance of $5,000 on a personal note, dated July 18, 1872. There seemed to be no distinction in his operations between public and private funds. In the treasury vault were found purses, beaded bags and other family effects. A little satchel purse, containing pieces of silver and gold, which had belonged to a deceased child, was discovered along with objects belonging to the state.

On the other hand, certain operations of Tate clearly branded him as an embezzler and swindler. He had gambled heavily in stocks, many of which were in the nature of "wildcat" ventures. Apparently these had been purchased with state funds. Moreover, on leaving, Tate had carried away a satchel filled with the commonwealth's money. He escaped, possibly to foreign soil, and apparently was never again seen by a Kentuckian. Incidentally, as might be well imagined, with feeling soaring wildly (and the excitable and voluble lawmakers in session) Tate's family was not treated very kindly.[4]

In June criminal proceedings against Tate began in Franklin County, where he was indicted on several counts of embezzlement. Meanwhile, the legislature, to guard against another such episode, created the office of state inspector and examiner. The inspector was to be appointed by and removable by the governor, and he was required to examine annually the management of the auditor's and treasurer's office, as well as all public institutions and all other officers entrusted with property of the state. The inspector was also required to be present at each monthly settlement between the auditor and the treasurer, and to report his findings to the governor.

Greatly reducing the total money reported stolen were due bills and other evidences of indebtedness, to the amount of $59,782.80. After interminable battling in the courts, the Appellate court held, in 1895, that the bondsmen were not liable, the opinion against the Commonwealth having been handed down by the Chief Justice, William S. Pryor. However, the state ultimately lost no more than $40,000.

The episode had been like a nightmare. Seemingly nothing that ever happened in Kentucky caused wilder excitement and sensation. Almost overnight the people of the state seemed to suspect and distrust state officials and clamored for circumscription of their powers. Apparently too it began to be thought by some that the legislative sessions, as often as not, had been in recent years little better than nuisances and a drain on the state's finances. The Tate defalcation incident unfortunately affected even the philosophy and language of the state constitution of 1891.[5] Had it not been for "Old Bolivar's" firm and calm leadership, the possibility of violence would have been much greater.[6]

Legislative Achievements, 1887-88

The initial experience of Governor Buckner with the state's lawmakers was indeed not a pleasant one. The sturdy governor had repeatedly urged them to enact needed laws with dispatch; begged them to eschew special private legislation and to adjourn in February. He enjoyed no such good fortune. The session finally adjourned on May 4, 1888. No fewer than 1,571 acts and 86 resolutions, covering 3,400 printed pages, were passed, of which only 168 acts, covering 216 pages, were of a general nature.

The lengthy session was more than a "do-nothing" legislature, however. After electing Beck senator over Bradley by a 94-31 margin, the lawmakers turned to other tasks. They enacted a provision for a second vote (August 1889) on the proposed constitutional convention. The General Assembly recodified the school laws, revised the revenue laws, and continued the Geological Survey for another two years. They appropriated $150,000 for the completion of Eddyville penitentiary—which would accommodate over 400 prisoners—and launched a system for paroling prisoners. Agricultural experiment stations, a state board of pharmacy and a provision for fire escapes in large city buildings over three stories were all established.

Governor Buckner incurred the ill-will of the lawmakers by his numerous (60) vetoes of private bills, designed all too frequently to help some person or persons at the expense of the state. After a few weeks of these vetoes, the friends of Buckner could say, as was said of Grover Cleveland, in connection with his vetoes, "We love him for the enemies he has made." Henry Watterson, who had been courageously exposing legislative abuses for years, was delighted with the doughty old warrior. "The Governor of Kentucky," he declared, "has by use of his veto power rendered an inestimable service to the state. Clear in his conceptions of duty," the editor continued, "firm in his convictions, insisting on a strict interpretation of the law and rigid obedience to its requirements, he has awakened throughout the state a new regard for Democratic principles and a new respect for its authority of government. The direct and indirect influence of his messages is very great," Watterson averred. "It will result in official recognition of the forms of law and it will inspire the people with greater confidence in its authority."[7]

Robert Kelly, editor of the *Commercial*, the state's leading Republican newspaper, was in accord with Watterson. "A few hard-working members," he wrote, "have made reputations during the present session of the legislature, but the only person who can truly be said to have strengthened himself with the people is Governor Buckner. . . . The *Commercial* opposed him [for governor]," continued the editorial, "because he was simply a piece of debris caught in a flood of war sentiments and swept into a nomination that he could never have secured under Heaven had he not been an ex-Confederate soldier. . . . It was under these adverse conditions," declared the editor, "that Buckner assumed the Gubernatorial chair. His appointments were submitted to close scrutiny. . . . His real work did not begin until the Legislature convened. His message was a thoughtful, wise, and earnest document, and its publication gave the people assurance that he would do his duty whatever course the General Assembly might choose to take. . . . Not the smallest matter has escaped his vigilant and critical eye."

The lawmakers soon learned that every measure passed would be subjected to a "Gubernatorial gauntlet, unsurpassed in the history of the State in point of technical and testy faultfinding. Bills of high and low degree," declared Kelly, "railroad bills, local option bills, bills creating eye-doctors, and bills for the regulation of cities, of towns, or of counties were measured upon the Governor's Procrustean bed, and were ruthlessly broken off at both ends to fit the brief, narrow and downless couch. It sprinkled vetoes. It rained vetoes. It fairly poured vetoes."

Rather interesting it is to note the reaction of the special interests. "Legislators growled," the *Commercial*'s editor declared. "Incorporators kicked. Lobbyists got out their black-list books and printed the Governor's name in red letters. But all to no purpose. He continued to send to both Houses 'a communication in writing' and at every stroke of the pen a bill tumbled into the waste basket."

Doubtless, not only the governor but the people generally— those who comprehended the situation—breathed a sigh of relief when the "legislative statesmen" at long last evacuated Frankfort. "All things come to him who waits," wrote the relieved Watterson. "Even the Kentucky Legislature, after waiting 127 days, at $1000 per day, came to a *sine die* adjournment yesterday at 1:00 o'clock. There have been worse Legislatures than the late lamented," declared the truculent editor. "The members of the House meant well, but didn't seem to know how to 'get there.' Every man was his own leader, and some strayed in peculiar paths. . . . Even the Republicans broke up in factions. . . . The Senate was a strong, conservative body far superior to the House. . . . In witnessing the return of the members to their homes, we trust that each may receive his just deserts from his constituents and that those who should never have been sent to Frankfort in the beginning may never be returned."

It is clear that the solons had not gained votes for the Democracy. Nor had the Tate defalcations strengthened the moribund "Bourbon Dynasty." In addition, Cleveland was not popular in the state. The result was, as one observer put it, "The defection to the party is said to be considerable. . . . A number of Democrats are going to vote the Republican ticket."[8] Offsetting the trend was the fact that Buckner had gained the confidence of the people generally. Except for this fact, the Kentucky Democracy might have fared badly in the national and state elections of 1888.

Elections of 1888 and 1889

As the 1888 canvass for the presidency developed, observers noted considerable apathy. There was little interest in the congressional races. Logically, this should not have been true, because economic conditions generally in the nation were not encouraging, and the incumbents were not in great favor. It seems that voters would have adopted the formula, "kick the rascals out." However, the people, satisfied with neither party, perhaps could not warm up to any of the old nostrums. Watterson had sought assiduously to persuade the Democrats to nominate someone other than Cleveland (with whom he had personally "fallen out") at the 1888 national convention. He disagreed with Cleveland's civil service reform measure and was fearful that the President was pulling away from his former stand for "tariff for revenue." For his part, Cleveland was quite bitter against "Marse Henry." Tariff reform was Watterson's "cloud by day and pillow of fire by night." To his mind it was the most important question on the political horizon.[9]

Under the circumstances, the state's Democrats in 1888 did far better than might have been expected, although John G. Carlisle, one of the ablest men in the party, barely squeezed through for

248

reelection to Congress from the northern Kentucky district. And Carlisle was Speaker of the House in Congress. Kentucky again went Democratic, with approximately 175,113 votes for Cleveland and 148,716 for Harrison. A total of 323,829 votes was cast. The Republican gain in votes (1888 over 1884) was approximately 1,000 as compared with 22,000 for the Democrats.

Generally speaking, eastern Kentucky voted Republican, while the western and central sections went Democratic. There were some exceptions. The Democrats elected nine congressmen; the Republicans, two. The county elections had been held on August 6; no general state elections were necessary. Judge Pryor was returned to the Appellate Court without opposition.[10]

Although only one state officer, the treasurer, was to be elected in 1889, both parties held state nominating conventions and adopted platforms. The Democratic convention, meeting in Louisville on May 9, nominated the incumbent treasurer, Stephen G. Sharp, and adopted a platform designed to appeal to the workingman. This platform gave an indication that a third group—neither Bourbon nor New Departure—was now rising. A resolution declared that the laborer should be "protected against the oppressions of combinations and monopolies." In that interest, it called for passage of "such laws as will guarantee to working-men the most favorable conditions for their labor in the way of proper ventilation and other safeguards for life and health in mines, factories, and railroads, and the sure and prompt payment of wages, and also laws as will facilitate the collection and dissemination of information relating to the interest of labor." The platform endorsed impartial arbitration between employer and employee. The fact that the erstwhile agrarian-minded Kentucky Democratic leaders saw fit to make a decided "play" for the labor vote certainly reveals a changing policy.

The Republican convention assembled in Louisville on May 22, and nominated John G. Barrett (Greensburg and Louisville), prominent lawyer and banker, for treasurer. Barrett subsequently announced inability to accept and a second convention, held in

Lexington, nominated David G. Colson of Bell County. The Louisville convention adopted a platform bristling with condemnation of Democratic rule in the state for the past twenty years, quite naturally referring to the Tate defalcations in none too gentle a manner. It indicted the Democratic party for (1) squandering public funds and increasing taxes and (2) for failing to provide an adequate system of public education; and it again favored federal aid for public education (under the Blair Bill), as well as the calling of a constitutional convention.

The return indicated Sharp to be the winner. In the legislative races, the Democrats elected 31 senators to 7 for the Republicans, and 86 representatives, as compared to 14 Republicans. Again the constitutional convention call passed, this time with 31,931 votes in excess of the requirements. The convention therefore would start its work in 1890.[11]

General Assembly's 1889-90 Session

Events both exciting and important occurred during the last biennial legislative session of Buckner's administration. The Assembly, sprinkled with a few able, earnest men, convened December 30 in the house of representatives chamber at what is now known as the Old State House. So small is the chamber that it is difficult to understand how 100 representatives ever crowded into it, particularly when the avoirdupois and heavy attire are considered. Thinking of the excessive smoking (particularly of cigars), the prodigious chewing, the well-filled and ancient cuspidors, the frequent resort to stimulating bourbon by some of the "statesmen," the neglected opportunities for ventilation, the "air" constantly issuing from the raucous throats of some of the marathon "orators," one is tempted to believe that the scene would require the equivalent of Dickens to describe it properly.

On the first ballot, Harvey Myers, Covington, was elected speaker, receiving 81 votes, while Republican John W. Langley, representing Johnson and Floyd counties, garnered only 15. Again the governor submitted to the lawmakers for consideration a lengthy but able and statesmanlike message.

The initial paragraphs of the governor's report were devoted to a somewhat detailed report of the government's financial condition. The treasury had a balance of $73,000 as of June 30, 1889. The chief executive again called attention to the fact that nearly 58 percent of the state's entire revenue was devoted to "educational and other specific purposes" and that only 40 percent could be applied to governmental expenses; the general expenses of the state were defrayed on a tax of 20 cents on every $100 of assessed property valuation. Calling attention to the fact that property in the state amounting to $227,000,000 in value was exempt from taxation because of faulty law, Buckner urged the legislators to pass remedial measures, pointing out that proper action would not only help the state financially but provide relief to burdened taxpayers as well. Incidentally, the 1889 property assessment for taxation was nearly a half-billion dollars, one-fifth of which was in the city of Louisville. Needless to state, the governor's request was not gratified.

An interesting feature of the session was the election of a U. S. Senator. The leading candidate was J. C. S. Blackburn, who was seeking reelection. He had been one of the most persistent, as well as successful, ex-Confederate office seekers. Blackburn, familiarly called "Jo," was a bold, aggressive, and at times attractive fellow, a good "mixer" and hand-shaker. He had made a name for himself partly through his eloquence. He had "waved the bloody shirt" vigorously for more than a decade and had been a good Democrat. The Democracy owned him another term, he contended. The joint session unanimously reelected him on January 3, 1890.

More sensational than Blackburn's reelection was the election of John G. Carlisle to the United States Senate. This election was occasioned by the sudden death of James B. Beck. Scarcely had Beck been placed in his coffin before moves were afoot to name his successor. Partisans of Proctor Knott, William Lindsay, Laban T. Moore, of Louisa, James B. McCreary, Evan Evans Settle of

Owenton and the Republican, Silas Adams of Liberty, worked ceaselessly for the suffrage of the legislators. Carlisle was nominated in a scintillating speech studded with oratorical flourishes by the Irish wit and poet, Judge James H. Mulligan of Lexington. The Covington congressman, though bitterly opposed by Greenbackers, Populists, and Farmers Alliance men, won out on the ninth ballot; he took his senatorial seat shortly thereafter.[12]

Although the legislature, convening December 30, 1889, remained in session until May 27, 1890, as usual few bills of importance were enacted into law. Critics pointed out that, of the 1,900 measures passed, fewer than 100 were of a general public nature, and most of these of no great purport. Legislators spent a good part of their time in passing acts anticipating the constitutional convention, which was to assemble in Frankfort on the second Tuesday in September, 1890. Election of delegates, 100 in all, was to occur in the regular August voting.

Perhaps the worst bill introduced was that providing for reduction of the tax from 47½ to 42½ cents on the $100 of property. The governor, foreseeing a deficit should the measure pass, vigorously fought it. In a long message, he pointed out that the lawmakers had already made appropriations in excess of the probable income if the bill became law. "The people desire low taxation," he declared, "but they do not wish it at the cost of public dishonor." Many of the state's leading editors supported Buckner's view. However, demagogic men in both houses, perhaps thinking to make political capital back home, had pressed the reduction measure through. The governor promptly vetoed it. The bill was just as promptly passed overwhelmingly over his veto, and soon the state was in financial difficulties.

Many times during the long session Buckner had urged the lawmakers to get down to business and enact much-needed legislation. The warnings, however, went unheeded, and the solons continued to pass "special legislation" to please certain influential personages back in their counties, and "Old Bolivar's veto axe" fell heavily and fast (over fifty vetoes), much to the disgust of the

Senator J.C.S. Blackburn

Courtesy of The Filson Club, Louisville

Senator John G. Carlisle

Collection of the Kentucky Historical Society

"statesmen." Passage of the tax reduction act was the last straw. On the last day of the session, the embattled old soldier sent a "stinging" rebuke to both houses. He not only upbraided the lawmakers for passage of the unwise measure but also taunted them with the fact that "many other public interests are left unsettled." It was not his custom to mince words. "If I do not convene the General Assembly in extra session," he declared, "it is because suggestions which have not been considered during a prolonged session now about to cease would not be likely to receive attention if you were reconvened." The governor might have, had he chosen, derived some grim satisfaction from the reflection that the members of that session were not the worst in the state's history.[13]

As Buckner had predicted, there was a deficit by June 30 of that year, 1890. During the fiscal year 1890-91, money in amount of $229,000 had to be borrowed through warrants issued by the auditor, which meant a loss to the state. The chief magistrate, in order to give the treasury sufficient funds immediately needed, reportedly advanced perhaps as much as $75,000 from his own private fortune.

Strangely enough Henry Watterson, usually of the opinion that "nothing in its life so becomes it [the legislature] as the leaving of it," was inclined to defend the session of 1889-90. While admitting that it had done many things it should not have done and left undone many that it should have done, he stated that in the main it had devoted its time to the public interest, declaring that it had been charged less frequently with "improper influences and sacrifice of public to private demands than is usual in the history of such bodies." He expressed the opinion that overwhelming demands from people back home for "special legislation" and great expectations generally of legislative achievement worked against the harassed solons. Many citizens, he averred, confidently looked to the lawmakers "to remedy every wrong." He said that it was astounding "in the face of almost uninterrupted failure of legislation, that there should be a growing faith in its "powers and efficacy." Watterson declared that "we throw upon these bodies entirely too much work and enlarge the scope of their powers, with the inevitable result that none of the work is done as well as it should be done." Deploring the lack of leadership generally in Kentucky legislatures, he expressed the opinion that Kentucky's form of government was not divised to do "everything for the people," that if state socialism was the desideratum, if the state was expected to "usurp the functions of the citizens," then a new form of government should be devised. However, he did not believe that the form of government should be changed.[14]

Inclined to support Governor Buckner's position, the editor of the *Commercial* took an opposite view from Watterson. Republican Kelly thought the 1889-90 legislature a very poor one indeed. Describing the end of that session, he wrote: "A desperate double suicide occurred today [May 27] at noon. Death was nearly instantaneous in both cases, but, while the dying were in the death throes, Governor Buckner simultaneously preached the funeral of both. His last sermon," continued the sarcastic editor, "over the helpless and speechless bodies was without a word of praise, and dwelt only on their misdeeds." Though admitting that some important business had been transacted and that many able men were members of the body, the Louisville journalist, like Watterson, deplored the fact that leadership had not been concentrated any place and that no one seemed to take the initiative in legislative work.

The editor then launched into a discussion which seems meritorious. "As far as our State Legislature is concerned," he declared, "there is never any discussion before the people of the measures to come before the members when they assemble. Every member has some local bills he intends to put through, but not one in a dozen has given the least attention to the subject of general legislation, and not one in twenty has thought of any general scheme of work for the whole session. Subjects are acted upon," he stated, "according to the vigor and ability of the committee to which they are assigned, and measures get precedence and are acted on without regard to their relative importance."

Taking up another phase of the subject, Kelly argued that existence of a "jealousy of executive power, which is a survival from the time when executives claiming power from a higher source than popular power were dangerous, has made the Governors under our State Constitutions little more than figureheads, except in this matter of recommending measures for the consideration of the Legislature." He expressed the belief that if this power was "rightly used" able governors could make themselves "most useful to the State." He declared that "had Governor Buckner, with the aid of other state officials, worked out a program, he might have presented needed legislation to the Assembly, without interfering with legislative freedom, with fair promise of the program's being enacted ... now half the session is actually gone before general measures can be got in form, or the members know enough to shape and handle them. It would," the editor thought, "add to the dignity and efficiency of state politics if the Governor's measures should be advocated and opposed as administration measures."[15] Both editors had stressed as key points in their criticism both the lack of legislative leadership and the limited power of the governor. They looked to the constitutional convention to remedy these shortcomings.

XII

THE CONSTITUTIONAL
CONVENTION, 1890-1891

As early as December 7, 1867, Governor Stevenson had recommended in a message to the General Assembly that the question of calling a constitutional convention to revise the 1849 basic charter be submitted to the people for a vote. Obviously the old proslavery document, now that slavery had been abolished in the nation by the Thirteenth Amendment, was not only out of date but in violation of the federal Constitution. Furthermore, such matters as curbing special legislation and revising the judicial system were felt by many to necessitate the calling of a convention.

John M. Harlan and the Republican platform had supported the convention call in 1871, and in 1873 the General Assembly had drafted a bill to "take the sense of the people on calling a convention to revise the constitution." The question was before the people in the August election of 1874. The majority of those eligible to vote, required by the constitution, was not obtained. Following this test, the two major parties gave the call continuous endorsement at their quadrennial state nominating conventions until the vote was concluded in 1889. Besides the public's general lack of interest, as well as the general reluctance to most any change, and a well-nigh morbid fear of innovation and radicalism, together with almost fanatical dread by influential property owners that taxes might be raised, the 1849 constitution itself made the calling of a convention extremely difficult. It required that a convention call would have to obtain favorable vote of a majority of those entitled to vote for state representatives at two separate votings.

At last the constitutional requirement was made to appear satisfied by a rather circumventive legislative act of 1886 providing that those who came to vote in the general election of 1887 could be considered as the total entitled to vote for representatives. Under this arrangement 300,339 voters were registered, of whom 175,362 voted for the convention call. The same procedure was followed in 1889, when 296,700 voters were registered, of whom 190,280 voted for the call, thus assuring the convention.[1] The extreme difficulty experienced in calling the constitutional convention of 1890 should have taught the constitution makers the dangers of putting provisions in a basic instrument which make its legal revision practically impossible. The experience of the states has been that constitutions become antiquated and prevent progress in a state, thus causing the necessity of revision. Yet most of the states' constitutions have been difficult to alter. The usual experience has been that the people tolerate as much as they possibly can, then they violate their basic law in order that changes may be made to suit the demands of an advancing society.

The act providing for election of delegates to the convention stipulated that one delegate would be elected from each representative district for a total of 100 delegates. Although each district apparently gave some thought to putting forward its ablest men for the task of making a new constitution, the candidates were party selections, who ran as Democratic or Republican nominees. Consequently an overwhelming number of the delegates were Democrats. At the time, however, the Democrats were considerably split, with western Kentucky arrayed against the Bluegrass, and agrarian interests bitterly fighting the corporations. Farm interests not only formed the majority but dominated the convention. By 1890 the Farmers' Alliances definitely refused to compromise on questions which threatened a continuing agricultural supremacy. Consequently, the document prepared is rather an agrarian oriented instrument.

On the whole, the delegates were above average in ability and experience. Cassius M. Clay, Jr. was elected president of the convention; he might be said to have represented the well-to-do farmers' interests. Wealthy and conservative, he was not the type of man to champion measures proposed by either the Alliance or the Populists. As a matter of fact, Clay was uncommonly property-minded and a strong advocate of the gold standard; he did, however, favor curbing the corporations.

Edward J. McDermott of Louisville was the chief defender of the corporations, and probably prevented them taking a worse "beating" than they did. A bitter opponent of the L. & N. Railroad was William Goebel, who probably had more to do with the insertion of sections regulating the corporations than any other delegate. His chief ambition apparently being to become governor of Kentucky, Goebel sought to ally himself with agrarian interests and to distinguish himself as champion of the peoples' rights against the "bloated corporations." However, perhaps the bitterest opponent of corporate power was James F. Montgomery of Adair County.

The spokesman of eastern Kentucky, with its mining and miners' interest, as well as its poor people, was Laban T. Moore of Boyd County. Benjamin T. Birkhead of Daviess County and Dr. John D. Clardy of Christian County, ably represented the poor farmer interests of western Kentucky, as well as that section generally. The champion of public education, women's rights, and other humanitarian matters was Judge William M. Beckner, of Winchester. Peacemakers, sages, friends of the people, elder statesmen all, were Simon Bolivar Buckner, J. Proctor Knott, Curtis F. Burnam, William H. Mackoy, and Henry Davis McHenry, from Ohio County. (McHenry died during the convention.) The one hundred delegates convened in the house of representatives chamber on September 8, 1890.[2]

Unfortunately, the period, or time, was bad for the making of a constitution. Since the defalcation of James W. Tate, suspicion and distrust were leading characteristics of Kentucky political life. It was a day of agrarian unrest and prejudice against corporations, factories, and industrial development generally; a day favorable to

Cassius M. Clay, Jr., president of the
constitutional convention
*Reprinted from "Scrapbook of the Constitutional
Convention"*

William M. Beckner, active in various
reform movements

Reprinted from H. Levin, *Lawyers and Lawmakers
of Kentucky* (1897)

decentralization in government, isolationism, and localism; a day full of distrust and fear of legislators, judges, and other state officials. Road building and administration were chiefly private and local activities; education, though receiving state aid, was becoming largely a local affair. The idea of central control was abhorred. The experience with Frankfort and the spirit of localism had nurtured a belief that the powers of state officials should be curbed and restricted. This spirit was carried to the convention.

Most of the gentlemen of the convention reveled in debate—it being a day of excessive verbosity—and as there were strong group and individual differences, verbiage flowed incessantly, almost interminably. Debate on the Bill of Rights alone lasted almost a month, and in the end the Bill of Rights of the 1849 constitution was practically taken over bodily. Whereas the constitutional convention of 1792 had lasted 15 days and a document covering some 10 printed pages framed, the convention of 1890 lasted 226 days and produced an instrument requiring some 70 pages of printed matter. After studying each of the state's four constitutions, a reader is likely to be convinced that the fathers of the 1891 document were obsessed with distrust and fear, particularly of the legislature.

The delegates undertook in the new constitution to legislate for the future lawmakers. As Professor Coulter so aptly declared, "They attempted to legislate for all time." Actually, in closing the convention, Clay stated that "Future generations will read our names as the framers of the last constitution for Kentucky."[3] The convention was in session from September 8, 1890, to December 19, when it adjourned for the Christmas holidays. It reconvened on January 6, 1891, and sat until April 11, when the document was completed, signed, and sent to the voters for ratification, which was accomplished at the August election of that year. However, after ratification, the delegates reconvened on September 2 and continued until September 28. During that time much "smoothing over" was done and many changes, some fundamental, were made. In spite of the changes, the document was not

263

resubmitted to the people. It was signed again, proclaimed, and promulgated and the men "who came for dinner" at long last adjourned sine die.

Subsequently a suit (Miller *vs.* Johnson) was filed to restrain the secretary of state from recording the instrument, on the grounds that the document was promulgated with important clauses never voted upon by the people, the idea being that the convention in itself was not sovereign. The Court of Appeals, however, by a divided vote (Caswell Bennett vigorously dissenting), refused to invalidate the constitution. Chief Justice Holt (Owingsville and Frankfort) wrote the majority opinion.[4]

Reporters in Frankfort during the convention had issued so many reports critical of the delegates' work that many observers had believed the people would reject the document. Such things as the useless debates over the Bill of Rights, the wrangling over moving the capital, and adoption of the Australian ballot system annoyed and irritated leading editors, including Watterson. Finally when it was learned that the constitution was being cluttered up with purely statutory matter, authorities on constitutions became very suspicious and antagonistic.

One of the new provisions of which the convention seemed most proud was that prohibiting local, or special legislation. Because of the abuses of the 1889-90 Assembly, the delegates knew this relief to be timely. That assembly, sitting 149 days, had passed local legislation, covering 4,893 pages of legislative record, including index, at a cost in printing alone of $17,000, and in other respects its expenditures were $151,000. The average time and cost of the four preceding legislatures had been little different. The new instrument prohibits special laws on a large number of subjects, and in all cases where general laws can govern, and limits the legislature to a 60 days' session.[5]

Other important features set forward as improvements included forbidding of lotteries in the state; establishment of the secret, or Australian ballot; prohibition of convict labor outside the penitentiaries; provision for the government of cities and towns by uniform laws (strangely enough advanced as a gain); provision for a uniform system of courts; limiting the rate of local taxation; allowing county officers regular salaries, instead of fees; providing for what was recommended as an easy way of constitutional amendment, whereas amending under the old organ had been practically impossible; changing of the date of state elections from August to November; decreasing the number of grand jurors from 16 to 12, and provision that three-fourths of a jury might render a decision in a civil case; abolition of the slavery clauses; changing the date for beginning of legislative meetings from December to the first Monday in January of even numbered years; electing of senators for four years, representatives for two, with limits of 38 senators and 100 representatives; limiting state indebtedness to $500,000 unless the people vote otherwise; forbidding of the General Assembly to release or extinguish the contracts, indebtedness, liability, or obligation of any corporation or individual to the state, or to any county or municipality thereof; prohibition of giving or loaning the credit of the state in aid of any person, association, municipality, or corporation; refusal to permit the governor, lieutenant governor, and all elective department heads to succeed themselves in office; abolition of the Superior Court, although permission given to increase the number of Appellate Court judges from five to seven, all elective; provision for circuit courts.

In the reconvened session, the delegates, among other things, provided that special legislation might be allowed on questions of local option, turnpikes, bridges, public roads, public improvements and buildings, common schools, and paupers; that railroad commissioners be elected instead of appointed.[6]

Actually the constitution, in some respects, was out of date before it was ratified. Henry Watterson, who had been eager, even militant, for the convention call, bitterly opposed ratification of the convention's work. Among numerous other derogatory statements and after characterizing the new instrument as "confusion more confounded," he tersely wrote:

The new constitution is big with disaster, and it should be defeated. It contains mischief in every section. It is formulated on lines that mark a wide departure from anything we have known or conceived of relative to written constitutions. It is in no sense what a constitution is intended to be—It contains promises which it is not possible to fulfill. It is made the vehicle of personal ambition, and embodies special legislation of a most dangerous character. It violates every rule the convention has sought to impose on future Legislatures. . . . Had they [the delegates] confined themselves to their plain duty, and let the statutes alone, they could have adjourned in sixty days. . . . The convention, in fact, has ignored almost entirely the distinctions between the three departments, executive, judicial and legislative. Recognizing no limits to its power, it has failed to mark distinctly the divisions of the three departments of State. Only in the last few weeks was the fact brought to the attention of the convention that it has omitted the ordinary declaration to the effect that the government should be divided into three departments. Without debate that clause was inserted, but through all its deliberations the convention has ignored this principle with the result that confusion reigns every where.[7]

Historian Thomas D. Clark has made some pertinent general observations relative to the 1891 constitution. "Kentucky's fourth constitution," he wrote, "is not so much a fundamental rule of government as a piece of omnibus legislation. Apparently the new document is the handiwork of delegates who worked diligently in behalf of an embattled constituency. Implied powers," he states, "were eliminated wherever possible; nothing was left to interpretation or to changing conditions of the future. Delegates to the convention attempted to anticipate future needs of the government and provide for them in specific sections of the constitution." He also intimated that, in addition to the document's being agrarian in general flavor, it reflects the specific influence of the Farmers' Alliance movement, in such areas as salary and debt limitations, curbing of corporations, particuarly railroads, and ineligibility of state elective officials to succeed themselves in office.[8]

The constitution was under formidable attack by powerful metropolitan editors and by an influential section of the Democratic party when the state Democratic convention of May 14, 1891, assembled to nominate for state offices, so that the convention failed to endorse it. As a matter of fact, Cassius M. Clay, Jr., president of the convention, was defeated for nomination for governor by John Young Brown who seemed for the time being to oppose ratification of the new constitution. However, the Republican convention, May 20, 1891, with an eye to gaining Democratic votes, endorsed the new basic law.

Quite naturally, the delegates to the constitutional convention did not relish having their work repudiated by the people. They therefore (and they were powerful men locally) took the stump in their constituencies in defense of the document. Soon local editors sang praises of the new constitution. Journals, including the *Danville Advocate*, the *Benton Tribune*, the *Breckinridge County News*, and the *Henry County Local*, made strenuous local campaigns in its favor.

Watterson, however, doggedly kept up the fight against ratification. In an editorial of April 11, 1891, he wrote: "Let all who believe in popular institutions, all who believe that a Constitution should not embody a code of laws, but should be merely declaratory of fundamental principles of government, unite to defeat the proposed Constitution of 1891."

As the campaign proceeded, astute politicians realized, with the Republicans supporting and a powerful section of the Democrats actively campaigning for its ratification, that the constitution would be adopted. John Young Brown, the Democratic nominee for governor, in the midst of the campaign, announced that he would vote for accepting the instrument. The constitution, therefore, could have been worse and still have been ratified. It was accepted by a vote of 213,432 to 74,017.[9]

Following ratification came the "Long-Session Legislature," or the "Long Parliament," whose task it was to harmonize the statutes to the new instrument. A newspaper correspondent reporting the work of that session threw considerable light upon its tenacity and longevity.

> *I started in with them on the last day of 1891, stayed with 'em until the following June; pretended to suffer a 'breakdown,' went for several weeks for a visit among the parliamentary bodies of Brussels, France and England, came back and 'stayed with 'em' again for six months, took a Christmas holiday and a wedding trip, came back after Christmas, 'stayed with 'em' three months longer, and I had been at Chicago reporting the World's Fair for three months, when one day that summer the news came that the legislature had adjourned sine die, and that the state was probably sine a dime.*[10]

In addition to the "harmonizing" labors of the solons, three able lawyers—James H. Sims (Bowling Green), John D. Carroll (New Castle), and William C. McChord (Springfield)—were appointed as a commission to help make the statutes conform to the new basic law. Their work was notable. However, the task was never satisfactorily completed; such perhaps was an impossibility. The new constitution has been the bane of the Appellate Court's existence from that day to this.

XIII
LITERATURE AND THE
ARTS

For readers of serious works the English novelists still appealed. Theodore Hallam, prominent Covington attorney, wrote in 1875 that "there are only four authors that I know, Thackeray, Dickens, Bulwer and Scott." The large library of John Means of Ashland contained over 1,500 volumes, which he carefully listed in a catalogue. While perhaps not typical, this library does given some idea of reading tastes. It included works by Dickens, Scott, Thackeray and Tennyson, plus forty volumes on English poetry; the historians Macaulay, Froude and Gardiner were represented, as were their American counterparts Hildreth, Bancroft, Sparks, Prescott, Parkman, and Henry Adams. Aside from many books written by Cooper, Irving, Poe, and Bret Harte, Means had in his library very few works by other American authors. Copies of a few contemporary books, including Lew Wallace's *Ben Hur* and Helen Hunt Jackson's *Century of Dishonor*, appeared on his shelves, but he purchased the works of few modern authors.[1]

The most startling feature of Means' library was its nearly total omission of books written by Kentuckians. In view of the fact that in the late nineteenth century Kentucky was enjoying works by native authors that were attaining national fame, this paucity may seem strange. James Lane Allen, "the last champion of the Genteel Tradition," was then issuing some of his most popular books. Born near Lexington in 1849, Allen grew to maturity during the unsettled periods of war and readjustment in Kentucky. Graduation from Kentucky University in 1872 was followed by a dozen years as a teacher, a vocation that led him from Kentucky to Missouri, back to Kentucky, then to West Virginia, again Kentucky, then New York, Ohio, and Kentucky once more. It was in the Bluegrass country in the mid-1880s that the tall, slender, refined, sometimes austere man began to chronicle that area's habits and mores as a Romanticist. His first book in 1891, *Flute and Violin and Other Kentucky Tales*, was quickly followed by *The Blue Grass Region of Kentucky*, both portraying the Old South charm and its lingering influence on the New South. With the success of the latter book, Allen left Kentucky in 1893 seldom to return, except through his books' pages. There soon followed *A Kentucky Cardinal* (1894), *Aftermath* (1895), a sequel full of praise for rural life, and *The Choir Invisible* (1897), an immensely popular historical romance of the Early National Period, a work that enhanced Allen's reputation nationally.

Allen, accepted as a Romanticist, experimented, and stressed the duality in human nature between romance and realism. In this he was not overly successful. His *Summers in Arcady* (1896) dealt with the forbidden topic of sex, while *The Reign of Law* (1900) discussed science and religion and brought criticism from the clergy. He startled his own age by his boldness in handling social problems; yet critics of a later period took to task his writings dealing with the prewar civilization as sentimental. In Thomas D. Clark's estimation: "Allen was closely attuned to the soil and society of the Bluegrass. . . . He portrayed a social system caught in the new era without proper conditioning or bearings. . . . It was James Lane Allen who best portrayed for his age the confusion and frustrations which came with the birth of a more modern Kentucky." Neither Realist nor Romantic, Allen was a transitional figure in an age of transition.[2]

While Allen was making the Bluegrass one of the best known areas of America, John Fox, Jr., one of his students, was turning his attention to the eastern Kentucky mountains. Fox was born in December 1863 in Bourbon County. Fourteen years younger than Allen, he too attended Kentucky University (now Transylvania

Novelist James Lane Allen
Collection of the Kentucky Historical Society

University), but he left there for Harvard, graduating in 1883. Illness forced his return to Kentucky after a brief newspaper career. Joining his father—who had moved his family to Big Stone Gap, Virginia, in 1890—in a mining venture to eastern Kentucky, Fox soon developed an interest in the area and two years later his first work, *A Mountain Europa*, was published. But the short story which gave him his fame was "Hell for Sartain" appearing in *Harper's Magazine*. Paid six dollars for the piece, which was printed in the advertising section of the magazine, Fox followed this popular success with more articles—and with more financial success. His best known works, *The Little Shepherd of Kingdom Come* (which sold over a million copies), and *The Trail of the Lonesome Pine* (1908), came early in the next century. While perhaps not writing great literature, Fox attempted to do for the mountains what Allen was doing for central Kentucky. If he did not totally succeed, Fox nevertheless focused attention on a once-forgotten people and gave them a sympathetic hearing before the reading public. His writings were generally popular.[3]

Near Louisville, two authors had just begun their writing careers as the century ended. Mrs. Annie Fellows Johnston was born in Indiana in 1863 and came to Kentucky just before the turn of the century. Her three year stay gave her the basis for her "Little Colonel" series, which began with *The Little Colonel*. Writing under her maiden name of Alice C. Hegen, Mrs. Alice H. Rice published her immensely popular best seller, *Mrs. Wiggs of the Cabbage Patch* in 1901. Both women created a stereotyped image that reflected sheltered lives. Both gained wide popular acclaim.[4]

Kentuckians found their state's history being reexamined in this period. Some leading historical works appeared, beginning with William B. Allen's 1872 *History of Kentucky*. A large section of the book contained biographies of prominent state personalities. Richard H. Collins' revision and addition of another volume to his father Lewis' famous work made the joint effort a popular one, used by professional historians as well as school children, in another edition. The volumes published in 1874 made few attempts at historical interpretation but included a large amount of raw data that became the starting point for later historical investigation. The two-volume work has been a very fortunate contribution for Kentucky.

Within a three year period from 1885-88, three other useful works appeared. Former State Geologist Nathaniel S. Shaler published in 1885 his volume in the American Commonwealth Series, *Kentucky: A Pioneer Commonwealth*. Like others before and after him, Shaler depended heavily on Collins, Humphrey Marshall, and Mann Butler, but the result was a short, readable history that included recent state history and covered the Civil War from a Unionist point of view, although not failing to extol the deeds of valor of Kentucky Confederates. A joint effort by William H. Perrin, J. H. Battle, and G. C. Kniffin resulted in *Kentucky: A History of the State* (1885), a book that went through numerous editions. A hodgepodge of information and biographical sketches with about half of the narrative devoted to the prestatehood period, the compiled work served as a popular history. The authors also published several county histories in the period. Another author, ex-superintendent of public instruction Zachariah F. Smith, introduced his *History of Kentucky* in 1885. Published by subscription, the book included a brief historiographic essay on published sources and covered events down to 1884. A separate version for school work was introduced. Interest in the Civil War was reflected in several books about Morgan's raiders, the Orphan Brigade, and other units, chiefly Confederate. Several local histories appeared, often as promotional tracts, with George W. Ranck's *History of Lexington* (1872) among the better historical ones. Near the century's end, Elizabeth S. Kinkead published her brief *History of Kentucky* (1896) which served for several years as a textbook.[5]

Not all the material Kentuckians read was as scholarly as history books, or as well written as an Allen novel. Dime novels (which often really sold for a nickel) became the popular fare for thousands. Crude, chaste, and filled with ethics, these works featured the escapades of Nick Carter, Deadwood Dick, and other heroes whose names were familiar to schoolboys. Irvin Cobb later remembered those days as only Cobb could:

> *I read them at every chance; so did every normal boy of my acquaintance. We traded lesser treasures for them; we swapped them on the basis of two old volumes for one new one; we maintained a clandestine circulating library system which had its branch offices in every stable loft in our part of town. The more daring among us read them in school behind the shelter of an open geography propped up on the desk.*
>
> *Shall you ever forget the horror of the moment when, carried away on the wings of adventure with Nick Carter or Big-Foot Wallace or Frank Reade or bully Old Cap, you forgot to flash occasional glances of cautious inquiry forward in order to make sure the teacher was where she properly should be, at her desk up in front, and read on and on until that subtle sixth sense which comes to you when a lot of people begin staring at you warned you something was amiss, and you looked up and round you and found yourself all surrounded by a ring of cruel, gloating eyes?*
>
> *...In a five-cent story the villain was absolutely sure of receiving suitable and adequate punishment for his misdeeds. Right then and there, on the spot, he got his. And the heroine was always so plu-perfectly pure. And the hero always was a hero to his finger tips, never doing anything unmanly or wrong or cowardly, and always using the most respectful language in the presence of the opposite sex. There was never any sex problem in a nickul librury. There were never any smutty words or questionable phrases. If a villain said "Curse you!" he was going pretty far.*[6]

In the more refined field of poetry, Robert Burns Wilson and Madison Cawein rose to prominence in this period. As a young man, Wilson settled in Frankfort and gained widespread recognition as an artist before he began publishing poems, first in *Harper's*, then in a book entitled *Live and Love* (1887), perhaps his best-known work. His *Chant of a Woodland Spirit* and his last book of lyrics, *The Shadows of the Tree* (1898), both reflect "the strain of melancholy, the reflections of a brooding spirit and a persistent note of sadness" that characterize his works.

Cawein was born as the last year of the Civil War raged in 1865. His father's search for medicinal herbs in the woods near Louisville perhaps gave Madison the basis for what would become a stress on nature in his poems. After attending Male High School in Louisville, Cawein tried a business career but met with financial failure. Soon afterward his first book of verse appeared, a collection of school-boy poems entitled *Blooms of the Berry* (1887), and within a year the Louisville papers and *Harper's* both were noting the young poet's promise. A friend of Fox and Wilson, Cawein finished what may be his best work, *Myth and Romance*, as the nineteenth century ended. Known as the "Kentucky Woodland Thrush" or the "Kentucky Keats," Cawein was perhaps the most talented of the nineteenth century Kentucky poets.[7]

Young poets James Thomas "Cotton" Noe of Washington County and Edwin Carlisle Litsey were only beginning their work in the 1890s. Noe's most successful poems were short, humorous, earthy pieces depicting persons he remembered from his early life, including "Tip Sams," "Wagoner Joe," "Umbrella Jim," "Fiddlin' Mose," and "Thin Britches Dick." Henry Thomas Stanton, Kentucky's unofficial Poet Laureate, was nearing the end of his work by the 1890s. Born in 1834, Stanton had been a major under Confederate General John S. William, had practiced law, and had become editor of the Maysville *Bulletin*. His most popular work was "The Moneyless Man" (1871). Humorist Irvin S. Cobb was only twenty-four at the century's end and his best years still lay ahead.[8]

When James Lane Allen remarked in 1892 that "Kentucky has little or no literature," he was doubtless referring to her past. By the 1890s Kentucky fiction and poetry were in full flower. For whatever the reason the circumstances of these authors' youths brought out their full creative spirit and the first "golden age" of Kentucky literature had arrived.

Poet Madison Cawein

Reprinted from Otto Rothert, *The Story of a Poet* (1921).
Filson Club Publications: No. 30.

Poet and artist Robert Burns Wilson
Collection of the Kentucky Historical Society

The most common reading material was not the Kentucky authors' books, but the newspapers of the period. In the early 1870s, the state press numbered little more than one hundred papers, most of them weeklies, and fully a fifth of them in Louisville. By the end of the century three times that number were in operation—more than three hundred, with over fifty publications centered in Louisville, including one Negro paper and three German language papers. Besides the simple numerical expansion, other changes occurred in the newspaper business. Editors in the 1870s printed sheets of four to eight pages devoted largely to political news and advertisements. By the century's end newspapers had expanded and incorpoated more specialized features, including a women's page, large print headlines, sketches, and pictures. Newspapers appealing to specific groups appeared in the form of the *Thoroughbred Record* (1875) and the *American Stock Farm*, which together had a circulation of over 10,000. The semi-monthly Louisville *Home and Farm* (1875) went to over 80,000 homes.[9] Kentucky newspapers by 1900 did not differ significantly from twentieth century ones.

The antebellum tradition of personal journalism died hard, however. Newspaper editors still traded barbs with their competitors, and papers still reflected their editors' personal styles in the way the papers were run. Outstanding among these editors of the 1865-1900 period was Henry Watterson, a colorful editor known across the nation. Born in 1840, son of a Tennessee congressman, Watterson had worked for various eastern papers before the Civil War. Early enlisting in the Confederate army in Tennessee, Watterson served as a scout and, perhaps more valuably, as publisher of the Chattanooga *Rebel* for a year. His success in various ventures after the war caught the eye of the aging George D. Prentice (1802-1870), who brought him to Louisville in 1868 as managing editor of the *Louisville Journal*. The consolidation of that paper with the *Louisville Courier* and the *Louisville Democrat* gave Watterson and Walter N. Haldeman a powerful national voice. The *Courier-Journal* became one of the leading newspapers in the

South and the nation. For a half century, Watterson stressed the importance of a progressive program, a "new departure" for Kentucky, and called for fellow Democrats to heed his call. An enemy (sufficiently important) was likely to receive editorial criticism; a friend would likely expect friendly counsel. Watterson personified the best—and occasionally the worst—of Kentucky journalism in the nineteenth century.[10]

The *Courier-Journal*'s dominance of Kentucky journalism did not go unchallenged. Emmett Garvin Logan of Shelby County, together with E. Polk Johnson of Jefferson County established the Louisville *Times* in 1883 and began writing editorials that almost rivaled Watterson's. The paper's 32,000 circulation in1897 exceeded the *Courier-Journal*'s by some ten thousand. Richard Knott's Democratic daily, the Louisville *Evening Post* (circulation 12,000) gave that party three strong newspapers in the area. The Republican *Louisville Commercial* (circulation 18,000), under able editor Robert M. Kelly, was influential in shaping that party's policies.

Lexington, the site of Kentucky's first newspapers, still had several fine papers. The old *Observer and Reporter* had ceased publication in 1873, but the *Press* began production in 1870, under the guidance of Hart Foster and Henry T. Duncan. The *Morning Transcript*, for a time edited by Judge James Hillary Mulligan, author of "In Kentucky," was founded in 1878. The two papers merged on January 1, 1895, appeared as the *Press-Transcript*, and later as the daily *Morning Herald*. By the late 1890s the *Herald* became nationally known, as the editorials of W. C. P. Breckinridge and his son Desha thundered their attacks on William Jennings Bryan and William Goebel. The paper remained independently Democratic. The Republican counterpart in Lexington was the *Kentucky Leader*, launched in May, 1888, by Samuel J. Roberts of Canton, Ohio. A close friend of William McKinley, Roberts sought to strengthen the Republican party in central Kentucky. The paper devoted considerable attention to community affairs, and used special departments to attract more readers.

Richard W. Knott of the Louisville *Evening Post*
Reprinted from Ben LaBree, ed., *Notable Men of Kentucky* (1902)

Emmett G. Logan of the Louisville *Times*
Reprinted from Ben LaBree, ed., *Notable Men of Kentucky* (1902)

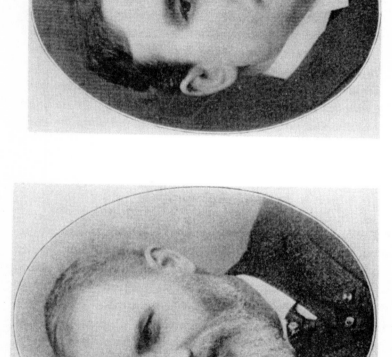

Samuel J. Roberts of the Lexington *Leader*
Reprinted from Ben LaBree, ed., *Notable Men of Kentucky* (1902)

Robert M. Kelly of the Louisville *Commercial*
Reprinted from Ben LaBree, ed., *Notable Men of Kentucky* (1902)

Both it and the *Herald* later included a literary page, a gossip column, book reviews, and other features.

Throughout the state many other influential papers appeared daily as did numerous well-edited weekly county papers. Urey Woodson's *Owensboro Messenger*, established in October, 1881, voiced its policies as a powerful organ of the western Democracy. In Covington, the *Commonwealth* was established in 1878, but its more than 5,000 circulation was doubled by the *Kentucky Post*, which challenged it after 1890. The only other state newspaper whose circulation exceeded 5,000 was the weekly edition of the Paducah *News*. Among the best smaller papers were W. P. Walton's Stanford *Interior Journal* (established in 1872) and H. A. Sommers' Elizabethtown *News* (founded in 1869).

Bitter attacks of editors on each other showed that these Kentucky newspapers, despite their more modern format, still had not freed themselves of their past traditions of personal journalism. Breckinridge would remark that "a newspaper can be a gentleman,"[11] but it was not always that way.

Sculpture and Music

James Lane Allen once observed that it was well that sculptor Joel Tanner Hart was born in 1810, for Allen feared that if born later, Hart would have run for Congress. Unfortunately, his observation was too true. Other pursuits lured talented Kentuckians and, aside from Hart, few sculptors of note appeared.

A similar situation existed in the musical field. Of the less than a dozen professional symphony orchestras established before 1900 in the United States, Kentucky had none. Only German-born, Louisville-raised Gustave Kerber (1857-1923) stood out in the field of opera. Director of New York's Casino Theatre, he wrote "Belle of New York" (1897), the first operetta to have that city as its setting. While that operetta enjoyed more success in England than the United States, Kerber's "The Telephone Girl" (1898) found more favor with American audiences. Kentucky produced a great deal of original material in her folk songs and ballads but music critics paid little attention to that music in the nineteenth century. Nameless songwriters produced works that would be sung from generation to generation, finding their way into print only decades later.[12]

If Kentuckians were not outstanding producers of musical works, they nevertheless enjoyed the popular songs of the time. Religious hymns enjoying a wide popularity included "Rescue the Perishing," "Onward Christian Soldiers," "When the Roll is Called Up Yonder," "Saved by Grace," and other, older ones. The numerous popular bands of the era and local barbershop quartets gave communities their renditions of popular songs, while Gilbert and Sullivan dominated the stage with their "The Mikado" and other productions. As ragtime gained favor, vaudeville replaced minstrelsy in popularity and by the 1890s John Phillip Sousa's works began to win an audience.

The songs people heard included "Carry Me Back to Old Virginny" (1878), "Down Went McGinty" (1889), "Frankie and Johnnie" (1890s or earlier), "After the Ball" (1892), "Daisy Bell" (1892), "The Sidewalks of New York" (1894), "The Band Played On" (1895), "There'll Be A Hot Time in the Old Town Tonight" (1896), Sousa's "Stars and Stripes Forever" (1897), and "On the Banks of the Wabash" (1897).[13] Kentuckians listened, enjoyed, and praised the music, but did little to produce their own.

Postwar Architecture

Following the Civil War, some of the well-to-do in Kentucky began building Italian villa style residences in both country and city. Good examples are Cassius M. Clay's "Whitehall" near Richmond, Colonel Atwood Hobson's "Riverview" near Bowling Green, "Hollywood" and "Glengarry" near Lexington and "Maxwell Place" and "Lyndhurst" in Lexington.

The taste of the period, however, was not characterized by sensitivity and refinement. It was notable for the rococo and the excessively ornate and showy. Perhaps far too frequently, edifices of this post-war period were characterized by overdoing. There were towers, mansard roofs, pedimented pavillions, deep bracketed cornices, narrow tall windows nearly reaching the floor, with narrow lower windows square-headed below and arched above, bay windows, iron work, three-arched side porches, very high ceilings, and small arched iron-bordered coal-burning grates surmounted by ornamented Victorian marble mantles.

Somewhat later began an era of what was known as eclectic architecture—that is, selecting the best style that seemed appropriate and functional for the time. During the Civil War tastes generally became coarsened. Following the conflict came a horde of generally uncultured adventurers who had profited fabulously by the war. These *nouveaux riches* sought to advertise their wealth and importance by building huge, showy, often atrocious looking "castles," especially in the large cities. Money was plentiful and uninhibited architects had a free hand. Fortunately for America, however, a few able architects who had studied in Europe came home to build after European models—English, French, Italian, and Spanish. And so, in addition to Italian villas, there were erected fine French Renaissance, Romanesque, and Neo-classical edifices. Kentuckians, who never quite lost their taste for the classical, profited architecturally by the new knowledge. In Louisville, for example, Henry Whitestone and Charles D. Meyer planned tall, narrow homes, and buildings with fascades of florid cast iron grids and large Palladian motifs. A native Louisvillian, Mason Maury built his hometown's first skyscraper, a six-story affair, in 1885.

Unfortunately some cheaper houses, many of them frame structures especially in the small towns, contained excessive ornamentation—modified towers, turrets, cupolas, high gables, elaborate cornices, and other extras that had no bearing upon the general design of the house. The idea was to imitate and "show off." Many of the simple houses of working people often displayed better taste than the more expensive dwellings. Many of the tenants' houses, unless antebellum, were cheap and plain; Negro tenants frequently occupied old log cabins.

In the mountains the design of the log cabins—many of which were still used—remained the basic architectural plan. In numerous cases, owners added to existing cabins, or frame facsimiles, in front, side, or back. They clapboarded some of the double cabins, both one and two stories, and in many cases added two-story porches in front. Two-story frame houses modeled after these, with wings to the rear and with considerable "gingerbread," became notable. Frequently called "mountain mansions," these large clapboarded, perhaps log, mansions were usually occupied by heads of the best-known families of eastern Kentucky, families whose prominence initially resulted from their large land holdings and shrewd husbandry.

James Lane Allen believed Kentucky homes, no matter what their style, contained "tasteless surroundings." A more modern writer echoed this opinion, calling the middle-class homes of the time "a museum of aesthetic horrors."[14] A slowly evolving art, architecture in few places evolved more slowly than in Kentucky.

Artists

Somewhat more promising was the work done by Kentucky artists. While only simple pictures, often of a religious nature, hung in most rural homes, many houses owned by the wealthy contained old oil portraits, individual and family group, painted by competent artists. While interest in good art was not widespread, a small spark developed. Artists Samuel Woodson Price (1828-1891) and Edward Troye (1808-1874), famous for his sporting prints, did the bulk of their work early in the period. A national trend toward landscape art affected Kentucky somewhat. Some of the state's best landscape painters appeared during this period, among them Paul Sawyier, Robert Burns Wilson of Frankfort, and Carl Brenner of Louisville. Living at the same time, however, was Frank Duveneck of Covington, who directed his genius in different directions.

Of the Kentucky artists, Duveneck earned a greater national and international reputation, perhaps, than any other Kentucky artist. Born in Covington in 1848, he left school to work as a decorator of Catholic churches. In 1870, he went to Munich, Germany and learned the "Munich style," with its realistic vision, avoidance of hard colors, dark and warm tones, heroic subjects, and dashing displays of brush strokes. Broad lights brushed into a dark, red-brown, shadowy background were characteristic of the school. Returning to America in 1873, Duveneck painted portraits for a time in the Cincinnati area and two years later exhibited his works at the Boston Art Club. He became overnight a national figure in art. Returning to Munich, he set up his own school, later moving to Florence. Duveneck returned to the United States after the death of his wife in 1888. He spent the rest of his life as head of the Cincinnati Art Academy, dying in 1919. His technique had made him famous. The art work in the Cathedral Basilica of the Assumption (St. Mary's) and the Mother of God Cathedral, both in Covington, give inspiring evidence of his genius. Another of Duveneck's great contributions was his school in Cincinnati and the influence it exerted upon the many artists who studied under him. Artist John Singer Sargent called Duveneck "the greatest talent of the brush of this generation."[15]

Carl C. Brenner, born in Lauterecken, Germany in 1838, the son of a glazier and wine merchant, received a small town education which included drawing courses. A talent for art resulted in a commission to the Munich Royal Academy of Art. His father refused to allow him to attend. After the family arrived in Louisville in 1854, Brenner found some solace in his profession of "sign and ornamental painter." He was fond of wandering through the forests and over the fields around the city. Nature inspired him: "I love nature for its own sake and do not think it can be improved upon," expressed his artistic faith. By the early 1870s he began producing the works that made him famous. In 1874 Brenner exhibited his paintings at the Louisville Industrial Exposition and two years later his canvasses at the Philadelphia Exposition

Artist Frank Duveneck
Portrait by Joseph DeCamp, courtesy of the Cincinnati
Art Museum, gift of J. R. DeCamp

Duveneck's "Whistling Boy"
Courtesy of the Cincinnati
Art Museum, gift of Frank Duveneck

featured the beech trees found in and around Louisville. Over the next decade his striking treatment of these trees made him very successful. He and Governor Proctor Knott became close friends and Brenner frequently painted in a room in the governor's house.

Brenner's heart was in those beech woods. The glint of sunlight on the whitened bark, the deep shadows relieved by the sunshine on the cool waters of a small stream characterize his best works, such as "Beech Woods, Autumn" (1884). Influenced by the Hudson River School of landscape painters, Brenner modeled his mature work upon their compositional schemes. If not truly original, he showed growth and maturity as an artist.[16] His death in 1888, before his fiftieth birthday, ended a life full of still more promise.

By the time of Brenner's death, Robert Burns Wilson had attained artistic prominence in Frankfort. Born in Pennsylvania in 1850, Wilson received his early schooling in western Virginia, then studied art in Pittsburgh. At the age of nineteen, he began portrait painting and came down the Ohio by canoe to Kentucky in 1871. After completing a portrait of "Marse Henry" four years later, Wilson removed to Frankfort where S. I. M. Major, the editor of the Kentucky Yeoman, commissioned him to do his own portrait. Wilson liked the green hills and the blue Kentucky River around the city and remained. His work brought him numerous commissions, and with more pictures came more fame. His watercolor landscapes of the picturesque Kentucky and Elkhorn valleys were collected in 1884 for exhibitions in Louisville and New Orleans. While sentimental in spirit, the blue shadowings and hazes of the pictures gained for the artist further favorable recongition. A personable, pleasing man, Wilson enjoyed wide popularity in Kentucky. On his death in 1915 he left behind scores of paintings, including "Omar's Rose," "The Quiet Fields," "The Cedars of Colmers Hill," and others as his legacy.[17]

Paul Sawyier, like Wilson, did much of his best work after 1900, but his career began before the turn of the century. Born in Ohio

Artist Paul Sawyier
Collection of the Kentucky Historical Society

Sawyier's "Portico, Old Capitol Hotel"
Collection of the Kentucky Historical Society

in 1865, Sawyier was brought by his parents to Frankfort as a young child. His interest in art included advance study at the Cincinnati Art Academy. After pursuing portrait painting with moderate success, he reluctantly entered his father's Frankfort business. Disappointed in this, Sawyier again studied art, first with William M. Chase of the New York Art Students League, then with Duveneck in Cincinnati.

Returning to Frankfort at the age of twenty-six, Sawyier spent the next twenty-two years there. This period saw the death of his parents and dissolution of family ties. But at the same time he produced the main body of his works. Using his water colors to portray the calm and conflict of the Kentucky River, its cliffs, bridges, and valleys, he conveyed a type of technical impressionism in a pleasing color, form and mood. Somehow he was able to put an enchanting blue in his Kentucky River—Elkhorn paintings. In his canvasses he captured the charm of rock and creek, of leaf and bark, of mist and rain, and of boat and shack. He appealed to nostalgia even in his day by painting subjects with the aura of the past. Works such as "View of Wapping Street," with its stress on a quiet stroll before a tree-lined sidewalk, or "Old Capitol Hotel," or "Scene on Elkhorn Creek," or "Rainy Day in Frankfort" remain as Sawyier's tribute to the simple elements of nature. For reasons of economic necessity he left Frankfort for New York, turned more to oils, and devoted more time to coastal themes. He died in the Catskills in 1917, a lonely man.[18]

Individuals, including Duveneck, Sawyier, Allen, and Fox, overshadow the age. Some truly excellent individual work was produced, but only in certain fields was overall depth of artistic success achieved. The problem continued to be the public in Kentucky. Mass illiteracy did not encourage culture and as one writer observed of Kentucky's upper class, "the highest mark of the gentleman is not cultivating the mind, not intellect, not knowledge, but elegant living."[19] A mixed picture of broad successes and equally broad failures resulted. The last quarter of the nineteenth century in Kentucky was notable in literature and art.

Though perhaps not "a golden age," it was nevertheless outstanding. The bright achievements in these fields occurred during a period of much mediocrity and general lack of education and culture.

XIV

AGRICULTURAL AND
INDUSTRIAL DEVELOPMENT

Agricultural Development

Agriculture functioned as Kentucky's basic economy. In 1888 for example, 226,000 rural households outnumbered the 124,000 in cities, towns, and villages. The average size of the farm in Kentucky steadily declined, however, from 211 acres in 1860 to 158 in 1870 (nearly the smallest in the South) to 129 in 1880. Small farms (less than fifty acres) had greatly increased in number since antebellum times, while larger ones (more than five hundred acres) had decreased. The steady decline in average acreage per farm continued to 1900. This decline conformed to patterns in surrounding states, north and south.[1]

Despite this trend, Kentucky agriculture was in a healthy condition. The valuation of farm lands in the state rose from $311,000,000 in 1870 to $428,000,000 in 1890. Farm products in 1900 were valued at $123,000,000, best in the South—except for Texas. Lands throughout the period were surprisingly cheap and still somewhat plentiful. Winston J. Davie, Commissioner of Agriculture, reported in 1878, for example, that good land was available at from thirty to a hundred dollars per acre, while less fertile land sold for as low as ten dollars an acre. Vast tracts of timber lands could be purchased very cheaply, often as low as fifty cents or a dollar an acre.[2]

Kentucky boasted one of the soundest and most diversified agricultural economies of any southern state. In 1870 the state ranked first in the nation in tobacco production, first in hemp, third in mules, fifth in swine, fifth in rye, sixth in corn, and eighth in wheat and flax. The wheat centers of Kentucky were Logan and Christian counties, the tobacco centers were Daviess, Christian, and Henderson counties, as well as several in the Bluegrass region, and the corn and dying hemp crop center was central Kentucky. Corn, wheat, and tobacco production increased throughout the rest of the century, with occasional setbacks. Wheat production more than doubled from 1870-1900 and tobacco poundage increased over 70 percent. Bushels of corn produced increased from 50,000,000 in 1870 to over 63,000,000 in 1896, while hay production in tons, increased from 180,000 in 1889 to 925,000 just seven years later. While some Kentucky livestock evidenced large gains—cattle and sheep almost doubled in value in only five years, from 1889-1894—overall the picture was not as bright. After a 43 percent increase in stock value between 1880-1890 a very slight overall decrease followed over the next ten years. Since the national average showed a large increase, Kentucky livestock production was in a mild depression, though still best in the South, again save for Texas.[3]

These fragmentary statistics indicate the diversity of Kentucky farm economy. Perhaps it was for this reason that although the farmers of Kentucky in 1893-1894 reportedly suffered greatly from depression, they were better off than most of those of other states. They were far better off certainly than most public labor, for throughout the nation employment slumped tremendously, and in the nation manufacturing, mining, and transportation were practically at a standstill; the unemployment situation was critical. Merchants and business houses failed every day. The Kentucky commissioner of agriculture optimistically reported the state's farmers as "holding their own and enjoying a good degree of prosperity." Though prices were low, the farmer could live very cheaply, for "a bushel of wheat," he declared, "brings more pounds of sugar or more yards of cotton than at any time in memory." He asserted, however, that some farmers were doing a great deal of "grumbling." Advocating the raising of "less corn and more hell" was a sentiment peculiar not only to Kansas. The

Commissioner did call the situation in the western Kentucky dark tobacco belt critical; he believed that this was caused more by the fact that white burley had superseded dark tobacco than by the depression.

As late as 1870, only dark tobacco was manufactured in this country. At that time the surplus of western tobacco found its way to New Orleans for foreign shipment. That market, however, was soon glutted, so that New Orleans merchants could make no profit, and they went out of business. New York then became a haven for shipments, but that city fared little better than the Crescent City, mainly because British and German agents began buying directly from Kentucky, Tennessee, and Virginia. Transportation, as well as middlemen, took a heavy toll of profit. With New York closing down, with Britain and Germany acquiring more than they needed, with acreage constantly increasing, a tremendous over-production occurred and prices went to the bottom. Kentucky producers could make profits at from eight to twelve cents a pound, but at no lower price; in 1867 the average price of tobacco was thirteen cents a pound, five years later it stood at ten and by 1878 through 1880 it dropped to five and a half cents, below the cost of production.[4] Many farmers seemed to believe that the more they produced, the more they would make. Europe, Africa, Central and South America, as late as 1888, required only 122,000 hogsheads of American tobacco. Yet, the crop of dark tobacco for export that year exceeded 200,000 hogsheads and there were already, at that time, 152,262 hogsheads of stock stored away.

All the while tobacco experts were calling for Kentucky growers to curtail production, cut acreage drastically, fertilize and produce a better grade of leaf. They believed that by proper selection of soils, fertilization, and scientific care, an acre could be made to yield three times as much, and that a far better quality would thereby be produced. The answer seemed to be white burley, which was developed in central Kentucky.

The origins of white burley tobacco remain somewhat obscure.

One tradition suggests that a Brown County, Ohio man discovered it in 1868 when he ordered seeds from the Department of Agriculture. When they matured, he found lighter colored stems and large light colored leaves. This variety quickly found its way to Kentucky. Another variation of the story suggests that tenants from Brown County, Ohio crossed the Ohio River to the farm of George Barkley in Bracken County, Kentucky and obtained plants which developed into light colored tobacco. Saving these seeds, the men planted more of the variety and from these came white burley. Whether grown first in Ohio or in Kentucky, white burley began to revolutionize tobacco growing.[5]

Farmers in western Kentucky gave up the old ways slowly and held to their unwanted dark tobacco to the bitter end. Some idea of the decline of the dark tobacco belt may be obtained from a report made by M. B. Nash, leaf tobacco broker, Paducah. He reported for the Paducah market: a decrease from 22,269 hogsheads worth $2,673,280 in 1876 to 13,254 in 1888 worth $1,723,000.

As the demand for dark tobacco decreased, the demand for white or light burley increased. In the depression, western Kentucky growers found that prices offered for their inferior weed would not pay the cost of production, while Bluegrass growers of burley made a profit.[6]

The western Kentucky growers became vociferously disgruntled. They blamed buyers, manufacturers, transportation men, capitalists, the tariff, the Republican Party, and at the same time they grew even more bitter toward central Kentucky and the Democratic leaders of the Bluegrass. They sought relief through political action by joining the Alliance, and finally by splitting the Democratic party in the state.

Apparently most of the agrarian distress in the state centered in western Kentucky, because the statistics of production and values received do not indicate widespread depression. Moreover, a study of farm mortgages in the nation shows Kentucky in favorable condition. Figures for 1890 note that in the United States almost

28 percent of farms were under mortgages. In Kansas, 55.5 percent of farms were under mortgages and many other states were similarly high. But in Kentucky only a little over 4 percent of farms were mortgaged. Reports for the depression year of 1894 indicate that over 95 percent of the state's farm-owning families had no debt whatsoever on their farm property.

One reason for discontent was not heavily mortgaged property but increasing tenantry. Fewer farmers owned their land as the century progressed: tenants made up one-fourth of the farm population in 1890 and one-third a decade later. Share tenants' farms averaged only forty-nine acres, as compared with an average of 112 acres for other farms. One written tenant agreement gave the tenant a house and garden for his use while in return he would cultivate eight acres of tobacco plus some corn, with the profits, if any, to be divided equally. Terms and shares varied according to personality and locality.

All these trends in tenantry were in line with southern ones—but that meant little to the tenant struggling on his little plot. In contrast to southern trends, however, black tenantry remained a fraction of the total. Negroes operated fewer than 5 percent of all Kentucky farms. While these farms were valued at only one-half the white average (and that already one-half the national average), they were worth much more than the national average for black farms.[7]

Increasing tenantry, marketing abuses, high taxes, and decreasing prosperity introduced economic factors that, united with social ones, brought about increased interest in farm organizations. In the early 1870s the Grange spread throughout Kentucky. Beginning in Todd County in 1871, the Grange quickly grew in number from around 20 chapters in November, 1873, to a reported 116 in December of that same year. Strong in the western part of the state, it grew sporadically and the Farmers' Alliance, organized statewide in the 1880s, expanded the aims. By 1890 the Christian County Agricultural Wheel was dissolved in name and reorganized as the Farmer's and Laborer's Union. With an estimated two thousand members, the strong Christian County organization listened to appeals such as the one that argued, "the time was, but is past, when a farmer could stand isolated and alone and succeed financially and socially." Farmers ready for action joined together in an effort to better their lot—whether the flatland farmer of the west or the hill and valley farmer of the east. Both areas supported the Alliance movement; both would give the politically-oriented Populists some support. As a Kentucky farmer observed, "We have reached the stage where slow reasoned arguments cannot any longer affect us, neither the ties of partisanship or political loyalty. It is a question of bread and meat, and we are ready to fight."[8]

Industrial Development

Kentucky began the decade of the 1870s under a burden, for within three years a nation-wide depression occurred. The Panic of 1873, precipitated by the failure of the banking firm of Jay Cooke and Company, did not immediately affect Kentucky seriously, although banking houses in Elizabethtown, Shelbyville, and other places were compelled to suspend temporarily because of the "unlooked-for stringency in the money market." With falling prices and mounting unemployment, however, Kentuckians, particularly farmers, after a time began to feel the pinch of the depression. Tobacco prices fell from ten cents a pound in 1872 to six cents in 1878, ruining a large number of one-crop farmers. In 1874 a Kentuckian wrote that "For the last three years the decline in the products of our farmers has been such as to dishearten and disappoint the very bone and sinew of our country; lands—Blue Grass lands—the best on God's green earth, have, owing to the stringent contraction, declined in value by at least a third."[9]

Industry was affected as well but soon recovered, and changes began to occur. Railroads, along with urbanization, changed the Kentuckian's life-style more than anything else in the late nineteenth century. Rural areas, to which neither factor extended, remained much as they were in antebellum times. But in areas where railroads came, life-styles changed. Closer markets, cheaper goods, expanded shopping possibilities, and increased mobility—all these contingencies resulted. Railroad mileage tripled between 1870-1900 and the "Age of Railroads" arrived.

Towns vied with their neighbors for subscription to stock in railroad lines, which the citizens believed would aid their area. Louisville had an indebtedness to railroads of nearly four million dollars. The story was the same elsewhere as small towns and large alike spent funds on stock. With this financial backing, during the decade, 1870-1880, mileage increased by 50 percent. In 1884 and 1885 more than 190 miles of track were laid, to be surpassed in 1887 with 244 more miles. Railroads' earnings in the state had increased 13 percent over the previous year. By 1889 railroads operated 2,835 miles of rail.[10]

In order to encourage railroad construction in the state, legislatures chartered companies upon the most generous terms, even making their tax problem merely nominal, and counties and towns floated bonds in profusion to aid in the furtherance of pet railroad projects. Millions in debt had been contracted in this way. Even as late as 1884, a law was passed exempting from taxation for a period of five years all additional roads built by companies already chartered as well as those to be chartered. Actually much of the bonded indebtedness was never liquidated. Thus "special-privileged" and, in many instances, becoming rapidly prosperous and affluent, the railroads not only soon began showing monopolitistic tendencies but also began striking for significant influence in state government, especially enough control to prevent passage of legislation inimical to their interests. Farmers, however, turned upon the roads with great bitterness, even sending agrarian-minded representatives to the legislature for the express purpose of both curtailing the railroads' power and of requiring them to pay taxes in equitable proportion.

A bill had been passed in 1878 providing for fair assessment of railroad property and tax on it at the same rate as on other real estate. Unfortunately, however, only about half as much tax was collected under the new system as the old, probably because of under assessment of rail property. The railroads seemed always to "have a way" with state and local politicians. As early as 1876 the agrarians had been able to make their influence felt in the General Assembly. In the session of that year, railway lawyers, fearful of their clients' interests, resorted to many sharp and clever practices to circumvent the "country yokels." The barristers then operated generally with a remarkable degree of success.[11]

In 1880 under Governor Blackburn's administration, the Railroad Commission Act was passed, setting up a board of three, appointed by the governor with the consent of the senate, to serve terms of two years. One member was to be selected from agricultural interests, one from mercantile, manufacturing, or mining, and one was to represent the railroads. The commission was to prosecute all violators of railway laws and have power to examine accounts and papers, take testimony, and subpoena witnesses. It was required to make annual reports to the governor, along with suggestions on classifying and rating passenger fares and freight rates. The duties of the 1878 railroad board of equalization and taxation devolved upon the railroad commissioners, and the old board was abolished.

An additional railroad act was passed by Blackburn's General Assembly of 1882. Intended "to prevent extortion and discrimination in the transportation of freight and passengers and to establish a board of railroad commissioners and define its powers and duties," this act set up penalties for unjust passenger and freight rates, discrimination in charges, rebates, evasions, and extortions. Three railroad districts—Eastern, Middle, and Western—were created, and the commissioners were to receive salaries of $2,000 each a year, with offices at Frankfort. Then too, each railroad, on or before September 1 of each year, was required to submit, under oath, "a full and true statement of the affairs of said corporation as the said existed on the first day of July preceding." The commission was authorized to hear and determine complaints. Cases involving more than $20 might be appealed to circuit courts.[12] The first three commissioners appointed by the governor were D. Howard Smith, former United States Senator W. B. Machen, and William M. Beckner. Even after passage of the federal Interstate Commerce Act, agitation in the state against railroads continued.

Professor Arndt M. Stickles pointed out that Governor Buckner antedated by a decade the later railroad reform work of Robert M. La Follette, of Wisconsin, and other progressive leaders. Perhaps it should be stated that, although a leading figure in an unpleasant altercation with the Louisville and Nashville Railroad during the Civil War, Buckner apparently felt no personal grievance against the railroads. Conscious of abuses on the part of the roads, however, and of the desirability for reform, he tried to act in what he perceived as the public interest. He was fully aware of the power wielded in Frankfort by the L. & N. lobby under the direction of the road's aggressive young president, Milton H. Smith. This lobby controlled a number of the lawmakers by means of gifts, liquor, food, and flattery. So overbearing did it become during the 1887-88 session that the solons set up a committee to investigate its operations, hiring a Pinkerton detective to ferret out its concealed machinations.

The report of the committee revealed startling activities. It indicated that the lobby sought to have the General Assembly abolish the railroad commission, which had increased the road's assessment and disclosed gross discrimination and abuses. It revealed, too, that the lobby conducted "an organized, subsidized press bureau to help its cause." The lawmakers generally deprecated the sinister operations of the lobby. However, seemingly intimidated, they refused to act upon Buckner's recommendations. Nevertheless, perhaps because of fear of the governor, the lobby discontinued its effort to have the railroad commission abolished. But railroad lobbying did not cease in Frankfort.[13]

Two lines dominated these Kentucky railroads. The Louisville and Nashville from its Kentucky headquarters controlled a large part of the South-central market. Part of its dominance was due to the efforts of Albert Fink. A highly educated German immigrant who never lost his accent, Fink began as bridge engineer for the L & N in 1857. Three years later he became chief engineer of the railroad, and in 1865 was promoted to general superintendent. During the next decade he built up the line and as an engineer completed his crowning work, the bridge over the Ohio River at Louisville. Over one mile long in total length, it was the longest truss bridge in the world at that time. In 1869, Fink was given more power as vice-president and began publishing vital information in his annual reports. He analyzed and standardized railroad rates and his 1874 report—the "Fink Report on Cost of Transportation"—became the foundation for railway economics. His work withstood its stiffest test during the Panic of 1873 when the L & N was one of the very few lines which escaped bankruptcy. Fink resigned in 1875, but continued in other railroad work for several years.

Dr. Elisha D. Standiford—banker, physician, politician, industrialist—served as the L & N's president during those crucial years, and Milton Smith became the road's chief executive officer in 1882. Three years later his line had 835 of the 1,887 miles of Kentucky track (and this did not include the hold the L & N had on other lines through overlapping directorships, etc.) Its 1890 report noted that passengers paid an average rate of 2.4 cents per mile and travelled, on the average, 36 miles.[14]

Chief competitor to Smith and the L & N was Collis P. Huntington's reorganized Chesapeake and Ohio. Taking over the line in 1869, Huntington incorporated into it several smaller lines, including the Elizabethtown, Lexington, and Big Sandy. The Kentucky Central, consisting of a hundred mile line between Covington and Lexington and a branch line half that length between Paris and Maysville, came under Huntington's control in 1887. But mismanagement and hard times hit the C & O system and J. Pierpont Morgan reorganized it. The line gradually recovered, but in 1890 it was forced to sell the Kentucky Central to the L & N. The L & N and C & O left little room for serious competition, but a few short systems still operated in the state.[15]

Kentucky, by and large, did not control her railroads; the owners, generally, lived in New York, not Louisville. Then too, the great coal and timber reserves were developed by outside magnates, who apparently had little, if any, thought of preserving the lands and resources for future generations. Corporate exploitation all but destroyed the fine virgin forests without regard for the people or the land, and big coal companies soon began to change eastern Kentucky. Company stores soon adversely affected the mountaineer's life and increasingly his valued individualism suffered. Much land became pockmarked by the new industrialism. There was no adequate legislation regarding land use. For example, the Cincinnati and Green River Railroad Company, organized in 1885, built a line to tap the timber in Casey, Russell, and Adair counties, stripped the forests, then ceased operations and disappeared by 1893. It left behind bare land, spur line cuts, and little else.[16] Unfortunately this type of pattern occurred again and again throughout Kentucky.

Railroad "mania" brought a system based on haphazard planning. Parallel lines and high rates, however, did bring the system under attack, often from small farmers. This agitation was responsible in 1880 for the Railroad Commission, which was given more regulatory powers as the century progressed. Involvement in politics by the L & N, especially under President Smith, won the line political favors—and political enemies, chief among whom was William Goebel. By the century's end, railroad growth had nearly stopped.[17] But the effects remained: increased cultural opportunities, added industrialization, expanded mobility, and a whole new world that heretofore isolated Kentuckians had seldom if ever known. The railroads' excesses often blinded men to the roads' ameliorative effects and their accomplishments, which in turn caused others to overlook their errors. However, for better or worse, the railroad changed Kentucky's way of life.

Often railroads even changed a whole countryside. This is a case in point: In 1888 the town of Cumberland Gap, thirteen miles from the railroad, had only half a dozen houses and one store. The next year the valley looked "as if it were occupied by an army." An English firm headed by Alexander A. Arthur formed a syndicate to buy up the mineral rights in the section. It also made plans to industrialize the area and run a railroad tunnel through the Gap. Borrowing from a Yorkshire, England borough, the new city was named Middlesborough.

The town was like a gold-rush camp; pistols were carried openly and killings were common. Sons of prominent English and eastern families mingled with rough laborers. "Silk hats, spats, and morning coats . . . monocles and walking sticks" competed with the miner's garb for attention. Speculation fever seized the locality as prices spiraled; town lots sold for as high as four hundred dollars a foot. The tunnel completed, a hotel built, coal, iron, and steel mills operating, a main street with ten blocks of stores—Middlesborough was said to be an investor's dream, an Eldorado, another Chicago or Birmingham. But with a disastrous fire that destroyed Main Street and the failure of the British banking firm of Baring Brothers, coupled with the 1893 depression, the bubble burst and depression and despair struck Middlesborough. Half the population left. The crash even drove some insane over their losses. The investors' "Camelot" disappeared.[18]

Railroads went into other mountain areas as well. James Lane Allen found a "new Pikeville" only five years after he first visited it; new because railroads and mining had made it more urban, more cosmopolitan, more "civilized."

Early Kentucky mines, still operating in the 1880s—Mud mine (1856) in Muhlenberg County, Morehead slope (1859) in Union County, and McDougall (1862), also in Muhlenberg—had all been slope or drift mines. The earliest shaft mines appeared in Henderson County in 1870 and by the mid-1880s all shaft-type mines operated in the western Kentucky fields. Several employed from 100-450 miners.

Southeastern Kentucky lagged far behind the western area. While coal had been dug since the 1840s, only the Woods Creek mine (1872) in Laurel County still operated by the 1880s. Most of the mines in the area had opened since 1880. Virtually centered in Clay, Laurel, Pulaski, and Lee counties, the mines in the area slowly expanded to their coal-rich counties. To the northeast a few mines began operation, starting with an Ashland Coal and Iron Railway Company mine in 1871. Overall in 1884, the western field's 47 mines produced 875,000 tons, the southeastern's 21 mines some 384,000 tons and the northeastern's 8 mines 278,000 tons. Coal-cutting machines and power drills had only recently been introduced, but improved methods, better transportation, and more capital resulted in larger mines and more yield.[19]

Coal production, in the west and in the newly developed eastern mines of the state, jumped from almost 170,000 tons in 1870 to 1,000,000 in 1879 to 3,000,000 in 1892 to 5,300,000 by 1900. Oil production also increased rapidly, doubling between 1880-1890, but the 1893 depression hit that industry particularly hard and the 9,000 barrels of oil in 1891 dwindled to only 322 barrels six years later. A spectacular increase came with better times and by 1900 the state was producing 62,000 barrels of oil a year.[20] Both industries survived the depression to become important in the state's industrial future.

While largely an agricultural state, Kentucky was making notable gains in manufacturing. Manufacturers produced articles valued at $54,625,809 in 1870 and employed over 30,000 people. Ten years later the value of products had grown to over $75,000,000. In 1890 it passed the $125,000,000 mark and the number of employees surpassed fifty thousand, and by 1900 the manufactured goods were worth over $150,000,000 and the industry included more than sixty thousand wage earners. Total value of products almost tripled in the thirty years and twice as many people were employed in manufacturing—a rosy picture indeed.[21]

The increasing commercial spirit in Kentucky centered in Louisville. An Arkansas paper's report in 1874 that they knew "no market but Louisville" could be repeated throughout the South. Aided by the L & N and the widely circulated *Courier-Journal*, business from Louisville looked southward for trade. Drummers drifted from town to village to country store to individual homes peddling their wares. Gifted story-tellers, men of wit, these travelling sales representatives varied their dress with the section, from elegance and aristocracy to slouch hats and rough boots. Their titles of Major and Captain suggested their background, and it was a foregone conclusion that the ranks were not acquired in the Union army. The John P. Morton Textbook Company, "publishers to the Lost Cause," employed teachers and preachers to sell their publications. All the drummers cooperated; if they could not fill orders for their own firm, they tried to fill for another Louisville firm. This, plus the L & N rate privileges, gave them further advantages.

Payment often came in the form of cotton, tobacco, sugar, and coffee, and some merchants in the city became entrepreneurs of the goods. The city's chief exports for sale in the southern market were hardware, dry goods, stoves, and plows. J. Bacon and Sons who published *Bacon's Home Journal*, a mail-order catalogue that circulated in eleven southern states, and the New York stores (later Stewart's Dry Goods Company) both did well in the southern trade. Firms, including W. B. Belknap Hardware and Manufacturing Company, Carter Dry Goods Company, the city's second largest in 1900, employed over two dozen salesmen to advertise their products. Bamberger and Bloom, largest dry goods store in the South, led city receipts in 1869 with over $276,000.[22]

The city's wealth was described in a toast by Henry Watterson: "A union of pork, tobacco, and whiskey will make us all wealthy, healthy, and frisky." Of the five largest firms in 1869 all produced these products. Taking from New Orleans the leadership in tobacco, Louisville had six of the twenty-three largest manufacturers of plug and smoking tobacco in 1871. Five years later the Falls City firms handled between two-thirds and three-fourths of all whiskey manufactured in the state, and the largest distributor of Kentucky bourbon was the Newcomb, Buchanan Company, until its 1882 failure. The pork business grew as well.

Louisville was the home of the largest plow factory in the world, the B. F. Avery firm, which sold southern farmers thousands of their products. Founded by Benjamin Avery, who came to Louisville in 1847 and supported the Union during the war, the company turned out up to 600 iron plows a day and employed 250 men. By 1868 Avery paid more individual taxes in Louisville than any other person ($62,324), save one.

The older business leaders in Louisville had had similar careers that usually included a run on the river, then a dry-goods venture, or perhaps cotton-liquor-tobacco dealings, then banking, railroads, and real estate. Families or small partnerships dominated the 1870s, but with a more complex society came more diverse arrangements. The Guthrie and Speed families had been the dynamic elements in early Louisville society. The leaders of what was described as "a class conscious society" in the 1870s included W. H. Dulaney (bank director, property owner worth $934,000), Walter N. Haldeman (publisher), J. P. Morton (textbooks), R. A. Robinson (L & N director, tobacco, banking), W. B. Hamilton (packer, L & N director), William Gay (wholesale grocer), Joseph T. Tompkins (dry goods), George Ainslie (steamboats), James Bridgeford (foundry, bank president), and J. S. Lithgow (stove manufacturer).

Two decades later the shift in wealth was evident: Haldeman, Dulaney, and Robinson remained among the wealthiest Louisvillians, but other millionaires included Avery, Dennis Long (pipe manufacturer), W. C. Hall (Texas land and railroads), C. P. Moorman (distiller), George H. Moore (distiller, banker), plus the estates of B. F. Guthrie, G. W. and W. F. Norton, Nathan Bloom (dry goods).[23] Industry and commerce in Louisville remained strong throughout the century.

Louisville's successful business ventures helped the South in manufacturing. Yet the success was deceptive; Kentucky trailed much of the rest of the nation and was not catching up. Her per capita wealth ($533 in 1877), while highest in the South, lagged far behind the national average of $870. Kentucky's overall indus-

S. L. Avery

Reprinted from *The City of Louisville and a Glimpse of Kentucky* (1887)

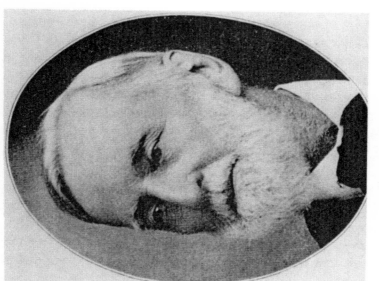

Walter N. Haldeman

Reprinted from Ben LaBree, ed., *Notable Men of Kentucky* (1902)

trial ranking in the nation, 1880-1900, varied between sixteenth and eighteenth, behind even Rhode Island. Her industrial production increased nearly 70 percent between 1880-1890, approximately the national average, and more than 20 percent from 1890-1900; this was far behind the over 40 percent national increase.[24] Thus while many citizens praised the state's advancements in industrialization, in truth there was no advancement when compared with the national gain. Industrially, Kentucky was struggling just to hold her place in the race. The brightest hope for industrial-minded Kentuckians lay in their success in changing the ethos from agriculture to industry. As to effecting this change they could not be certain.

Labor

Labor unions, never strong in the nation during the nineteenth century, gained few sympathetic supporters among Kentucky leaders. During the summer of 1877, the lot of railway workers became so wretched, as a result of repeated slashes in wages, that rail workers in many parts of the nation struck. In many cases, notably in Pittsburgh, violence and bloodshed occurred. In Louisville workmen struck against the Louisville and Nashville road and almost immediately violence broke out. On the whole, the city's press, prior to the outbreak of violence, had been moderately inclined toward the workers, as had Mayor Charles D. Jacob. However, on the evening of July 24 a mob of perhaps 2,000 hooted the mayor at the courthouse and even smashed the windows of his and other houses.

At that point Henry Watterson, no friend of unions, lost patience. "The disorderly proceedings of last night," he wrote, "are not to be submitted to for a single day, or night, by this community." Averring that the violence was perpetrated by "thieves, dead-beats, and bummers," he inveighed upon the poorly paid railway workers, who had received "full, just, liberal consideration," to rally to the side of law and order and disclaim any and all connection with the "hoodlums." In quick succession, both Mayor Jacob and Governor McCreary issued stern proclamations, making it clear that they were prepared to use armed force. By nightfall, over 700 militia reinforced the 175 policemen on duty. On the following day, the Governor sent in 400 troops. A few arrests and some small fines resulted.[25]

The trouble in Louisville, as far as it concerned the public, vanished almost as quickly as it had developed. The event served to demonstrate that organized labor's use of the strike would have tremendous difficulty in capturing much public sympathy in capitalistically-minded Louisville, or even in rural, agriculturally-inclined Kentucky.

By 1880 Louisville had thirty-six local assemblies of the strongest national labor union, the Knights of Labor, which had rapidly gained strength since 1877. However, the organization suffered a sharp decline during the 1890s. Regarding publicity, the unions found a voice first in the Louisville *Labor Record* (1884-1888), then in the *New Era*, and finally in the Kentucky *Irish-American* in 1898—that journal displayed the union label. But while these helped, they could not overcome the disorganized state of labor in the Commonwealth.

The failure of forty-one businesses in Louisville in 1893 left an estimated ten thousand people unemployed and for those who were able to keep jobs, the city's wages were considered the lowest in the south central United States. That same year, the L & N cut its wages 10 percent; the largest strike in the city's history, to that point, resulted. Over 1,400 workers struck in protest. However, hard times and weak organization forced them back within two months.

Overall, Louisville, with the strongest unions in Kentucky, experienced over 140 strikes between 1880-1900, mostly over wages. The Brakeman's Union, for example, struck every year from 1886 to 1893, and the peak strike years in the city coincided with national strikes, in 1886 (Haymarket) and in 1892-1894 (Homestead and Pullman). While several strikes were successful,

Police battle strikers in Louisville, 1877
Reprinted from Allan Pinkerton's *Strikers,*
Communists, Tramps and Detectives
Reprinted by Arno Press, Inc., 1969

the overall picture was less than bright. A fledgling American Federation of Labor was rising, but the depression's effects were still evident and labor would make no significant gains until the next century.[26]

Outside the cities and away from organized labor, farmers also experienced problems. The heavy migration of Negroes to urban areas after the war caused farm labor shortages south of the Ohio. Even in Kentucky these labor needs were felt. For instance, the Fayette (County) Farmers Club sent agents all the way to New York City to try to procure three thousand Scotch laborers to work on the farms for twelve dollars a month. The efforts were futile. Occasionally other methods succeeded in getting black labor. Some cases were extreme. An 1871 advertisement promised a five dollar reward for a "Bound Girl Runaway . . . Caroline Shepard . . . about 16 years old, a bright mulatto and has one wrist broken." In the 1880s, the Bourbon County Circuit Court sentenced black vagrants to serve one to three years to anyone who paid the vagrant's fine.[27] However, such cases had no effect in relieving the labor stringency.

Average wages for laborers fell from $20 in 1865 to $15 in 1878. By 1880 whites on farms earned from $15-$18 a month, "with house and an acre of garden. . . , the use of a cow . . . and firewood." Black laborers received the same benefits and $8-$10 in money. There was another difference according to the commissioner of the Kentucky Bureau of Agriculture: "White laborers are always treated as part of the employer's family, eating at the same table with the family & c.; with colored laborers this is not expected, and would not be tolerated." The optimistic prediction that there was "about to break the dawn of a new prosperity in Kentucky"[28] was never realized by the turn of the century. Economically, Kentucky entered the twentieth century in the same relative condition that had existed in 1865.

XV
POLITICAL EVENTS OF
THE 1890s

The Gubernatorial Election of 1891

As the state political conventions of 1891 approached, rising forces made the outcome even more uncertain than usual. Discontent among a section of the farm population resulted in widespread disaffection in the dominant Democratic party. As far back as 1885 agrarian forces had organized two societies, known as the Wheel and the Farmers' Alliance, in an attempt to reduce taxes and curb railroad excesses. They set up numerous local chapters, which joined together generally to support Buckner and the Democrats in 1887. Some legislation favorable to the organization had resulted. But more accomplishments were sought and in February 1889, the two farm organizations merged as the Farmers' Alliance and held a convention at Paducah. They elected John G. Blair of Carlisle as president and adopted a platform favoring free silver, popular election of United States senators and all state officials, a graduated income tax, salary reductions for governmental officials, state control of railroad rates, low tariffs, and increased appropriations to the Kentucky Agricultural and Mechanical College at Lexington.

To effect the election of persons favorable to its demands, the Alliance threw its support to the candidate—whether Democrat or Republican—appearing more likely to support its platform. With an estimated 80,000 members in October, 1890, the western section of the state "wild with enthusiasm," and the mountains well organized, their political support was eagerly sought by both major parties. The Alliance and Republican-backed candidate in the ninth district lost to free silver Democrat Thomas H. Paynter by 5,000 votes that fall. The alliance helped elect, to the constitutional convention, some eighteen delegates favoring "the Alliance idea."[1]

By early 1891 the Alliance boasted of 88 country chapters with 2,400 sub-unions. Under the name of the Farmer's and Laborer's Union, the organization became more politically oriented. County platforms repeated the 1889 demands and the programs advocated appealed to more and more as the hard times continued. By May, 1891, the membership had passed the 110,000 mark. They were a formidable force.

But on whose side? Occasionally the pattern was that the agrarian interest united with the party out of power locally. In usually Republican Christian County a fusion was effected with the Democrats, but in the Democratic second district overall an alliance was made with the Republicans. No all-prevailing pattern surfaced, however, as local politics confused the picture even more.[2]

The Alliance disposed of Blair in 1891 and chose Thomas T. Gardner, a more moderate leader, as president. He would eventually support the Democratic nominee that fall, despite his adherence to the gold standard. Gardner refused to sanction any third party movement. But not all of the disillusioned and embittered farmers followed their president. Blair led a group to the Populist party convention at Cincinnati, and returned across the river to Covington to organize the Kentucky Populists. He called for Alliance support of the new People's party. Henry Watterson, Richard Knott, Sam Roberts and many other leading editors ridiculed everything that smacked of Populism, in biting and truculent language. Earlier the *Leader* characterized the Alliance leaders as "broken down lawyers and worn out seedy politicians" whose party was but "a dead cock in the pit."[3] Now, however, political analysts saw a strong, rising agrarian force, one to be feared by Democrats and Republicans alike.

Politicians seeking the Democratic nomination for governor in 1891 had to seek the Alliance's support. Cassius M. Clay Jr.'s correspondence that year illustrates this circumstance, and also reveals the factors at work in campaigns throughout the previous decades.

Son of Brutus Clay, nephew of the old abolitionist, Cassius Clay, Jr. had served as presiding officer at the 1891 constitutional convention. He sought the Democratic nomination as a representative of agrarian interests since he himself owned a large agricultural estate. A Simpsonville (Shelby County) resident suggested that Clay "connect yourself with alliance, but *of course* make the race as a Democrat." Another writer suggested that he join the organization: "It would do you good and no harm." Advice continued to come from almost everywhere; a Louisville insurance salesman wrote him that "anything you can do to soft soap the Alliance will go down to your Interest." But another candidate, Dr. John D. Clardy of Christian County, an Alliance member, sought the small farmer's vote more successfully than Clay, who came under attack by him as representing the landed gentry.[4]

Clay did gain some support, however, simply because he was a Clay. Several voters, confusing Clay's paternity, reacted like Henry Clay Jones who said he did not know the candidate but would support him "by the force of family traditions and inclinations."[5] The issues remained as Patrick Henry Bridgewater asked them to Clay: "(1) how were your simpathies [sic] during the late war . . . ? (2) how do you stand in the principles of the Farmers and Laborers Union of America Alliance?" If Clay answered him correctly, the letter continued, then he would be given support. "In the event you are elected Governor remember me If I should want an office in your gift." The Confederacy, the Alliance, and the patronage interested voters. Another candidate, John Young Brown of Henderson, used his oratory to present his stands on these issues in a most favorable light.

As Clay, Clardy, Brown, and "Wat" Hardin campaigned, reporters found both apathy and intense excitement throughout the state. In one area the fight might be between Hardin and Clay, in another Clay and Clardy, in a third Brown and Clardy. A Breathitt County attorney called on one candidate to visit the mountains, where votes would easily be gained: "the mountain people are the easiest people in the world to get excited if a candidate will handle them properly."[6] Such "handling" often resulted in the election violence that rekindled smoldering feuds.

Political feuds would make the upcoming convention, a writer predicted, "the hottest and most demoralizing ever held in the state." Just prior to the beginning it appeared that Brown led the field. On the first ballot his 275 votes barely topped Clay's 264, while Clardy (190) and Hardin (186) trailed. For nine more ballots the vote changed little. The chair announced that the candidate with the fewest votes would hereafter be dropped. Clardy's vote went almost equally to all three. Then Hardin was forced out. His supporters turned to Brown, who secured the nomination on the thirteenth ballot.[7]

Clay and Clardy had split the farm vote while Hardin and Clardy did the same among the free silver delegates. Bourbons united behind Brown, who they knew was conservative and "sound" on the money question. They forced him through what perhaps was a "cheap money" convention, since the western section of the state had long been extremely critical about not having one of her sons accorded the nomination. Brown—from Henderson—satisfied that demand. A staunch pro-Southerner, Brown had not alienated the Alliance interests. Thus appeased, the farmers of western Kentucky had been made to feel that their section's day of leadership in the party was at hand.[8]

Notwithstanding their power to pick the gubernatorial nominee, however, the conservatives were either unable or disinclined to dictate the naming of the other candidates to run with Brown on the ticket. The personnel of the ticket consisted of Brown; Mitchell Cary Alford of Lexington for lieutenant governor; Henry S. Hale of Mayfield for treasurer; Luke C. Norman for auditor; William Jackson Hendricks of Flemingsburg for attorney-general; Ed. Porter Thompson of Metcalfe and Owen counties for superin-

Governor John Y. Brown
Collection of the Kentucky Historical Society

tendent of public instruction; Green Berry Swango of Wolfe County for register of the land office.

The platform adopted dwelled more on national affairs than on state. It demanded tariff reform, denounced the McKinley Tariff as "the most outrageous measure of taxation ever proposed in the American Congress," commended the Democrats in the last Congress for favoring free coinage of silver, and demanded silver's restoration to the position of equality before the law (16 to 1). The convention failed either to endorse the new state constitution or to approve Cleveland as the 1892 national standard-bearer of the Democracy. Upon such important state matters as public school expansion, industrial improvement and extension, financial adjustment, and law enforcement, the platform was rather noncommital. Smoldering factionalism and bitterness from many causes were so highly charged that even a minor incident might have caused a politically destructive explosion. Robert J. Breckinridge, Jr., writing to his brother, Congressman W. C. P. Breckinridge, declared, "I am glad you were not at the convention. There was, and is, much bad feeling . . . underlying the placid surface of things. . . . Some who are in public life . . . and were at the convention, I am satisfied . . . wish they had remained away."[9]

The Republicans held their convention in Lexington on May 20. After Bradley's promising race nearly four years before, it might have been thought that great enthusiasm would have prevailed and that a strong demand for Bradley to run again would have gone up. Neither occurred. Apparently, an understanding had been reached by the state central committeemen that Colonel Andrew T. Wood of Mt. Sterling would be nominated for governor. Wood was described as "a fine man, but poor politician." Some expressed the opinion that Bradley, believing that 1895 would be a more propitious year for the Republicans than 1891, did not choose to run.

Along with Wood, the convention named Henry E. Huston of McCracken County for lieutenant governor, Eli Farmer of Pulaski County for treasurer, Charles Blanford of Breckinridge County for

319

auditor, L. J. Crawford of Campbell County for attorney-general, L. V. Dodge of Madison County for superintendent of public instruction, W. J. A. Rardin of Greenup County for register of the land office, and it expressed a preference for E. R. Blaine of Fayette County for clerk of the Court of Appeals.

The platform adopted championed the national Republican platform of 1888, praised the Harrison administration as "pure, wise, and patriotic," opposed the "free and unregulated" coinage of silver, and endorsed the new constitution. A resolution supporting Harrison for renomination aroused so much opposition that a vote was not taken on it.[10]

The Populist party convention met in Covington, May 20, 1891. A full list of candidates was put forward for the state offices. Pollock Barbour of Louisville, chosen as their nominee for governor, declined the honor on the grounds that his Alliance opposed the political orientation of the People's party. The group then turned to Samuel B. Erwin of Fulton County for governor. They chose S. F. Smith of Franklin County for lieutenant governor, I. G. Sallee of Trigg County for treasurer, W. G. Fulkerson of Ohio County for auditor, G. F. D. Guffey of Morgantown for attorney-general, W. W. Morris of Ballard County for superintendent of public instruction, T. B. Herold of Butler County for register of the land office, and they expressed preference for John Blair for clerk of the Court of Appeals.

The convention adopted a platform that supported free and unlimited coinage of silver, and opposed organization of more banks of issue, and alien ownership of lands. It called for laws to prevent dealings in futures in agricultural and mercantile products, for legislation against taxation in class interest, for a bureau of labor and statistics, for the government's paying ex-Union soldiers the difference between currency and specie at the time they were paid paper money (with interest added) and declared that to meet such payment Congress should provide for issuance of treasury notes, making them full legal tender for all debts, private and public. The platform also came out for the state tax of $.50 being taken off mortgages, for reduction of all fees and salaries of national, state, and county officers, for working convicts only inside the prison's walls, for abolition of employment of children under fourteen years of age, and for making the mechanics's lien law the same as that of Ohio (prohibiting a lien for indebtedness on a workman's wages).[11]

A fourth party convention, the Prohibition's, was held in Louisville on May 29, and chose Josiah Harris of Paducah for governor, H. M. Winslow for lieutenant governor, J. M. Holmes of Daviess County for treasurer, W. W. Goddard of Mercer County for auditor, E. J. Polk of Louisville for attorney-general, A. B. Jones of Anderson County for superintendent of public instruction, Bradford McGregor of Kenton County for register of the land office, and R. S. Friend of Floyd County for clerk of the Court of Appeals.

The platform adopted not only favored legalizing the prohibition of alcoholic beverages in the state, but also the eradication of "all other wrongs that rest upon the people as the result of partisan, class, and corrupt legislation." The Prohibitionists also favored a larger circulating medium "in our national currency."[12]

The canvass, in spite of many parties in the field and widespread discontent, failed to generate great enthusiasm. Brown, conscious of the impending danger of losing thousands of farm votes, wooed the Alliance as assiduously as possible, even taking a stand against the proposed Louisville and Nashville Railroad monopoly, which was designed to take over the Chesapeake, Ohio, and Southwestern Railway system. In the midst of the campaign, he endorsed the new constitution. As a matter of fact, a surprising interest was shown by the people in the new basic charter.

Perhaps equally surprising was the large vote received by the Democratic ticket, and the unexpected strength of the Populists. Brown's vote was 144,168; Wood's 116,087; Erwin's 25,631; and Harris' 3,292. The Populist vote (almost 9 percent of the total) not only voiced protest and distrust of the major parties and disbelief in their promises, but also indicated that in an election anything like close, it would be a decisive factor, perhaps against

1891 ELECTION

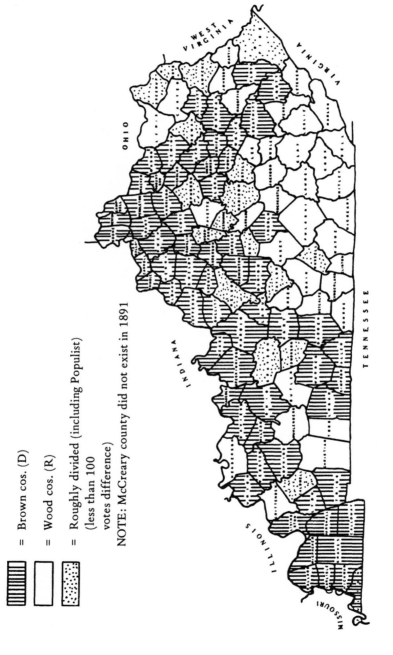

	= Brown cos. (D)
	= Wood cos. (R)
	= Roughly divided (including Populist) (less than 100 votes difference)

NOTE: McCreary county did not exist in 1891

Source: *Official Manual of Kentucky, 1895*

1891

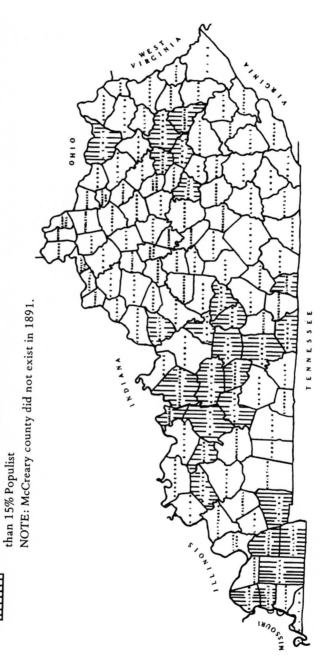

Counties whose vote was more
than 15% Populist

NOTE: McCreary county did not exist in 1891.

Source: *Official Manual of Kentucky, 1895*

the Democratic party. To the state senate, 27 Democrats, 10 Republicans, and 1 Populist were returned. To the house, 70 Democrats, 17 Republicans, and 12 Populists were elected.[13]

Inauguration of John Young Brown

The inauguration ceremonies were conducted in Frankfort, September 1, 1891. The press gave the retiring governor, "Old Bolivar," more attention than it did Brown. Buckner had greatly endeared himself to the people because of his continuous efforts in behalf of good government and in faithful discharge of public duty. Perhaps the feeling of most of the citizens was expressed by editor Richard Knott. "Kentucky loses from its executive chair today," he wrote, "one of the best governor's that ever 'steered the Ship of state.'" Knott admitted not having been enthusiastic about the General at first and that he had even believed his nomination a mistake. However, he declared, "From the time he took his seat until the present day he has made an exceptionally brilliant record. He has," continued Knott, "run the state on business principles, and he has had sufficient courage at all times to do and say whatever he believed to be right. He has not been a politician in office. He has studied the needs of the state and, as far as possible, has endeavored to supply them."

Concerning other matters, Knott stated that Buckner had not allowed "the many shortcomings of the Legislature to go unnoticed, but has called attention to them in vigorous English. He has raked judges, and other officials who were derelict in their duties .... He has used the pardoning power sparingly and with intelligence. In short, he has made a model governor. ... He is a grand old man, and we love him."

Buckner's farewell address was brief and sensible. He stated that "the paramount duty of the chief executive is to exert all the authority vested in his office by the organic law to protect the right and interests of the people, to enforce their laws, and to maintain the honor and dignity of their Commonwealth." Such a statement uttered by most political figures would have seemed trite indeed, but coming from Buckner, it carried conviction because the elderly man had truly striven with all his strength to do just that. The retiring governor, unassuming as always, gave high praise to Brown, admonishing him just once, with "As integrity is the essential of true manhood, so is the faithful discharge of public duty the essence of patriotic and good citizenship."[14]

John Young Brown, who probably little realized how difficult was the job of being governor of Kentucky at that particular time, delivered a fairly brief address, devoting a good deal of time to the subject of law enforcement. "The certainty of punishment for crime," he contended, "is the surest restraint of the vicious." He thought the governor should not interfere unduly, but that "he should take care that the law be faithfully executed."[15] The speech contained a good deal of the "oratorical" popular at that time.

The "Long Parliament"

Governor Brown devoted the first few weeks of his administration to the matter of appointments. One of his first was that of John W. Headley of Louisville to the office of secretary of state. Brown then named Charles B. Poyntz of Maysville, Charles C. McChord of Springfield, and Urey Woodson of Owensboro to the railroad commission. Apparently, the members of the official family were not companionable. It seems that Brown and Headley, most of the time, were at dagger's point, "politically, if not personally," with Treasurer Hale, Auditor Norman (who built up a strong machine) and Attorney General Hendricks. Both sides had their partisans throughout the state offices and in the General Assembly, which sat for parts of three years. The schism spread down all of the party avenues, growing wider with the passing of time. The principal point of difference was occasioned by the "free silver" issue. Brown, Watterson, Buckner, Breckinridge, and many other prominent Democratic leaders opposed free silver.

Legislative Session, 1891-1892

The legislature convened December 31, 1891. William M. Moore, of Harrison County, was elected speaker on the first ballot by a 76-17 vote over Republican hopeful Silas Adams, of Casey County. The Populists put forward Thomas Pettit, of Daviess County, who received only four votes—all from representatives of western Kentucky. Addressing the legislature, Brown stated that already he had appointed a commission of able lawyers, consisting of William C. McChord of Springfield, John D. Carroll, and J. S. Sims, which had been working assiduously testing the statutes against the new constitution. Then he announced that there was an actual deficit of over $229,000 in state funds, and put forth the estimate that at the close of the fiscal year 1893 there would be a deficit of almost half a million dollars.

The chief executive pointed out that the new constitution prohibited tax exemption, except as provided in the instrument itself, and, following Alliance proposals, he called for passage of legislation requiring railroads exempted from taxes to pay the regular state tax of 42½ cents on the $100 property valuation. He declared that $8,117,300 of railroad property was free of tax. Obviously, with the treasury empty and a constitutional mandate to tax, it would be assumed that the lawmakers would lose no time in getting through an adequate law. At the same time, the governor recommended a tightening of law enforcement relating to county and state taxation of distilleries.

Yet Brown was conservative. Nothing better illustrates his philosophy than his statement regarding the Geological Survey. He declared "that advantages commensurate with the cost of the Geological Survey" had not accrued to the state and therefore recommended that no further appropriation be made. Actually, the Survey's work had significantly aided the industrial development of eastern Kentucky. Moreover, Brown's reference to public education, although rather eloquent, was only thirteen lines in length, as compared with one hundred and seven devoted to the penitentiaries, exclusive of fifty lines or more on the parole system.[16]

The first of the long sessions of the General Assembly adjourned on August 16, followed by an extra session called to convene August 25. This special session continued until November 1. Apparently, some felt that the lawmakers were simply killing time, rendering no helpful service to the state and at the same time drawing pay from the public treasury. Absenteeism was constantly so heavy that quorums could not be obtained. A Louisville editorial of August 10 stated: "Both houses had quorums today. The attendance was fuller than for many weeks. Whether the consciences of the absentees had begun to prick them . . . whether their respective constituents made it so warm for them that they could stay at home no longer, will always remain open questions in the field of conjecture." It declared that for a solid month the largest attendance in the house (of 100 members) was 61.

Perhaps the greatest alarm sustained by the few who kept posted on legislative maneuvers was that the "statesmen," in spite of the empty treasury, would vote additional money for themselves. The House made such a move. Before the maneuver gained strength, however, the *Courier-Journal* screamed out in bold headlines, "SALARY GRAB. A BIG FAT HEN ON IN THE ASSEMBLY AT FRANKFORT. THE SOLONS MAY HAVE THEMSELVES PAID DURING VACATION." The article continued with, "This economical-third-party-Farmers-Alliance Legislature on the eve of a salary grab for which the Democratic party will be held responsible."[17] Apparently the solons took fright, because the project "died a-borning."

One reason Brown called an extra session immediately was the fact that several important bills he had vetoed needed to be rewritten and introduced again. Moreover, he had signed some bills which needed amending. Revenue and taxation, corporations, suffrage and elections, redistricting the state into circuit court districts, classification of cities, fiscal courts, and other matters growing out of the new constitution required attention. Another reason for the call was to get certain bills passed constitutionally. Many of the new statutes had been passed without majority vote of the legislature, and Brown feared tests in the courts. Be it said to his credit that the governor, upon discovering the facts, had vetoed many acts illegally passed. Some of these vetoed bills certainly were of such importance as to warrant reconsideration. However, another session of course would give the lawmakers, some of whom had seldom attended a session, opportunity to "plunder" further the bankrupt treasury.

The principal legislative measure, or at least the most pressing, was that pertaining to revenue. The senate, apparently under the influence of the railroads, had refused to agree that the roads exempt from tax be required to pay, even though it would mean an additional $300,000 annually to the state. The special session worked out a compromise measure. The railroad commission's assessment was taken as the true value of the railroad's real property in the state. The difference between the assumed capital stock and the assessment given the franchise was the basis upon which the regular tax rate was levied. Previously, the roads had insisted upon using their own assessment figures, and the state had insisted upon using official assessor's figures.[18]

Another bill causing long and excited discussion was one designed to provide separate railway coaches for whites and blacks. Negroes staged many demonstrations opposed to what they correctly deemed discriminatory and segregationary legislation, although the bill provided for "equal facilities." The Republicans and most Populists opposed the bill, as did a few Democrats. The combination was able to muster only 25 opposition votes in the house when the bill passed.

Other noteworthy bills enacted included one dividing cities and towns of the state into six classifications according to population; one creating the "Office of Inspector of Mines," and a resolution proffering sympathy to the strikers against Carnegie Steel at Homestead, Pennsylvania, and deploring use of Pinkerton detectives by company operators; another provided for Kentucky's participation in the Chicago World's Fair.[19]

The Presidential Election of 1892

As time for selecting delegates to the National Democratic Convention of 1892 approached, the Democracy was far from united. Perhaps the rank and file wished Cleveland, who had been defeated by Harrison in 1888, again to be the standard bearer. But many powerful elements opposed him. In the strategic state of New York (Cleveland's home) dissension was rampant, with the popular David B. Hill, governor of the Empire State, a bitter and implacable foe of the "stuffed prophet" (so dubbed by Watterson). Moreover, free silverites and cheap money men, as well as tariff reformers, opposed Cleveland.

Casting a weather eye over the discordant elements, "Marse Henry," perennially popular with the national Democracy, concluded that a renomination of Cleveland would be for the Democracy something like "walking through a slaughter house into an open grave." He put forward his good friend John Griffin Carlisle as the best possible man for the Democratic presidential nomination. His reasoning was expressed in a very able editorial, which attracted nationwide attention.[20]

The state Democratic convention met in Louisville, May 25, 1892, to elect delegates to the national conclave. There, the faction opposed to the renomination of Cleveland gained a decisive victory in electing as temporary chairman Charles R. Long of Louisville over Charles J. Bronston of Lexington (427 to 290). The platform indicated that the cheap money men were in control of the convention. The Watterson forces (strongly "sound money") were able, however, to dictate a "tariff-for-revenue-only" plank, which was perhaps some consolation to the outnumbered "gold" men. Among other things, the platform castigated the Republicans for "iniquitious tariff legislation" in the form of the McKinley Bill, as well as for their advocacy of the "force bill" (a proposal that would require Federal troops in the South to enable Negroes to vote). Taking the Republicans to task for wasting money, the convention demanded a sound and stable currency "composed of, or redeemable in, gold and silver dollars," as well as legislation for the free coinage of silver "without detriment to any business interest and to the great relief of overtaxed and debt-ridden people." The best that the anti-Cleveland forces could achieve for Carlisle was an uninstructed delegation to the forthcoming Chicago convention.[21]

The National Democratic Convention opened at the "Wigwam" in Chicago on June 21. It was of special interest to Kentuckians for two reasons—namely, the effort to nominate Carlisle and the influence Watterson exerted on the tariff plank of the platform. However, Watterson, in opposition to the Cleveland-inspired tariff declaration of the resolutions committee, took the floor and eloquently advocated a tariff for revenue only, declaring anything more to be unconstitutional and denouncing Republican protection as "a fraud, a robbery of the great majority of the American people for the benefit of the few." He carried the convention 564 to 342. Thus ruling the day once more with his "Star-eyed Goddess," as well as cramming her down the furious Cleveland's throat, "Marse Henry" was ready to return home and work for a Democratic victory, especially since the convention refused to declare for free and unlimited coinage of silver. It should be observed that Cleveland, although he captured the nomination rather handily, was not popular generally with the delegates. They liked neither his political nor personal policies. But they did believe that he was the only Democrat who could win the presidency that year. This was the feeling in Kentucky also.[22]

Two other national conventions of interest to Kentuckians were those of the People's party and the Prohibition party. The former nominated the old Greenback leader, General James B. Weaver, on a free silver platform; and the latter nominated John Bidwell, a colorful California pioneer and the proprietor of extensive ranches in that state, on a national prohibition and free silver platform.

After the normal fanfare, the normal pattern resulted: Cleveland, 175,461; Harrison, 134,441; Weaver, 23,500; and Bidwell, 6,424.[23]

The "Long Parliament" Reassembled

In January, 1893, the legislature reconvened for a session extending to July 3. The first matter of great interest was electing someone to fill the unexpired term of United States Senator John G. Carlisle, who had resigned his seat upon appointment as Secretary of the Treasury. In the contest William Lindsay, Democrat from Clinton and Frankfort, won over Augustus E. Willson, Louisville Republican, by a vote of 79 to 19. The term would expire March 4, 1895.

The old perennial question of moving the state capitol to another city arose, like Banquo's ghost, to plague the lawmakers. As usual, it generated tremendous heat. Partisans of Louisville, Lexington, Danville, and Bowling Green pressed claims vigorously. Although the name of Louisville was selected to fill the blank space in the bill, the legislators, their prevailing prejudice against that Falls City in evidence, voted it down with unusual dispatch, energy, and decision. Whereupon the elated citizens of Frankfort celebrated another of those rousing and unrestrained victories periodically enjoyed since 1792.

During the session the legislators saw fit to aid struggling Kentucky State College by passage of a bill accepting the provisions of the Congressional Morrill-Nelson Act of 1892, applying a portion of the proceeds from the sale of public lands to "the more complete endowment and support of the colleges for the benefit of agricultural and mechanical arts." This enabling act cost the state no money; nor did it change one jot or tittle the General Assembly's policy of niggardliness toward State College, which was never properly supported. Other acts provided for regulation and ventilation of coal mines, fixing the compensation of the governor at $6,500 annually, and division of the state into 38 senatorial districts.[24]

Senator William Lindsay
Reprinted from Ben LaBree, ed., *Notable Men
of Kentucky* (1902)

Following the mandate of the new constitution, the 1893 state elections were held in November. Although the vote was light, the Democrats showed gains, attributed somewhat to redistricting of the state. The Populists lost heavily. Even their leading candidate, Thomas S. Pettit,[25] was defeated for the legislature by a large Democratic majority. The Populists's losses may be attributed partly to the poor record made by the "Long Parliament," said to have been influenced by Alliance-People's Party elements. There were approximately 75 Democrats and 25 Republicans in the house, which, looking backward, marked a gain for the Republicans.

Legislative Session of 1894

The new General Assembly, the first elected under the new constitution, convened on Tuesday, January 2, 1894. It could boast of several able men, including Thomas J. Winfrey (Adair County), Charles F. Weaver (Boyd County), Judge William M. Beckner, Charles Finley (Whitley County), William Krieger (Louisville), Harvey Helm (Lincoln County), and John Crepps Wickliffe Beckham (Nelson County). A. J. Carroll, Louisville Democrat, was elected speaker over Thomas S. Kirk, Republican of Johnson County, by a vote of 73 to 23.[26]

Although necessarily devoting a sizeable portion of his message to recommending ways and means of clarifying and making legally workable various sections of the new constitution, Governor Brown offered suggestions upon several subjects of more than passing public interest, including a plan for making management of the penitentiaries more efficient,[27] and for expediting public printing, a matter left in an unfortunate condition by the constitution makers. His report concerning state finances, however, was altogether too sanguine. He contended that the treasury was in good condition, and even thought that the lawmakers might frame legislation designed to reduce somewhat the state property tax.

Being a competent lawyer, Brown reported on the proposed

consolidation of the Louisville and Nashville with the Chesapeake, Ohio, and Southwestern railroad. As a matter of fact, he had followed very closely the maneuvers of the roads' managers and attorneys to circumvent the Kentucky constitution quietly and quickly and had checkmated the counsel at every turn. He was thoroughly conversant with the railroad's hedging, as well as the efforts to compromise in the matter of paying full property tax on lines formerly exempted from taxation.

In recommending prevention of the consolidation of the two powerful roads (two-thirds of the state's mileage) and requesting that power of rate-fixing be accorded the state railroad commission, the governor not only followed the tendencies of the other states but also fulfilled a mandate of the new constitution.[28] Though his actions suited the Populists quite well, Brown was not attempting to please the People's party followers. He had no love for Populism.

The measure evoking the fullest amount of excited discussion and contention was Judge Beckner's bill concerning husband-wife property rights. Introduced on January 5, it was debated off and on until March 13, two days prior to adjournment, when it finally passed the house. It provided that marriage would give to the husband, during the life of the wife, no estate or interest in the wife's property, real or personal; that during the marital connection the wife could hold and own her estate to her separate and exclusive use and free from the debts, liabilities, or control of her husband, her estate being liable for her own debts only; that she might acquire property and sell and dispose of it in her own name, exclusive of her husband; that she could make contracts, sue and be sued, rent, collect, and receive; that the husband would not be liable for any debt of the wife incurred before or after marriage, except to the amount of property he might receive from or by virtue of marriage, but should be liable for necessaries furnished to her after marriage; that after the death of either the husband or wife the survivor should have an estate for his or her own life in one-third of all the real estate owned by the deceased, "or held by anyone to his or her use during coverture; and an absolute estate in one-half of all the surplus personalty left by such decedent"; and that the wife, if she be of sound mind and twenty-one years of age, might dispose of her estate by last will and testament, "subject to the provisions of this act."[29] Had it not been for the efforts of Judge Beckner, who championed other civil and educational reforms, the state's married women might have waited longer for the already tardy bestowal of such obvious rights.

A matter of considerable interest to the Democrats in the General Assembly was a resolution of particular political significance. This resolution, addressed to the United States senators from Kentucky, requested and instructed those gentlemen to refrain from voting to confirm any presidential appointee to the Supreme Court who was not a good Democrat, asking that they see to it that the recipient of their vote be able to establish "his devotion to the organization as well as to the cardinal principles of the Democratic party." The resolution failed to pass.

On the whole, most of the legislation passed during the session was still for the purpose of harmonizing the law with the constitution. The lawmakers, though adjourning sine die at the end of the 60-day session, failed to complete this Herculean task. In fact, the solons had insufficient time for many other important considerations. For example, no time was available, or at least taken, for devoting attention to serious labor unrest, particularly to strikes and violence among the coal miners.

Be it said to their credit, however, that by and large the work of the lawmakers won general public approval. One Louisville editor, palpably pleased, wrote that the wisdom of the 60-day session was completely vindicated by the "present legislature" which had completed the business "so thoroughly that there is no room for suggestion that an extra session is necessary." He contended that "the few laws passed promised to be beneficial." Declaring that the state's press generally had praised the session's work, the editor stated that "nobody can recall a legislature which received that sort of commendation."

The same editor took the legislators to task, however, for failure to correct a glaring defect in the new constitution pertaining to honest elections. Although the framers of that instrument had provided for the Australian ballot system of voting, they had made no other provision for honest voting nor for honest counting, which was actually a duty of the legislature. "The first elections under the new system showed glaring defects," he declared, "by which boodlers and corruptionists could and did falsify the will of the people. The defects of the primary laws," he declared, "were called to the attention of the legislature, but it refused to rectify them. The opportunities for fraud," he continued, "utilized in the general law were opposed to it and it refused to act. The provisions allowing ballots to be destroyed immediately after the count at the precincts, and the provisions for appointing election officers give all the chances for fraudulent manipulation of elections."

The editor charged that ballots were destroyed in Louisville immediately after the last election "to prevent the discovery of frauds, and there has never been a fair and honest appointment of election officers here." He insisted that the legislature, in dealing with election laws, "acted as a partisan body, and as such it decided to leave the doors for fraud open."[30]

The Elections of 1894

The political contests during the summer and fall of 1894 were extremely torrid and sensational. People were generally restive under the weight of "hard times." A good measure of blame for unsatisfactory conditions quite naturally was hurled at the Democratic party, in power in both nation and state, and considerable disaffection developed. Under the circumstances, therefore, the contest between the Republican and Democratic parties was of more than passing interest. What further inroads the Populists would make on the Democratic majorities was a matter of anxious speculation by the Democratic managers. Contests for congressional seats in the seventh and eleventh districts and the races in

Louisville and Jefferson County were highly turbulent. The Republicans, realizing the unpopularity of the Cleveland administration, as well as the tendency for political change during a depression, and displeasure with old Democratic abuses in the state, made a strenuous effort to win.

In the Eleventh Congressional District, the Republican incumbent, ex-Colonel Silas Adams of Liberty, Union hero of Wolford's celebrated First Kentucky Calvary Regiment, sought the Republican nomination. Strong opposition developed and abusive personal charges entered the canvass. Adams was defeated. Notwithstanding this, he ran in the final as an Independent and was again defeated by his former Republican opponent.

In the Seventh, Ashland or Lexington District, a bitter primary contest developed for the Democratic nomination to unseat the "Silver-tongued orator," W. C. P. Breckinridge, erstwhile idol of the Democracy. In the sensational Madeline Pollard damage suit, a sordid affair involving illicit sexual relations, the reputation of Breckinridge, a married man with five children, had been greatly damaged. The fall of Breckinridge was like that of an archangel, because everywhere the gifted "Billy" was virtually apotheosized. Realizing that the Colonel's loss of reputation might enable some other Democrat to win the Ashland seat, William C. Owens of Georgetown and Evan Evans Settle of Owenton announced for the nomination. The loyal friends of Breckinridge made a bitter, desperate primary fight, but Owens, former speaker of the Kentucky house of representatives, won by a plurality of 255 votes.[31]

In Louisville, the November election was of transcendent importance. Contests involving county offices, an Appellate Court judgeship, and a congressional seat were bitterly waged. For Congress, Edward J. McDermott ran on the Democratic ticket against Republican Walter Evans. St. John Boyle, son of General Jeremiah T. Boyle and a prominent Republican lawyer, contended against Democratic incumbent Judge Sterling B. Toney for the Court of Appeals.

A Breckinridge campaign poster in Lexington
Collection of the Kentucky Historical Society

Congressman W.C.P. Breckinridge
Reprinted from George L. Willis, Sr.,
Kentucky Democracy (1935), vol. III

"Boss" John Whallen
Reprinted from Ben LaBree, ed., *Notable Men
of Kentucky (1902)*

For years the city Democratic organization—in fact, the city of Louisville—had been ruled by a "boss," Colonel John Whallen, former Confederate soldier, who had settled down in Louisville after the war, and amassed a handsome fortune. He became a member of the Democratic State Central Committee. Whallen's principal legitimate enterprise was the burlesque show business, at the Buckingham Theater, the "Buck." The whole of the corpulent, genial, and generous Whallen's operations has never been revealed. It can be stated, however, that the Colonel maintained a suite of fine offices at the "Buck," and was very accommodating, and popular, particularly with the sporting men and politicians.

Colonel Whallen became quite interested in policemen—because they could be useful to him. There was, however, not much use trying to control policemen unless higherups were amenable. If he expected to keep his business operations out of the courts and give protection against the law to his friends and allied interests, he would more or less have to control the dominant Democratic party in the city and county. It appears that his ambition in this respect was realized, because by 1894 the center of city government was, it seems, Room 40 of the "Buckingham Palace."

The police force, reputed to "wink" at good-paying "vice rackets," was largely controlled by the "Duke of Buckingham" and his lieutenants, and the county judge and sheriff were said to be controlled by the "Duke." It appears that one of the most effective means of continuing in power was "stealing elections." Candidates could not win without the blessings of the genial "Duke," who was reputedly not inclined to "bless" anyone unwilling to ignore his profitable operations. The city was "wide-open" and "the goose hung high," according to some of the good citizens. It appears that Whallen maintained a little "flying squadron" of policemen who could be counted upon to beat-in the faces of any would-be reformers who became too troublesome.[32]

By the fall of 1894 the allegedly corrupt Louisville government under "Boss" Whallen and the "Buckingham gang" had become

340

Whallen's Buckingham Theater

Courtesy of the R. G. Potter Collection,
Univesity of Louisville

almost as notorious as that of the earlier "Boss" William Tweed of New York City. Never, however, had the "Duke" been in a stronger position. The county judge, William B. Hoke, running for re-election, was accused of being putty in his hands, and the sheriff, Henry Bell, was thought to be altogether amenable. Moreover, the policemen and council on public safety were listed as his men.

"Boss" Whallen, realizing the importance of the 1894 election and conscious of prominent citizens' opposition to his rule, determined, apparently, to take more than usual care to get the Democratic slate elected. Through Judge Hoke's connivance, he got the names of 4,000 Republican voters removed from the list and prepared to man the polls with thugs. At that point Democratic editor, Richard Knott of the *Evening Post*, revolted and called upon the "decent" citizens to vote Republican all down the line. Incidentally, both Walter N. Haldeman and Watterson, heads of the *Courier-Journal* and the *Times*, stuck with the "Buckingham" ticket and strove strenuously for its election. All the while the Republican *Commerical* poured forth a stream of scathing and truculent editorials, together with savagely satirical, though clever, cartoons scourging and flaying the "Buckingham gang" and fairly screaming for the decent citizens to rise up and smite the diabolical conspiracy. "Good Government" Democrats, surfeited with "Buckingham Palace" rule, went along with Knott and voted Republican. The blow was heavier than "Boss" Whallen had anticipated. Prepared to intervene in force though he was, Whallen simply could not withstand the devastating onslaught of the embattled citizens.

The morning following the election, the *Commercial* carried a story with the screaming headlines,

REDEEMED FROM GANG RULE. LOUISVILLE AND JEFFERSON COUNTY SWEPT BY AN UPRISING OF DECENT CITIZENS. THE NOTORIOUS BUCKINGHAM MACHINE ANNIHILATED AND ITS RULER FOREVER WIPED OUT.

The account declared Republican Walter Evans elected to Congress by a majority of 4,336. It boldly stated that "4,336 appear on the returns and 4,000 more represent the stealage, making 8,336 the fair figure. The decent Democrats of the district," it asserted, "disgusted with Buckingham rule, have at last risen to an assertion of their self-respect and their rights as citizens, and have overthrown their bosses and the hoodlum methods of the Buckingham rule." Continuing, the bold article declared that this was done in spite of the fact that "the Buckingham Committee, through its weak and pliant tool, Judge Hoke of the County Court, removed practically all the Republican election officers . . . and put in place of them thugs and bums, who were ready for any crime, to defeat the will of the people."

The story carried the charge that the sheriff, Henry Bell, "did all in his power to turn over the election to these thugs," illegally appointed as election officers. It was asserted that the sheriff had moved his headquarters to a room of the Buckingham Theatre, and that ballot boxes had been taken there prior to the voting and sent out "with shameless effrontery." Declaring that "on perjured testimony" the "Buckingham gang" had attempted to have 4,000 names stricken off the list, the article pointed out that too few ballots had been delivered to some voting precincts, while too many had been taken to others—all done to work to the "gang's" advantage—and that Negroes were refused admittance to the polls, while "trusted Democrats" were admitted by "the back way."

At the polls, "The Democratic election officers," according to the *Commercial*, "on orders from Buckingham and backed by policemen, refused to let any but Democratic inspectors enter. One of the city's most prominent citizens, Charles C. Mengel, Jr., was brutally assaulted by the blue-coated men of the Board of Safety, and thrown out of the polls, notwithstanding his legal credentials as an inspector."[33]

Watterson's *Courier-Journal* answered the *Commercial's* charges with attacks of its own. Republican inspectors, the paper charged, tried to force their way into the voting areas before the voting had

343

ceased—a violation. Seeking to stuff the ballot boxes, the Republicans had been rebuffed by Democrats who tried to keep the ballots unblemished by fraud. Reports of fraudulent voting by Negroes were repeated by the *Courier-Journal* staff. The paper expressed surprise but gave no explanation for the large turnout in several districts. In the Shivley precinct—where only 23 voters had cast their ballots in the previous year—now more than 250 had voted. Twenty-six other precincts ran out of ballots, resulting in a mass of confusion. Seventeen precincts called for supplemental ballot boxes to hold the excess ballots. The *Courier-Journal* happened to print the ballots and the shortage resulted in their plant's operation that day.

Knott had seen Sheriff Bell with ballot boxes and had assumed they were bogus, stuffed ones, said the *Courier-Journal*. Not so. The Sheriff simply sought to take the empty boxes to precincts which required them. Knott called Bell "an infamous liar" and the Sheriff got angry, but both men expressed regret over their actions. Later an editorial admitted that fraud did occur, but stressed the bi-partisan nature of the fraud: "There would to-day be fewer of both Republican and Democrats out of jail if every man who transgressed the election laws should be undertaken to end this state of affairs, for there is just about as much of this sort of lawlessness in one party as in the other."[34]

Declared the jubilant Louisville Republican lawyer, Harvard-educated Augustus E. Willson, upon being interviewed, "I love the Old Kentucky home, and I care more for the hope of the day when it will throw off the incubus of prejudice than for any other news on earth. Kentucky will be redeemed."

Richard Knott declared that the Democratic defeat was due to bossism:

Our people will no longer respond to the party lash, and they will no longer submit to those who assume to speak in the name of the party organization. Unless the Democratic party can give us an economical government; unless it can keep the bench above reproach; unless it can compel its own members in public office to obey the law, then there is no longer any excuse for its existence. . . . When John Whallen is the Democratic Party of Louisville, when Croker is the Democratic Party of New York, then have we surrendered our liberties and become the subjects of the most obnoxious form of tyranny.

Wrote the editor of the *Commercial*: "Mr. Knott deserves the thanks of the community."[35]

Following the election, prominent citizens, both Republicans and Democrats, organized a "Citizens Committee of 100" for the purpose of indicting and bringing to trial Whallen and his lawbreakers. Colonel Mengel was elected chairman. It was, however, a long time before Louisville's government was "laundered," although a staggering blow had been struck at "bossism and vice" and the "Duke" was on his way out.[36]

In the state the Democracy that year suffered the severest setback since the Civil War. Six Democrats and five Republicans were elected to Congress, the largest Republican gain to that time; there was but one Republican from the state in the preceding Congress. Undoubtedly, disaffection of the Populists (who had maintained candidates in nine congressional districts) played a part in Democratic losses. As to the vote, a total of 324,124 ballots had been cast. The Democrats received 156,195 votes; the Republicans, 147,277; the Populists, 18,437; the Prohibitionists, 2,215. The congressional vote in 1892 had been 174,539 Democratic to 121,858 Republican, and 23,736 Populists.[37]

Although a section of the state's Democratic press was inclined to minimize the seriousness of disaffection in the party's ranks, saying the setback was due to overconfidence, most of the leaders realized that a crippling split was approaching and they resorted to desperation tactics. On the eve of the election, an article in the *Mt. Sterling Advocate* stated: "Today tells the tale. Shall we have men whose party is mainly composed of negroes to fill our offices, or shall we have men who are representatives of white men to fill them?"[38] Among other disabilities, the Democratic party had been in power too long in the state. A veritable host of "sins," both commission and omission, had grown to plague the party. Contrarily, the party could not point to a record of outstanding progressive achievement. Great industrial development, educational progress, social advancement, and economic prosperity had not occurred. Instead the nation was in the throes of a devastating depression, and the Cleveland administration was unpopular even with the Democrats. There was also the bitter fight between cheap money and gold standard men, a struggle threatening to wreck the party. Added to all these ills was the fact that thousands of Democrats had become thoroughly dissatisfied with the old Bourbon leadership, continuously in power since the Civil War, and had demanded a change. The star of a young man named William Goebel was rising. The jealousy of the western Kentucky Democrats against central Kentucky no longer could be minimized. Adding to the Democracy's afflictions was the fact that several powerful Democratic leaders coveted the United States senatorial seat held by Jo Blackburn, a silverite and agrarian, who would come up for re-election in 1895.

Adding one more straw to the donkey's almost broken back was the fact that John Young Brown and his administration were popular neither with the jealous and ambitious leaders nor with the people. Wrote a prominent Louisville editor; "John Young Brown, who has done nothing since he went into office three years ago, but make himself the most cordially hated man in public life in this state, is so enveloped in a thick robe of self-conceit and so closely guarded from the outside public by the half-dozen members of his official family, who, from pity or prejudice, still adhere to him, that he really believes that he may yet be sent to the Senate in the place of Jo Blackburn."[39]

Neither the governor nor his administration accomplished anything bordering upon greatness. Little in the way of reform was achieved. He left a legacy of frustration and a hopelessly divided party.

XVI

THE CHANGING CENTURY

William O'Connell Bradley's Election

The 1895 Democratic state convention met at Louisville in the Music Hall on June 26. Badly split on the money question, with hard times converting thousands to cheap money, the Kentucky Democracy was seriously affected with the silver virus. In May of that year John G. Carlisle had made a speaking tour over the state, pointing out the evils of free and unlimited coinage of silver. Henry Watterson, militantly anti-free silver man, was lavish in praise of Carlisle, as well as of United States Senator William Lindsay, who was also doing yeoman service in behalf of sound money on various platforms in the state.

In spite of the fact that the sound money faction, with the help of Haldeman, Whallen, and the "Buckingham Palace Gang," was able to organize the convention and get adopted a more or less sound money plank, a silverite, "Wat" Hardin, principally because of his immense personal popularity, was nominated for the governorship—to the great disgust of Watterson, Haldeman, Breckinridge, Lindsay, John M. Atherton, Alexander P. Humphrey, and many prominent editors. These had favored the nomination of Cassius M. Clay, Jr. The other nominees on the ticket were Robert T. Tyler of Fulton County for lieutenant governor, incumbent treasurer Henry S. Hale for secretary of state, incumbent Luke C. Norman for auditor, R. C. Ford of Clay county for treasurer, incumbent William J. Hendrick for attorney-general, Ion B. Nall of Louisville for commissioner of agriculture, and incumbents Ed. Porter

Thompson for superintendent of public instruction, and G. B. Swango for register of the land office.

Pandemonium broke out when John S. Rhea of Russellville arose in the convention and tried to jam through resolutions favorable to "free silver" and opposing endorsement of the Cleveland administration. The clamor became so wild and tumultuous that the hard-pressed permanent chairman, state Senator Albert Seaton Berry of Newport, felt obliged to have a drink of bourbon whiskey before he could proceed with voting. Perhaps the bourbon helped. The Rhea resolutions were voted down, but in the teeth of powerful and bitter opposition.

If it had not dawned upon them at the time that they had nominated a silverite to run on a gold platform, the Democrats might have learned next day through the Republican *Louisville Commercial*. Its bold headlines read:

FREE SILVER HARDIN ON A STRADDLE GOLD STAN-DARD PLATFORM. FREE SILVER HARDIN BEATS SOUND MONEY CLAY BEFORE THE DEMOCRATIC CONVENTION. A RIDICULOUS CONVENTION. AFTER INDORSING CLEVELAND THE CONVENTION NOMI-NATES AN ANTI-CLEVELAND MAN.[1]

The Republicans, conscious of the Democratic disaffection, met in Louisville and did what they probably would have done with or without schism in the Democracy. They adopted a platform standing for high protection, the gold standard, and internal reform. This done, they nominated their ablest Kentucky campaigner, William O'Connell Bradley, to be their standard bearer. "Bradley and Sound Money!" was their battle cry. Democratic leaders started counter-Bradley propaganda. Richard Knott of the *Evening Post* wrote: "Bradley stands for nothing but the office. He represents no great measure of reform, has never exhibited any executive ability, and beyond being an attractive stump-speaker and retailer of anecdotes, more or less risque, Bradley has no qualities necessary to the successful candidate."

P. "Wat" Hardin, Democratic gubernatorial
candidate of 1895
Collection of the Kentucky Historical Society

Knott, nevertheless, was bitterly opposed to free silver, and despised Jo Blackburn, whom he characterized as an "adventurous, noisy charletan who had brought his party to the verge of ruin." The *Press-Transcript* (Lexington) and the *Courier-Journal* very gingerly and perfunctorily went along with Hardin, but the *Post* left his name off the list of candidates.[2]

The ticket nominated along with Bradley consisted of William J. Worthington of Greenup County for lieutenant governor, Charles Finley of Whitley County for secretary of state, Samuel H. Stone of Madison County for auditor, George W. Long of Grayson County for treasurer, William Sylvester Taylor of Butler County for attorney-general, William Jefferson Davidson of Pulaski County for superintendent of public instruction, Charles O. Reynolds of Lexington for register of the land office, and Lucas Moore of Marion County for commissioner of agriculture.

The sensational feature of the florid gubernatorial campaign was a series of joint debates between Hardin and Bradley. The Populist Pettit, however, was not included in the debate arrangements,[3] which contemplated stands at Louisville, Mayfield, Hopkinsville, Bowling Green, Leitchfield, Eminence, Covington, Cynthiana, Nicholasville, Winchester, and London—closing the joint meetings at Morganfield on September 9.

The opening of the canvass in Louisville on August 19 at the Auditorium attracted a capacity crowd of more than 3,000 auditors with, it was stated, some 400 platform sitters. Hardin opened the debate, making a play on the Civil War and recounting the horrors of Carpetbag reconstruction under Republican rule. He intimated that if the Republicans were elected in Kentucky the citizens of the state would learn first hand what Republican Carpetbag despotism really was. Soon the audience was tired of the "bloody shirt." Someone cried out, "The war is over; give us something else." Then Hardin shocked sound money Democrats by stating that he stood for no discrimination between gold and silver (ratio of 16-1) and that the coinage of each metal should be free.

Thomas Pettit, Populist leader
Reprinted from "Scrapbook of the Constitutional Convention"

According to a news correspondent, "General Wat's old rabble-rousing magic" had failed him for the first time. Louisville had not been swept off her feet and Bradley, clearly aware of Hardin's mistakes, eagerly awaited his turn. He arose, expressed a few pleasantries, and then entered into a defense of the Republican party and of his own family—a defense reported as eloquent. Thus warmed up and having captivated at least the assembled Republicans, Bradley proceeded to "devastate" the free silver "fallacy," taking the word of leading Democrats for his authority. He closed with an appeal for progress.[4]

The "Great Debate" was carried in journals throughout the state and editorial comment was free and extensive. Even "Marse Henry" was of the opinion that Colonel Bradley had lost "none of his cunning in juggling with words." Richard Knott, the crusader, having little praise for either candidate, stated that "in the second round (rebuttal) the Democratic candidate appeared somewhat groggy and winded" and that "the [Democratic] party needs a leader; Hardin has abdicated." The *Louisville Commercial*, partisan and of the opinion that Bradley had "wiped up the earth" with Hardin, carried the headline that "Hardin Gets His Written Speech Mixed Up And Then Gets Rattled And Makes A Failure."[5]

The campaign was vigorously waged throughout. The Democrats were not united.[6] However, the best silverite "spellbinders" took the stump. Bradley, as usual, bore the brunt of the Republican campaigning, assisted at every turn, however, by his able campaign manager, John W. Yerkes.[7] At the Eminence meeting, Bradley was shouted down. Twelve times he attempted to speak— all to no avail. Thoroughly disgusted, the "gallant Wat," by the side of Bradley, left the platform and refused to speak. Bloody encounters over the state were not unusual as the feeling mounted. Several were killed, a circumstance which by the year 1895 disturbed few in Kentucky.

The election returns indicated Bradley as the winner by a 9,000 majority over Hardin. The Populist candidate, Pettit, received nearly 17,000 votes. "Billy O. B." had gained 4,000 "Gold

1895 ELECTION

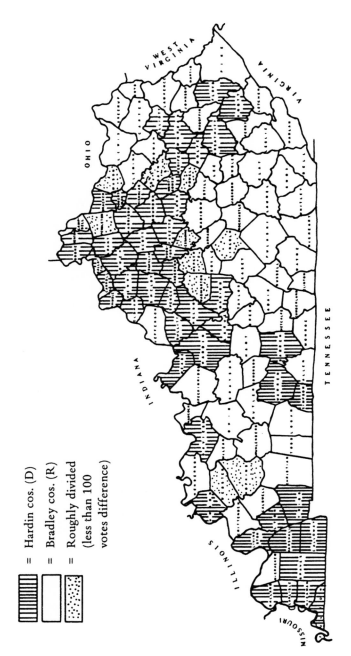

= Hardin cos. (D)

= Bradley cos. (R)

= Roughly divided
(less than 100
votes difference)

Source: *Official Manual of Kentucky, 1895*

Democrats" in Louisville.[8] A Republican had won, thirty years after the end of the war.

Stormy Weather

Perhaps the happiest day in Bradley's life was when, together with retiring governor John Y. Brown, he alighted from the white horse-drawn carriage at the Capitol in Frankfort to be inaugurated as governor.[9] He had fought hard and long for the office he was about to occupy. One of the largest crowds ever seen at Frankfort had come to wish Bradley well. He was Kentucky's first Republican governor, and the *Press-Transcript* noted the enthusiasm of the thousands who flung their hats into the air and shouted themselves hoarse. "The scene as Bradley mounted the stand beggars description," it stated. Bradley, taking no notice of a few partisan remarks, warmed graciously to the occasion and pleased the multitude.

The governor-elect asked the people not to expect miracles. He promised to be the governor of the whole people and to strive for educational, ballot and tax reform, for economy, and for an end to violence. He hoped that the "bonds of the Union" and "the love between the states" would "grow stronger." The speech ended, Chief Justice William S. Pryor of New Castle administered the oath.[10]

True to his promises, Governor Bradley recommended a full program of reform to the General Assembly which met in January, 1896. He asked that a constitutional amendment be offered to authorize the city of Louisville to exercise local self-government; he called for abolition of the offices of commissioner of agriculture and commonwealth's attorney; sought submission to the people for vote the question of erecting a new capitol and a new mansion; supported the establishment of a house of reform for correcting first offenders, so as to separate them from hardened criminals; advocated reforms in the fee system to attorneys for prosecuting criminals; urged investigation by experts into all state departments, in order that a correct statement could be made of the state's assets and liabilities. Bradley stated that he would not recommend an increase in tax rates, because he believed that, if property were fairly assessed, the state would have ample funds for running expenses. He expressed alarm at the growing tendency of mob violence in connection with the destruction over the state of tollgates and houses, acts perpetrated at night and designed to make travel on the turnpikes free. He felt that property should be protected as provided in the law and that the General Assembly should pass whatever additional legislation might be needed, and he reiterated his intention to enforce the law."[11]

Unfortunately, the new governor could not count upon the support of the legislature.[12] The senate named William Goebel president pro tem; by a 54-45 vote the house elected as speaker Charles Blanford of Breckinridge County, a Republican, over A. J. Carroll, sound money Democrat of Louisville. On joint ballot the two parties were about equally divided. One of the two Populists usually voted with the Republicans. Early in the session, committees were appointed to investigate contested seats. In the house, three Republicans and two Democrats were named to the committee. Charges of "no election" were not made, however, until toward the close of the session.

The only question of real interest to most of the lawmakers was that of electing a United States senator. This matter came up for vote early in the session. The free silver Democrats determined to return Jo Blackburn, who was on hand to push his candidacy in every way possible. Except for Blackburn, the Democrats, many of whom disliked him heartily, might have carried the day in short order. At the caucus held to name a party candidate, a determined minority held out implacably against him.

The Republican caucus selected Dr. W. Godfrey ("Gum Shoe") Hunter of Cumberland County and the balloting began. The sound money Democrats put forward James B. McCreary, who never received more than 13 votes. At various times, Brown, Carlisle, Watterson, Walter Evans, Buckner, Judge William H. Holt of Mt.

Sterling, William Murphy Reed of Benton and Paducah, Judge James S. Hazelrigg of Mt. Sterling and Frankfort, Judge John R. Grace of Cadiz and Frankfort, A. E. Willson, E. C. Bate, and others were nominated. On January 30, the vote stood: Hunter, 66, Blackburn, 57, Buckner, 9, Brown, 1, and Willson, 1. On the 28th ballot 9 votes went to Watterson. Meanwhile, the silverites challenged the naturalization of Dr. Hunter, born an Englishman. Investigation revealed that he had taken out first papers in 1859 as a minor and that he had taken his final papers in 1865. It was also learned, however, that as a surgeon in the army, Hunter's case could come under a federal statute permitting aliens who served in the army to be naturalized without any preliminaries.[13]

One of the acts associated with the contest was indictment of Hunter for bribery. No proof, however, could be found to convict him, so that he was forthwith acquitted. Following this incident, the contest continued, with tempers becoming shorter every day and hatred mounting to a dangerous height. Then in March the contest committee went into operation. One Democrat was unseated in the house and two Republicans in the senate.

When the vote was taken in the senate to unseat Republican senators Dr. A. B. James of Muhlenberg County and Dr. J. Walton of Hart County, wild excitement prevailed. A group of heavily armed partisans of Blackburn guarded the doors, swearing that James and Walton would never escape to the house, there to continue voting in the senatorial race. Walton had already slipped out, however, and James was roughly handled while trying to escape. Six outsiders, partisans of Blackburn, were quickly sworn in as deputies by the sergeant-at-arms of the senate.

Reporters repeated the rumor that all but a score of the 132 members had one or two pistols concealed, to say nothing of knives and other weapons. Even the most peacefully disposed legislators, wrote a correspondent, were tempted to arm for self-defense, and both parties had chosen leaders and stationed them on watch at strategic points about the hall. James and Walton, whose presence was obnoxious to the Democrats, were placed among Republican associates, and one of the most fearless of the party, well armed, was reported to have been deputed to open fire on any one who attempted to molest them. The silver men had several trustworthy persons in position to cover this Republican in case of a signal for action. The Democratic leader, seated in the center aisle near the door of the senate chamber, was another storm center.

Meanwhile, the leading journals of the nation were announcing in screaming headlines details of the sorry spectacle being provided by the Kentucky "statesmen." Nearer the wild scene, Henry Watterson found difficulty in restraining his feelings:

> The legislative halls of Kentucky, supposed to be the source of the State's law, were in possession of mobs which set at defiance all law. Turbulence, ruffianism, madness, anarchy, reigned; and that blood did not flow and death crown the orgy of passion, was a miracle not to be explained by the absence of death, and desperadoes to wield them. It is an outrage upon the fame of a nation which never knew such disgrace; it was a mockery of civilization, a prostitution of political methods to the ends of insane partisanship and brutish barbarism.[14]

One of Watterson's reporters issued a graphic account of the proceedings following the ousting of Drs. James and Walton. "The lobby," runs the account, "separating the Senate door from the House door was made almost impassable by a crowd of Republican and Democratic rowdies. At the critical moments not less than twenty stood with hands on handles of the weapons in their pockets. The noise was like the roar and din of an angry mob." "Senator Bronston," continued the report, "stood at the head of the Democrats at the House door, and trembling from excitement, shouted to those at hand to keep out the unseated Republicans. Curses and oaths," the correspondent declared, "echoed from the dome of the library building, and as the mob swayed in the direction of the Floor of the Representatives' Hall, the feeling and excitement was so intense that those who were not participants hid behind every door-sill or corner to avoid possible danger. . . ." As though timed in the best comic opera manner, at the dramatic moment, Senator Blackburn reportedly emerged from the senate cloakroom to be acclaimed by his boisterous partisans.[15]

By March 15 disorders had broken out all over Frankfort. Drunken rowdies, abetted reportedly by a few prominent citizens, obstructed the street and yelled, "until Frankfort was turned into a Bedlam." Realizing that neither the Frankfort authorities nor the county sheriff would do anything to preserve law and order and knowing that destruction of life was imminent, Governor Bradley called out the state militia. This action brought forth a local indignation meeting. While the meeting was in progress, "crowds of drunken rowdies" practically took over the town.

Bradley's action in calling out the militia appears to have been wise. The famous Louisville Legion, under command of Colonel John Breckinridge Castleman and Colonel Edward H. Gaither, moved to Frankfort and took up positions at strategic points. Leading Democrats, among whom were Louisvillians Richard Knott and W. H. Dulaney congratulated the governor for his actions. Some of Blackburn's supporters, however, were reportedly furious. But order was quickly restored. There was still no elected senator.

Before adjourning sine die on March 16 the senate sought by resolutions to "convict the Governor of interference" and to fine him $500 and sentence him to six months in jail. Some of the silverites had boasted that they would put Lieutenant Governor Worthington "in hoc." They would then be free to put President Pro Tem Goebel in the governor's chair, after removing Bradley. A committee headed by Senator Goebel was appointed to investigate Governor Bradley. It appears, however, that the committeemen were rather discomfited by Bradley.[16] Had Bradley been less strong, it is believed, he might have been thrown out of the office by force, so great were the resentment and rapacity of the silverites. As a matter of fact, less than four years later, that very fate befell a Republican governor less strong than Bradley.

Adjournment found the solons no nearer agreement on the election of a United States senator than they had been at the outset, and practically the entire time of the session had been devoted to the problem.

The modicum of important legislation passed can be listed in a small amount of space. Less than 40 bills introduced became law and 9 resolutions were passed. Significant bills enacted provided for two houses of reform—one for boys and one for girls; for free turnpikes and gravel roads; and for compulsory education by requiring that every child of school age attend school not less than twelve weeks in each year and forbidding the employment of children who had not attended.

Perhaps the most reprehensible deed of the senate was its failure to pass the revenue bill, obviously to embarrass the administration. The treasury was empty, the state practically bankrupt, and Bradley had nothing on which to run the state. It was bitterly disappointing to him that his reform program was not enacted. This new insult aroused the governor's fighting spirit considerably. His supporting paper, the *Commercial*, proclaimed the end of the legislative session in these bold headlines:

THE LEGISLATURE ADJOURNS UNDER MILITARY PROTECTION. GOVERNOR BRADLEY'S COURAGEOUS COURSE PRESERVED THE HONOR OF KENTUCKY. THE MOST DISGRACEFUL SESSION OF KENTUCKY'S GENERAL ASSEMBLY DRAWN TO CLOSE. THE STATE LEFT BANKRUPT.[17]

The Presidential Election of 1896

On the heels of the political disturbances at Frankfort came the political conventions to nominate delegates to the national conventions to select candidates for the presidency and the vice presidency. The Republican convention met in Louisville, April 16 and 17. The delegates were instructed to vote for Bradley for the presidential nomination. If Bradley's name were withdrawn, they were to support William McKinley. The platform adopted favored the protective tariff, support of the Monroe Doctrine, sympathy for Cuba, extending the free school system, and the gold standard. Aside from the last provision it was innocuous.

The Democratic convention assembled in Lexington, June 3. The silverites, with a decisive majority, elected Charles J. Bronston to the temporary chairmanship by 691 to 206. All the delegates chosen for the national convention at Chicago were free silver men, and they were instructed to vote for J. C. S. Blackburn for president. The platform expressed opposition to the national bank system and retirement of the greenbacks, declared for tariff for revenue only, favored bimetallism and demanded free and unlimited coinage of silver at the ratio of 16 to 1, with equal legal tender power.

The Populist convention met in Paducah, July 20. It opposed the plan for adoption by its national convention of the Chicago (Democratic) ticket, which had nominated William Jennings Bryan, and the Chicago platform. However, a plan for fusion with the silver Democrats was arranged September 22, by which two of the Populist electors were to be placed upon the ticket and the other withdrawn.[18]

The National Democratic Party convention assembled at Louisville, on August 25. The "gold" Democrats of the state, refusing to go along with Bryan and the Chicago platform, decided to join the National Democratic Party formed in Chicago on July 23. They believed Bryan to be a Populist, "pure and simple," and were convinced that those in control of the old party were in no sense Democrats. One of the leaders of the national organization was Walter B. Haldeman, part owner of the *Courier-Journal* and owner of the *Louisville Times*. Some of the national party leaders had hoped that Watterson would run for president, believing that he would receive sufficient votes to make McKinley a certain winner and to give Watterson control of the regular Democratic party after Bryan's defeat. However, Watterson was in Europe and Buckner desired the vice presidential nomination, so that Haldeman, who kept in close communication with "Marse Henry," discouraged the proposal.

The state convention of the National Democrats elected former lieutenant governor James R. Hindman of Columbia temporary chairman and J. Q. A. Ward permanent chairman. Wrote Haldeman: "We had a grand State Convention in Louisville on day before yesterday, and nearly all the counties of the state were represented by the best Democrats in Kentucky." The convention declared for the gold standard, with a bank currency well secured and redeemable in gold, "with the use of silver and other metals within the reasonable limits prescribed by convenience and safety and to be kept at par with gold," and for tariff for revenue only. It declared the candidates and platform of the Chicago convention un-Democratic, and advanced twelve reasons for so pronouncing. Bryan, the convention charged, was a Populist, and Arthur Sewall (wealthy Democratic leader of Maine), his running mate, "a subsidized shipbuilder and high protectionist." Holding the action of the Chicago convention to be "unauthorized and revolutionary," the platform stated that there was no moral obligation to support it. It endorsed Buckner for vice president.[19]

There is little doubt that the delegates to this convention were among the most prominent men in the state. In fact, the register of the Galt House at Louisville at that time reads like a Kentucky social register.[20] The gathering, devoid of "radicals and rabble," was genteel and conservative. From the outset, they felt that their action was not only patriotic but would work the salvation of the party. Hindman, in the opening speech, referring to the Bible, said it was written that ten righteous Lots could have saved Sodom; he believed there were enough righteous Lots assembled to save the Democracy of Kentucky. The highlight of the occasion was a speech by W. C. P. Breckinridge, whose vicissitudes had failed to diminish his oratorical wizardry. Hardly less able was the effort of Carlisle who took the principles of Jefferson as his text, declaring that "agrarianism, communism, Populism and fiatism have no place in the Democratic creed, and can not be incorporated in it." An encouraging telegram was received from Senator William Lindsay, confined by sickness to his residence in Frankfort.

The most acrid campaign denunciations emanated perhaps not from the Republicans but from the pen of Henry Watterson. He felt that Populism was something evil and was convinced that Bryan was a Populist. "Marse Henry," a rugged individualist, deprecated governmental interference and governmental aid. The very thought of government ownership of property and economic support of the citizens drove him to anger. Even limited governmental regulation of individual enterprise aroused his ire. He believed apparently that the Populists were bent upon a war on property. "If once begun," he declared, "the revolution, like that in France, will go on and land will be taken too." He was not convinced, however, that all farmers were in debt and that they wished "to pay in dishonest money." He asserted that the Populists wanted the government to take over the land, that they insisted land was the common property of all, that no man had a right to own it. "They deny," he continued, "that any compensation should be paid for it. If the war on property led by Bryan and Sewall succeeds, does any one imagine that the revolution will stop there?" He begged the forces of order, including the farmers, to stand together against Populism. "No Compromise with dishonor" became his battle cry. All the while subscriptions to the *Courier-Journal* dropped at an alarming rate.[21] "Marse Henry" was no longer spokesman for the Democrats in Kentucky. Agrarianism had triumphed.

The gold Democrats (National Democrats), unable to accept Bryan, held a convention at Indianapolis on September 2 and nominated for President and Vice-President General John M. Palmer of Illinois and General Simon Bolivar Buckner—they were old adversaries at Fort Donelson. President Cleveland and all his cabinet except Secretary of the Interior Hoke Smith of Georgia, supported the Indianapolis ticket, which polled only 134,645 votes on election day.

As expected, the canvass in Kentucky was explosive. The National Democrats including Watterson, Breckinridge, Buckner, and Carlisle, politically more akin to McKinley and Bradley than to Bryan and Blackburn, worked diligently, though indirectly, it was charged for a Republican victory. The silverites, brought the "Boy orator of the Platte" to the state for speaking engagements. On the other hand, Republican orators, once more feeling the exhilarating sensation of approaching victory, were also plentiful. Some indication of the mood of the campaign may be gained from the "Covington Incident." There in his own home town, Carlisle, attempting to speak, was "pelted with rotten eggs and other offal" by silverites. Palmer, Buckner, and other men on the platform were confronted by "angry mobs who hooted and jeered them and tried to disperse their meeting."

As to the election results, once more the commonwealth went Republican. McKinley received 218,171 votes and twelve of the state's thirteen electoral ballots. Bryan was given 217,890 votes, and Palmer, 5,114. The Republican candidate had a plurality of only 281 votes. Instead of the results having a sobering effect upon the silverites and causing some degree of contrition, just the opposite was the case. The spirit of bitterness, violence, and vindictiveness, together with seemingly an inordinate personal ambition to "rule or ruin" was more evident in the years immediately following than in the year 1896. Those who lost most were the Populists, who had gambled all and lost all. That year too, A. Rollins Burnam, Richmond Republican, defeated the prominent and widely known Judge Pryor for the Appellate Court.[22]

Legislative Sessions, 1897-1898

After the riotous legislature of 1895 adjourned without having elected a United States senator, Governor Bradley appointed Andrew T. Wood to serve, beginning after March 4, 1897, if the legislature in the meantime had failed to make a choice. He then called a special session for March, 1897. At that session, the old contest between Hunter and Blackburn continued in all its fury. Ballot after ballot was taken and the deadlock continued. Completely exhausted, seeing no hope of breaking the deadlock and under constant attack, Dr. Hunter withdrew from the race, and the Republicans substituted St. John Boyle. The grim business continued. Boyle, seeing little hope of winning, also withdrew. The Republicans then put forward William J. Deboe, an imposing giant from Marion, who on the 112th ballot received a majority and election. During the special session, the "gold" Democrats had been supporting Henry L. Martin, prominent political and business leader of Woodford, Blackburn's home county. At the end he had 13 votes, Blackburn 50, Deboe 71, and Stone 1.[23] Deboe became Kentucky's first Republican United States senator.

Also during the special session, the lawmakers passed a bill designed to relieve the embarrassing financial condition of the state treasury. Provision was made for issuance of bonds in amount of $500,000 to bear interest at the rate of 4 percent. The effort, however, was of no avail, because the Appellate Court ruled the law in violation of the constitutional limitation of $500,000 indebtedness, declaring that the state already had a bonded indebtedness in excess of $2,000,000. The solons began to realize what a straitjacket the framers of the constitution had placed them in. Bradley, unlike Buckner, had no personal fortune to place at the disposal of the bankrupt state.

The most exciting feature of the year to the sensation-loving people was the race for clerk of the Court of Appeals, the only state officer to be elected. Democrats, Republicans, Populists, and Prohibitionists put forth candidates. With the injection once more of the "free silver" issue, the canvass became extremely acrimonious and violent. Hatred and vindictiveness magnified the contest out of all proportions to its actual importance. On election day a bloody encounter developed in Frankfort, resulting in the death of three men and the wounding of two others. At Mt.

Vernon an election-day disturbance ended in a shooting affray between rioters and the sheriff and his deputies. Three deputies were killed.

The regular (silver) Democratic candidate, Samuel J. Shackelford, won with 187,482 votes. The Populist candidate, Joseph A. Parker (whose platform was thought by some unusually radical) received only 7,374; the Republican, James G. Bailey of Magoffin County, 169,687; and the National Democratic nominee, James R. Hindman but 9,562.[24] The shrinkage of the Populist vote was very notable. By the end of this contest it was evident that a quasi-Populism had captured the Democratic party in the state. It was clear, too, that party control by conservative, aristocratic, ex-Confederates was passing. It seemed that politicians ready to please tenant farmers and labor were taking control. Most of the gold Democrats, including Watterson (his paper almost bankrupt) joined the new order. Many went over to the Republicans. Some, including Breckinridge, wandered from one party to the other, finally to return after 1900 to the Democrats.[25]

Bradley's Final Effort for Reform

The regular session of the General Assembly convened January 4, 1898, with the Democrats approaching the old time majorities.[26] Boyish J. C. W. Beckham was elected speaker over Republican John P. Haswell, Jr., Hardinsburg, by 70 to 24. William Goebel again was elected president pro tem of the senate. It was during this session that the two later-to-be "bosses" and political masterminds of the Democracy, Percy Haly of Frankfort and William F. ("Billy") Klair of Lexington made their debut on the state scene. Haly was elected sergeant-at-arms of the house, and Klair assistant sergeant-at-arms of the senate.[27]

Either uninformed or unmindful of the intentions of the Democratic legislature, Bradley sent another message to the General Assembly replete with recommendations for passage of his reform legislation. Though devoting a good part of the message to

A political rally of the 1890s
Collection of the Kentucky Historical Soc.

vigorously informing the solons of the seriousness of the tollgate war and of widespread lawlessness, the governor presented stark facts concerning the treasury's deplorable condition. Then he plunged into a discussion of possible means of economy, centering upon the idea of cutting salaries of state officers; he advised also that numerous fees be eliminated, fees and costs in connection with prosecuting, convicting, confining, and keeping criminals. "The present salaries," he stated in support of financial conservatism, "are in nearly every instance twice as much as they were at the conclusion of the war, when the premium on gold was greater than ever before. . . . Extravagance should not be tolerated," he declared. Bradley called attention to considerable possible saving, if the legislature would cut off political "hangers-on," abolish the sinecures, and eliminate the "political gravy."

One of the recommendations asked for by the governor was that control of the eleemosynary institutions be put in the hands of a nonpartisan board trained in social and institutional work. "The charitable and penal institutions of the Commonwealth," he stated, "should be placed on a thoroughly nonpartisan basis, and officers appointed on account of their especial fitness and experience. Charities," he declared, "should not be used to promote political ends. Such a practice most frequently results in 'stealing the livery of Heaven to serve the devil in.' " In general Bradley simply wasted breath and paper. But not all was lost. The legislature did pass an act providing that management of the prisons be taken from the commissioners of the Sinking Fund and placed under a commission of three, appointed by the governor, with salaries of $2,000 annually plus traveling expenses.

The governor ventured to inform the lawmakers that the capitol was falling to pieces, a part of the ceiling of the Appellate Court chamber having been propped up by iron bars to protect the pates of the learned justices. He declared also that a part of the ceiling of the representatives' chamber had already fallen, and asked authorization for repairs. He believed the governors' mansion so unsafe that he made an out and out recommendation for building a new one.

Bradley's recommendations for educational reform were striking. Placing public education as first in importance, he asked that the old district system, with its numerous trustees, be abolished, and that the county system, with superintendent and county board, be established. He thought uniform school taxes on a county-wide basis would provide enough money for running the system adequately; that not only the superintendent, but board members as well, should be required to possess satisfactory educational qualifications, and that some compensation should be given them for services. He believed that county boards, and not district trustees, should appoint teachers. Bradley, recognizing the evils of the system of adopting textbooks, asked that uniformity in adoption be established, and that overpaying for books be eliminated. He made an eloquent plea for fairer support of black education and recommended establishment of a normal school for Negroes in western Kentucky.

The governor also called for repeal of the "Separate Coach Law." He pointed to the Negroes' record of service to southerners during the Civil War. "Left in charge of the wives and children of Confederate soldiers," he reminded them, "who were fighting to perpetuate their bondage, when their liberty was trembling in the balance, not one instance is recorded in which they were faithless, or in which criminal assault was made, or torch applied to the house of their masters." He contended that every citizen "should be judged according to his conduct, decency and good citizenship, rather than his color, and the slave who, side by side with his master, drove the carriage or played upon the green with his children in old slave days can not disgrace him, now that he is free, by riding in the same coach provided that his conduct and character are good." Bradley's recommendation appeared to elicit little but indignation from the Kentucky legislators.

In addition, the governor recommended that requirements for licenses to practice law be stiffened, that penalties be passed for certain unethical practices by some lawyers at the bar; also that the statute requiring an involvement of as much as $100 in property for a case to go to the Appellate Court be amended to $300—this to relieve the hard-pressed Court of Appeals.

Although Bradley's legislative message was conciliatory throughout, the lawmakers were generally in no mood to enact his recommendations into law. They did pass a pure food and drug act which became law without Bradley's signature. But their principal considerations were partisan.[28] One of their first actions was to pass a resolution calling upon Senator William Lindsay to resign his seat in the United States Senate, on grounds that he no longer represented his party. The measure passed 25 to 10 in the senate and 55 to 35 in the house, the Republicans and "gold" Democrats voting against the resolution. Lindsay, it is recalled, had refused to support either Bryan or "free silver." His defense in the senate was that he represented, as expected, the people of Kentucky, a majority of whom had in 1896 voted against Bryan and the Chicago platform. Lindsay declared that he was not required to vote according to the wishes of a faction of one party.[29] (Earlier Henry Clay had undergone the same experience.) Lindsay's statement did not fill Kentucky silverites with joy. Nevertheless, he remained United States Senator.

More to the interest of the lawmakers was the "Goebel Election Law." The acrimonious debates on this highly controversial measure aroused the wrath of many and the indignation of others, who believed it was coldly thought out and designed not only to give the silverite Democrats control of the state but to make Goebel governor, regardless of the wishes of the people. The act provided for the creation of a state election commission of three, for four year terms, to be appointed by the existing General Assembly. The state board was empowered to appoint annually three commissioners in each county, who, in turn, were to appoint all the elective and registration officers for their respective counties. Vacancies occurring on the state board, when the General Assembly was not in session, were to be filled optatively by the board's members. The measure empowered the state board to remove members of county boards at any time without showing cause. The state commission could be composed altogether of members of one party, although the county boards were required to select the election officers from the two leading parties. The county commissions were empowered to count the votes and issue certificates of election, said certificates to be sent to the state board, which, if satisfied, was to make duplicate certificates for those having the highest number of votes. In the event of a tie, the contest was to be settled by lot. Election contests were made impossible, because, it was advanced, going behind the returns of the county boards was not permitted.

Heated debate was to no avail. The bill passed as Senator Goebel had planned, and Bradley promptly vetoed it. It was almost immediatley repassed over the governor's veto. Goebel then picked the three men to be state election commissioners and the legislature, most of the Republicans refusing to vote, went through the motion of naming them. The men selected (surprisingly prominent) were Captain William T. Ellis of Owensboro, Charles B. Poyntz, and Judge Pryor (all Democrats)—to the shouts of "Hurrah for William the Conqueror, William One, William the Czar!"[30]

Then the legislature adjourned. Wrote Edward A. Jonas, a Louisville reporter, "What Senator Goebel proposed was that elections be held by officers to be selected by a partisan county board, that board to be appointed by, and therefore to become the creature and the servant of, a partisan state board. This last," he declared, "was to be named by one party in the Legislature and to be self-perpetuating. These canvass returns and decide contests. In practice, what this intended," he asserted, "was that every election would be at the mercy, not of one party but of whatever faction of that party chanced to be on top. And so," Jonas concluded, "he not only destroyed self-government but party government in the broader sense."[31]

Watterson likewise found little good in the Goebel bill. Under an editorial entitled "Of Imminent and Deadly Peril to the State," he compared the proposal to the Force Bill. The Goebel bill "makes no claim or show of fairness" and places the entire election in the hands of "three irresponsible persons." This triumvirate would decide who could hold office and who could not, the fiery old editor predicted.

The author of the bill received much of Watterson's attention:

> *Self-possessed, able and tireless, and fearless, he seems to belong to the category of born leaders. Such men are capable of great public good, or great public mischief.* The Courier-Journal *would not summarily, nor willingly, dismiss Senator Goebel to this latter classification. The measure [however] . . . is of sweeping viciousness and far-reaching evil.*

A young, ambitious, aspiring man, Goebel sought the governorship, thought Watterson, and "he thinks he sees a ready chariot to bear him thither in the Election Bill that bears his name." With this law, "his ambition may be, probably will be, gratified."

But such must not be the case, Watterson warned. The people's wrath and outrage will give those responsible for "this monstrous usurpation of power" their just reward—"everlasting ignominy and disgrace." Calling on delegations to assemble in Frankfort to protest the law, "Marse Henry" asked the masses "to call off the maddened dogs of war whom passion and faction have let loose at Frankfort, and who, having a taste of blood, would rend the very eagles that guard the Commonwealth limb from limb, leaving the people only the bare and worthless bones."[32]

Soon after adjournment, Richard Knott wrote that "There are indications already that the gentlemen responsible for the Goebel force bill are becoming alarmed at the popular revolt against them and their machine. The people of Kentucky," he declared, "are wide awake . . . suspicious of the men who have been dominant at Frankfort, and more intolerant than ever of the scheme to overthrow popular institutions." Knott asserted that this "force bill" was a "direct blow at the fundamental principle of republican institutions" and that it "must be destroyed or Kentucky can not claim that she today has even the form of republican government." By and large, many thoughtful people in the state seemed to feel as Knott did.

Attorney General William S. Taylor contended that the measure was destructive of the basic principles of republican government and tended to destroy local government and to concentrate power so that one man might have full control. He charged that the law was "corrupt and dishonest in purpose" and held that it was unconstitutional. The auditor thereafter refused to honor the requisitions of the newly appointed commission, which threw the measure into the courts. In a strictly partisan decision the Appellate Court, by a four to three vote, decided that the Goebel law did not conflict with the state constitution—and the legislation stood. Some suggested that Senator Goebel, in his obvious determination to make himself governor, had overlooked only one item—the possibility that the members of the state election commission might be honest.

A section of the Goebel law concerned contests over the election of governor or lieutenant governor. In such cases, a special board was to be selected by lot from the legislature to examine the contests and report to the General Assembly. As the Democrats were usually overwhelmingly in control, this constituted an additional blow at Republican chances of having another governor.[33]

The War With Spain

After the sinking of the *Maine*, political quarrels were, for a time, put aside. While some newspapers, including the *Lexington Herald*, cautioned patience, most called for war. The populace supported the call to arms when it came. Kentucky's State Guard quickly offered its services to the governor. Consisting of three regiments, the Guard had as its senior officer John B. Castleman of the 1st Regiment, the Louisville Legion. Equipped with four artillery pieces, four Gatling guns, and 700 "trap door" Springfield rifles, the Legion was the best supplied of all three regiments.

Companies from central Kentucky made up the 2d Regiment commanded by Colonel Edward H. Gaither, while Colonel Thomas J. Smith's 3d Regiment had been recruited from western Kentucky.

At first Governor Bradley ordered the regiments brought to full strength—12 companies of 103 men each—but the lack of equipment caused him to reduce strength to 84 men each. Even then not enough modern arms could be procured. On April 23, 1898, when the call for volunteers came, the State Guard stood ready to fill Kentucky's initial quota. Mobilizing in Lexington, the 2d and 3d Regiments went to Camp Collier—in the south end, where horse barns housed some of the men—and the 1st camped on the Chautauqua grounds near "Ashland," home of Henry Clay.

The initial delay caused by lack of equipment was furthered by another delay while doctors conducted rigorous physical examinations. Castleman's and Bradley's long distance battle of words made for interesting reading in the press but did little to get anxious troops to the seat of war. But finally the 1st Regiment received orders to go to Puerto Rico. Once there the men were assigned to garrison duty. They saw little action and were mustered out in February 1899. Meanwhile an epidemic of mumps, "measles and mosquitoes" struck the 3d Regiment at Fortress Monroe, Virginia and delayed their departure for Cuba until January 1899. They were mustered out in Georgia in May.

The men of the 2d Regiment suffered more than those of other regiments from Kentucky. Assigned to Camp George H. Thomas at Chickamauga, Georgia, they, along with over 40,000 other soldiers there, bore the full brunt of army inefficiency and War Department mismanagement. Crowded conditions, poor sanitation, improper clothing, diseased and unfit food ("Rotten Bully Beef") —all made war for these soldiers what Sherman had said it was. Conditions improved noticeably in August when W. C. P. Breckinridge's brother, Major General Joseph Cabell Breckinridge returned from Santiago, where he had seen action at El Caney and San Juan Hill, to take over command of Camp Thomas. With conditions

Return of the Louisville Legion from the
Spanish-American War

Courtesy of The Filson Club, Louisville

"close to anarchy," he put crews to work burning garbage, deepening latrines, and improving hospital conditions. Breckinridge ordered tents placed further apart and organized sporting events to improve morale. Just as these improvements came the 2d was ordered to Anniston, Alabama. From there they went to Lexington and the disgruntled soldiers were mustered out in October, 1898.

The War Department had authorized a fourth regiment of Kentucky infantry and David G. Colson of Middlesboro was named its colonel. Recruited from the mountains, the 4th Regiment mobilized in Lexington in June, went to Anniston also and was mustered out there in February, 1899. Two troops of Cavalry volunteers and a number of Negro recruits—assigned to the 10th United States Cavalry—made up the balance of Kentucky's contribution to the war.

Governor Bradley borrowed $3,000 from a Frankfort bank, subject to General Assembly approval, and equipped hospital trains to return sick Kentucky soldiers. Seventy-five were brought from Chickamauga and a hundred from Fortress Monroe. But eighty-four did not return. Their deaths resulted from accident or disease, not from battle. For those returning soldiers—including Corporal Henry Watterson, Jr., Sergeant Polk Laffoon, Lieutenant Edwin P. Morrow, Lieutenant Desha Breckinridge, and Colonel Morris B. Belknap[34]—war had brought victory but few laurels.[35]

Their disillusionment was shared, perhaps, by Governor Bradley as he came to the end of his term "bloody but unbowed." His administration wrecked by hostile legislators, he had tried diligently and unsuccessfully to enact into law some reform measures. But aside from having been a strong executive, he could not point to great achievement.

XVII

LAWLESSNESS AND VIOLENCE

Introduction

As observed earlier, the Civil War was responsible for long enduring hatred and violence in the border states. Kentucky endured a full measure of it. Many elements caused disorder. Among them were guerrillas, Ku Kluxers, Loyal Leaguers, Regulators, and many other lawless organizations, as well as individuals bent on settling personal grudges.

Local law enforcement officials generally failed to discharge their duties, so that numerous counties fell prey to marauders, banditti, and vendettas. Moreover, at least one governor pardoned criminals on a large scale—many even before they came to trial. This was one reason for the rise of a sort of vigilante, which took the law into its own hands, ferreted out supposed bad characters, dragged them from their homes at night and often hanged them to convenient trees.

Reference has also been made earlier to the fact that some Democrats sympathized with the so-called Ku Klux and were not desirous that its members be punished; while on the other hand, some Republicans favored the Loyal Leaguers. However, both Democrats and Republicans were among the Regulators, who were often as violent as the dreaded guerrillas. The experiences of the war had made the people callous. Some appeared to enjoy an exhilarating excitement derived from violence and bloodshed. Public morals were woefully low, with a resultant lack of desire for law enforcement.

Still another factor was the bad blood engendered in communities by opposed Confederate and Union sympathizers. Such antagonism was perhaps worse in eastern Kentucky, where bloody feuds ensued, than in any other section. However, some antagonism existed in all sections of the state. Intimidation, attack, and reprisal were common throughout the Commonwealth.

Unfortunately, too, the feeling between Democrats and Republicans became so bitter in many places that assassination and violence were defended by supposedly respectable citizens, and, throughout the period, scores of men were killed in election-day brawls. The people of eastern Kentucky, many of whom were as clannish as their Scottish highlander forebears, were particularly given to free and bloody reprisal, so that one assassination might lead to many.[1] Of course partisans in the toils of the law expected those with power in the political party to get them off, or if in the penitentiary, to get them out.

Lynch Law

Instances of "lynch law" were quite numerous. One example was an occurance in and around Lebanon on November 25, 1866. On that night, three prisoners—Crowdus, Stephens, and Goode—were taken from the Marion County jail in Lebanon and hanged. Lieutenant J. R. King, United States Army, who was in the vicinity at the time, reported that the local authorities had received ample warning of the proposed tragedy; that they not only failed to call for the support of his troops stationed nearby, but also actually declared that the prisoners "deserved hanging." He stated that the mob consisted of 100 to 150 men from Perryville, Springfield, Haysville, and Mackville, with some young men from Lebanon. It was reported that in Marion and Boyle counties "the sway of the mob was almost undisputed."

Earlier, on the night of October 19, 1866, Lebanon had suffered another outrage. A gang of from 25 to 40 mounted men, said to have been under the command of a native outlaw (fictitiously dubbed "Captain Skaags"), who boasted a command of 120 irregular cavalrymen subject to bugle call, gallopped into the Negro section of Lebanon, dismounted, plundered the houses, insulted and frightened the occupants, wrecked the interior furnishings of the houses, even tore off roofs and chimneys, and then harried the helpless blacks out of the country. Brigadier General Jefferson C. Davis, United States Army, investigating the outrage, reported that the local authorities not only knew about the raid but were acquainted with many of the bandits who perpetrated the crime. Apparently no one was ever indicted for either outrage at Lebanon. Except for the dispatching of a large force of federal troops, Marion County might have been taken over completely by outlaws.[2]

In southern Kentucky near Bowling Green, desperados, in October, 1866, held up and derailed a pay train. They threw the engine and pay car off the track and seriously injured the conductor. The locomotive having rolled down the bank, the bandits boarded the train and at gun point seized and escaped with $12,000 to $15,000, leaving behind a smoking train and badly frightened passengers.

In November of the same year a formidable band, in the same manner, threw an L & N train off the track near Franklin—fortunately failing to injure anyone—and lined up the passengers and robbed them of their money, jewels, and other valuables. The express car caught fire, so that the thugs failed to extricate the safe, thereby losing their intended prize. Six of the gang were afterward arrested and brought to Franklin for trial.

Greatly perturbed by the mounting lawlessness and violence, Governor Bramlette appealed to the legislature (1866) for help. "Jails are forced by them," he declared, "and their victims ruthlessly torn from legal custody and murdered. Those standing on bail, who are obnoxious to their murderous wrath, are dragged from their homes and executed. . . . Within the last few days, during the session of the Boyle Circuit Court, these murderers took from the jail of that county a man there confined, to answer on indictment, and hung him to death within the limits of the town." The governor also noted an instance where the house of a citizen had been burned because his son had resisted the outlaws' authority. He related another instance, of a soldier being warned by a lawless group to leave the county. His "crime" had been his expressed purpose to help his younger brother, a man ordered to leave the area.

Bramlette concluded that under existing laws rewards could not be offered for the apprehension and conviction of the criminals except upon the petition of the circuit or county judge of the county in which the crimes were committed. He stated, however, that no applications had been made.[3]

Known as "Regulators," the band operating in Marion, Boyle, and Mercer counties professed to execute justice in cases where civil authorities were ineffective. There seems to be little doubt that the officials in these, and many other counties, failed to do their duty. However, the Regulators were as guilty of murder and lawlessness as some of those they hanged. They ordered out of the country any who protested their actions. Printed warnings appeared, and the arrogant malefactors even went so far as to order the governor of the Commonwealth to stop his attacks on them. If he refused to heed them, the Regulators warned, he would taste their vengeance.

In September, 1867, Governor Stevenson ordered all lawless groups disbanded. His proclamation asked Kentuckians to obey the legal authorities, but soon after, on October 1, a group called "Rowzee's band"—organized to fight Regulator activity—killed two people in Marion County.

Stevenson sent Adjutant General Frank Wolford to investigate and gave him authority to call out the militia, if necessary, to end the killing. Wolford called out three companies, and "Rowzee's gang" vanished. Another company rushed to Boyle County to assist civil authorities there. Such moves by the governor and by the soldiers involved brought some semblance of law and order to Marion, Boyle, Mercer and Lincoln counties.

Governor Stevenson, in his determined effort to break up lawless gangs, was ably helped by a few prominent editors. Henry Watterson, through the *Courier-Journal*, waged war relentlessly upon the lawless, regardless of political affiliations. "The desperado," he wrote, "who, calling himself a Ku Klux puts on a mask and mounts a horse at midnight to prowl about after the weak unprotected, is merely a brutal assassin, without one solitary picturesque or dramatic quality. He is an enemy of his race, a foe to society, a cruel monster who should be shot down in his tracks like any other wild animal. But, pretending to be a Democrat and relying on the want of Democratic legislation, he is the most fatal of Radical emissaries, who is mightily undermining the foundations of State authority, and piling up fuel for the partisans of Federal usurpations."[4]

One reason why the lawless gangs had not been broken up was the fact that numerous prominent local and state Democrats seem to have "considered the Ku Klux as political allies, allies not sought but accepted." Realizing its politically unfavorable stand, the Democratic party, at its 1871 state convention, approved a resolution condemning lawlessness "on whomever it fell and from whatever quarter it came."

In the legislative session of 1871-1872 several legislators sought to enact law against the prevalent lawlessness. After much discussion the act finally was defeated in the house. Thoroughly disgusted, Henry Watterson denounced this reactionary legislature, which "whilst it lived," he declared, "was regarded as incapable," and "now that it is dead . . . will be remembered only as the weakest assembly that was ever elected in the state."[5]

The following year Governor Preston H. Leslie made determined efforts to stamp out both the Ku Klux (if such an organization then existed) and the Loyal League. He did secure from a new Assembly a measure against lawbreakers, particularly groups organized for the purpose of violence.[6]

By the spring of 1873, the "gangs" of lawless men were either falling apart of their own weight or were driven out of existence by the new law. Wrote Professor Coulter: "They [the lawless bands] left a heritage, which has been a curse to the state since, a weakened respect for state authority. Lynchings continued long as outcroppings of this spirit, though gradually becoming more infrequent; and feuds grew up in the mountains of the eastern part of the state, spectacular though deadly, to give the state a fame all its own."

Another form of lawlessness, however, was still being perpetrated by the legislature. It was the passage of acts for the relief of sheriffs. This abuse was so frequent and glaring that it became something of a "racket." In a scathing veto message of March 19, 1870, Governor Stevenson wrote that this character of legislation was "partial, mischievous and unjust." He declared that "its direct tendency in the past has been to encourage official delinquency, and neglect in the discharge of official duty." "Litigation," he continued, "and immense pecuniary loss, amounting to nearly a million dollars in the Revenue receipts of the Commonwealth during the past ten years illustrates the impolity of such legislation. If this act be passed," he declared, "fifty applications for similar extensions will be sought at your next session, and our annual receipts of revenue will be diminished to the extent of the relief granted."[7]

The Governor issued this challenge: "While declaiming against invasions of our Federal Charter, let us prove ourselves worthy of the high character of enlightened freemen, by setting the example of a faithful observance of all the mandates of our own Constitution." Two days later he vetoed a bill for the relief of the late sheriff of Grayson County from paying a judgement of $3,198.21 for money that officer had failed to pay to the state, money collected by him in 1860. "I cannot think," wrote the governor, "that age, want, or present poverty is any ground for releasing sureties on a sheriff's bond."[8]

One of the boldest acts committed by lawless bands was that perpetrated at Frankfort on February 25, 1871, while the legislature met. Shortly before dawn of the twenty-fifth, a band of armed men, 75 to 100 in number, freed from the Franklin County jail a white man charged with murdering a Negro. The shock given the public was perhaps enhanced because of its having quickly succeeded an outrage committed early in January upon Negroes at Stamping Ground, only a few miles distant. There a Negro shoemaker, named Cupin, was killed by seventeen "Kukluxers." After this murder the band attacked Negroes at Watkinsville, near Stamping Ground. There the blacks held their ground and drove off their assailants, but they suffered three casualties. The Negroes in the vicinity fled to Frankfort, the seat of the state government, where it was thought they would be protected. Though citizens and authorities had assured them of safety in the capital city, the Frankfort outrage completely terrified and dismayed them.

The Frankfort authorities had stationed four militiamen to guard the jail, to ensure protection of the prisoners. But the lawless band had planned and organized well. Leaving their houses across the river, they posted their own guards along the approaches to the jail, which stood at the rear of the courthouse. The gang captured the night watchman, then the four guards, and finally the jailer, who was forced to unlock the prisoner's cell. The band quickly fled. Later, the jailer reported that he had seen some seventy-five masked men, armed with shotguns. According to him, they were complete strangers.[9]

A few weeks earlier a Negro railway mail clerk, on the Lexington-Louisville run, was assaulted when the train stopped at North Benson station, nine miles from Frankfort. One of four white intruders quickly entered the mail car and grappled with the clerk. The assailants, vowing to kill the Negro, attempted to drag him from the train. However, as the vehicle pulled away quickly and increased speed readily, the intruder jumped off without his quarry. When report of the incident was transmitted to the federal authorities, ten troops were assigned to accompany the mail agent. After a few days and further threats, the Post Office Department discontinued mail service on the line altogether. This led to a loud outcry from persons living along the line, and Congressman James B. Beck denounced the action on the floor of the House.

Republicans acribed the attack to white Democrats prompted by political and racial motives, while Democrats attributed the incident to Republicans jealous of the Negro's holding a job which several white Republicans desired. Governor Stevenson ordered his adjutant general, J. Stoddard Johnston, to investigate the affair. The report was conveyed by the governor to the General Assembly, with a message strongly denouncing the violence and urging that body to pass a law to aid in the capture of the offenders. The matter was referred by each house to special committees. However, no one was either apprehended or punished. Ultimately the mail service was restored.[10]

A singularly brutal crime was perpetrated at Owingsville, in Bath county, during the early morning of October 20, 1872. Twenty-five armed men on horseback broke into the county jail, seized a Negro (Sam Bascom) confined on a charge of attempted arson, took him to a field near the town and hanged him. Persisting in declaring his innocence, the Negro pleaded for mercy. As a matter of fact, there was no convincing proof that the man was guilty of the crime with which he was charged.

Watterson was again deeply stirred by these crimes, especially the hanging of Bascom:

> The act was cowardly as are all such midnight outrages; it was to be excused not by the poor plea of popular indignation, for guilt of the Negro was by no means conclusive, nor was his offence of capital nature, if even he were guilty; it was a piece of mob law such as has been almost unprecedented in the criminal history of the state, and the participants should be hunted down with all the appliances of the law, and punished without mercy. The crime committed in this little interior town reflects upon the whole commonwealth, and if the local authorities be not sufficiently energetic and willing, then let the people of the state demand of them the energy and the disposition to discover and prosecute the murderers to the extremist limit of the law.

Watterson was certain that the culprits could be found, and he urged the people of Bath County to run them down. "We call upon the people of Bath County," he challenged, "to rid themselves of the foul stigma upon their name and fame stained in the bloody outrage. . . . We repeat that these cowardly murderers *can be found*, and there is not a recess in Bath county, nor in the caves or defiles of mountains nearby, that should protect them from the vengeance of the law they outraged."[11]

Violence in the Mountains

While decrying the fact that men were being hanged by the score in central and western Kentucky, the metropolitan press paid scant attention to bloody occurrences in parts of isolated eastern Kentucky. An outbreak in 1878 in Breathitt County, however, attracted attention.

This act was perpetrated during the Amis-Strong feud. After Bob Little, a nephew of Captain William ("Bill") Strong, had been killed and an Amis seriously wounded, affairs became more serious. A mob formed and attacked a prisoner being escorted by the sheriff and twenty-five deputies. In the shooting that followed, the guards fled and one of them—County Judge John Burnett—was killed. A state of near anarchy prevailed. William Randall, presiding judge of the criminal court, had said that his court would see that criminals were punished; this precipitated the uprising. Randall's court was disrupted and the judge fled the country. As the lawlessness grew worse, Governor McCreary sent in the military to restore order.

The state militia troop left Jackson in March, 1879, and returned to Frankfort with thirteen of the "principal actors" as prisoners. A report stated that "it was generally considered that the disorders there had not grown out of the barbarism, or any relapse from the social status." It declared that an "imperfect organization has resulted from the practical isolation of the people, the unlettered authorities, and the absence of schools and moral example. They need," it averred, "the contact of more advanced communities."[12]

Eastern Kentucky Regulators

Such communities apparently were not found in Carter, Boyd, and Lawrence counties in the spring of 1880. The "good" citizens of Carter felt obliged to request Governor Blackburn for troops to suppress "a band of cut-throats in that region" who "style themselves 'regulators.' " A company of state guards stationed at Maysville was consequently ordered to prepare for duty in that county.

The rampaging Regulators in the three counties seem to have taken their work seriously. They pillaged, maraudered, broke into jails, and murdered—all in the name of popular justice. This band was remarkable among the vigilante in respect to numbers and power exercised, for numerous leading citizens belonged—citizens who believed they were doing a public service. It completed what it considered its work of destroying or driving out certain lawbreakers and broke up of its own accord, two hundred men surrendering to civil authorities at Louisa. Those who surrendered furnished the names of eight hundred others for presentation to the grand jury.

Apparently the Regulators felt that their work had been successful, and the editor of the *Greenup Independent* wrote an epilogue: "Inefficient men have been in office, the laws were not enforced and justice went by default, encouraging crime and iniquity, until the people, propelled by natural laws of reaction, put a stop to it."[13]

Unfortunately, one of the three counties, Boyd, continued for a short time to be disturbed. It appears that the Regulators there had been instrumental in bringing about the arrest of two alleged criminals named Neal and Croft. During their incarceration attempts were made to lynch them. Whereupon state troops, under Major John R. Allen, were rushed in to protect the court and prisoners at Catlettsburg. A change of venue to Carter County was granted Messrs. Neal and Croft. Circuit Judge George N. Brown of Catlettsburg directed that the prisoners be taken to Lexington for safe keeping. While embarking on a steamer with the prisoners, the troops were threatened by a mob from Ashland. A short time later they were attacked from a ferry boat while leaving that city. Members of the mob fired into the troops, wounding several people. The embattled militiamen then returned the fire, killing some on the ferry boat and others on the wharves. Following this disturbance, the prisoners were taken on to Lexington without further incident.[14] "Justice" outside the law again had brought further violence.

Rowan County Violence

On June 22, 1887, a bloody battle was fought at Morehead that again called the attention of the nation to the fact that Kentucky was truly a "dark and bloody ground." On that day the Tolliver feudists, who had turbulently ruled Rowan County, more or less as outlaws, were virtually wiped out, and a new day dawned in the history of the luckless county.

The trouble had its origin as far back as 1874 when Captain Thomas F. Hargis of Carlisle, late of the Confederate Army, was running as Democratic nominee for circuit judge against George M. Thomas, a prominent Republican of Vanceburg. The race was spirited. Thomas' partisans charged that Hargis was ineligible for the office because of not having been admitted to the practice of law long enough, as well as not having reached the requisite age. Unable to find records to prove his eligibility and accused of having destroyed them himself, Hargis (admitted to the bar at Morehead) was defeated—in a Democratic district.

Feeling had run so high that a desire for revenge existed among many of Hargis' friends, particularly in Rowan County. This ill-feeling seemed to mount instead of subside. Making matters worse was the fact that perhaps no county in the state experienced deadlier hatred between Democrats and Republicans (nearly evenly matched in numbers) than Rowan did. Later Hargis defeated Judge William Holt, a prominent Republican lawyer of Mt. Sterling, for the Appellate bench, following the death of Judge John Milton Elliott in 1879. This contest had been so bitter that the press of the entire state followed it with interest, particularly the *Maysville Eagle*, whose fiery editor, Thomas Marshall Green, bitterly and scathingly denounced Hargis.

The strife had been so acrimonious in closely contested Rowan County that every neighborhood, almost every household, became embittered and dangerously partisan. Each succeeding minor political contest served "to open old sores and to inflict new wounds, adding material for the spirit of revenge to feed upon."

In those days the Australian ballot system had not yet been introduced, and Kentucky's constitution required that a voter cast his vote publicly. Vote buying was rather common. Under the viva voce system, the buyer could make certain that the seller voted as promised. In addition, whiskey was promiscuously used on election days in virtually every county of the state. Candidates served it freely by the barrel, hoping to influence voters in their favor. "Election contests," one writer pointed out, "frequently excite the most staid and conservative citizens, but when whiskey is added it is certain to arouse passions which might, otherwise, have slumbered on."[15] The result was brawls and fights, with the free use of knives, pistols, shotguns, and rifles. The real threat of serious injuries, or even death, kept from the polls thousands of those classed as good respectable citizens.

In 1884 a heated race was run between Democrat S. B. Goodan and Republican W. C. (Cook) Humphrey for sheriff of Rowan County. The contest was close, with Humphrey winning by a twelve vote margin. Money and whiskey had been used, and fights had ensued throughout the day. During one of these, John Martin, son of a wealthy and highly respected farmer, was badly injured. He immediately drew his pistol, and a general melee ensued, resulting in the death of Solomon Bradley and the serious wounding of Adam Sizemore. Martin and Bradley, both Republicans and friends, were closely related and members of the leading families of the county. Bradley's death was deeply resented. It appears that Martin had been struck down by Floyd Tolliver, a brother of Craig Tolliver, who later gained the reputation of a cruel, blood-thirsty man.

A short time later John Martin felt he had been insulted in a saloon by the same Floyd Tolliver, who drew his pistol. Before he could fire, however, Martin fired and "Big Floyd" fell dead. A gathering of relatives and allies from Rowan, Carter, Morgan and Elliott counties soon resulted, with Craig Tolliver taking command of the one, and young Cook Humphrey the other. The Logans, Republicans and highly reputable citizens, were allied with the Martin faction.

Following the death of Floyd Tolliver, John Martin surrendered to the authorities and was incarcerated at Morehead. County Attorney Taylor Young realized that Martin was not safe there, and had him taken to Winchester. A few days later, the Tollivers, forging a court order for Martin to be returned to Morehead, caused the luckless man to be taken on board the evening Chesapeake and Ohio train. At Farmers, a few miles from Morehead, a band of the Tolliver vendetta boarded the train and riddled the hand-cuffed man with bullets. Martin's wife, riding on the same train, was unaware of her husband's whereabouts until she rushed back and found him dead.[16]

Following this cowardly murder, a reign of terror almost unprecedented for ferocity, depravity, and violence set in. All manner of crime went unpunished by the law, stated one writer. Many of the officers of the courts were partisans and participated actively in the conflict. Circuit Judge A. E. Cole, who leaned toward the Tolliver faction, made little effort to perform the duties of his office.[17]

Soon after John Martin's burial, County Attorney Z. Taylor Young, thought by the Martins to be of the Tolliver faction, was shot from ambush but not killed. Then a Martin man, Deputy Sheriff Baumgartner, was murdered. Reprisal after reprisal followed in the bloody feud. As town marshall, Craig Tolliver and his band intimidated and controlled Morehead, whose population had decreased from 700 to less than 300 in less than two years' time. Setting up his headquarters in a hotel known as The American House, Tolliver took control of the whiskey business, which he operated without license. This threw the town wide open for crime and violence. Tolliver made himself police judge of Morehead and assumed operation of the local machinery of government.

At one time Governor Knott sent Attorney General Hardin to prosecute for the Commonwealth, but all he got for his pains were a few indictments for the carrying of concealed deadly weapons. At another time, Knott dispatched troops under Captain R. W. McKee of Lawrenceburg. All went well while the troops occupied Morehead, but when they left the bloody reign began afresh. Just before the troops were dispatched, Asher Graham Caruth, Louisville attorney and later a member of Congress, was sent by the governor to investigate and to prosecute. He succeeded in getting Cook Humphrey and Craig Tolliver to sign statements promising to leave the county permanently. Humphrey kept his word, but not Tolliver. Then followed the burning by the Tollivers of the Martin home, and the brutal murder of the Martin women. On the heels of this came the cruel murder by the Tollivers of two young Logans, twenty-five year old W. H. and John B., eighteen, sons of John B. Sr. By that time "Tsar" Tolliver felt strong enough to punish those offering even faint criticism of his rule.

At last Boone Logan, whose father had been feloniously arrested, and who was a cousin of the murdered boys, could stand no more. Logan was soft-spoken, serious-minded, intelligent, and a promising lawyer. He conferred with Hiram M. Pigman, a respected citizen, formed an alliance, and drew up a plan. On June 16, 1887 he went to the governor for help. Knott refused again to send troops and stated his inability to furnish arms from the state arsenal. The quiet-mannered Logan, however, realized that Knott was deeply sympathetic. At that point Boone Logan is reported to have said: "Governor, I have but one home and but one hearth. From this I have been driven by these outlaws and their friends. They have foully murdered my kinsmen. I have not before engaged in any difficulties—but now I propose to take a hand and retake my fireside or die in the effort."[18]

Without any prospect of governmental aid, Boone Logan then went to Cincinnati and purchased several hundred dollars worth of Winchester rifles, pistols, shotguns, and an ample supply of ammunition. All this was sent to Rowan County without being discovered by the Tollivers. The citizens of the county who could be counted upon to fight for law and order were organized, warrants were issued, and Morehead was quietly surrounded on the morning of June 22, 1887, by the Logan-Pigman forces. Most of the Tollivers, posted in The American House, were arrested before they fully realized what was happening.

Pigman's force approached from one side of the town; Logan's, from the other. Craig Tolliver and the remaining gang were caught between crossfire at The American House, which was soon riddled with bullets and in flames. Threatened with being burned to death, the Tollivers made a break. With a lack of restraint that Tolliver would have approved of, the Logan men all but wiped out the remaining Tollivers. Craig died with his boots off, as he had desired. After the battle, troops were belatedly sent in to protect Logan and to help restore order. Their earlier absence had caused private citizens to take the law into their own hands and use, for a time, the same methods as Boone Logan and Hiram Pigman. It is interesting to note that the legislative committee investigating the Rowan County disorders recommended abolishing the County.[19]

Pike County Violence

Early in January, 1888, the inhabitants of Pike County petitioned Governor Buckner for arms and ammunition to defend themselves against threatened attacks from West Virginia. To understand the cause for threatened invasion, the student must go back many years to when the Hatfield-McCoy feud was in full fury. The trouble grew out of alleged hog-stealing by the Hatfields and then received its strongest impetus from an election day dispute in 1882, which was considerably stoked by corn whiskey. This affray was between members of the Hatfield family, who resided across Tug River in Logan County, West Virginia, and of the McCoy clan, on Blackberry Creek of Tug River in Pike County. The terrain of that section was wild, rugged, heavily-wooded and mountainous. There were deep ravines, rapid-running creeks, lonely trails and isolated log cabins. At the head of the Hatfield clan was Captain William Anderson ("Devil Anse") Hatfield, and the titular chief of the McCoys was the aging Randolph McCoy.

On the fateful election day a Hatfield suffered fatal knife wounds at the hands of a McCoy. Four McCoys, though arrested by civil authorities, were captured by the Hatfields and carried into West Virginia. One was a brave little lad fifteen years of age. A few days later, the Hatfields secretly brought back the captives to Kentucky, tied them to trees and killed them, the plucky teenage lad included. Three of Randolph McCoy's sons thus perished.[20]

Desultory fighting continued thereafter until September, 1887, when Governor Buckner offered $500 reward for the murderers of the McCoy brothers. Buckner at that time made an unsuccessful requisition upon Governor Emanuel Willis Wilson of West Virginia for delivery of the murderers. This request and a lengthy word battle ensued between the two governors which not only attracted nationwide attention, but also brought the two states to the verge of war.

Unsuccessful in this effort, Governor Buckner appointed Pike countian Frank Phillips as special deputy assigned to the task of seizing the wanted Hatfields. Phillips was amazingly, almost uncannily, successful. His very first sally into West Virginia netted him three members of the Hatfield clan. These were lodged in the jail at Pikeville.[21] He did not, however, trap "Devil Anse." At that

"Devil Anse" Hatfield

American Journal of Sociology (1901),
Reprinted from Virgil C. Jones, *The Hatfields and the
McCoys* © 1948 by the University of North Carolina Press

point, the Hatfields, Republicans generally, took a hand unsuccessfully in the Pike County elections.

The West Virginia clan, rebuffed in their political efforts and smarting at having some of their number languish in a Kentucky jail, resolved to retaliate. On a biting, cold New Year's night, 1888, they stole up Blackberry Branch, attacked the surprised McCoy homestead and burned it. The McCoys, taken completely by surprise, had little chance to escape. The attackers clubbed the aged Mrs. McCoy into insensibility, murdered a daughter and another son. Old Randolph somehow made his escape. He immediately organized a force strong enough to deal with the Hatfields. Logan County, West Virginia, was invaded by thirty of the McCoy clan. Two Hatfields were killed. A few days later deputy Phillips captured six additional of the Hatfield clan and lodged them in the Pike County jail. About the middle of January, Phillips made a second raid on West Virginia; it netted an additional Hatfield.

Later in the month Governor Wilson sent a special agent to Governor Buckner to ask for the surrender of the captured Hatfields. His mission was fruitless. The West Virginia governor then appealed to Judge John Watson Barr, of the United States Circuit Court of Appeals, for a writ of habeas corpus. After a hearing, however, Judge Barr decided that the prisoners were properly in the custody of Kentucky authorities.

During July, August, and September, 1888, encounters continued on the border between members of the two clans.[22] Following several murders, Governor Buckner increased the reward to $5,000 and, early in 1889, he stationed a company of state militiamen at Pikeville to prevent a threatened rescue by the Hatfields of their incarcerated kinsmen.

Trials were conducted at Pikeville and one of the Hatfield clan, Ellison Mounts, was convicted of murder and sentenced to be hanged. The day of the hanging was a gala one indeed. All the mountaineers for miles around came to Pikeville to witness the affair. Even babes in arms were brought by their mothers. Whiskey flowed freely, and the town bristled with Winchester repeaters. A heavy cordon of troops and deputies guarded the place against a Hatfield attack. A short time after one o'clock the lifeless form of Ellison Mounts dangled from the gallows-beam.

Sometime later, under a new governor, the Hatfields began depredations in West Virginia. At last West Virginia officials realized that the Hatfield clan contained some of the most dangerous and desperate of outlaws and they organized a large attacking force, which old Randolph McCoy was permitted to join. The Hatfields were invested in their mountain lair, and most of those remaining were wiped out. Old "Devil Anse," however, escaped to live to the ripe old age of ninety. Before the end he professed Christianity and was baptized.[23]

Other feuds of the "bloody eighties," all with political implications, were the Howard-Turner (1884-1889) in Harlan County, the French-Eversole (1887-1894), in Perry County, and the Hargis-Marcum-Cockrell-Callahan (1879-1912), in Breathitt. Though not as deadly as the Hatfield-McCoy vendetta, these wars took scores of lives and added additional reproach to the "dark and bloody ground."

Strangely enough business rivalry and "a woman" seem to have been the basis of the notorious Perry County outbreak. This struggle was made famous, not only by the bloody battle of Hazard (which left the Courthouse a shambles), but also by the animated word battle between Governor Buckner and Circuit Judge Henry Clay Lilly, who insisted upon the protection of state troops before attempting to hold court in Perry, Letcher, and Knott counties.[24]

The Howard-Turner vendetta had its origin apparently in a political quarrel preceding an election in 1884, when Wilson Howard shot and killed one of the Turners. Thereafter three additional Turners were murdered, the last just prior to the August election of 1889. The county was Republican, and the Howards were believed to control the party in the county, but not in the town of Harlan. It appears that no effort was made to arrest the guilty. In fact, a Howard was sheriff, and the county judge seems to have been friendly to the numerous Howard clan.

When a new county judge, Wilson Lewis, applied to Buckner for troops, the governor's only answer was that a posse comitatus of one hundred men be collected to capture the outlaws. Only nine men responded. Led by Judge Lewis they attacked the outlaws and were defeated, with three of their number killed, and the judge himself narrowly escaping with his life. Soon thereafter troops were dispatched. These attacked the Howards on October 21, 1889 near the Harlan Courthouse. The Howards suffered a crushing defeat. Six were killed but the leader, Wilson, escaped and left the country. Some semblance of order thereafter returned.[25]

The Breathitt County "War"

In many respects lawlessness in Breathitt was more notorious than in the other counties. Feuding had characterized the county since the Civil War. The most famous vendetta was the so-called Hargis-Cockrell-Marcum-Callahan Feud. The cause of this seems to have been altogether political. In a county race during the late nineties the Democratic ticket, headed by James Hargis for county judge and Ed Callahan for sheriff, was declared elected. The fusion ticket, however, declared that Hargis and Callahan had stolen the election, and instituted proceedings alleging fraud. Unfortunately, the partners of the leading law firm of the county were retained on different sides—John B. Marcum, one of the outstanding lawyers of the state, by the Republicans and the fusionists, Ott Pollard, by the Democrats.

During the process of taking depositions in Marcum's office, Marcum, Pollard, Hargis, and Callahan had heated words and pistols were drawn. Marcum ordered them all out of his office. Police Judge Cardwell issued warrants, and Marcum at once surrendered and paid his fine. Hargis, however, declaring Cardwell his enemy and refusing to appear before that judge, surrendered to a friend, Magistrate Edwards, which raised a question of jurisdiction. To allay the trouble, Marcum, a United States Commissioner, a leading state Republican and a trustee of State College, moved dismissal of the case against Judge Hargis, which was done.

But dismissal did not end the troubles. In making the arrest of Judge Hargis, the town marshal of Jackson, Tom Cockrell, assisted by his brother James, was said to have drawn a gun on Hargis; and it was alleged that only the intervention of Sheriff Callahan had prevented the Cockrells from killing Hargis. This charge the Cockrell brothers indignantly denied. Hargis swore that they would pay for the insult to his dignity.

Numerous unsavory charges followed on one side and the other. Marcum accused Ed Callahan of assassinating his uncle, Captain Bill Strong, a Union Army officer and leading Republican, from ambush. Then came a pistol duel at the "blind Tiger" saloon in Jackson between young Tom Cockrell and Ben Hargis, brother of James, in which Hargis was killed on the spot.

From that time on Cockrell was doomed. Yet Marcum volunteered to defend him, and Dr. B. D. Cox, perhaps the town's most prominent and highly respected citizen, backed him to the limit. Unfortunately, shortly thereafter, John "Tige" Hargis was killed by Jerry Cardwell. The Cardwells were, of course, friends of the Marcums, Cockrells, Coxes, and their companions. Though the evidence clearly proves that "Tige" Hargis, who had been drinking, was entirely to blame, Judge Hargis apparently thought only of revenge. How to get his "enemies" killed without losing his own life—that seemed to be the question.

Judge Hargis laid his plans well. It was charged that he surrounded himself with paid killers. Perhaps Curtis Jett was the most notorious of these. First came the murder from ambush of Dr. Cox, who was going on a call one night. His murder occurred at a point just opposite Judge Hargis' stable. Then fell Jim Cockrell, murdered in broad daylight by an assassin hidden in the Courthouse. Hargis and Callahan looked on, but did little or nothing either to prevent, apprehend, or punish, although the two were county judge and sheriff.

People about the town refused to testify for fear of being murdered. Then it came time for the life of Marcum, who had steadily refused to quit the county, insisting upon his rights to life, liberty, and happiness as an American citizen. He was foully murdered one morning while standing in front of the courthouse. He lay bleeding for fifteen minutes before anyone gathered the courage to attend to him. It was then too late. Hargis and Callahan, seated in front of the former's store across the street, were among those who saw all that occurred.[26]

Following this tragedy, a reign of terror began, one so formidable that state troops were sent in. Safety thus seeming assured, Captain B. J. Ewen, who was standing with Marcum at the time of the murder, decided to tell all he knew on the witness stand. Then Ewen's hotel was burned. Though indicted for murder, Hargis and Callahan were acquitted. At least thirty-seven members of the two factions were killed between 1901-1902, but few murderers were indicted; even fewer were convicted.[27]

Judge Hargis enjoyed unusual political power. He controlled Breathitt county completely, exerted strong influence in other counties, had a certain power at Frankfort and in the state Democratic party. A staunch supporter of William Goebel, Hargis exerted a powerful influence in his favor in the notorious Music Hall convention of 1899 at Louisville. Hargis influenced Goebel partisan Judge D. B. Redwine of Breathitt county who was chairman of the convention which nominated Goebel for governor. Many observers later commented on Hargis' ability to obtain pardons from Goebel's successor, Governor Beckham. This may or may not be true. Whatever else is said, however, it may be confidently asserted that Hargis enjoyed a strange immunity from punishment by the Commonwealth.

But, as though in fulfillment of some prophecy, the judge met his death violently. He was murdered during the winter of 1908 by his own son, Beach Hargis, whom he had angered. Apparently,

John B. Marcum
Reprinted from R. L. M'Clure, "The Mazes of a
Kentucky Feud," *The Independent*, IV (1903)

Tom Cockrill, James B. Hargis and Jim Cockrill

judging by the desperate fight she made to keep the boy from the penitentiary, Mrs. James Hargis sympathized strongly with the dull-witted, hard-drinking Beach. The last of the Mephistophelian cabal, Ed Callahan, tormented by the dread of assassination, was shot from ambush and killed in May, 1912, while working in his store. This incident did not end violence in Breathitt county, but the "Terror" was at an end.[28]

The history of the principal Kentucky feuds reveals certain factors more or less common to all. Both blood ties and strong political partisanism played a part, as did local officials who were frequently incompetent, ignorant, and violent. Furthermore, general ignorance and lack of respect for law and order were evident. Most of the feuds revealed excessive brutality, depravity, criminality, and cowardliness. It may be asserted likewise that, despite writings to the contrary, there was a total lack of the romantic and glamorous in the vendetta, which instead created much pitiousness, horror, and grief—the plight of Mrs. Martin and Mrs. Marcum being striking examples. An additional characteristic was the inevitable drawing into the frightful disruptions of good, intelligent, and worthy citizens, who often lost their lives or committed deeds totally beneath them. Perceptive observers blamed the feuds on endless land disputes, blood relationships, the weakness of the courts, isolationism, and a fighting spirit.[29]

Violence in the Bluegrass

The mountainous section of the Commonwealth did not have anything like a monopoly on homicide. The entire state shared in the dubious honor. Lack of law enforcement and prevalent violence had made Kentucky notorious in the eyes of the nation as early as 1882. E. L. Godkin, editor of the New York *Nation*, stated that there were "more homicides in Kentucky in 1878 than in the eight states of Maine, New Hampshire, Vermont, Massachusetts, Rhode Island, Connecticut, Pennsylvania, and Minnesota with an aggregate population of ten millions."

At the height of the Rowan County war, Henry Watterson wrote: "One would suppose that the reign of terror existing in certain sections of the state, and the immunity enjoyed by criminals of every degree everywhere, would have unanswerable arguments to the lawmakers which would at least have made their enforcement possible, but it was not so. Certain privileges and prerogatives were looked upon as vested rights, and the Legislature adjourned leaving the law-abiding citizens at the mercy of the murderer or marauder." He declared that "cold blooded, malicious murderers go scott free, or are acquitted," that "officers refuse to enforce the law," and that the "jury system is a complete failure."[30]

The Assassination of Judge John Milton Elliott

On the steps of the side entrance to the famous old Capitol Hotel in Frankfort at about one o'clock in the afternoon of March 26, 1879, Thomas Buford of Henry County murdered Appellate Court Judge John Milton Elliott. The weapon used was a double-barreled shot gun loaded with twelve gauge buckshot in each barrel. Elliott was unarmed. Buford belonged to the distinguished Buford family of Woodford County. He was born at "Woodburn," and was the brother of General Abe Buford.

The assassination arose out of an Appellate Court decision which left Buford virtually penniless. Some years previous Buford had invested his entire fortune, together with the whole estate of his sister, Mary, in a tract of land in Henry County, belonging to George J. Roland and wife. The Bufords, having paid $10,000 in cash and executed three notes, one for $10,000, which was paid, and two for $6,250 each, had discovered that clear title to the property could not be made. The latter two notes were assigned to James Guthrie, of Shelby County, who brought suit on them, asking that the lien be foreclosed and the entire tract be sold for the lien debts. Miss Buford filed her answer and asked that the entire contract be rescinded, stating that the title to the land was not good.

A change of venue to Fayette county was granted. The Fayette judge ordered the land sold for the debt of $12,500; whereupon the plaintiff, James Guthrie, bought the whole tract for the amount of the claim, causing the Bufords to lose $20,000. The case went to the Appellate Court, which affirmed the decision of the lower court. These events left Buford bitter and possibly mentally deranged.

His assassination of the popular Judge Elliott caused a tremendous sensation in and around Frankfort. A change of venue to Owen County was granted, and Colonel Buford's trial was conducted at Owenton. The attorneys on both sides were singularly distinguished. Among those for the Commonwealth were Judge O. D. McManama, W. C. P. Breckinridge, John Rodman and Jerry Lillard. For his defense Buford had obtained the services of Judge George M. Curtis of New York, W. R. Kinney of Louisville, Phil Thompson of Harrodsburg, Theodore Hallam of Covington, Evan E. Settle, Judge Thomas Gordon, and Judge J. W. Perry, all of Owenton.

On January 11, 1881 the jury was completed, all members being farmers. For defense Buford pleaded insanity. The speech of Judge Curtis was eloquent, brilliant, and moving. The jury finally adjudged the defendant insane, and the court ordered him committed to the asylum for the insane at Anchorage. After a brief confinement, however, Buford escaped into Indiana, and the Hoosier governor refused extradition.[31]

Less than a decade later, on November 10, 1889, citizens of the Bluegrass country were shocked to read that, on the preceding day, prominent lawyer and Republican leader, Colonel Armistead M. Swope, and Judge William Cassius Goodloe, also a prominent lawyer and Republican leader, had killed each other in an altercation in the Lexington post office. Goodloe actually did not die until forty-eight hours after the fight, which occurred at about 1:30 p.m.

According to one account, Goodloe's uncle, fiery old Cassius M. Clay, had earlier asked him, "William Cassius, is it a fact that you have said . . . that you were not armed the other afternoon?"

"Yes, Uncle Cass," Goodloe replied.

Taking a knife from his large assortment, Clay gave it to his nephew, saying, "Now you take this knife. If Armistead Swope insults you again and you don't kill him, you're no Clay. I never want to see you again."

Later, both Swope and Goodloe went to the post office for their mail. The box of one being immediately above the other and both trying to get their mail at the same time, Judge Goodloe accused Colonel Swope of blocking the way. The men were bitter enemies of long standing. Swope declared he was insulted by Goodloe's addressing him and said he didn't give a damn if he did block the way. Both men backed away and on this slight pretext reached for their weapons. Goodloe used the long knife, somewhat like a Bowie knife, given him by his uncle Cassius. Swope used a thirty-eight caliber Smith & Wesson revolver. Swope fired two shots, the second taking effect in the lower abdomen of his enemy. Goodloe meanwhile repeatedly plunged his blade into Swope's body, inflicting up to thirteen separate wounds, until Swope fell dead.

Colonel Swope, a former Union officer on Buell's staff, had been appointed Kentucky internal revenue collector at Lexington by President Arthur and had moved to Lexington from Paris. He had been reared in Lincoln County, only a short distance from where Goodloe was born. From the time of the internal revenue appointment, there had been bad blood between the two. Goodloe, said to have been small in stature, was irasible and aggressive; he denounced Swope in letters and at Republican political conventions. Swope, a large man with splendid physique, was somewhat arrogant and dictatorial. Both were extremely ambitious for political honors and for party leadership. A bitter quarrel ensued on the floor of the Republican convention at Louisville in 1888, which almost, but for the intercession of friends, led to a duel. At the time of his death, Goodloe was internal revenue collector for the Lexington district. Saddened by the death of his favorite nephew, Clay still was proud that Goodloe had behaved as a Clay should. Tears rolling down his cheeks, he turned to a friend and said, "I couldn't have done better myself."[32]

The Toll-Gate War, 1896-1898

Until the second decade of the twentieth century the turnpikes were more or less locally owned and operated. Roadbuilding was so expensive that, in order to obtain sufficient capital for construction, corporations were organized, stock sold and dividends on toll returns distributed to stockholders. So well did the roads pay that the commissioners of the Sinking Fund had invested through the years several thousands of dollars in turnpike stock; the state was a heavy investor. Counties too had invested heavily in turnpike corporations. Some controlled certain roads and even levied taxes for their upkeep. Apparently Buckner believed that the counties should own the roads, because in 1889 he asked the General Assembly to pass a law providing for a superintendent of roads in each county and a county road fund under county control.

Tollgate houses had been built at intervals of about five miles along the roads to collect charges. The usual charge at a tollgate was five cents for a horse and rider, and ten cents for a vehicle, the prices depending on the number of horses or mules and passengers. Though travelers would sometimes pull off the road into the woods and drive around a tollgate to avoid paying (a process known as "shunpike"), returns from the "gates" were quite remunerative; and the roads, especially through the Bluegrass country, were usually kept in excellent condition.

By the early eighties considerable opposition was voiced against the tolls and especially against the road owners, who were accused of operating solely for profit. Many contended that the fees were exorbitant. As a result, the poor keepers of the "gates" were recipients of more than a generous amount of epithets and threats.

Even the editor of the Lexington *Daily Transcript* on February 24, 1882, inveighed against the system. "Such absurd restrictions as the tollroads," he declared, "are utterly too medieval for a rejuvinated Kentucky." The agitation for free roads began in earnest in 1890. The cry was for "free roads." However, many property-owners opposed the idea on the grounds that county-owned roads would greatly raise taxes. Nevertheless, many intelligent persons were convinced that the tollgate system was outgrown, a relic of the past.

During Bradley's administration the long threatened "war" broke. The lawless element, styling itself "turnpike regulators," issued warnings to the keepers not to collect any more tolls. As J. Winston Coleman has stated: "When these warnings were not heeded, the tollgate houses were raided and burned, the 'gates' cut down, and occasional horsewhippings administered the toll-keepers." The raiders operated at night and, for that reason, were often called "nightriders." Notices such as the one issued in December 1896 to one luckless "keeper," William Mattingly of Mercer county, were numerous:

Toll Gate Raiders Notice

We ask you not to collect no more tole, you must not collect one cent if you do we are a Going to Destroy your House with fire and Denamite so you must Not collect No more toll at all. We Don't want to do this but we want a Free Road and are agoing to have it, if we have to Kill and Burn up everything. Collect no more Tole we mean what we say, so fair warning to you.[33]

As can be seen in this notice, the tollgate raiders were largely composed of an uneducated and violently inclined class of people. They were, nevertheless, organized in bands, under mounted leaders, just as the earlier guerrillas and Ku Kluxers. The most serious outbreaks occurred in Washington, Anderson, Marion, Mercer, Franklin, Woodford, and Jessamine counties, where, as Coleman states, "nearly all the toll-houses were burned and the 'gates' cut to pieces and pitched over the side of the road." Those counties also had been a prey to postwar lawlessness generally and had suffered under ineffective county officials. Roads were abandoned and deteriorated rapidly.

Numerous were the wild raids. Families along the roads, especially women and children, were frightened almost out of their wits, and life was made frightful in the extreme for the keepers and their families. It was a dreadful experience to be aroused from sleep by rough masked men, many criminally bent, many drunk, to be rushed outside, shivering and frightened, and to watch the house go up in flames. The victims were always warned upon penalty of death not to reveal identities, so that few indictments were returned. The county officers for the most part proved to be no better than those in the mountain counties during the feuds. Those keepers brave enough to defend their homes were murdered. It was unfortunate that men who winked at the law controlled the dominant party in those counties most affected.

Governor Bradley, in the legislative session of 1898, scathingly denounced local officials and called for stringent action. Turnpike raids, he declared, had increased. The Martin law, offering rewards, was not enough. He said that he had tried faithfully to enforce that law, offering rewards and even employing detectives, but did not know of a single conviction. In many localities, he averred, public sentiment was reported as "endorsing that kind of crime." Peaceful citizens were overawed and the turnpikes so depreciated in value that counties could buy them up at nominal prices. Many counties therefore had become beneficiaries of crime, he charged—a condition which would not have occurred except for the "cowardice of officials and the corruption of citizens, who openly countenanced the lawbreakers."

Turnpike stock owned by the state and valued at $400,000 three years before was reported as practically worthless. Bradley declared that in many places turnpike officials feared to ask for guards lest their homes be burned and they themselves murdered.

Worse still, peace officers in many localities sympathized with the mobs. Actually, raiders themselves had been appointed as guards in some places, thus "surrendering to the outlaws," Bradley said. Occasionally arbitrary prices had been set and owners were forced to sell, or cease to collect toll. In at least one instance, the gate keeper had been robbed of his tolls by the raiders.

Lately the "knights of the road," Bradley charged, had undertaken to "regulate" the amount of tobacco a farmer could cultivate, destroying his plants if he dared disobey; had begun to warn millers that they should not sell flour for more than the price fixed by the raiders; had even threatened with shotguns farmers who posted their lands against hunters. The people of the state had so long fed on contempt for law that the Commonwealth was beginning to reap the whirlwind of its folly.

In view of these conditions, Governor Bradley called for the passage of laws making the county responsible for losses of property and death caused by such violence. In addition, he asked that the Martin law be strengthened, that guards be assigned in places where violence was threatened, and, if guards could not be found, the governor be empowered to place troops at the gates, with authority to collect the toll. He declared that the county involved should be required to bear the expense. Though recognizing the severity of the recommendations, the governor asserted, "better severity than anarchy."[34] The bitterly partisan Democratic legislature, was in no mood, however, to humor the first Republican governor. The prevailing political philosophy, decidedly in favor of permitting local authorities to do as they pleased, kept state interference at a minimum.

With little help forthcoming from the state, citizens in some of the counties, believing that unless drastic steps were taken anarchy would follow, finally began obtaining indictments against some of the known "nightriders." According to Coleman, Anderson County citizens were credited with bringing the first indictments and causing the first arrests, in April, 1897. Bold citizens in other counties followed suit, and the lawlessness was finally suppressed, but not, however, before the tollgates were put out of business.[35] The 1890s were too late for so archaic an institution as tollgates in Kentucky, but that fact did not justify the criminal destruction of private property. The "Tollgate War" was just another example of the seeming penchant of far too many Kentuckians for lawlessness and violence as a solution to problems, of the prevalence of weak local officials, and of the apparent lack of interest on the part of "good citizens" in requiring enforcement of the law.

A few comparative statistics will perhaps suffice to indicate Kentucky's relative standing in crime. In 1890 Kentucky reported 425 homicides, which is a number actually smaller than the total number killed, because in some counties men were murdered with no official notice whatsoever being taken. The Commonwealth that year had the largest number of homicides of all states save New York. The Empire state, with a population of 5,997,853 to Kentucky's 1,648,690, reported 442 homicides. Ohio had 207; Indiana 209, while Tennessee had only 285.[36]

Governor Buckner wrote that "nothing is more common than to find civil officers disregarding their plain duty, either by failure to issue proper process, or by neglecting, and even refusing, to serve process placed in their hands for execution." He declared that "citizens, too, when summoned to aid in the arrest of offenders, often fail and frequently refuse obedience to the summons." And no attempt was ever made "to bring these infractions of law before grand juries, or if their attention is called to these neglects, they are usually ignored." "In every case of lawlessness on an extended scale, which has been investigated, the cause is directly traceable to the neglect of civil officials," Buckner concluded.

Honest "Old Bolivar" struck at one of the most serious evils when he inveighed against the buying of elections. He declared that:

The evil has already attained magnitude which seriously endangers the interests of society. Not only of candidates for political and municipal offices, but it seems certain that judicial elections are conducted with equal disregard of law; and when it is considered that there is but one step between the purchase of judicial position and the sale of justice, the people may well despair of the proper administration of the laws under so vicious a system of election as is so often pursued.

The chief executive pleaded with the lawmakers to enact a measure to punish the purchaser of votes as severely as the seller. Above all, he asked that something be done to force the officers to enforce the law.[37] But like Bradley later, he got little response from the legislature.

At the end of the "Tollgate War" many thought Kentuckians would be satiated and disgusted by the plethora of perennial lawlessness, violence, and crime that ran through a generation. Law enforcement, peace, and calm, they assumed, would soon follow. Such an assumption was erroneous. A writer for a national magazine in 1900 described the Kentuckian as "a man of war, quick to take affront, and ever ready for a personal test of courage." The reputation for violence was well earned, he believed, for even the leadership had "a singular disregard for the sacredness of human life." While the mountaineers deserved the notoriety they received, he noted, the gentlemen of the Bluegrass were also "careless of life."[38] His interpretation was one with which many Kentuckians could agree.

Poor education, outdated philosophy, and ineffective politicians were all part of the problem; but all these factors could be found elsewhere. Attention focused on the mountains, but widespread violence belonged to all sections. What made Kentucky different was that the hard-to-define abstraction, "the Kentucky character," contained elements which in the late nineteenth century combined to produce a bloody epoch in the state's history.

XVIII

GOEBEL!

On the stump in 1899, William Goebel represented few of the stereotypes usually associated with Democratic candidates of the preceding quarter-century. In a state that valued family ties, his name had little impact compared with that of a rival, P. Wat Hardin. Goebel's German origins flew in the face of Kentuckians' pride in their English forebears. Son of an immigrant, Goebel lacked ties to Kentucky's past. More than that, the preceding thirty years had been dominated by ex-Confederates in government. Goebel, too young for war, could claim only an uncle on the side of the South. Worse still, his father had fought for the Union. Beyond all this, cries of "Black Republicans" echoed throughout the entire period. And Goebel now openly sought black votes.

Even the man's campaign style seemed a rejection of Kentucky traditions. Cold and reserved, Goebel rarely functioned well in large gatherings. The hand-shaking, back slapping, joke-telling style typical of the era's politicians was not Goebel's forte. He stood awkwardly out of place mingling with the common man. On the platform his speeches lacked the smooth, soothing force of orators like W. O. Bradley, J. C. S. Blackburn, or W. C. P. Breckinridge. Beardless, looking younger than his forty-three years, Goebel gave little indication that his appeal to Kentuckians in 1899 would be anything but negligible. Yet he became the Democratic gubernatorial candidate and his appeals found willing followers—and equally willing opponents. Disliked, hated, admired, loved, William Goebel, if nothing else, aroused Kentuckians' party passions.

William Goebel

Collection of the Kentucky Historical Society

The Making of a Candidate

Goebel's father had left Goettingen, Germany for America, married a German-born immigrant, and built a log cabin in Pennsylvania. On January 4, 1856, William Goebel was born in Sullivan County. A premature baby, weighing less than three pounds, the child struggled and survived. Not until after his fifth birthday did he speak English; the German language remained a part of his heritage. When ten, Goebel moved with his family to Covington. While his father worked as cabinet maker, railroad workman, and at various other jobs, Goebel became a jeweler's apprentice in his mid-teens.[1]

Ambitious, he hoped to be a lawyer. Ex-governor John W. Stevenson allowed him to study in his office. Later Goebel graduated from a Cincinnati law school and attended Kenyon College. On his return, another influential northern Kentuckian, John G. Carlisle, then congressman, later Speaker of the House, United States senator, and secretary of the treasury, took him in. When Stevenson's partner died, Goebel moved to join his firm in 1883. Leading conservative Democrats backed the rising young barrister.

Through a lucrative practice that earned him up to $25,000 a year, Goebel became established in Covington. Shy, an avid reader, a man who rarely visited the theater and who was "timid and awkward in the company of women," bachelor Goebel devoted little time to social matters: "His social qualities were not winning," a judge remembered. The black, slicked-down hair, yellowish skin and coal-black eyes that often seemed oblivious to events before them reinforced the aura of coldness surrounding the man. Yet at the same time Goebel encouraged his brothers, took a deep interest in their affairs, and gave them financial aid. He told one brother, Justus, that he almost wept when he saw his brother Arthur win an honor at Yale. That side of Goebel seldom appeared before the public.

Editor Richard Knott, like many of those opposed to Goebel, left little doubt of his feelings. While Goebel's intellect was clear and his mental methods incisive, "he was by nature an autocrat, but an autocrat not born to the purple." A man born out of his time, he had no sympathy with popular government, according to Knott. Goebel, with none of the "traditional graces of an orator," rarely excited enthusiasm, and seldom stopped to placate men. "Hate could burn in him to a white heat but he could not conceive that men would sacrifice a political career to a political principle."

Young *Evening Post* reporter Irvin S. Cobb had strong and mixed feelings about Goebel. No one he ever knew matched him in intellectual strength, Cobb wrote in 1940, but "he loved power as drunkards love their bottle." No man numbered himself as an intimate friend of the Covington lawyer. Goebel reminded Cobb of a synthetic "self-assembled mechanism." His description of Goebel typified many men's perceptions: "He had audacity, ruthlessness, a genius of leadership, an instinct for absolute despotism, a gift for organization, a perfect disregard for other men's rights or their lives where his own wishes were concerned; the brain to plan and the will to execute."[2] In 1887 he used some of these characteristics to gain his district's senate seat. Over the next thirteen years he would gain a reputation in some circles as a progressive reformer.

At Frankfort, Goebel moved in ways that angered influential men. He sponsored a law that would reduce toll charges on several Covington roads, roads in which John Sanford owned stock. An ex-Confederate banker, Sanford blocked Goebel's elevation to the Appellate bench. Others joined him in opposition. Theodore F. Hallam had become angered when Goebel refused to yield him the fraction of a vote he needed for a nomination. Harvey Myers, Jr. joined Sanford and Hallam and sought to halt the march of the "Kenton King." By 1895 they supported eventual candidate Hardin over Goebel's choice, "sound money" man Cassius M. Clay, Jr.[3] The northern Democracy was deeply split.

Goebel focused his legislative attention on railroads. Though often absent at the Constitutional Convention of 1890-1891, he led the fight to incorporate the Railroad Commission as a permanent feature of the new document. Two years later, Goebel helped guide through—over Governor John Young Brown's veto—a bill prohibiting rebates and discriminatory freight rates. Railroad employees who struck in sympathy with Pullman strikers in 1894 found the Covington state senator ready to defend them gratis. His "fellow-servant" bill designed to make railroads—not their employees—bear the financial burden in accidents was vetoed by Governor Bradley after a session ended. Goebel aided the effort to investigate the railroad lobby, led by ex-Confederate General Basil Duke. He also gave active support to Charles C. McChord's bill (eventually vetoed) that gave the Railroad Commission the right to hear evidence, decide guilt, fix rates—if considered discriminatory—and then to fine the offender.[4] Kentucky railroads, especially the L & N, found little in the record of William Goebel to attract them.

If railroad opposition, together with factionalism in his home territory, were not enough, Goebel soon incurred additional enemies. Convinced that Republican fraud had deprived Bryan of the state's electoral votes in 1896, Goebel had sought to remedy that situation. Under the old system, the judge, sheriff, and clerk of each county functioned as the county board of election and sent returns to Frankfort.[5] Local political realities were recognized. Democrats regularly charged that heavily Republican eastern Kentucky returned fraudulent counts, while Republicans made the same charge toward heavily Democratic western Kentucky. The 1898 law bearing Goebel's name changed all this. The Democrats sponsored the bill centralizing power in Frankfort.

As stated previously, the Goebel law empowered the state election commission to appoint the county boards. These local commissioners would then select officers to preside at the polls. The Democratic legislature named William S. Pryor, a recently defeated Court of Appeals judge, ex-Confederate and former congressman William T. Ellis, and Charles P. Poyntz, former state senator with Goebel and member of the Railroad Commission. All were Democrats. They chose two men from their party and one

Republican for the county boards, even in heavily Republican areas. The fears of prominent Democrats who had opposed the bill, including Watterson and Breckinridge, now seemed realized.[6] The partisan appointments strengthened already strong Republican fears regarding "Boss Bill."

The Fight for Nomination

Three men sought the 1899 Democratic nomination. Hardin, the 1895 choice, initially led in the pre-convention fight for delegates. His chief contender seemed to be William J. Stone, who found support in western Kentucky's rural areas. Past Speaker of the Kentucky House, former congressman, the crippled ex-Confederate who had lost a leg while serving under Morgan had strong backing among free-silver, populist-oriented Kentuckians alienated by Hardin's supposed L & N ties.[7]

Goebel's mood fluctuated between optimism and complete dejection in these months. In the fall of 1898 he told a brother of his certainty of nomination. "The fighting Democrats are for the Election Law and for me," he wrote, adding that he would soon seek the support of a factional opponent, J. C. S. Blackburn. But by winter, gloom replaced his cheery predictions. Actions of men he considered to be his Covington allies brought a long, angry outburst in a letter to his brother Justus:

> I shall not permit any man to be elected mayor on the Democratic ticket unless he is entirely satisfactory to me. I shall beat any man that I do not like with the Election Commission. I turned over to [J. W.?] Pugh the entire matter of appointing election officers this year. Next year I shall attend to the matter myself, whether I am nominated for governor or not.
>
> There is going to be a hot fight between me and Hardin for the nomination.[8]

In February, 1899, Goebel believed that persons pretending to be his friends had betrayed him and destroyed all chances of victory. "I can not be nominated," he wrote, and he spoke of his inclination to withdraw. A week later he stated that he cared nothing for the governorship. A postscript added, however: "the Louisville crowd is no good to me, and I want to smash them anyhow."[9]

As Goebel, Stone, and Hardin sought delegates in the spring of 1899, the usually stormy political seas of Kentucky grew even stormier. Editor James M. Richardson of the *Glasgow Times* echoed part of the Democratic fears throughout the state. The party faced "the supremest peril in its existence. The battle of its life is just before it. It must be bold." To repeat the Republican victory of 1895 would mean four more years of black rule, of bayonet rule, and of military usurpation.

The opposition press warned of the fraudulent, evil, corrupt, and "communistic" influence of the party of Bryan. Democrats sought to halt the state's progress by attacking railroads. They wanted to take men's property by supporting an inflationary free silver scheme. They hoped to rob the victors of rightful victory by enacting a corrupt election law. They would replace majority rule with mob rule. Democratic victory, as the Republicans and Gold Democrats pictured it, would bring anarchy.[10] Calm political discussion would not be a feature of the 1899 campaign.

In this political climate, the three candidates crossed the state seeking to line up delegates. Each man sought to outdo the other in placing the onus of "boss rule" on his opponents. Behind Hardin stood Louisville politico John Whallen, who had purchased the financially troubled Louisville *Dispatch* to aid the cause. The L & N was rumored to support Hardin and the *Dispatch* as well. The paper began attacks on the selfish demagogue who had none of the "chivalric spirit of a Kentuckian," none of the devotion to friends. Goebel's supporters retaliated by attacking the Whallen machine, the L & N, and the lies from the "false and craven throat" of the *Dispatch*. Their candidate's life, they stressed, was but one long battle against corporation influences.[11] Speaking at Bedford on

May 30, Goebel himself answered his detractors in a widely reprinted speech. "I have not had a powerful family connection nor wealth to aid me. I am not the chance bearer of a great name made famous by somebody else," he said in reference to Hardin. Goebel scornfully repudiated the boss politics of the "Frankfort dynasty" and "Tateism."[12]

Areas began to select delegates for the convention, called to meet on June 20. Rumors spread throughout the state telling of a Goebel-Stone "deal." The two men would organize county conventions jointly to overcome frontrunner Hardin. In Louisville events in a primary foreshadowed the problems. The *Dispatch* reported that "Goebel's gamblers," with the police, clubbed and drove citizens from the polls. Before noon, the city and county committee declared the election "null and void on account of the fraudulent interference of the police." Intimidation, they said, had prevailed throughout the city. The editor of the Whallen-backed *Dispatch* blamed the affair on Walter Haldeman of the *Courier-Journal* and Mayor Charles P. Weaver, "a venal character . . . who cares nothing for the good name of the city he disgraces, a cowardly inciter of riot, a disturber of the peace, a highwayman . . . , a man sunk to the lowest depths of political if not moral depravity. . . ." The *Courier-Journal* answered, claiming that when the Whallen forces saw their defeat they abandoned the field. Other officials simply took their place, so that voting—despite the declaration of the committee—continued until the evening. The results stood.

The next day the *Dispatch* suggested that armed citizens might be necessary to prevent a repetition of lawless interference in the convention to select delegates. "On the verge of anarchy," the city should be policed by a hundred or more armed citizens, "to preserve order." A gang of "political cut-throats and highwaymen"—the forces of Haldeman, Weaver, and Goebel—would again attempt fraud and violence as they had recently, if men armed with Winchesters "and well supplied with ammunition" did not stand up to them. The call to arms, the continuing tendency of each side to respond by appeals to force, not law, would not end in Louisville in mid-June.

The mass convention in the city and county on the seventeenth came off without violence. Hardin captured 49 votes and Stone 35 in Jefferson County. Stone and Goebel made plans to contest the results, as they would in many counties. They had to. The preliminary results gave Hardin 362 votes, Stone 271½, and Goebel only 231½ as the convention drew closer. The rest of the vote stood uncommitted. Opponents of the man from Kenton, "the most despicable demagogue of the age" to their eyes, were overjoyed. Goebel could not win, for he trailed the field.[13]

At the Music Hall

Just before the Convention assembled at the Music Hall in Louisville, rumors continued of a Stone-Goebel deal. On the nineteenth Ollie James and John S. Rhea, Stone managers, met with Urey Woodson, Sam J. Shackelford, Henry Hines and C. M. Lewis, all Goebel leaders. The two sides parleyed for a time and the proposed arrangement became open knowledge. Stone managers feared that Goebel might dump their candidate and "march off with the entire reward" if they united with him. Finally though, on June 21, 1899, Woodson later wrote, the two men agreed to aid each other and signed a memorandum. They would throw out Hardin's Louisville vote and divide the vote between them. If one withdrew all his support would go to the other. The same day the *Dispatch* headlines proclaimed: "Stone-Goebel Deal Made."[14]

Both men agreed to perfect the organization in their favor. Ex-governor John Young Brown, they concluded, would make a good temporary chairman, but he declined. As the convention opened on June 20, James, a Stone man, nominated a minor politician, Judge David B. Redwine of Breathitt County, as chairman. When Woodson, a Goebel man, seconded the nomination, the rumored deal became apparent. Hardin men put forth a former Goebel ally, now an opponent, William H. "Roaring Bill" Sweeney of Marion County. The band played "Dixie" over and over, followed by the inevitable rebel yells, the heat grew more and more oppressive, and the candidates lobbied for votes as time drew near for the selection of a chairman. Meanwhile Philip Preston Johnston of Lexington, a Whallen supporter and state party chairman, arbitrarily decided who would be allowed to vote, for contested delegations were extremely numerous. Generally, but not always, he recognized local party authorities. This was in line with precedent, for delegations which held credentials signed by the local party chairman usually voted until unseated. With 551 1/6 votes to Sweeney's 529 5/6, Redwine had ten more than needed.[15] He would preside.

The contested votes—vital to Stone or Goebel if they hoped to overcome Hardin's lead—would be decided by the Committee on Credentials. Only four of the thirteen men appointed by the committee favored Hardin. As they debated the final outcome, in the convention Sweeney and John B. Thompson, Harrodsburg, managers for Hardin, asked that the delegates recognized by Johnston be allowed to vote—as was the custom—until the final report was made. This motion Redwine ruled out of order.[16]

"UNDER CONTROL OF OUTLAWS. Music Hall the Scene of Wild Disorder and Terror, and for a Time on the Verge of Bloodshed," headlines proclaimed. The preceding day, the 23rd, had been one of confusion and bitterness. Each side blamed the other for the debacle. Hardin men claimed that Redwine, as Goebel's lieutenant, packed the hall with thugs, gamblers, Weaver's policemen, and firemen. They wanted to prevent any voting until the Committee on Credentials reported in favor of Goebel. Stone-Goebel allies argued that it was Whallen's thugs and gamblers who had been present to intimidate the chair. Weaver and his chief of police Jacob H. Haager had only been asked to send police to disperse the mob.

Redwine, seeing the impossibility of proceeding, had called for adjournment. Every attempt to vote had been met with catcalls, loud hissing, and other noise. Charles J. Bronston asked that

Redwine's decision to adjourn be put to a vote. He sought to remain and vote Hardin men in. Again, Redwine refused to allow the opposition forces' wishes. Angered, Bronston later shouted out that his party could not be controlled by "cutthroats and assassins." Cheers and boos drowned out his voice. He continued and was stopped time and again as he castigated the Redwine rulings. Backed by "Roaring Bill" Sweeney, Thompson, and even some Stone supporters, Bronston threatened to bolt a convention dictated by one man, oblivious to parliamentary law. Finally, however, cooler times brought adjournment.[17] Decisions made the next day, Saturday, would be crucial.

The majority report of the Credentials Committee decided for Stone or Goebel in 26 of the 28 contested cases. A shift of 159 1/3 votes from Hardin to Goebel and Stone would be the result, if the report was approved. A minority report, signed by the four Hardin supporters, gave him the contested votes generally. Chairman Redwine ruled that only uncontested delegations could vote on whether to accept the minority report over the majority one. Thus nearly one-third (322 delegates) would not vote. Most were Hardin men, since the majority report gave their seats to the Stone-Goebel combination. The vote, 441-328, rejected the minority report. Hardin's hopes for victory again declined.

Seeing this, Hardin came forward and withdrew his name from contention. His followers did not accept their hero's move, however, and some voted for him as the balloting began. When the clerk announced Jefferson County, the leader of the Goebel forces there announced that all the county's votes would go to Goebel. The earlier agreement with Stone promised him half of that vote. Without those votes he would lose to Goebel. The ex-Confederate's managers, angered by the treachery as they saw it, planned to change their votes to Hardin. If they were to be beaten, better by their enemy than to be betrayed by a professed friend. Augustus Owsley Stanley of Henderson, later a Kentucky governor and senator, climbed on a box, balancing himself on a chandelier and American flag. He changed Henderson's vote to Hardin. Woodson, realizing what was occuring, changed his Daviess County delegation's vote to Stone in order to keep the bargain that he had witnessed. Before the changes Goebel had received 520 votes, Stone 428½ and Hardin 126½. Hardin supporters—seeing the split in their opposition—returned to their candidate, while some Stone supporters gave him votes. Even a few of Goebel's allies left him, angered by the Louisville move. A recapitulation of the first ballot reversed the results: Stone, 395 5/12, Hardin, 359 11/16, and Goebel 330 2/3. Ten more ballots followed until adjournment just before midnight. The final ballot left the men even closer: Stone 376 3/4, Hardin 365 1/2, Goebel 346 3/4. The day of rest would be welcomed.[18]

On Monday the delegates returned to the Music Hall to find it patrolled by police. The anti-Goebel *Dispatch* reported that some delegates were refused entrance, alternates were ordered away, and even members of the unfriendly press were turned down in their requests. Those inside the hall found more than 200 policemen, friendly to Mayor Weaver and Goebel, and all present by Redwine's request.[19]

John Rhea of the Stone camp demanded that the chair order the police removed from the hall, Redwine declared the motion out of order. Ex-congressman Willard Mitchell appealed the ruling. That appeal was then declared out of order. Bronston, Rhea, Sweeney, James, Thompson and others all rose in protest. No parliamentarian anywhere would support the chair's refusal to allow an appeal of his decision, Bronston argued. Wheeler too said that nowhere can a ruling not be appealed. Redwine stood firm. He ordered the roll call to begin for selecting a nominee.

Stone and Hardin men, angered by the rulings, refused to allow the convention to proceed. An uproar ensued. The clerk's voice: "Adair county." Jeers and hoots made it impossible to hear. Men on chairs shouted for attention, various delegates argued and some fought, others blew tin horns. "The whole floor," one reporter noted, "was a howling, excited pandemonium." Reporters from the pro-Goebel *Courier-Journal* wrote that Whallen, Basil Duke, and his L & N agents had a hundred men on the floor to break up the convention. Songs began to break out, among them "Hang Judge Redwine to a sour apple tree." The chairman asked the secretary to read the rules allowing him to clear gallery and lobby. James, "his face white with rage," thundered that no rule gave Redwine the right to clear the floor, or eject a single delegate. Shouts of "Put us out if you can" supported him. Forty minutes or more of pandemonium passed with nothing done. Cries of "Appeal" answered Redwine's attempt to begin a vote.

Finally amid shouts, songs, and jeers, a roll call began. The noise made an accurate vote impossible. Several counties refused to vote. The result—according to the chair—gave Goebel 352½, Stone 261½ and Hardin 67. Another quick ballot ended in similar results. James asked the chair if Goebel was elected since he had a majority of the votes cast. Redwine so ruled. James answered that if so the nomination "would not be worth a baubee [sic]." Goebel sent a messenger, telling Redwine that he would accept only if an absolute majority (547) voted for him. The convention adjourned.[20]

As the voice of Whallen, Hardin, and the L & N, the *Dispatch* told its readers the next day: "This is no schoolboy game that is now being played in Kentucky. It is genuine political war of the most desperate character." The "revolutionary" methods of Goebel justified the "most vigorous and far-reaching plans of opposition."

That same day the "war" ended. Stone called on the convention to adjourn sine die. Hardin made the same appeal. Ex-governor James B. McCreary rose for the first time to speak and called for a continuation. A move was made to adjourn. Redwine began his ruling, correctly stating: "I lay no claim to being a good parliamentarian." He declared the resolution to adjourn out of order. An appeal on his ruling was similarly ruled out of order. Mitchell rose and said that his forces would not disrupt the convention as they had the previous day. They would accept today's verdict.

On the fourteenth ballot it was Stone, Hardin, and Goebel, in that order, but no more than twenty votes separated anyone. For the next six ballots this continued. Goebel's strength continued to be in urban areas and northeastern Kentucky, not the Populist-oriented west. On the twenty-first Stone's total rose to 398, Hardin had 355, and Goebel, 328. Stone still needed almost 150 more votes to gain the nomination. More ballots. A resolution was introduced to drop the lowest man after the twenty-fifth ballot. Redwine allowed a vote on the resolution, which was adopted (572-520). Both James and Mitchell bitterly attacked the chair's ruling since the resolution to adjourn, made earlier that day, had been declared out of order. The decision stood.

The crucial twenty-fifth ballot saw a drastic shift: Goebel now led with 389, Hardin continued second with 382¾, and Stone trailed with 319¼. Stone was dropped. The next ballot would decide the nominee. Of the first six counties formerly in the Stone column, five went to Hardin as the balloting began, including James' Crittenden. The urban centers of Fayette, Jefferson, and Daviess, divided previously, now gave their entire vote to Goebel. The decision was still uncertain. When the clerk called Union County, a Stone stronghold on earlier ballots, the county's sixteen votes went to Goebel, and with them went the nomination. Had Hardin received the votes a tie would have resulted. Goebel had 561½, Hardin 529½ in the final tally.

As was the custom, leaders of the opposition pledged to support the ticket, though with little enthusiasm. Rhea, Sweeney, James, Bronston, Wheeler, and others gave the decision their qualified blessings.[21] The convention chose the rest of the slate quickly. The nomination for lieutenant governor went to young (not yet thirty), aristocratic J. C. W. Beckham of Nelson County. Goebel had openly questioned the wisdom of Beckham's selection since former Speaker of the Kentucky House Ben Johnson had voted Nelson County for Hardin. Friends finally persuaded Goebel to keep the legislator. Beckham offered the ticket some of the things Goebel could not, including a long family tradition of leadership. For similar reasons Judge Robert J. Breckinridge, Jr., an old ex-Confederate from Danville, was given the nod for attorney general in part to satisfy voters discontented with Goebel's Unionist background. Others on the ticket were: Gus G. Coulter (Graves County), auditor; Judge S. W. Hager (Boyd County), treasurer; Judge R. Breck Hill (Clark County), secretary of state; Harry V. McChesney (Livingston County), superintendent of public instruction; and editor Ion B. Nall (Louisville), commissioner of agriculture.[22]

Watterson's *Courier-Journal*—whose news reports had been pro-Goebel, though the paper remained silent editorially—now stated that the paper would "be compelled to support the ticket." A few days later the paper began to take up the Goebel theme of L & N oppression. This young man's movement, shown in the youthful nominees, steadied by "an eloquent and brilliant old stager like Robert J. Breckinridge," would roll to glorious victory. While not acknowledging the paper's strong opposition to the election law, the editorial did suggest that nothing could beat the Democrats, "Goebel law or no Goebel law."[23]

Serious defections from the Democratic party had already begun. Both the Louisville *Dispatch* and W. C. P. Breckinridge's Lexington *Herald* deplored the outcome. On the day following Goebel's selection the *Dispatch* refused to support the nominee. A strong advocate of free-silver and Bryan, the paper believed the support of the *Courier-Journal*, only recently opposed to both, proved that Goebel was not a true Democrat. In the mountains of Kentucky another free-silver, almost Populist paper, the Hazel-Green *Herald*, echoed Bronston's words when it said that "the convention seems to have been in the hands of assassins, cutthroats and thieves."[24] In the Lexington *Herald* congressman-turned-editor Breckinridge struck out at the ticket during the campaign despite his brother's presence on it. Kentuckians should unite against that system called Goebelism, he advised. It was a disease, a madness, a "moral aberration" threatening the manhood of Kentucky. "The most expert political schemer, trickster and charlatan" in Kentucky, King William I advised lawlessness, in

Breckinridge's version. His followers were but Hessian mercenaries led by a German general.[25]

The Republicans and Mr. Taylor

Prepared to wage war on these "mercenaries," Republicans assembled in convention, confident of victory. Though they disliked and feared Goebel more than the other Democratic contestants, at the same time they thought that the Music Hall fiasco made him especially vulnerable. The Republican delegates began to believe that their nominee might really win the race after all—if the party could avoid the bitter factionalism of the Democrats.

Early indications made that possibility more remote. While lame-duck Governor Bradley supported Judge Clifton J. Pratt of Hopkins County, editor Sam J. Roberts of the *Leader* and John W. Yerkes backed state auditor Sam H. Stone of Richmond. Senator Deboe gave his blessings (and some of his federal patronage) to Bradley's attorney general, William S. Taylor. Some politicians had virtually abandoned the gubernatorial field early because they foresaw a Republican defeat, but events at the Democratic convention changed their evaluation of the possibilities. Meanwhile "Tom Tit" Taylor organized—like Goebel—a strong machine that swept most county delegations. He seemed assured of nomination.

Bitter at his party's repudiation of his candidate, Bradley boycotted the convention. Negro leaders threatened to follow him, for they believed Taylor represented the western "lily-white" branch of the party. Black newspapers suggested a separate convention and a third party if Taylor won, as seemed the case. In an effort to strengthen his November chances, Taylor made a Negro leader permanent secretary while promising offices to other blacks. According to rumor, Taylor also offered to make Bradley's nephew, Edwin Porch Morrow of Somerset, the nominee for secretary of state if the governor would campaign for the ticket. Bradley refused.

Despite the factionalism, Taylor won the nomination, as expected. All other candidates, facing certain defeat, withdrew. The convention chose as lieutenant governor candidate John Marshall, a young Louisville lawyer who had studied under John Mason Brown. The ticket also included young (thirty-one) Caleb Powers, superintendent of the Knox County schools, for secretary of state and Judge Pratt for attorney general. Others nominated were the Reverend John S. Sweeney of Bourbon County for auditor; young Walter R. Day of Breathitt for treasurer; John W. Throckmorton of Fayette for commissioner of agriculture; and John W. Burke of Campbell County for superintendent of public instruction.[26]

The head of the ticket represented a world very different from the polished urban background of Goebel. Born in a Butler County log cabin near Morgantown, Taylor received only a cursory education because of his family's poverty. Farmer, rural school teacher, and then county clerk, he rose to the position of county judge. He had remained a local politician until selected attorney general in 1895.

Taylor—like Goebel—won office less through personal attributes than through organization. Even Taylor's friends saw some elements of the man they knew in the Democratic picture. "Hogjaw" Taylor, an unfriendly paper noted, was "a slouch in his gait, a boor in his manner, and the butt of the entire bar of Kentucky." While industrious, "Taylor knows nothing of social or political amenities. If he is in a crowd and desires clear space he shoulders everybody within reach out of his way." The editor noted Taylor's financial condition—he and his wife kept a Frankfort boarding house—and concluded: "Taylor is the personification of all the low and degrading in human tendency." Irvin Cobb later described Taylor as a well meaning "but a poor enough creature," only putty—and not high grade at that—in the hands of others.[27] Both candidates represented a political type that had not often appeared in the state arena before.

The "Brownies"

The election would not be only a two-candidate affair. A third

The Republican Leadership of 1899, The back row includes, from left to right:
Caleb Powers, John Marshall, W. J. Deboe, W. S. Taylor, C. J. Pratt and Sam D. Brown
Reprinted from Robert E. Hughes, *et. al.*, *That Kentucky Campaign (1900)*

group threatened to enter the field. Dissenting Democrats continued to attack Goebel, Redwine, and the Music Hall convention. Former Congressman William M. Beckner spoke for many when he maintained that Goebel's election would set the state back a generation in development. A vote for the Kenton King signified sympathy with poolrooms "and every form of vice," in Beckner's eyes. Worse, it would encourage young men to believe "that straight methods do not bring honor in Kentucky."[28]

Other Democrats agreed that only they could restore honor to the state. A call to meet in convention at Lexington met an enthusiastic response. Those present once represented, and in many cases still represented, the leadership of the state Democratic party. Editors Breckinridge of the *Herald*, Knott of the *Evening Post*, and Charles I. Stewart of the *Dispatch* joined the northern Kentucky faction of Myers, Hallam, and Mackoy. Boss Whallen and reformer Beckner both led delegates. Politicians and some former congressmen supported the "revolt": "Roaring Bill" Sweeney, past speaker of the Kentucky House William C. Owens of Scott County, and Phil Thompson—all were present. The convention chose ex-Governor Brown to head this conservative "revolution." Their candidate spoke to them of their dear old homes, fragrant flowers, beautiful daughters, the glorious American Revolution, Robert E. Lee, Henry Clay, and, finally, Goebel. "Has manhood fled to brutish beast and are we to be called up and voted like dumb driven cattle?" he rhetorically asked. The "true" Democrats would "save" the old party's standards and reject these anarchists. He declared: "I won't bow my neck to the usurpation of the Louisville convention." Brown quoted Watterson's own words attacking Goebel two years before as proof of the lack of principle in the opposition. The Brown Democrats had their leader.

His subordinates included the lieutenant governor candidate P. P. Johnston of Lexington, L. P. Tanner of Daviess County for attorney general, Frank A. Pasteur of Caldwell County for auditor, John C. Droege of Kenton County for treasurer, and E. L. Hines of Warren County for secretary of state.[29]

The "Brownies" received immediate attention—little of it favorable—from the Goebel forces. Watterson attacked the movement's
L & N ties and "holier-than-thou" attitude, "questionable at its
very best." The Glasgow *Times* more bitterly noted that Breckinridge and Owens were practically Republicans anyway, while
Beckner had not a Democratic bone in his body. The editor
concluded that Whallen "wouldn't know a political principle if he
met [it] in the road." The comment of another paper seemed
particularly apropos as the canvass opened: "It is hard to tell who
is for and who is against the several tickets."[30]

The Search for Votes: Goebel

Goebel took the field first. Just after the Democratic convention he told a brother of the changes in him: "The nomination
has given me a power that nothing else could have given me; and if
I am elected my power will be still further increased. I do not
doubt my election." Later in the same letter Goebel repudiated
Stone's post-convention charge of betrayal. "I took Stone away
from Rhea and company and used him," he wrote, but he never
promised to nominate him. A determined candidate told his
brother, "I have made up my mind not to be beaten, no matter
what is done by the L & N and [Mark] Hanna. And I shall not
take any chances. So far as I can do so, I shall make my election
certain."[31]

Plans for victory were being made by a committee headed by
Blackburn, who finally pinned his senatorial hopes to Goebel's
lapel. Ex-Alliance leader J. D. Clary, former conservative governor
McCreary, and young Beckham guided the campaign, aided by
Percy Haly, secretary at the Goebel headquarters. The candidate
made Allie Young of Morehead chairman of the state committee.
The opening speech would be given in the Democratic stronghold
of the Jackson Purchase.

On August 12, some 3,000 gathered at Mayfield to hear Goebel
and new ally Blackburn flay the opposition. After a less than

successful attempt at mingling with the voters on the hot day, Goebel turned to speaking. He spoke clearly and made his points through a deep, almost harsh voice that carried well. Suddenly, in the midst of an attack on his opponents, Goebel collapsed. While aides sought to revive the candidate, Blackburn hastily took the stand and made his usual talk. He then yielded to Goebel, who had recovered from his heat exhaustion.[32] As omens go, it was not an auspicious beginning.

Goebel's speech—after the interruption—contained themes he had stressed all his life. The L & N monopoly directed by the New York Belmonts and foreign investers must be controlled, he stressed.[33] Concentrated, outside corporate wealth wanted to select Kentucky's governor rather than allow the people's will. The question, he proposed, was "whether the trusts or the people shall rule . . . , whether the Louisville and Nashville Railroad Company is the servant or the master of the people of this Commonwealth."

To Goebel, the L & N was an economic vampire, seeking to suck the lifeblood from the Commonwealth, enriching outside interests. Goebel's earlier tendency to invent opposition or to exaggerate its evils now came to full fruition. If events had not gone as he hoped in the past, friends became—to his view—enemies, and sincere opposition turned into a secret conspiracy against him. Very real problems did exist and reform was needed in the L & N; its opposition to him in the form of contributions was not, however, a new feature of Kentucky politics. Given a basis for some of his fears, he exaggerated and magnified the evil so that it became something he must conquer, no matter what the cost—or it would conquer him: "I ask no quarter and fear no foe."[34]

The Search for Votes: Taylor and Brown

The Republican campaign opened in the party's stronghold, the eastern Kentucky mountains. At London before a crowd of some 5,000 that included Deboe, Powers, and former gubernatorial

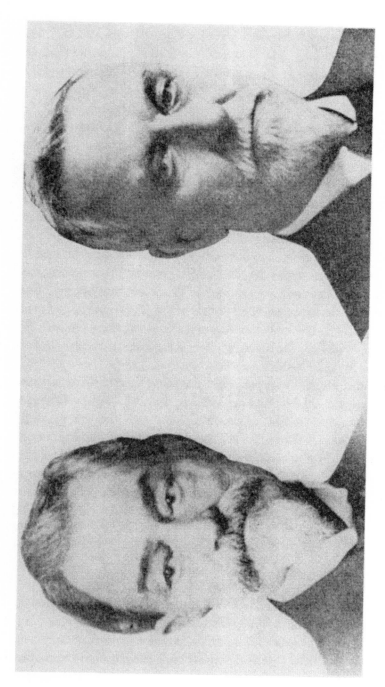

Two of Goebel's Bitter Foes
Basil W. Duke (left) Milton H. Smith (right)
Reprinted from Urey Woodson, *The First New Dealer* (1939)

candidate Thomas Z. Morrow, Taylor began his two and a half hour talk by stating that slavery never had flourished in the mountains and political slavery would not now. Organize well, he advised, to insure a fair election. "This is your only salvation. If it fails you then the deadly coils of tyranny will tighten about you and crush to death your political liberties." Taylor routinely defended Republican state finances, praised McKinley prosperity and supported the new acquisitions in the Pacific and Caribbean.

In a later speech at Clinton, Taylor focused on similar issues. "A government by force and fraud is about to be established. The ballot box is intended to be robbed," he warned. Was this not the end of republican government? "Is this election law to voice the will of the people, or is it to subserve the ends of men who lust for office, overide and stifle the will of the people?" As voters, they must act now, for once intrenched in the executive branch, Goebelism would be supreme. The battle cry: "The Goebel bill must be destroyed."[35] The two candidates gave voters their choice: Was the elusive "will of the people" being subverted by the L & N machine or by the Goebel machine?

Brown and his allies increasingly supported Republican answers to that question. In his opening speech, the ex-governor defended his administration while questioning the sincerity of Goebel's free-silver views. A bitter attack on Redwine and his conduct of the Music Hall Convention ended with Brown asking if a John C. Breckinridge or a Lazarus W. Powell, or other great Democrats would have approved of such proceedings. He concluded with an attack on the Goebel law as "oligarchy." "Home rule is murdered in it."[36]

The Campaign Intensifies

To this point papers throughout the state could well praise the "gentlemanly" speeches that focused on the issues. But as party speakers spread throughout the state, issues became subordinated to personalities. Bitter denunciations replaced cool deliberations.

One of the "Brownies," Theodore Hallam, a shrewd ex-Confederate follower of Morgan, had supported Sanford and was a long-time friend of the L & N. He became one of Goebel's harshest critics. Cobb remembered Hallam as "a battered-looking, hard-hitting, hard-drinking little Irish lawyer" who "was perhaps the greatest natural orator in a state of natural orators." At a Bowling Green speech earlier a Goebel supporter had asked Hallam if he had not said following the Music Hall Convention that even if the Democratic party nominated a "yaller dog" for governor he would support him.

"I did," answered Hallam.

Why, then, did he repudiate Mr. Goebel now? the questioner asked, smiling.

Hallam waited for absolute quiet. "I admit," he said blandly, "that I said then what I now repeat, namely, that when the Democratic party of Kentucky, in convention assembled, sees fit in its wisdom to nominate a yaller dog for the governorship of this great state, I will support him—*but lower than that ye shall not drag me.*"[37]

Speaking in the same city later, Goebel countered. Hallam was but "a drunkard and debauchee"; Basil Duke of the L & N lobby, only "a professional corruptionist"; Myers, a recipient of illegal lottery money while a legislator; Owens, a gambler angry because he (Goebel) had tried to make roulette a felony; Mackoy, an owner of toll roads, and—referring to his problems in the Pollard affair—W. C. P. Breckinridge: "I need only to mention his name."[38]

The response came quickly. Duke called his attacker "a liar, a slanderer and an assassin," while Breckinridge concluded that "a gentleman cannot be made out of a vulgarian." When such replies brought further venom from the Democrat, Breckinridge remarked: "Poor Goebel: one of the most pitiable sights to a hunter is to see a snake writhing in agony from poison injected by itself in a mad and futile passion."[39]

The growing intensity of an already fiery campaign, expected to be close, made every vote even more important. Two voting blocs—the Negroes and the Confederates—became vital to each side's hopes for victory. Each bloc gave indications that it would not be as solid as in past elections.

Goebel's Unionist background, his centralized Goebel bill, and his identification with bossism made him odious to many Confederates, especially among the officer class. The issue that had additionally turned many against him now re-emerged in the campaign. Sanford, an ex-Confederate who had served under generals Humphrey Marshall, William Preston, and John C. Breckinridge, had been Goebel's bitter rival in the 1880s. An April 11, 1895 meeting between them outside a Covington bank had resulted in bloodshed. Both men drew—witnesses were unsure which drew first—and both fired. Sanford fell, shot in the head; Goebel (unharmed) looked at his victim, put the pistol in his pocket, walked away, and surrendered to the police. A grand jury failed to return an indictment.

Sanford's death five hours after the shooting left a blot on Goebel's record. He remained an assassin to the opposition press. Confederates had deserted him even before his nomination. After it, John R. Boyd, president of the Confederate Veterans Association in Kentucky, led a Lexington rally in opposition to the "Kenton King."[40] The *Dispatch* reprinted a story telling how Sanford's widow, a niece of General Marshall, had to be placed in the state lunatic asylum. The account ended by saying, "She has been gradually losing her mind ever since the awful shock occasioned by the bringing home of her husband's bloody dead body."[41]

When supporters of Goebel—including Blackburn—denied that their candidate had authored a newspaper article which supposedly had been the immediate spark of the Sanford incident, the *Dispatch* quickly printed a photograph of a manuscript, written in Goebel's hand, which had attacked "Gonorrhea" Sanford in other equally unchivalrous terms. The paper later asked: "What husband, if he has the manhood, the chivalry of a gentleman, can look into the innocent and trusting face of his wife and tell her that he voted to elevate to the gubernatorial chair the man whose vile obscenity in the public press sent Sandford [sic] to his grave and Sandford's wife to an asylum for the insane?"[42] Angry ex-Confederates made it uncertain whether they could be counted in their usual Democratic column.

On the other hand, Negroes seemed to be departing from their usual voting patterns as well. The typical cry of Negro domination did not come from Goebel, as it had from some other Democratic candidates. Earlier, he had not voted on any questions involving the Separate Coach bill, though present at the sessions. Negroes began organizing Goebel clubs as the 1899 campaign began. Black speakers stumped the state for the Democrat and an Independent Colored Voters League presented Goebel a bouquet of flowers following one Louisville speech.[43]

Attorney-General Taylor's refusal to take a stronger stance on the Separate Coach Bill and his actions at the convention clearly had angered black voters. The president of the Afro-American League of Kentucky and moderator of the General Assembly of Colored Baptists of Kentucky, the Reverend G. W. Balin of Elizabethtown, called for the election of a Republican who really opposed the bill. The Reverend S. E. Smith of Owensboro, chairman of the Baptist organization, stated his belief that Taylor favored segregated rail facilities. He appealed to the estimated 65,000 black voters to register their feelings at the polls.

Though Goebel sought to woo black voters from the Republicans, his actions threatened to alienate many of his own supporters. He tried to tread a cautious middle course that could keep both groups safely in his camp. That was difficult. Finally, after repeated questioning, he admitted at Cloverport that he favored the separate coach bill and would oppose its repeal. Goebel stressed, however, his desire to see accommodations made equal. A little over a week later Taylor (who hoped to do the same thing Goebel had attempted) reluctantly admitted that he opposed segregated cars. Thereafter Rev. Smith and other blacks came out for Taylor. Their real ally was Bradley, "the friend and champion of all the people, be they white or black," but they now believed Goebel's treatment of Negroes showed insincerity. They went for Taylor.[44]

Still, when the election came, apparently not all Negroes followed their leaders. A Henderson paper reported "a number of negroes stamped under the rooster for the first time. . . . Here in the city some negroes voted for Goebel, while hundreds of others were easily persuaded to stay away from the polls. More surprising still, a number of negroes in the county precincts voted for Goebel." McCreary earlier noted in Richmond a stronger disposition "than he had ever known" among blacks to go over to the Democrats.[45] If the race were not complex enough, now Confederate Republicans and Negro Democrats confused an already murky politics.

The Populists, whose support Goebel could have expected, had nominated their own slate, headed by John G. Blair. While denouncing the school book "trust" monopolies and supporting free silver—stands favored by Goebel—the convention had specifically disapproved of the Goebel law and its author. Though some Populist leaders, including Thomas S. Pettit, spoke in his behalf, Goebel found others on the opposite platform.[46] In danger of losing his Confederate, Populist, and conservative Democratic supporters, Goebel turned with renewed effort to a man whose ability to garner votes in the state stood unchallenged.

The name William Jennings Bryan united many of the warring factions. Brown Democrats, as well as the Goebel wing, supported Bryan, while he still remained a hero to many Populists. Goebel's initial efforts to bring Bryan to the state were rebuffed, reportedly because the Kentucky candidate used language that offended the fundamentalist. Finally, however, "the Great Commoner" agreed to campaign for the ticket. Beginning at Mayfield the train carrying Goebel and Bryan continued across the state in a whirlwind tour that included six or more speeches a day. Bryan called on western Kentucky Populists to vote for Goebel, not trusts; he appealed to urban Negroes to abandon the Republican policy of imperialism and black subjugation; he called on Brown Democrats to follow him to Goebel. In three days the two men travelled an estimated thousand miles, speaking to 150,000 Kentuckians.

Goebel generally abandoned his former defensive stance, striking out at the railroads again and again on the tour. Comparing his fight to Andrew Jackson's with Nicholas Biddle and the Bank of the United States, he called the Honest Election League of Louisville, organized by Whallen, Duke, and others, "a combination of the Pharisee and the blackleg."[47] As Bryan returned to Nebraska, Democrats in Kentucky, for the first time in a long while, felt more confident of victory. Some—but by no means all—of their wounds had been healed by the Bryan trip, while the Republicans continued to be divided between Bradley and Taylor-Deboe forces.

That confidence was quickly shattered. As soon as Bryan departed, the Republican's old war horse, "Billy O.B.," took the stump. Bradley started his "swing around the circle" at Louisville, before an audience of some 4,000. He began the widely reprinted speech by saying that while the Democrats had to import an orator, the opposition did not, for all the state's best men had now deserted the "Kenton King." Goebel's old benefactor, Carlisle, and Lindsay, Breckinridge, Brown, Hallam, Owens, even Hardin and Stone, had left the nominee of the Music Hall Convention. As to his motive in taking to the campaign trail at this late date, Bradley insisted that he only sought to defend his administration. (Watterson soon suggested that Taylor's promise of support for his senatorial bid might be a truer motive.)

Bradley appealed to black voters not to desert their party. He cited his appointments of Negroes as director of the Central Lunatic Asylum, as a member of the Agricultural Board, as trustee of the Colored Normal School, and as Lumber Inspector for the state. What had the Democrats done for blacks, except to pass a Separate Coach Bill? "I have never been ashamed of being the friend of the negro. . . . I have never been afraid of the bugbear of

A Goebel speech in Owenton

Reprinted from *Harper's Weekly* (1899)

'social equality.' " He sought only more kindness and more justice to the Negroes of Kentucky, he added near the end of his long speech.

To this point Bradley had not mentioned his party's nominee. Finally, he closed his talk by saying: "And go to the polls and elect Taylor." As the cheering continued after the dramatic pronouncement, Louisville Republican leader (and later governor) Augustus E. Willson whispered to the governor, "Bradley, that's the slickest thing you ever did in your life."[48]

Together Willson and Bradley made their own whirlwind campaign, outdrawing Taylor. A Democratic paper reluctantly noted that the governor's speeches were "the equal of any Republican speech heard in any Kentucky campaign for a long time." Bradley now spoke almost fondly of "Bill Taylor," and speakers introduced the governor as the next senator from Kentucky. With Brown injured and confined to his wheelchair for the last two weeks of the campaign, his party not drawing well, it was clear that the contest stood Goebel–Blackburn versus Taylor-Bradley.[49]

The Last Days

Both parties agreed that the Louisville vote would be crucial and both made strong last-minute appeals in the city. Goebel again devoted most of his talk to the bossism of the L & N. He gave his full support to laborers who went on strike for higher wages and portrayed the Republicans as the party owned by trusts. At another speech, before a predominantly German-American audience, the immigrant's son opened by speaking in his parents' native tongue. Republicans tried to counter Goebel's urban appeal with their own speakers.[50]

The tense political atmosphere had not lessened as the campaign dragged on through the hot summer. Both sides talked of the violence and fraud certain to be perpetrated by the other. Careless words bandied from speaker to speaker. An opponent would be characterized as "the little guttersnipe from the slums of creation," and warnings were given that fraud in the election would result in "ornaments never dreamed of by an architect" hanging from local bridges.[51] Charges of lying and deceit were hurled against prominent leaders by men who had been their closest friends only months before. Each side feared—and expected—the worst from the other.

In Louisville Republicans and Brown Democrats, recalling the preconvention vote in that city, warned citizens to resist by force if necessary attempts to deprive them of their vote on election day. When Mayor Weaver, a Goebel supporter, added some 500 private police to the city force just prior to election day, Republicans feared possible intimidation. The mayor had proclaimed that the rumors of "riot and bloodshed" would not be allowed to become more than rumors, in defense of his actions. After consulting Duke, Knott, Stewart, and others, Governor Bradley ordered the militia readied in order to prevent possible disturbances. The day before the election Democrats replaced several Republican election officials. *Courier-Journal* headlines on election day proclaimed "BAYONET RULE" in response to Bradley's warning alert. The opposition *Dispatch* warned against riots: "If there must be a row let it be started by the Goebelites." As election day neared, the anti-Goebel *Harper's Weekly* saw "no more important struggle against corrupt government and the ascendancy of the criminal in politics . . . going on in the country."[52]

Election and Question

Surprisingly, election day passed quietly in Louisville and elsewhere, with the usual few exceptions. Watterson's paper even reported less disorder in the city "than usually results from excessive partisan zeal." Fewer than a dozen men were arrested, mostly on disorderly conduct charges. The militia made a brief march to investigate rumored trouble but quietly returned when none was discovered. Over the state the tardy results made it apparent: "Slow Returns and Close Finish." The Democratic belief was that

Goebel's margin remained small but safe. The Republicans answered: "God Reigns and the Government in Frankfort Still Lives."[53]

The question of religious sanction aside, it became clear that the closeness of the vote meant that the Goebel-appointed Board of Electoral Commissioners would have the power to decide the election. Dire warnings and charges of fraud in the voting appeared almost as quickly as the polls closed. The *Dispatch* cautioned that Goebel must be met by bold measures for he was willing, they believed, "to take the risk of precipitating civil war." In Lexington Breckinridge and Bronston told a rally that the Republicans had won fairly and should hold their office by force if necessary.

Democrats charged fraud. In Nelson County, where 1200 ballots bore the name "W.P." rather than "W.S." Taylor, they called for these votes to be rejected. Knox and Johnson County Democrats charged that "using thin tissue" ballots, so thin that a voter's pencil marks could be seen through them, made these illegal votes as well. Allie Young called for the entire Louisville count (Taylor had over a 3,000 vote majority there) to be thrown out, on the grounds that the militia intimidated voters. Actually, both Republicans and Democrats could argue persuasively that their candidate had been deprived of some votes through fraud. Both would be correct.

The powerful and widely-read *Courier-Journal*, noting the "very grave" situation, admitted that Louisville had had "a most orderly and peaceful election." The paper declared that the results of the State Board should be accepted as final: "If the Republicans are declared the victors, nobody will block their way to Frankfort." Smaller papers agreed that the Republicans had probably won, and memories of 1877 when Samuel J. Tilden—they believed—had been cheated out of victory by Republican Rutherford B. Hayes still haunted them. "Better that a Republican should hold the office forever," one declared, "than that the Democratic party should dishonor itself by Hayesing it to Goebel. A free ballot and a fair count is our program."[54]

1899 ELECTION

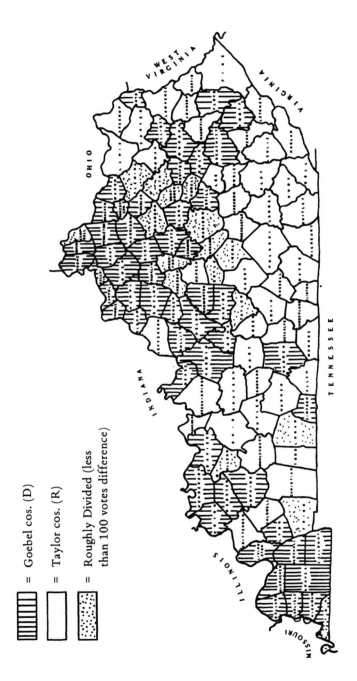

= Goebel cos. (D)

= Taylor cos. (R)

= Roughly Divided (less than 100 votes difference)

Source: *Official Manual of Kentucky, 1900*

Governor Bradley feared that no Democratic acquiescence would result. As the date for the election board hearing grew nearer, he asked President McKinley for aid. In a letter conveyed by Senator Lindsay, Bradley wrote of his fear "that I may not be able to crush the spirit of lawlessness and preserve the peace. . . ." He appealed for a thousand regulars to be sent to Fort Thomas, plus ammunition (50,000 rounds), rifles (890 Springfields), blankets, and overcoats for the militia. Whether his request was met or not, he concluded, "I will not surrender to a lawless mob."[55]

Despite Bradley's fears, the initial election ruling favored the Republicans. The Court of Appeals announced that the Nelson County vote should remain in Taylor's column, for voters obviously cast their ballots for him, whether W. S. or W. P. But the ruling of the election board might be a different story. Two of its members, Ellis and Pryor, had openly campaigned for Goebel and all three owed their selection to him.[56]

Small bands of Republicans began arriving in Frankfort just prior to the board's meeting. Taylor later admitted that he advised them to do so, believing their presence would "exercise a moral influence on the contest." The Democratic press called them "the advance guard of the army of intimidationists." Some 500, supposedly from the mountains, eventually arrived. Resolutions from their home counties, passed just prior to the board's decision, called Goebel a "vicious serpent," a tyrant, a monster, and usurper. "Before this ring of looters shall deprive us of the victory we have won in this contest, we will shoulder our guns and march to the music of war." Similar resolutions from Knox County proclaimed that the men there would tender their services "to the end." Taylor, Powers, and the others would be inaugurated, "by peaceful means if we can, by forcible means if we must."[57]

Amid this charged atmosphere Republican lawyers led by Gus Willson presented their arguments, while Frank Peake of Shelbyville and Louis McQuown of Bowling Green gave the Democratic version. The board announced its decision quickly. Taylor received the certificate of election by a surprising 2-1 vote. Pryor and Ellis in the majority stated that the board had no judicial powers in the governor's race and thus could not hear proof or swear witnesses. This only the legislature could do. They hinted that, given these broadened powers, Louisville's vote would have been thrown out. But as it stood Taylor was governor. The announced vote: 193,714 for the Republican, 191,331 for Goebel, 12,140 for Brown and 2,936 for the Populist Blair.

Less than a week later, on December 12, 1899, Taylor was inaugurated as Kentucky's thirty-third governor. His brief speech portrayed the election as a mandate for civil liberty over a partisan machine in a contest between the "infamous" Goebel law and a true ballot.[58] Peace at last had arrived.

Gentlemen May Cry "Peace" . . . .

Two days later the Democratic State Central, Executive, and Campaign committees met in Frankfort with McCreary, Young, Woodson, Chinn, McChord, Trimble, Haly, and scores of other leaders present. As chairman, Blackburn pushed for a resolution calling on Goebel and Beckham to contest the election. The committees agreed. While Goebel's inclination had been to let the matter drop (and seek a United States senate seat in 1901), he and Beckham followed their party's wishes. Watterson's paper praised the decision as "A Brave Venture"; Republicans, heavily outnumbered in the legislature, saw the affair in a somewhat less courageous light.[59]

In a Democratic caucus just prior to the opening of the legislature, state senator Goebel nominated Blackburn as the party's choice for senator. In a joint ballot later, "Old Jo" won easily over Bradley by a 75-54 vote. In the House, a straight 57-40 party vote made Trimble Speaker and the senate officers were chosen by another party vote of 25-12.[60] With the preliminaries out of the way, the legislature turned to choosing the membership of the decisive joint committee to decide the contested governor's race. Their findings would be subject to legislative review.

The existing division of the chambers made it likely that the eleven-man committee would contain approximately four or five Republicans. Names were placed in a box. It was examined, then shaken vigorously. The selections were drawn. The names were called out: a Democrat, another. Finally all had been called—ten Democrats and one Republican would decide the governor's race. Nine of the eleven chosen to decide the lieutenant-governor's race were Democrats as well. While Republicans did well overall in the other committee selections, the make-up of the decisive one brought them to charge fraud. They suggested that the slips of paper had been folded in such a way that Republican names filtered to the bottom of the box when shaken. Democrats, "greatly elated" over the results, laughed off the allegations and prepared to hear witnesses in the case.[61]

At the same time, legislators began their own investigation of another serious matter. At the Democratic caucus, Senator S. B. Harrel of Logan County had dramatically charged Whallen with offering him a $4,500 bribe to vote for Taylor in the legislative battles. Holding up a key, he said the money could be found in a Louisville bank. A grand jury investigated the charges and found the money. Vaultkeeper James Speed, Jr. swore that Whallen, Harrel and Charles Ryan of Russellville had jointly rented the box.

Defended by Hallam and Hardin, Whallen struck back, charging Harrel with obtaining money under false pretenses. He swore that the Logan County senator told him that Goebel supporters had promised him $1,000 in cash plus the superintendency of the Western Lunatic Asylum if he would give them his support. Harrel then proposed, said Whallen, that for enough money to live "without pecuniary loss" (since he would not get the cash or job from Goebel), he would tell all. Whallen gave him $5,000 the affadavit continued, of which Harrel apparently had used $500. When the case went before a judge, Whallen introduced as evidence a paper signed by him, Ryan, and Harrel, and witnessed by two other men. The document substantiated Whallen's version. Harrel denounced it as a forgery. Neither Harrel's nor Whallen's case went to trial and General Assembly efforts to reach a decision ended without resolution.⁶² Tensions rose and each side saw the affair as substantiating its basest fears of the other.

With this controversy in the background, the contest committee began hearings on January 15 in the Capitol Hotel ballroom. Before them stood Bradley, Breckinridge, Sweeney, and others as Taylor's counsel. The Democratic side included less well-known lawyers. The initial conduct of the proceedings brought immediate objections. The "alleged trial" was merely a farce, one argued, for the committee upheld all Democratic objections and overturned all Republican ones. After that first day, Republican leaders met at Louisville's Galt House. Taylor, Marshall, Deboe, Willson, Knott, John M. Atherton, George Denny, Edward C. O'Rear, and James P. Helm, among others, pledged to resist Goebelism to the end.⁶³

As the committee continued to hear testimony, Frankfort once again filled with men, mostly from the mountains, only this time in larger numbers. The L & N had transported them to the city without charge, Democrats suggested. Headlines screamed: "ARMED MOB OF MOUNTAINEERS Invade Frankfort to Bully the Legislature." Papers of a different persuasion reported the more than a thousand men were only lawabiding citizens there to "protect their liberties," to protest the crime being perpetrated by the legislature. These papers defended the citizens' right to peacefully protest and praised their "commendable self-restraint."

But even defenders of the mountaineers recognized the dangers involved. Rifles and pistols everywhere focused attention on the possibilities of violence. Even though some of the "outside" men stacked their weapons in the Commissioner of Agriculture's office, both sides remained well-armed. Open threats kept men alert and apprehensive. A single incident could spark bloody warfare. Breckinridge and other leaders opposed to Goebel privately condemned the presence of the men and counselled Taylor to order their withdrawal. The next day most of the men departed, as suddenly as they had arrived. Still, some two or three hundred remained, in a silent vigil, awaiting the decision.[64]

The verdict would come within a week. Thirteen legislative contests, involving seven Republican seats, would be decided then, perhaps in such a way as to give the Democrats an even larger majority. On January 29, testimony ended before the contest committee. After closing arguments, their decision would be announced within days.[65]

A Clear January Morning

On the morning of January 30, Goebel, Chinn, and Eph Lillard, warden of the state penitentiary, met in the Capital Hotel lobby. As usual the two men left with Goebel as he started for the senate chamber. They crossed the railroad tracks and entered the capitol yard. Considering the number of men usually there, the area was unexpectedly clear. As they approached the fountain outside, Lillard moved ahead of the other two men to make certain that there would be no problems ahead in the lobby. A loud report caused him to turn hurriedly. Goebel fell to his knees, then to his side, shot. "Goebel, they have killed you," Chinn cried to the fallen man. Sounds of more shots, more muffled ones, caused him to call out, "Lie down, they will shoot you again." Goebel replied weakly, "That's right." Lillard quickly glanced toward the executive building and thought he saw a raised window in the secretary of state's office.[66] He saw no one and turned away to help several men carry Goebel to the senator's room in the Capital Hotel. Twenty minutes later doctors examined him. He was bloodless, his skin cold, his body wet with perspiration. The bullet had entered the right lung, passed through the body, shattering ribs, and then exited near the spinal cord. The "quite profuse" bleeding continued and only later could doctors slow it. They gave Goebel a saline solution. None of the physicians expressed optimism over his chances of recovery.[67]

Outside all was chaos. Rumors spread rapidly. Goebel was dead,

The Assassination of Goebel
Reprinted from the Cincinnati *Enquirer*,
January 31, 1900

said one; no, wounded, said another. Would Taylor be shot in revenge? Who had shot Goebel? Legislators who quickly came out of the capitol saw Goebel being carried off. Scores of men hurried about trying to find a suspect, a clue. Troops appeared, adding to the uneasiness.

Some seven hours after the assassination attempt, the contest committee met at the Frankfort city hall, since soldiers blocked entry into the capitol. Breckinridge and Bradley appealed to the men to defer action because of the emotional atmosphere. The committee adjourned for over an hour. Returning, the joint committee by a strict party vote stated that Goebel and Beckham received the highest number of votes and therefore were "elected to their respective offices." No specific count was given. The Republicans on the committee filed a minority report.

A little over an hour after that decision, Governor Taylor declared a state of insurrection in Kentucky. He ordered the General Assembly to adjourn and meet in London. Republican legislators complied with the order, though many believed it unconstitutional. The next day Democrats sought to meet, in order to adopt the majority reports and declare Goebel legal claimant while he still lived. At the capitol, then to the opera house, the city hall, the courthouse—everywhere soldiers blocked their attempts to gather. The legislators returned to the hotel, went separately to Judge Pryor's room and signed the majority report. The 19 senators and 57 representatives declared Goebel governor. Taylor, the proclamation said, fraudulently and unlawfully tried to prevent the General Assembly from meeting. No violence, except by "reckless armed men" brought to Frankfort by Taylor, existed.

Chief Justice James H. Hazelrigg swore in Goebel and Beckham the same day. In the governor's first action, he signed an order commanding the troops to disperse and return to their homes. The troops remained. Later the Democrats met at the Capital Hotel and in joint session again declared Goebel governor. To insure the legality of the earlier actions, he was given the oath of office once more, by Circuit Judge James E. Cantrill this time.[68]

Goebel's condition worsened. With his lungs full of blood and pneumonia beginning, doctors administered oxygen. Nothing helped. In the early evening of February 3, William Goebel died. A spokesman told reporters that his last words had been "Tell my friends to be brave, fearless and loyal to the common people." Cobb—present at the time—later gave a different version. Newspapermen scoffed at such death-bed eloquence, he argued, for Goebel all his life had displayed no such oratory. They dutifully filed their stories, but many—like Cobb—believed another report. In that account, Goebel ate one of his favorite foods just before he went into a coma. His last words, in Cobb's version: "Doc, that was a damned bad oyster."[69]

Whatever the correct version, the one the newspapermen reported spread across the state. In death Goebel became what he had never been in life—a charismatic hero, a man worshipped. Thousands attended his funeral on a cold, rainy day. Blackburn delivered an impassioned eulogy. Watterson's printed tribute began with "He lies dead at Frankfort." An ambitious man, Goebel wished to do the state service, however. The leader whom corruptionists feared now was gone. Though his paper denounced the Goebel law, said Watterson, he supported its author because he beat "the combination of brute force and money" in the Music Hall Convention. "His death unites the Democrats of the United States," he added.[70] In Kentucky men who had turned from the party only recently now returned. Republican hopes of holding office sank into the ground with Goebel's coffin. A martyr they could not defeat.

Answers and Hopes

Strong leadership could have changed ensuing events. But Governor Taylor was not such a leader. After Goebel's death he walked the floor, "his bony arms flailing the air, the skirts of his dismal coat flapping like black distress flags, his famous under-slung jaw adroop until it seemed ready to come undone and fall off, and his haggard eyes streaming." He cried out asking why men persecuted him, then at the next minute swore that he would die before yielding his office. One of his counsellors, W. C. P. Breckin-ridge, recognized the problems and saw Taylor as "an irresolute, unstable and indecisive man—incapable of either making up his mind or keeping it made up. . . . He is patriotic, well-meaning and perhaps with physical courage; but wholly unfit for leadership in times like these. . . . I am sorry for him."[71]

Goebel's death removed one of the obstacles at least to reason-able discussion. Within forty-eight hours, both parties met and drafted a proposed peace. Taylor and Marshall would step down and be given immunity from prosecution; all legislative actions would be postponed for a week and "all partisan considerations" eliminated from contests of election "as far as may be." A new, "absolutely fair" election law would replace the present one, and the militia would be withdrawn from Frankfort. Willson and five other prominent Republicans signed the proposal, as did Black-burn, McCreary, Woodson, Robert J. Breckinridge, Jr., and four more Democrats. After conferring with his attorneys and friends for several days, Taylor announced on February 10 his decision not to sign. He instead issued an order lifting the ban on the legislature meeting in Frankfort.

By February 19, the legislature reassembled in the capitol with two sets of officers. Republicans in the senate obeyed only Lieutenant Governor Marshall, for example. Taylor's attorneys filed suit to enjoin Beckham from exercising authority; Beckham answered with a suit seeking possession of the capitol and execu-tive building. The suits were consolidated by mutual agreement for a decision before Judge Emmet Field of the Jefferson cir-cuit court. Both sides agreed to abide by the final court deci-sions, since the case undoubtedly would be appealed. Field re-fused to go behind the legislative decision and on March 10 ruled for Beckham.

"The Seal of Kentucky—Revised"

Reprinted from Robert E. Hughes *et. al.*,
That Kentucky Campaign (1900)

The minor state offices went to the Democrats as well. Unlike the governor and lieutenant-governor race, the Goebel law gave the State Board of Election, sitting as a Contest Board, power to decide the other offices. After the initial decision favoring Taylor, the two men who voted for him had resigned. Provisions of the Goebel Act allowed the sole remaining member—who voted for Goebel—to appoint a replacement, and the two in turn would select a third member. Two strong Democrats were chosen. Taylor's efforts to invalidate the process failed. On February 26 the Contest Board threw out the Jefferson County ballots on a charge of voter intimidation and four mountain counties' votes because of their ballots. The change gave Democrats all the minor posts. Judge Cantrill ordered the Republicans to turn over their offices. Their appeal to the state's highest court failed.[72]

On April 6, the Court of Appeals by a 6-1 vote declared Taylor legally unseated. Two Republicans joined four Democrats in the majority. The decision was appealed. The Republican governor declared: "I am not a criminal, neither shall I be a fugitive from justice. Whenever indicted, if such an outrage should be committed, I will appear for trial." At that time Secretary of State Powers was being held for planning the Goebel assassination, along with other men suspected of the assassination itself. Their cases would drag on for years as partisanship marked the trials.

On May 21, 1900, the Supreme Court ruled on the Taylor case. They refused to overturn lower court decisions. Harlan dissented. Taylor fled the state, travelling in secret. He remained in Indianapolis practicing law until his death in 1928.[73] Beckham stood unchallenged as governor of the state.

As men and women looked back over the past three decades, the violence of the past months seemed only a logical step in a sequence: Ku Kluxers, Regulators, feudists, personal duelists, tollgate destroyers, and then Goebel. But the past campaign suggested that the old political alliances might be breaking down. Perhaps at

Governor J.C.W. Beckham

Collection of the Kentucky Historical Society

last the Commonwealth would achieve the lofty expectations voiced throughout the last few decades. A new century was eagerly awaited. What it might bring no one knew, but many were hopeful. The young governor symbolized their hopes. The first days of the twentieth century grew nearer.

APPENDIXES

APPENDIX I

Kentucky Population, Urban and Rural Statistics*

	1860	1870	1880	1890	1900
Population	1,155,684	1,321,011	1,648,690	1,858,645	2,147,174
Decennial rates of increase in population over preceding census	17.6	14.3	24.8	12.7	15.5
Increase in population over previous census	173,279	165,327	327,679	209,945	288,539
Population per square mile of land area	28.8	32.9	41.0	46.3	53.4
Membership of House Representatives at each apportionment	9	10	11	11	11
White population	919,484	1,098,692	1,377,179	1,590,462	1,862,309
Percentage increase in white population over preceding census	20.8	19.5	25.3	15.5	17.1
Negro population	236,167	222,210	271,451	268,071	284,706
Percentage increase in Negro population over preceding census	6.9	5.9	22.2	1.2	6.2
Urban population	120,624	195,896	249,923	356,713	467,668
Percent urban increase over preceding census	63.4	62.4	27.6	42.7	31.1
Rural population	1,035,060	1,125,115	1,398,767	1,501,922	1,679,506
Percent rural increase over preceding census	13.9	8.7	24.3	7.4	11.8
Percent of urban to total population	10.4	14.8	15.2	19.2	21.8
Percent of rural to total population	89.6	85.2	84.8	80.8	78.2
Number of farms	90,814	118,422	166,453	179,264	234,667
Acres in farms	19,163,261	18,660,106	21,495,240	21,412,229	21,979,422
Acres improved land in farms	7,644,208	8,103,850	10,731,683	11,818,882	13,741,968
Cropland harvested, acres	....	....	5,245,337	5,616,453	6,349,926
Percentage increase in farm population	17.6	14.3	24.8	12.7	15.5
Percentage increase in number of farms	21.4	30.4	40.6	7.7	30.9
Percentage increase of land in farms	13.1	2.6	15.2	0.4	2.6
Percentage increase of improved land in farms	28.1	6.0	32.4	10.1	16.3

*From Donald B. and Wynelle S. Dodd, *Historical Statistics of the South, 1790-1970* (University, Ala.: University of Alabama Press, 1973).

APPENDIX II

Kentucky Agricultural and Industrial Statistics
1860-1900*

	1860	1870	1880	1890	1900
Average acreage per farm	211.0	157.6	129.1	119.4	93.7
Percentage increase in cropland harvested	...	...	...	7.1	13.1
Value of farms, dollars	291,496,955	248,991,133	299,298,631	346,339,360	382,004,890
Value of farms, percent increase	88.0	14.6	20.2	15.7	10.3
Average value per farm, dollars	3,210	2,103	1,798	1,932	1,628
Farms operated by owners	...	...	122,426	134,529	157,602
Value of livestock on farms, dollars	61,868,237	53,029,875†	49,670,567	70,924,400	73,739,106
Average value of livestock per farm, dollars	681	448	298	396	314
Production of cotton in commercial bales	...	1,080	1,367	873	1,369
Production of corn in bushels	64,043,633	50,091,006	72,852,263	78,434,847	73,974,220
Percent of total production of corn	7.6	6.6	4.2	3.7	2.8
Production of tobacco in pounds	108,126,840	105,305,869	171,120,784	221,880,303	314,288,050
Percent of total production of tobacco	24.9	40.1	36.2	45.5	36.2
Number of manufacturing establishments	3,450	5,390	5,328	7,745	9,560
Capital of manufacturing establishments	20,256,579	29,277,809	45,813,039	78,811,980	104,070,791
Average number of wage earners	21,258	30,636	37,391	56,558	62,962
Total wages	6,020,082	9,444,524	11,657,844	21,326,831	22,434,185
Cost of materials used in manufacturing	22,295,759	29,497,535	47,461,890	63,677,583	82,830,415
Value of manufactured product	37,931,240	54,625,809	75,483,377	126,719,851	154,166,365

*From Donald B. and Wynelle S. Dodd, *Historical Statistics of the South, 1790-1970* (University, Ala.: University of Alabama Press, 1973).

APPENDIX III

A Brief Sketch of the Kentucky Governors, 1865-1900*

*From G. Glenn Clift's *Governors of Kentucky, 1792-1942*

Thomas Elliott Bramlette. 1863-1867

Born 1817. Son of a Kentucky state senator, Bramlette lived in Cumberland (now Clinton) County and represented that county in the 1841-42 legislature. He was admitted to the bar, after a common school education, in 1837, and was appointed Commonwealth's Attorney, 1848-50. Following his move to Adair County in 1852, Bramlette was elected judge for the sixth circuit. After raising and commanding the Third Kentucky Infantry in 1861, he resigned the next year to become United States District Attorney. He defeated Charles A. Wickliffe in 1863 for governor. Bramlette lost an 1867 United States Senate bid, and went to Louisville. He died there in 1875.

Bramlette married Sallie Travis (1819-1872) in 1837 and, following her death, married Mrs. Mary E. Graham Adams.

John Larue Helm. September 3-7, 1867

Born 1802. Son of Kentucky legislator George Helm, John L. Helm had private tutors and a common school education. His career advanced quickly as he was admitted to the bar (1823), appointed Meade County Attorney (1824), elected to the legislature (1826-1838), selected Speaker of the House (1836, 1842, 1843), and chosen to the state senate (1844-1848 and 1865-1867).

In 1848 he was elected Whig lieutenant governor, and on John J. Crittenden's resignation two years later he became governor. Helm served as president of the Louisville and Nashville Railroad from 1854-1860. Following his 1867 election as governor, over William B. Kinkead and Sidney Barnes, he lived but five days after his inauguration.

He married Lucinda B. Hardin, daughter of Ben Hardin, in 1830.

John White Stevenson. 1867-1871

Elected lieutenant governor in 1867, Stevenson took office as governor following Helm's death. In a special election in 1868 he defeated Republican R. Tarvin Baker. He resigned his office after his election to the United States Senate and served there from 1871-1877.

Born in 1812 in Richmond, Virginia, Stevenson was the son of Andrew Stevenson, Speaker of the United States House of Representatives from 1827-1834. John Stevenson was educated first by private tutors, then attended Hampden-Sidney College, and graduated from the University of Virginia in 1832. He married Sibella Winston in 1843. A Covington lawyer following his move to Kentucky in 1841, Stevenson served Kenton County as legislator

460

(1845, 1846, 1848) and as delegate to the 1849 constitutional convention. He served in Congress from 1857-1861.

Following his term in the Senate he taught in the Cincinnati Law School, chaired the 1880 Democratic convention, and served as president of the American Bar Association in 1884. He died in 1886.

Preston Hopkins Leslie. 1871-1875

Taking office on Stevenson's resignation, Leslie later won the 1871 election by defeating John M. Harlan.

Born in 1819, he grew up on a Clinton County farm and began to study law in 1838. Two years later he was admitted to the bar and one year after that he entered Monroe County political life as county attorney. Leslie served in the Kentucky house (1844-1845, 1850-1851) and in the senate (1852-1859). He became a Democrat in 1854, and, following the Civil War, again won election to the senate (1867-1871).

After leaving the governor's chair, Leslie practiced law in Glasgow, was appointed circuit judge in 1881, and President Grover Cleveland appointed him governor of Montana (1887-1889). Leslie settled in the West, served as United States District Attorney for Montana from 1894-1898, and died in 1907.

He married Louisa Black in 1841. Following her death in 1858, he married Mrs. Mary Maupin Kuyendall in 1859.

James Bennett McCreary. 1875-1879

Born in 1838, McCreary graduated from Centre College in 1857 and Cumberland University's law department two years later. Soon after his admission to the bar, he joined the Confederate Eleventh Kentucky under Brigadier General John Hunt Morgan, eventually attaining the rank of lieutenant colonel. He married Katherine L. Hughes in 1867. Two years later he began a six year stint representing Madison County in the Kentucky house; the last four of those years he was selected speaker. He defeated John M. Harlan for governor in 1875.

Following his term as governor, McCreary served in the United States House of Representatives from 1885-1897. He won election to the senate and sat there from 1903-1909. In 1911 McCreary defeated Republican Edward C. O'Rear and became governor for a second time. He lost congressional bids in 1896, 1908, and 1914. McCreary died in 1918.

Luke Pryor Blackburn. 1879-1883

Born in 1816 in Woodford County, Blackburn received his education in the common schools and at Transylvania University. He earned an M. D. degree in 1834 and began his practice in Lexington. After representing Woodford in the state legislature in 1843, he removed to Natchez, Mississippi, and sought to combat yellow fever epidemics in the area. During the Civil War he served as a surgeon for Confederate forces and in 1867 settled in Arkansas.

In 1873 he returned to Kentucky. Then two years later he again went south to treat yellow fever patients. He came back to his home state and was elected governor in 1879 over Republican Walter Evans. Blackburn died in 1887.

In 1835, he married Ella Gist Boswell, a granddaughter of Christopher Gist. She died in Natchez in 1856 and a year later Blackburn married Julia M. Churchill, of Louisville.

James Proctor Knott. 1883-1887

Born on August 29, 1830 in Marion County, Knott as a young man moved to Memphis, in Scotland County, Missouri and began the study of law there in 1846. In 1857-1858 he served in the Missouri legislature, and in 1859 was appointed to the unexpired term of the attorney-general of the state. He won that office in 1860 but military authorities declared his office vacant and disbarred him in Missouri in 1861 for his refusal to take the test oath.

Knott returned to Kentucky in 1862, began his practice in 1863 at Lebanon and in 1867 won a seat in Congress. He served until 1871, did not run for re-election, then was elected again, from 1875-1883. He defeated Republican Thomas Z. Morrow in 1883 for governor.

In 1890 he was selected as a delegate to Kentucky's constitutional convention, and two years later became Dean of Centre College's law department. Knott married Mary E. Froman in 1852 and she died less than a year later, in 1853. In 1858, he married Sarah R. McElroy of Bowling Green. Unsurpassed as an orator, he was a brilliant constitutional lawyer and a charming raconteur. Retiring in 1902, he died in Lebanon on June 18, 1911.

Simon Bolivar Buckner. 1887-1891

Born in 1823 in Hart County, Buckner received a common school education, followed by attendance at West Point Military Academy where he graduated in 1844. After fighting in the Mexican War, he returned to teach at West Point and then served at various military posts. He resigned from the army in 1855, and engaged in business in Chicago for several years. In 1861 he was appointed Kentucky Inspector-General by Governor Beriah Magoffin. After declining a commission as brigadier in the Union Army, he was appointed a brigadier general in the Confederate Army, September 14, 1861. He surrendered Fort Donelson in February, 1862, and soon thereafter was exchanged. He returned to command a division at the Battle of Perryville, and reached the rank of lieutenant general and chief of staff to Kirby Smith on September 20, 1864. He returned to Kentucky after the war and served for a time as editor of the *Louisville Courier*. Buckner defeated Republican William O. Bradley in 1887 in the governor's race. At the 1891 constitutional convention he represented Hart County. Buckner ran as the vice presidential candidate on the Gold Democratic ticket of 1896. He campaigned for his former son-in-law, Republican gubernatorial candidate Morris B. Belknap, in 1903. Buckner died in 1914.

Following the 1874 death of Mary J. Kinsburg, his first wife, Buckner married Delia Claiborne, one of Virginia's "most noted beauties," in 1885.

John Young Brown. 1891-1895

Son of a Kentucky legislator and 1849 constitutional convention delegate, Brown was born in 1835 in Hardin County. He was educated in the Elizabethtown schools and graduated from Centre College in 1855, after which he studied law. From Henderson, he was elected to the Thirty-sixth Congress in 1859, though he had not attained the necessary age of twenty-five. He took his seat in 1860. Brown also served in the House of Representatives from 1873-1877, prior to his 1891 defeat of Republican gubernatorial candidate A. T. Wood.

Following his governor's term, Brown was defeated as the Democratic congressional candidate in 1896 against Republican Walter Evans, and again in 1899 as the independent Democrat's gubernatorial candidate in opposition to William Goebel. He defended Caleb Powers in Powers' first trial. Brown died in 1904.

He married Lucie Barkee in 1857 and following her death the next year, married in 1860 Rebecca Hart Dixon, a daughter of former United States Senator Archibald Dixon.

William O'Connell Bradley. 1895-1899

Kentucky's first Republican governor was born in 1847 at Lancaster in Garrard County. A special legislative act gave him his law license at age eighteen, and he never attended college. During the Civil War, he twice left home to join the Union forces but was returned both times because of his youth. In 1870 voters elected him county attorney of Garrard County. Defeats followed: in 1872 and 1876 for Congress and in 1887 for governor. He defeated Democrat P. "Wat" Hardin in the 1895 governor's race. After four unsuccessful attempts, he was elected to the United States senate in 1908 but died in 1914 before the end of his term.

Bradley married Margaret R. Duncan in 1867. Later Republican governor Edwin Porch Morrow was Bradley's nephew.

William Sylvester Taylor. 1899-1900

Taylor was born in 1853 in Butler County. After a common school education, he entered politics, first as clerk of the county court (1882-1886), then as county judge (1886-1894), and finally as attorney-general of Kentucky (1895-1899). The State Election Commission declared Taylor victor in the 1899 gubernatorial race over Democrat William Goebel. The General Assembly removed him from office and after adverse court decisions against him Taylor left the state and went to Indianapolis, Indiana. He practiced law there and served as vice president of a life insurance company. Taylor died in 1928.

He married Sarah B. Tanner in 1878, and in 1912 took as his second wife Norah A. Myers.

APPENDIX

William Goebel. 1900

Son of a German immigrant, Goebel was born in 1856 in Pennsylvania. His family came to Covington and Goebel received a public school education there. He studied law both at the Cincinnati Law School and under John W. Stevenson. First elected to the state senate in 1887, Goebel served in that body until 1900. His narrow defeat in the 1899 gubernatorial election brought him to contest the election. In the midst of debates over that issue, an assassin shot Goebel. The legislature quickly named him as governor, but he died soon afterwards. Goebel was a bachelor.

APPENDIX IV

Various Kentucky Officials, 1865-1900

United States Senators from Kentucky, 1865-1900

James Guthrie	1865-1868	Garrett Davis	1861-1872
Thomas C. McCreery	1868-1871	Willis B. Machen	1872-1873
John W. Stevenson	1871-1877	Thomas C. McCreery	1873-1879
James B. Beck	1877-1890	John S. Williams	1879-1885
John G. Carlisle	1890-1893	J. C. S. Blackburn	1885-1897
William Lindsay	1893-1901	William J. Deboe	1897-1903

Speakers of the Kentucky House of Representatives

Harrison Taylor	1865-1867	Mason County
John T. Bunch	1867-1871	Louisville
James B. McCreary	1871-1874	Madison County
W. J. Stone	1875-1876	Lyon County
E. W. Turner	1877-1878	Madison County
J. M. Bigger	1879-1880	McCracken County
William C. Owens	1881-1882	Scott County
Charles Offutt	1883-1886	Bourbon County
Ben Johnson	1887-1888	Nelson County
Harvey Myers	1889-1890	Covington
W. M. Moore	1891-1892	Harrison County
A. J. Carroll	1894	Louisville
Charles J. Blandford	1896	Breckinridge County
J. C. W. Beckham	1898	Nelson County
South Trimble	1900	Franklin County

Chief Justices, Court of Appeals of Kentucky, 1870-1900

Rufus K. Williams	1870
George Robertson	1871
William S. Pryor	1872
Mordecai R. Hardin	1874
Velvard J. Peters	1876
William Lindsay	1878
William S. Pryor	1880
Martin H. Cofer	1881
Joseph H. Lewis	1882
Thomas F. Hargis	1884
Thomas H. Hines	1885
William S. Pryor	1886
Joseph H. Lewis	1887
William H. Holt	1888

APPENDIX

Caswell Bennett	1893
Isaac M. Quigley	1894
William S. Pryor	1895
Joseph H. Lewis	1897
James H. Hazelrigg	1899

Lieutenant Governors of Kentucky, 1865-1900

John W. Stevenson	1867	
William Johnson	1867-1869	(Acting Lt. Gov.)
Preston H. Leslie	1869-1871	(Acting Lt. Gov.)
G. A. Christian Holt	1871	(Acting Lt. Gov.)
John G. Carlisle	1871-1875	
John C. Underwood	1875-1879	
James E. Cantrill	1879-1883	
James R. Hindman	1883-1887	
James W. Bryan	1887-1891	
M. C. Alford	1891-1895	
William J. Worthington	1895-1899	
John Marshall	1899-1900	
J. C. W. Beckahm	1900	
Lillard H. Carter	1900	(Acting Lt. Gov.)

Treasurers of Kentucky, 1865-1900

Mason Brown	1865-1867
James W. Tate	1867-1888
Stephen Sharpe	1888-1890
H. S. Hale	1890-1896
George W. Long	1896-1900
Walter R. Day	1900
S. W. Hager	1900

Attorney Generals of Kentucky, 1865-1900

John Rodman	1865-1875
Thomas Moss	1875-1879
Parker Watkins Hardin	1879-1889
William J. Hendricks	1889-1896
William S. Taylor	1896-1899
Robert J. Breckinridge, Jr.	1900

Secretaries of State of Kentucky, 1865-1900

John S. Van Winkle	1866-1867
Samuel B. Churchill	1867-1871
Andrew J. James	1871-1872
George W. Craddock	1872-1875
J. Stoddard Johnston	1875-1879
Samuel B. Churchill	1879-1880

APPENDIX

James W. Blackburn	1880-1883
James A. McKenzie	1883-1887
George M. Adams	1887-1891
John W. Headley	1891-1896
Charles Finley	1896-1900
Caleb Powers	1900
C. B. Hill	1900

NOTES

CHAPTER I

[1] E. Merton Coulter, *The Civil War and Readjustment in Kentucky* (Chapel Hill: University of North Carolina Press, 1926), 145 *et seq*. A good, brief account of the conflict is Lowell H. Harrison, *The Civil War in Kentucky* (Lexington: University Press of Kentucky, 1975).

[2] Coulter, *Civil War and Readjustment*, 145, 165, 166, 249, 250, 228.

[3] *Ibid.*, 228, 229, and *passim*. James Beauchamp Clark, born near Lawrenceburg, in Anderson County, Kentucky, described the conditions in his *My Quarter Century of American Politics* (2 vols., New York: Harper and Brothers, 1920), I, 73-75: "The land swarmed with cut-throats, robbers, thieves, firebugs, and malefactors of every kind, who preyed upon the old, the infirm, the helpless, and committed thousands of brutal and heinous crimes—in the name of the Union or the Southern Confederacy."

[4] William Elsey Connelley and Ellis Merton Coulter,*History of Kentucky*, edited by Charles Kerr (5 vols., Chicago: American Historical Society, 1922), II, 906; Coulter, *Civil War and Readjustment*, 258.

[5] Connelley and Coulter, *History of Kentucky*, II, 907. Palmer reasoned that the act of March 3, 1865—granting freedom to wives and children of ex-slaves in the Union army—affected 72,045 women and children. When added to the 28,000 black soldiers, some 100,000 ex-slaves were thus free. Assuming that half of the remaining 130,000 slaves belonged to the rebels, there were also free. Palmer calculated that the number of Kentucky slaves in midsummer 1865 numbered over 64,000. He set about to destroy this last remnant. *Cincinnati Gazette*, August 3, 1865; Coulter, *Civil War and Readjustment*, 269.

[6] Lewis and Richard H. Collins, *History of Kentucky* (2 vols., Covington: Collins and Co., 1874), I, 155; Coulter, *Civil War and Readjustment*, 261, gives a different vote.

[7] *Lexington Observer and Reporter*, April 29, 1865 (hereinafter *Observer and Reporter*); Coulter, *Civil War and Readjustment*, 265.

[8] Coulter, *Civil War and Readjustment, passim*. Kentucky Democrats capitalized on state ill-will toward congressional "Radicals," including Benjamin Wade, Zachary Chandler, Benjamin Butler, Thaddeus Stevens and others, and labeled their local opposition "Radicals." Actually this group often themselves attacked congressional "Radicals" and announced their support for the policies of Lincoln.

[9] *Ibid.*, 439; Nathaniel Southgate Shaler, *Kentucky: A Pioneer Commonwealth* (Boston: Houghton, Mifflin and Company, 1884), 385.

[10] *The War of The Rebellion: A Compilation of the Official Records of the Union and Confederate Armies* (128 vols., Washington: Government Printing Office, 1880-1901), Series IV, vol. I, 1094, vol. II, 585; Collins, *History*, I, 155; Thomas Speed, *The Union Cause in Kentucky, 1860-1865* (New York: G. P. Putnam's Sons, 1907), 259.

[11] Shaler, *Kentucky*, 325 and Speed, *Union Cause*, 260 offer contrasting views. A general source for the violence is Coulter, *Civil War and Readjustment*, chapters XV-XVI. The career of one Home Guard member can be followed in Frank F. Mathias, ed., *Incidents & Experiences in the Life of Thomas W. Parsons* (Lexington: University Press of Kentucky, 1975).

[12] Burbridge's career should be re-examined. Speed's *Union Cause*, for instance, presents the general's career in a far different light than, for example, Collins.

[13] Shaler, *Kentucky*, 369, 370.

[14] *Observer and Reporter*, February 2, 19, 1870; Collins, *History*, I, 208-46; *Appletons' Annual Cyclopaedia and Register of Important Events, 1871*, 433, 434 (hereinafter cited as *Annual Cyclopaedia*).

[15] Clark, *My Quarter Century of American Politics* I, 73-75. A Confederate sympathizer whose son was being held as a guerilla in 1866 wrote that the charge was "as false as perjury itself" but added: "I do believe there are and has been for years some of the meanest witches in human form [here] that ever lived." See Louise Horton, *In the Hills of the Pennyroyal: A History of Allen County, Kentucky, From 1815 to 1880* (Austin, Texas: White Cross Press, 1975), 53.

[16] Collins, *History*, I, 170-72; Connelley and Coulter, *History of Kentucky*, II, 915.

[17] Coulter, *Civil War and Readjustment*, 184, 185. Many Whigs went to the Democrats as well as the Republicans. William Preston, Preston Leslie, and Garrett Davis are examples.

[18] *Ibid.*, 185-87; Shaler, *Kentucky*, 363, 364; Collins, *History*, I, 137, 138, 163. The state elections featured the race for state treasurer. Conservative James H. Garrard's 42,187 votes defeated Radical candidate William L. Neale, who received 42,082. In congressional races two Conservatives and four Radicals won elections. The complexion of the General Assembly shifted, as Conservatives controlled both houses.

[19] Coulter, *Civil War and Readjustment*, 282; *Annual Cyclopaedia, 1865*, 465.

[20] *Cincinnati Gazette*, February 23, May 26, July 17, 1865; Coulter, *Civil War and Readjustment*, 279-85.

[21] Hambleton Tapp, "Incidents in the Life of Frank Wolford," *Filson Club History Quarterly*, X (1936), 97, 98 (hereinafter cited as *FCHQ*); Frankfort *Daily Kentucky Yeoman*, December 13, 1865; *Louisville Courier-Journal*, January 12, 1882 (hereinafter cited as *Courier-Journal*); *Journal of the House of Representatives of the Commonwealth of Kentucky* (1865) (Frankfort: State Printing Office, 1865), 75-77 (hereinafter cited as *House Journal*).

[22] Coulter, *Civil War and Readjustment*, 293, 295, 299.

[23] *Cincinnati Gazette*, January 12, 1866; *Annual Cyclopaedia, 1866*, 424; Coulter, *Civil War and Readjustment*, 301.

[24] D. Howard Smith to W. C. P. Breckinridge December 26, 1865, Papers of the Breckinridge Family, Manuscript Division, Library of Congress (hereinafter cited as Breckinridge MSS); Coulter, *Civil War and Readjustment*, 301.

[25] Collins, *History*, I, 171; Coulter, *Civil War and Readjustment*, 303.

[26] *Annual Cyclopaedia, 1866*, 425; Coulter, *Civil War and Readjustment*, 303.

[27] Coulter, *Civil War and Readjustment*, 305-09; Collins, *History*, I, 172; Ross A. Webb, "Kentucky: 'Pariah Among the Elect'," in Richard O. Curry, ed., *Radicalism, Racism and Party Alignment: The Border States During Reconstruction* (Baltimore: Johns Hopkins Press, 1969), 116-20.

[28] Coulter, *Civil War and Readjustment*, 309; Collins, *History*, I, 173.

[29] *Reminiscences of General Basil M. Duke; C. S. A.* (Garden City, N. Y.: Doubleday, Page & Company, 1911), 478; Otto A. Rothert, *A History of Muhlenberg County* (Louisville: John P. Morton & Company, 1913), 316, 317; *Observer and Reporter*, August 29, 1866. See also Webb, "Kentucky: Pariah Among the Elect," 122.

[30] Collins, *History*, I, 175. The votes were 57-27 and 24-9.

[31] *Ibid.*, 167; Connelley and Coulter, *History of Kentucky*, II, 914; *Annual Cyclopaedia, 1867*, 421.

CHAPTER II

[1] William E. Connelley and E. Merton Coulter, *History of Kentucky*, edited by Charles Kerr (5 vols., Chicago: American Historical Society, 1922), II, 914. Ross Webb, "Kentucky: 'Pariah Among the Elect'," in Richard O. Curry, ed., *Radicalism, Racism and Party Alignment: The Border States During Reconstruction* (Baltimore: Johns Hopkins Press, 1969), 123, suggests that "it was anti-congressional antagonism not pro-Confederate sentiment that motivated Kentucky Democrats."

[2] *Annual Cyclopaedia, 1867*, 422; Connelley and Coulter, *History of Kentucky*, II, 914.

[3] *Annual Cyclopaedia, 1867*, 423.

[4] Connelley and Coulter, *History of Kentucky*, II, 915; Lewis and Richard H. Collins, *History of Kentucky* (2 vols., Covington: Collins and Company, 1874), I, 180, 181. A good survey of Beck's house years is T. Ross Moore, "The Congressional Career of James B. Beck, 1867-1875," (M. A. Thesis, University of Kentucky, 1950).

[5] *Cincinnati Semi-Weekly Gazette*, March 27, 1868, and *Cincinnati Daily Commercial*, May 31, 1867, quoted in Connelley and Coulter, *History of Kentucky*, II, 915.

[6] Collins, *History*, I, 182, 203; E. Merton Coulter, *Civil War and Readjustment in Kentucky* (Chapel Hill: University of North Carolina Press, 1926), 392.

[7] Collins, *History*, I, 186. McCreery received 100 votes, the Republican candidate Sidney Barnes had 9, and third party candidate Aaron Harding garnered 5 votes.

[8] *Annual Cyclopaedia, 1867*, 423; Coulter, *Civil War and Readjustment*, 412.

[9] Being a Radical, or Republican, was hazardous in some localities. One Radical wrote scornfully: "Rob a man of the means of a livelihood, banish him from his native state, traduce his character, exclude him and his family from Society, drive the minister from his pulpit, compel the merchant to close his store, take his pupils from the teacher, patients from the physician, clients from the lawyer, and work from the mechanic, and yet say that men are not interfered with on account of their opinion. . . ." Quoted in Coulter, *Civil War and Readjustment*, 414, 415.

[10] *Annual Cyclopaedia, 1868*, 405; Collins, *History*, I, 192, 193. The *Cyclopaedia* gives a different vote.

[11] Connelley and Coulter, *History of Kentucky*, II, 917; Coulter, *Civil War and Readjustment*, 417, 420, 419.

[12] Coulter, *Civil War and Readjustment*, 425; *Daily Louisville Commercial*, August 6, 1870 (hereinafter cited as *Commercial*).

[13] Coulter, *Civil War and Readjustment*, 393; *Frankfort Commonwealth*, May 8, 1870; Collins, *History*, I, 199, 211, 207.

CHAPTER III

[1] The term "New Departure"—probably first applied to Henry Watterson's doctrine

by the *Yeoman*—referred to Clement L. Vallandingham's Ohio reform measures of the same name. Thomas L. Connelly, "Neo Confederatism or Power Vacuum: Post War Kentucky Politics Reappraised," *Register of the Kentucky Historical Society*, LXIV (1966), 257-69 (hereinafter *Register*), suggests that the struggle was commercial and sectional, a rivalry of cities, railroads, crops, industries, turnpikes, and leadership. He argues that "the struggle of these commercial blocs was a key feature of the political vacuum of the period."

[2] *Courier-Journal* (weekly), August 16, 1871.

[3] *Ibid.*, August 30, September 20, 1871.

[4] Joseph F. Wall, *Henry Watterson: Reconstructed Rebel* (New York: Oxford University Press, 1956), 91-94; Victor B. Howard, "The Kentucky Press and the Black Suffrage Controversy, 1865-1872," *FCHQ*, XLVII (1973), 222, 223, 227, 229; Howard, "The Kentucky Press and the Negro Testimony Controversy, 1866-1872," *Register*, LXXI (1973), 39-43, 46.

[5] Johnston, a nephew of General Albert Sidney Johnston, married the daughter of George W. Johnson of Scott County, Confederate provisional governor of Kentucky. For 17 years Johnston presided over the Kentucky Press Association and for years he was a member of the Democratic state central committee. He served as adjutant general in 1871 and secretary of state from 1875-79. See E. Polk Johnson, *A History of Kentucky and Kentuckians* (3 vols., Chicago: Lewis Publishing Company, 1912), II, 629, 630.

[6] E. Merton Coulter, *The Civil War and Readjustment in Kentucky* (Chapel Hill: University of North Carolina Press, 1926), 401; *Courier-Journal* (weekly), May 10, 1871; *Yeoman*, September 9, 1871 and *passim*; Francis B. Simkins and Charles P. Roland, *A History of the South* (4th ed. New York: Alfred A. Knopf, 1972), 304-19; Monroe L. Billington, *The American South* (New York: Charles Scribner's Sons, 1971), 208-15; T. Harry Williams, *Romance and Realism in Southern Politics* (Athens: University of Georgia Press, 1961), 46, 47. A leader of the Kentucky group called Bourbons attacked Watterson's New Departure as "a surrender . . . to Radical usurpation and Revolution." See *Observer and Reporter*, July 15, 1871.

[7] *Courier-Journal* (weekly), May 10, 1871; *Tri-Weekly Kentucky Yeoman*, May 4, 1871; *Paris True Kentuckian*, May 6, 1871; *Frankfort Commonwealth*, May 5, 1871. The latter characterized Leslie as "neither statesman, scholar nor distinguished in his profession." The editor declared: "He owes his elevation to the desire of the Louisville & Nashville Railroad to pay its debt of gratitude to him for defeating the Cincinnati Southern Railroad, and to jealousy of J. Proctor Knott's fame by some of his central Kentucky compeers. We do not believe that Preston H. Leslie can write grammatically a state paper." The editor later retracted his more derogatory statements and apologized. Leslie and former governor Bramlette, both from Clinton County, were close friends. See Louise Horton, *In the Hills of the Pennyroyal: A History of Allen County, Kentucky, From 1815 to 1880* (Austin, Texas: White Cross Press, 1975), 53.

[8] Lewis and Richard H. Collins, *History of Kentucky* (2 vols., Covington: Collins and Company, 1874), II, 43; *Biographical Encyclopaedia of Kentucky* (2 vols., Cincinnati: J. M. Armstrong and Company, 1878), II, 660, 661.

[9] *Courier-Journal* (weekly), May 10, 1871; E. Merton Coulter, "John Griffin Carlisle" in *Dictionary of American Biography*, Allen Johnson and Dumas Malone, eds. (20 vols., New York: Charles Scribner's Sons, 1928-36), III, 494, 495 (hereinafter cited as *Dictionary of American Biography*); *National Cyclopaedia of American Biography*, I, 461; *Woodford Weekly*, June 2, 1871.

[10] *Courier-Journal* (weekly), May 10, 1871; *Biographical Encyclopaedia of Kentucky*, I, 127, 572, 575, 300; H. Levin, comp., *The Lawyers and Lawmakers of Kentucky* (Chicago: Lewis Publishing Company, [1897]), 120; Basil W. Duke, *History of Morgan's Cavalry* (Cincinnati: Miami Publishing Company, 1867), 237.

[11] *Courier-Journal* (weekly), May 10, 1871.

[12] *Annual Cyclopaedia, 1871*, 436. Two Bourbon factional organs, the *Yeoman* and the *Louisville Public Ledger*, praised the convention almost without reserve. The editor of the *Ledger*, James A. Dawson, was on the state ticket. An ex-Union soldier, now a leader of the Bourbons, he represented the unusual: a Union man on the Confederate-dominated Democratic ticket.

[13] Collins, *History*, I, 214; *Courier-Journal* (weekly), May 24, 1871; *Woodford Weekly*, June 2, 1871.

[14] *Courier-Journal* (weekly), May 24, 1871; Coulter, *Civil War and Readjustment*, 434.

[15] *Courier-Journal* (weekly), May 24, 1871. Earlier, in December 1869, Republicans Benjamin H. Bristow, W. A. Meriwether, and A. A. Burton launched the *Daily Louisville Commercial*, edited by Robert Morrison Kelly. Law partner of Garrett Davis, his uncle by marriage, and a Colonel in the 4th Kentucky Infantry, Kelly held the editorial position until 1873. He was then appointed pension agent by President Grant, a post he held until 1886. However, he maintained a connection with the paper for many years. The paper's purpose was to oppose "Radicalism" and set up a "safe and sane" Republican paper. The paper, together with Albert G. Hodge's *Frankfort Commonwealth*, gave Harlan and other Kentucky Republicans a daily to challenge the Democratic *Courier-Journal*. See Z. F. Smith, *The History of Kentucky* (Louisville: Courier-Journal Job Printing Company, 1886), 768, 769 and *Cincinnati Semi-Weekly Gazette*, November 30, December 31, 1869.

[16] The Kentucky constitution retained all pre-war references to slavery, therefore violating federal law. The legislature's February 1866 Civil Rights Act repealed Kentucky's slave code, however. See W. E. B. DuBois, *Black Reconstruction in America* (New York: Russell & Russell, 1935), 568, and *Acts of the General Assembly of the Commonwealth of Kentucky* (Frankfort: George D. Prentice, 1866), 38, 43-44 (hereinafter *Kentucky Acts*).

[17] *Annual Cyclopaedia, 1871*, 436.

[18] *Courier-Journal* (weekly), May 24, 1871; Watterson, *"Marse Henry": An Autobiography* (2 vols., New York: George H. Doran Company, 1919), I, 177.

[19] Champ Clark, *My Quarter Century of American Politics* (2 vols., New York: Harper and Brothers, 1920), I, 63, 64.

[20] Louis Hartz, "John M. Harlan in Kentucky, 1855-1877," *FCHQ*, XIV (1940), 34, 37. The Paris   ntuckian, June 28, 1871 commented, "If political changes make a wise man, then Harlan's wisdom will compare with that of Solomon."

[21] *Courier-Journal* (weekly), August 9, 1871; Coulter, *Civil War and Readjustment*, 436, 437.

[21] Collins, History, I, 216; *Annual Cyclopaedia, 1871*, 438; Paris *True Kentuckian*, August 9, 1871; *Courier-Journal*, August 16, 1871. See J. H. Spencer, *A History of Kentucky Baptists From 1769 to 1885* (2 vols., Cincinnati: Privately printed, 1886), I, 40, 41, on Pratt.

[23] *Cincinnati Semi-Weekly Gazette*, August 8, 1871; *Frankfort Weekly Commonwealth*, August 11, 1871; *Courier-Journal*, August 10, 1871; *Cincinnati Gazette*, August

9, 1871. See Hartz, "Harlan in Kentucky," 39.

[24] Coulter, *Civil War and Readjustment*, 436; *Courier-Journal* (weekly), August 16, 1871.

[25] Leslie appointed William Samuel Pryor of Henry County to succeed Judge Robertson.

[26] *Courier-Journal*, September 6, 1871; Kentucky *House Journal, 1871-72*, 122-124.

[27] *Courier-Journal*, August 17, 1871; *House Journal, 1871-72*, 31-34.

[28] *Kentucky Acts, 1873*, I, 35, 36.

[29] Howard, "Press and Negro Testimony," 47-49; *Daily Kentucky Yeoman*, January 25, 1872; Collins, *History*, I, 224.

[30] Barksdale Hamlett, *History of Education in Kentucky* (Frankfort: Department of Education, 1914), 120-33; *House Journal, 1871-72*, 40.

[31] Hamlett, *History of Education*, 131; Stanford *Interior Journal*, May 31, 1872.

[32] The Sinking Fund, provided for in 1836, consisted of funds collected from specified taxes and dividends. This money was to be used in discharging the state debt. The fund grew steadily. Following the Civil War, the practice developed of the State borrowing money from the Sinking Fund in order to discharge its current obligations. See Collins, *History*, I, 40 and William E. Connelley and E. Merton Coulter, *History of Kentucky*, edited by Charles Kerr (5 vols., Chicago: American Historical Society, 1922), II, 836.

[33] *Kentucky Legislative Documents, 1871* (Auditor's Report), iii, iv, v, vii; *House Journal, 1871-72*, 28. The Commonwealth held sizeable claims against the federal government for advances made to the Union during the war. The "Kentucky War Claim" of approximately $1,200,000 was not finally settled until the early twentieth century.

[34] Collins, *History*, I, 222, 223, 227; *House Journal, 1871-72*, 29, 30, 49, 50.

[35] In December 1871 the state owned turnpike stock valued at over $250,000 and railroad stock worth over $134,000. *House Journal, 1871-72*, 25.

[36] Coulter, *Civil War and Readjustment*, 374; Collins, *History*, I, 211; *House Journal, 1871-72*, 55, 56.

[37] An excellent, concise account of the struggle is Leonard P. Curry, *Rail Routes South: Louisville's Fight for the Southern Market, 1865-1872* (Lexington: University of Kentucky Press, 1969). Other sources include Edward A. Ferguson, *Founding of the Cincinnati Southern Railway* (Cincinnati: Robert Clark Company, 1905), J. S. Hollander, "The Cincinnati Southern Railway," in *Johns Hopkins Studies in History and Political Science*, XII (Baltimore: Johns Hopkins Press, 1894), E. Merton Coulter, *The Cincinnati Southern Railroad and the Struggle for Southern Commerce, 1865-1872* (Chicago: American Historical Society, 1922), H. P. Boyden, *The Beginnings of the Cincinnati Southern Railway: A Sketch of the Years 1869-1878* (Cincinnati: The Robert Clark Company, 1901), Joseph G. Kerr, *Historical Development of the Louisville and Nashville Railroad System* [n. p., 1926?], *History of the Ohio Falls Cities and Their Counties* (2 vols., Cleveland: L. A. Williams and Company, 1883). The fight can be followed in the *Cincinnati Commercial, Cincinnati Daily Gazette, Courier-Journal, Observer and Reporter, Daily Louisville Commercial, Yeoman*, and *Western Railroad Gazette* from 1869-72.

[38] Curry, *Rail Routes South*, 37-50; Connelley and Coulter, *History of Kentucky*, II, 942.

[39] Curry, *Rail Routes South*, 65, 66; Connelley and Coulter, *History of Kentucky*, II, 953-56.

[40] Connelley and Coulter, *History of Kentucky*, II, 960; Curry, *Rail Routes South*, 74, 75; *Courier-Journal*, May 10, 1871.

[41] Connelley and Coulter, *History of Kentucky*, II, 962; William C. Davis, *Breckinridge: Statesman, Soldier, Symbol* (Baton Rouge: Louisiana State University Press, 1974), 601-04.

[42] Collins, *History*, I, 201, 202, 209, 211; Connelley and Coulter, *History of Kentucky*, II, 969, 970. A Lexington observer, quoted in the *Cincinnati Semi-Weekly Gazette*, October 20, 1871, wrote: "Louisville wars upon every scheme which proposes to give us an outlet south, except over the tortuous lines that now terminate in her limits."

[43] *Annual Cyclopaedia, 1871*, 431, 432. Economic desires of some of the central Kentucky Bourbons overcame their states' rights philosophy. A further irony was that Watterson's New Departure Democrats briefly opposed railroad construction while the Bourbons temporarily supported it.

[44] Connelley and Coulter, *History of Kentucky*, II, 980; *Courier-Journal* (weekly), May 10, 24, 1871.

[45] *House Journal, 1871-72*, 11; Curry, *Rail Routes South*, 119, 130.

[46] *Daily Kentucky Yeoman*, January 13, 15, 26, 27, 29, 1872; Curry, *Rail Routes South*, 132-35; *House Journal, 1871-72*, 239; *Journal of the Regular Session of the Senate of the Commonwealth of Kentucky* (1871-72) (Frankfort: Kentucky Yeoman Office, 1871), 271, 274, 275 (hereinafter *Senate Journal*).

[47] Connelley and Coulter, *History of Kentucky*, II, 982, 985; *Daily Kentucky Yeoman*, January 18, 19, February 27, 28, March 8, 12, 1872.

[48] *Annual Cyclopaedia, 1872*, 428, 429; *Daily Kentucky Yeoman*, March 28, 1872.

CHAPTER IV

[1] *Ninth Census: Population*, I, 3; *Twelfth Census: Population*, I, part 1, xxiv. See Appendix I.

[2] *Ninth Census: Population*, I, 31-32; Lexington *Observer and Reporter*, April 20, 1870; Lexington *Daily Press*, September 6, 1877; Hopkinsville *South Kentuckian*, April 22, 1879 (hereinafter *South Kentuckian*).

[3] *Ninth Census: Population*, I, 299, 310; *Twelfth Census: Population*, I, pt. 1, civ-cix, clxxiii-clxxvii; Thomas D. Clark, *Kentucky: Land of Contrast* (New York: Harper and Row, 1968), 201; Nathaniel S. Shaler, *Kentucky: A Pioneer Commonwealth* (Boston: Houghton, Mifflin and Company, 1884), 392-95. These German colonies will be described in John J. Weisert's "Lemcke Visits Kentucky's German Colonies in 1885," to be published in a future *Register*.

[4] *Twelfth Census: Population*, I, pt. 1, cxxxii, cxiii-cxlix, clix, cxix, 618, cix, cvii. Lexington ranked 12th nationally in percentage of Negroes, ahead of Richmond, Virginia, and New Orleans.

[5] *Ibid.*, lxix-lxx, lxxxiv. "Urban" was defined as over 4,000.

[6] Robert Peter, *History of Fayette County, Kentucky, with an Outline Sketch of the Blue Grass Region*, edited by William H. Perrin (Chicago: O. L. Baskin & Co., 1882), 273, 274; J. Winston Coleman, Jr., *The Squire's Sketches of Lexington* (Lexington: Henry Clay Press, 1972), 61, 68.

[7] Charles D. Warner, *Studies in the South and West* (New York: Harper and Brothers, 1889), 279; *Louisville Municipal Reports . . . 1877* (Louisville: J. P. Morton & Co.,

1878), 242, 310; James T. Wills, "Louisville Politics, 1891-1897" (M. A. thesis, University of Louisville, 1966), 304; J. Stoddard Johnston, *Memorial History of Louisville* (2 vols., Chicago: American Biographical Publishing Co., [1896]), I, 328, 354, 359.

[8] Charles M. Meacham, *A History of Christian County Kentucky* (Nashville: Marshall & Bruce Co., 1930), 220, 224; John E. L. Robertson, "Paducah: Origins to Second Class," *Register*, LXVI (1968), 135; William Morgan Beckner, *Handbook of Clark County and the City of Winchester* (Chicago: Arkansaw Traveler Publishing Company, 1889), 21.

[9] Lewis and Richard H. Collins, *History of Kentucky* (2 vols., Covington: Collins and Co., 1874), I, 235; Coleman, *Squire's Sketches*, 58-60, 64, 71.

[10] Collins, *History*, I, 229, 245; Meacham, *History of Christian County*, 207; Lexington *Kentucky Leader*, April 21, June 1 1890 (hereinafter cited as *Leader*).

[11] Diary, Laura Clay Papers, Special Collections, Margaret I. King Library, University of Kentucky (hereinafter cited as University of Kentucky Library), entries of July 14-21, 1878.

[12] *The Autobiography of Nathaniel Southgate Shaler . . .* (Boston and New York: Houghton Mifflin Co., 1909), 277; Allen, *The Blue-Grass Region of Kentucky* (New York: Macmillan, 1892), 188, 184.

[13] *Kentucky State Gazetteer and Business Directory 1887-8* (Detroit: R. L. Polk and Company, 1887), 73-698; Kentucky Writer's Project, *Union County: Past and Present* (Louisville: Schuhmann Publishing Co., 1941), 195.

[14] Gordon Wilson, *Fidelity Folks: A Visit to a Self-Sufficient Kentucky Village* (Cynthiana: Hobson Book Press, 1946), 204.

[15] Thomas D. Clark, *Pills, Petticoats and Plows: The Southern Country Store* (Norman: University of Oklahoma Press, 1944), vii, viii, *passim*; Warren B. Davis and Leigh M. Hodges, *A Boy from Kentucky* (Philadelphia: privately printed, 1938), 14.

[16] G. C. Swetman County Store Records, ledger dated April 1885—February (1886), University of Kentucky Library. These purchases do not take into account any purchases made by the wife in the family.

[17] Clark, *Pills, Petticoats and Plows*, 161-68; Arthur M. Schlesinger, *The Rise of the City, 1878-1898* (New York: Macmillan, 1933), 148-50.

[18] Clark, *Pills, Petticoats and Plows*, 172-83; Wilson, *Fidelity Folks*, 177, 178.

[19] *Abstract of the Eleventh Census* (2d rev. ed., Washington: Government Printing Office, 1896), 259, 260; *Ninth Census: Population*, I, 539, 513. 521. C. Vann Woodward in his *Origins of the New South, 1877-1913* (Baton Rouge: Louisiana State University Press, 1951), 449, 450, notes that 4 of every 5 rural southern churches had absentee pastors and 9 of 10 held services but once a month.

[20] *Courier-Journal*, March 1-4, 1885; *Leader*, August 11, 1890; Meacham, *History of Christian County*, 227, 229; Woodward, *New South*, 170; Francis B. Simkins and Charles P. Roland, *A History of The South* (4th ed., New York: Alfred A. Knopf, 1972), 393.

[21] William Moody Pratt Diary, vol. IV, April 25, 1873, vol. V, July 30, 1884; John Fox, Sr. diary, January 1, 1871, Fox Family Papers; Joseph U. Milward diary, May 16, June 21, 1892, all in University of Kentucky Library. The *Hazel Green Herald*, June 3, 1892 reported Beattyville churches as flourishing and prosperous.

[22] Simkins and Roland, *History of The South*, 414, 415.

[23] *Annual Cyclopaedia, 1882*, 452; Thomas D. Clark, *A History of Kentucky* (rev. ed., Lexington: John Bradford Press, 1960), 398; *Annual Cyclopaedia, 1874*, 440; William E. Connelley and E. Merton Coulter, *History of Kentucky*, edited by Charles

Kerr (5 vols., Chicago: American Historical Society, 1922), II, 992. Prohibitionists probably praised one effect of the 1893 depression: Over 300 distilleries closed because of the depressed market. *Annual Cyclopaedia, 1896,* 375.

[24] Hickman *Courier,* January 28, 1871; Guardian Angel Society Minute Book, The Filson Club, Louisville.

[25] Hickman *Courier,* June 24, 1871; *Leader,* July 2, 1897. Non-temperance proved occasionally useful. At an 1884 barbecue the people so disliked a speaker that they "got rid of the pest by getting him drunk and putting him to bed." Thomas M. Wood to Desha Breckinridge, October 20, 1893, Breckinridge MSS, vol. 460.

[27] Connelley and Coulter, *History of Kentucky,* II, 992; *South Kentuckian,* September 30, 1879; Polk's *Gazetteer,* 239; London *Mountain Echo,* March 11, 25, April 22, 1881.

[27] The following sketch of rural life is based in part on Kent Eubank, *Horse and Buggy Days* (Kansas City, Mo.: Burton Publishing Company, 1927), 11, 24-28, 59; Wilson, *Fidelity Folks,* 95-105, 115-20, 173; "Memoirs of Henry V. Johnson, of Scott County, Kentucky," unpublished MS, typed copy in Georgetown Public Library; Gabriel C. Banks, *Back to the Mountains* (n. p., 1964), 4-18; Alben Barkley, *That Reminds Me* (Garden City, N Y: Doubleday & Co., 1954), 24-53; Caleb Powers, *My Own Story* (Indianapolis: Bobbs-Merrill Co., 1905), 3-6; Edwin Green Bedford Diaries, 1870-75, 1884, University of Kentucky Library, and other diaries and autobiographical works cited elsewhere.

[28] Fred A. Shannon, *The Farmer's Last Frontier: Agriculture, 1860-1897* (New York: Harper and Row, 1945), 125-37, Thomas D. Clark, "Southern Common Folk After the Civil War," *South Atlantic Quarterly,* XLIV (1945), 136, 137.

[29] Harry M. Caudill, *Night Comes to the Cumberlands* (Boston: Little, Brown, 1963), 6-7; Connelley and Coulter, *History of Kentucky,* II, 1205.

[30] John Fox, Jr., *Blue-Grass and Rhododendron: Outdoors in Old Kentucky* (New York: Charles Scribner's Sons, 1901), 4, 18, 11, 13, 22, 28; Allen, *Blue Grass Region,* 230, 231, 235, 236; S. S. MacClintock, "The Kentucky Mountains and Their Feuds," *American Journal of Sociology,* VII (1901), 1-28. See also C. T. Revere, "Beyond the Gap: The Breeding Ground of Feuds," *Outing Magazine,* February 1907, 609-21.

[31] William H. Haney, *The Mountain People of Kentucky* (Cincinnati: Roessler, 1906), 51, 40, 47, 52-57; [Sam Johnson], "Life in the Kentucky Mountains," *The Independent,* LXV (1908), 73-82.

[32] *Ninth Census: Population,* I, 595; *Twelfth Census: Population,* II, pt. 2, clx; *ibid., Vital Statistics,* III, pt. 1, liv. The birth rate was 30.6/1,000 mean population, compared to a 29.6 rate in 1890, and the national rate of 27.2.

[33] Arthur Krock, *Myself When Young: Growing Up in the 1890's* (Boston: Little, Brown and Co., 1973), 13; Pattie French Witherspoon, *Through Two Administrations: Character Sketches of Kentucky* (Chicago: T. B. Arnold, 1897), 67; G. H. Clay to Susan M. Clay, July 28, 1889, Thomas J. Clay Papers, Manuscript Division, Library of Congress.

For example see W. Goddard Grundy letters to Lydia Huston, Grundy Family Papers; H. M, Mackoy Diary, 1890, 1893-97, Mackoy Family Papers; Margaret Means Diary, 1884-88, Seaton Collection, all in University of Kentucky Library.

[34] *Abstract of the Twelfth Census* (Washington: Government Printing Office, 1904), 186-90, 200, 208-13; *Municipal Reports, 1877,* 596; *Louisville Municipal Reports . . . 1895* (Louisville: Courier-Journal Job Printing Co., 1896), 146; Collins, *His-*

tory, I, 246i-246s; John J. Dickey Diary, October 3, 19, 1886, University of Kentucky Library.

[35] William A. Pusey, *A Doctor of the 1870's and 80's* (Baltimore: Charles C. Thomas, 1932), 23-53, 137; Medical Historical Research Project of the Works Projects Administration, *Medicine and Its Development in Kentucky* (Louisville: Standard Printing Co., 1940), 194-215.

[36] Clark, *Pills, Petticoats and Plows*, 191-211, quotes on pp. 204, 203, 208; *Kentucky Acts, 1872*, 56; Hickman *Courier*, January 28, 1871; London *Mountain Echo*, July 9, 1880; *Courier-Journal*, March 4, 1882.

[37] *South Kentuckian*, September 30, 1879; *Daily Kentucky Yeoman*, January 19, 1872; *Illustrated Kentuckian*, II (1893), 174; Arthur Krock, *The Editorials of Henry Watterson* (New York: George H. Doran Co., 1923), 219, 358; quoted in Clark, *History of Kentucky*, 405.

[38] Mary B. Clay, "Kentucky," in Susan B. Anthony and others, eds., *History of Woman Suffrage* (4 vols., Rochester: Susan B. Anthony, 1902), III, 818, 819; *South Kentuckian*, October 28, 1879. See also Lexington *Press-Transcript*, January 11, 1895 and Paul E. Fuller, *Laura Clay and the Woman's Rights Movement* (Lexington: University Press of Kentucky, 1975), 22, 23.

[39] *Daily Kentucky Yeoman*, April 27, 1880; Fuller, *Laura Clay*, 22-25, 12; Laura Clay Diary, July 26, October 25, 1874. See also letters from Lucy Stone and Susan B. Anthony to Mary B. Clay, Cassius M. Clay Papers, The Filson Club, Louisville.

[40] Fuller, *Laura Clay*, 34, 33, 39, 40, 47-49, 91; Lexington *Herald*, June 11, September 19, 1897; *Illustrated Kentuckian*, II (1894), 256; Simkins and Roland, *History of the South*, 376, 377; Schlesinger, *Rise of the City*, 127; Laura Clay, "Kentucky" in Anthony and others, eds., *Woman Suffrage*, IV, 670-77; *ibid.*, III, 821, 822. Herbert Finch, "Organized Labor in Louisville, Kentucky, 1880-1914" (Dissertation, University of Kentucky, 1965), 10, notes that women's wages in Louisville in 1903 averaged $.87 a day.

[41] Hickman *Courier*, May 20, June 17, 1871; *Municipal Reports, 1877*, 303; *1895*, 219; *Eastern Kentucky Lunatic Asylum Statutes and By-Laws* (Lexington: Transylvania Printing Company, 1883), 34; *Kentucky Acts, 1893*, 63. Lexington blacks, meeting in October, 1893, protested the Separate Coach Act and—led by local ministers—vowed to fight it. See *Transcript*, October 2, 1893.

[42] *South Kentuckian*, June 24, 1879; *Kentucky Documents, 1885*, No. 19, 19; *Daily Transcript*, September 13, 1881; Middlesboro *Weekly Herald*, August 7, 1896; Collins, *History*, I, 220; *Transcript*, September 16, 1893.

[43] Herbert A. Thomas, Jr., "Victims of Circumstance: Negroes in a Southern Town, 1865-1880," *Register*, LXXI (1973), 253-71.

[44] Allen, *Blue-Grass Region*, 46, 47; Dickey diary, November 18, 1883. See also James C. Klotter, "The Breckinridges of Kentucky: Two Centuries of Leadership" (Dissertation: University of Kentucky, 1975), 212-16.

[45] Collins, *History*, I, 221; Meacham, *History of Christian County*, 209, 228; Frankfort *Commonwealth*, August 18, 1871; Robertson, "Paducah," 134. See chapter XI for educational gains. Blacks—led by Isaac Murphy's three wins—rode Kentucky derby winners in 13 of the first 25 derbies. See William B. Strother, "Negro Culture in Lexington, Kentucky" (M. A. Thesis, University of Kentucky, 1939), 83, 84.

[46] Krock, *Myself When Young*, 8, 58, 62-65, 73-79, 91.

[47] James G. Speed, "The Kentuckian," *Century magazine*, LIX (1900), 946-50; James

Bryce to Edmund T. Halsey, Halsey Collection, The Filson Club, Louisville; Shaler, *Kentucky*, 404.

CHAPTER V

[1] John Fox, Jr., *Blue Grass and Rhododendron* (New York: Charles Scribner's Sons, 1901), 80; *Leader*, April 20, 1890; James Lane Allen, *Blue Grass Region of Kentucky* (New York: Macmillan, 1892), 29.

[2] William A. Pusey, *A Doctor of the 1870's and 80's* (Baltimore: Charles C. Thomas, 1932), 12; Francis B. Simkins and Charles P. Roland, *A History of the South* (4th ed., New York: Alfred A. Knopf, 1972), 371; unidentified clipping, Breckinridge MSS, box 1.

[3] Hickman *Courier*, January 14, 1871; Mrs. Arthur Peter to Phiny [Peter], March 8, 1890, Evans Papers, University of Kentucky Library.

[4] See for example, Middlesboro *Weekly Herald*, August 7, 1896; London *Mountain Echo*, January 14, 1881; *South Kentuckian*, May 27, 1879; Midway *Blue-Grass Clipper*, February 7, 1884 and *Leader*, August 29, 1890.

[5] German Club Record Book, 1884, The Filson Club, Louisville; *South Kentuckian*, June 10, August 5, 1879.

[6] *Leader*, April 27, 1890.

[7] Simkins and Roland, *History of the South*, 385, 386; Sallie Peter to Letitia Peter, December 21, 1879, Evans Papers; *Courier-Journal*, September 24, 1889. Booth and the company received $20,000 for a week's stand.

[8] *Collected Writings Related to Institutions of Louisville* (Louisville: Free Public Library, 1935), 177-81; *Courier-Journal*, March 5, August 1, 1882; *South Kentuckian*, April 22, 27, 1879; John E. L. Robertson, "Paducah: Origins to Second Class," *Register*, LXVI (1968), 133n.

[9] Simkins and Roland, *History of the South*, 386; *Observer and Reporter*, February 9, 19, January 19, March 5 and *passim* 1870; Lexington *Daily Press*, April 20, 1881 (hereinafter *Daily Press*).

[10] *Weekly Maysville Eagle*, September 6, 1876; *Leader*, September 16, October 3, 1890.

[11] J. Winston Coleman, Jr., *The Squire's Sketches of Lexington* (Lexington: Henry Clay Press, 1972), 58; *Morning Transcript*, September 2, 1892; Kentucky Writers' Project, *Fairs and Fair Makers of Kentucky* (2 vols., Frankfort: Kentucky Department of Agriculture, 1942), I, 174-87; Hickman *Courier*, July 15, September 20, 1871.

[12] *Annual Cyclopaedia, 1883*, 464 and *Courier-Journal*, August-November 1883.

[13] Hickman *Courier*, August 5, 25, September 9, 1871; *Transcript*, September 25, 1891.

[14] *Transcript*, September 24, 1891.

[15] Simkins and Roland, *History of the South*, 390, 391; Thomas D. Clark, *A History of Kentucky* (rev. ed., Lexington: John Bradford Press, 1960), 281.

[16] "The Running Turf in America," *Harper's Monthly Magazine*, XLI (1870), 252; Allen, *Blue Grass Region*, 144, 145.

[17] William H. Bishop, "Among the Blue-Grass Trotters," *Harper's Magazine*, LXVII (1883), 715-30.

[18] J. Winston Coleman, Jr., *The Springs of Kentucky* (Lexington: Winburn Press, 1955), 82; Frances Peter to Letitia Peter, August 27, 1877, Evans Papers.

[19] Coleman, *Springs*, 82-95; *Daily Press*, July 6, 1871; *Transcript*, August 2, 1882; *South Kentuckian*, July 4, 1879.

[20] *Kentucky Chautauqua Assembly . . . Program Handbook* (Lexington: n. p., 1888), 39, 49-51; "The Summer Assemblies," *The Chautauquan*, XI (1890), 493, 770; *Leader*, July 2-10, 1897.

[21] Simkins and Roland, *History of the South*, 391, 392; *Daily Press*, July 25, 1884; J. Stoddard Johnston, *Memorial History of Louisville* (2 vols., Chicago: American Biographical Publishing Co., [1896]), I, 121.

[22] *Confederate Veteran Association of Kentucky* (Lexington: n. p., [1893]), 10; *Courier-Journal*, September 20, 1889. The Rev. William Moody Pratt observed in his diary (vol. V, July 25, 1883, University of Kentucky Library) that the Morgan men gathered near Lexington, but he felt that "it didn't amount to much. Good many drunk."

[23] Allen, *Blue Grass Region*, 87, 88; Pattie French Witherspoon, *Through Two Administrations: Character Sketches of Kentucky* (Chicago: T. B. Arnold, 1897), 60-65; Thomas D. Clark, *Kentucky: Land of Contrast* (New York: Harper and Row, 1968), 239, 240; *Daily Press*, December 6, 1871.

[24] *Observer and Reporter*, April 17, 1867, August 27, 1870; *Frankfort Commonwealth*, September 2, 1870; *Daily Press*, August 14, 1875.

[25] *Daily Press*, August 13, 14, 1875; *Courier-Journal*, September 19, 20, 1889.

[26] Simkins and Roland, *History of the South*, 394; *Transcript*, April 10, 1880; Milton D. Feinstein, "History and Development of Football at the University of Kentucky, 1877-1920" (M. A. thesis, University of Kentucky, 1941), 7-24; Hardin Craig, *Centre College of Kentucky* (Louisville: Gateway Press, 1967), 105. A State College (University of Kentucky) team in the 1890s averaged 147 pounds.

[27] *Weekly Maysville Eagle*, January 3, 1877; *Transcript*, December 13, 9, 1893; Feinstein, "History of Football," 30-32; Lexington *Herald*, October 24, 1900; James F. Hopkins, *The University of Kentucky: Origins and Early Years* (Lexington: University of Kentucky Press, 1951), 181.

[28] *Daily Press*, February 4, 1881; Charles M. Meacham, *A History of Christian County Kentucky* (Nashville: Marshall & Bruce Co., 1930), 210; Coleman, *Squire's Sketches*, 71. See also *Leader*, July 10, 1897 and Middlesboro *Weekly Herald*, August 7, 1896.

[29] *Leader*, August 31, June 8, 1890; *South Kentuckian*, April 15, 1879; *Observer and Reporter*, February 5, 1870; James D. Bennett, "Some Notes on Christian County Grange Activities," *Register*, LXIV (1966), 230.

[30] Simkins and Roland, *History of the South*, 397, 398; Fox, *Blue-Grass and Rhododendron*, 80-82, 88, 184-86. See also *Illustrated Kentuckian*, II (1893), 188.

[31] Abby M. Roach, "Then—Girlhood in Louisville in the Nineties," *FCHQ*, XXXVII (1963), 137-41.

[32] Harry B. Mackoy Diary, 1890, University of Kentucky Library.

[33] *Ibid.*, 1890, 1893, 1897.

CHAPTER VI

[1] Joseph F. Wall, *Henry Watterson: Reconstructed Rebel* (New York: Oxford University Press, 1956), 96, 99-106; Henry Watterson, *"Marse Henry": An Autobiography* (2 vols., New York: George H. Doran, 1919), I, 239, 243.

[2] Both Blair and Brown had emigrated from Kentucky. Sons of Francis Preston Blair and Mason Brown, they were related to some of Kentucky's prominent families.

[3] Wall, *Watterson*, 106-08; *Courier-Journal*, May 17, 1872.

[4] Stanford *Interior Journal*, May 17, 1872.

[5] *Courier-Journal* (weekly), June 26, 1872. The *Interior Journal* felt that failure to adopt the Duke Resolution constituted "entirely too much pandering to the views of the Bourbons." The editor of the *Woodford Weekly*, June 28, 1872, believed that Duke's Resolution would have passed, if voted upon, but in doing so would have split the party.

[6] *Courier-Journal* (weekly), June 26, 1872.

[7] Ellis P. Oberholtzer, *A History of the United States Since the Civil War* (5 vols., New York: Macmillan Company, 1928-37), III, 49; *Woodford Weekly*, June 28, 1872. As editor of the New York *Tribune* before the war, Greeley had been an implacable foe of the South and the Democratic party.

[8] *Courier-Journal* (weekly), March 20, 1872; *Annual Cyclopaedia, 1872*, 428. Minority opposition to Grant was smothered in the convention. The aged and able Albert G. Hodges—who opposed Grant—simply discontinued publication of his famous paper, the *Frankfort Commonwealth*. See E. Merton Coulter, *Civil War and Readjustment in Kentucky* (Chapel Hill: University of North Carolina Press, 1926), 405.

[9] Coulter, *Civil War and Readjustment*, 405; Lewis and Richard H. Collins, *History of Kentucky* (2 vols., Covington: Collins and Company, 1874), I, 231, 235.

[10] Oberholtzer, *History of United States*, III, 64. Greatly dejected, Watterson wrote: "We are to have four years more of Radical domination and corruption, of rings, martial law and monopolies of all sorts." He added that "the results of the election show either that the Liberalism of the present year is four years in advance of the country, or else that popular government is gradually but surely going the way of its predecessors." *Courier-Journal* (weekly), November 13, 1872.

[11] *House Journal, 1873-74*, 19-29, 37.

[12] Barksdale Hamlett, *History of Education in Kentucky* (Frankfort: Kentucky Department of Education, 1914), 123.

[13] *House Journal, 1873-74*, 32-34, 46, 47.

[14] Shaler had become one of the nation's ablest geologists. He achieved an international reputation as a scholar and author, not only in the field of natural science but in history and literature as well. His successor as director of the Geological Survey, John R. Proctor was able; Shaler had trained him.

[15] *Annual Cyclopaedia, 1874*, 440, 441; *Kentucky Acts, 1873-74*, 10, 56, 57.

[16] *Kentucky State Gazetteer and Business Directory, 1887-8* (Detroit: R. L. Polk and Company, 1887), 37-39; *Eastern Kentucky Lunatic Asylum Statutes and By-Laws* (Lexington: Transylvania Printing Co., 1883), 7. Names of the institutions often changed.

[17] *Kentucky Documents, 1900*, No. 8, 16-21; No. 9, 18-21; *Louisville Municipal Reports . . . 1877* (Louisville: J. P. Morton & Co., 1878), 521-25, 561.

[18] *Annual Cyclopaedia, 1874*, 441. The successful candidates were A. R. Boon (1st district), John Young Brown (2nd), Charles W. Milliken (3rd), J. Proctor Knott (4th), Edward G. Parsons (5th), Thomas S. Jones (6th), J. C. S. Blackburn (7th), Milton J. Durham (8th), White (9th) and John B. Clark (10th).

[19] *Courier-Journal* (weekly), May 12, 1875; *Annual Cyclopaedia, 1875*, 416.

[20] *Courier-Journal* (weekly), May 19, 1875.

[21] *Tri-Weekly Yeoman*, May 15, 1875. Harlan's reluctance to accept the nomination centered on the necessity of his absence from his extensive law practice, and because of the strenuous regimens of campaigning, a good part of which still had to be done on

horseback. He apparently accepted on condition that he be relieved of a part of the campaign duties.

²² *Ibid.*, July 27, 1875.

²³ *Annual Cyclopaedia, 1875*, 416.

²⁴ Bristow attracted favorable notice for his honesty in the office of the treasury. He appointed capable revenue officers, removed corrupt ones, and helped break up illegal "rings," most notably the "Whiskey Ring." Deprived of the presidential support he sought, he finally resigned. Bristow and Harlan shared a law practice. See Ross A. Webb, *Benjamin Helm Bristow: Border State Politician* (Lexington: University Press of Kentucky, 1969).

²⁵ *Annual Cyclopaedia, 1875*, 416.

²⁶ Quoted in the *Yeoman*, August 31, 1875.

²⁷ *Daily Louisville Commercial*, June 28, September 10, 1875 (hereinafter *Commercial*). Thomas Speed wrote Bristow on July 2, 1875 outlining the problems and promises of the campaign:

> We could use a great deal more money than we can possibly raise—and I believe if we had about five times as much we could carry the State for General Harlan. The letters which came to our committees from all parts of the State are full of encouragement. It really looks like the scales are balancing in our favor. Our old union friends are coming back to us. . . .

Speed concluded that "we can very reasonably look for a reduced democratic majority." In Benjamin Helm Bristow Papers, Manuscript Division, Library of Congress.

²⁸ *Annual Cyclopaedia, 1875*, 417; *Tri-Weekly Yeoman*, August 24, 1875.

²⁹ *Courier-Journal*, September 12, 1875.

³⁰ A less than forceful leader, unable to control his legislatures, Leslie often placed too much trust in friends who should never have been trusted. The *Commercial*, September 10, 1875, did not let the ex-governor forget that: "If their [advisors] financial suggestions resulted immediately in financial benefit to members of the circle, this must have been solely because within the circle were to be found the men most fitted to carry through projects having a financial bearing, and as projects having a financial bearing are not worthy to be considered unless somebody gets profit from them, profits fell to the members of the circle."

³¹ A successful lawyer, McCreary tended to lean heavily on the legal aspects of questions confronting him. Affable and handsome, he worked hard. But his reluctance to commit himself upon any question unless certain that his course was the popular one brought him much criticism. Reform measures that might upset the status quo were not "safe" enough for the careful governor to support.

"Bothsides" McCreary, according to one story, became even more careful as time passed. As he and a companion rode along a road to Richmond, the companion looked out and said, "There goes a grey horse." Whereupon the governor answered: "It's grey on this side, at least."

³² *Courier-Journal* (weekly), September 8, 1875; *Tri-Weekly Yeoman*, September 4, 1875.

CHAPTER VII

¹ Thomas D. Clark, *A History of Kentucky* (rev. ed., Lexington: John Bradford Press, 1960), 415, 416; William E. Connelley and E. Merton Coulter, *History of Kentucky*,

edited by Charles Kerr (5 vols., Chicago: American Historical Society, 1922), II, 987.

[2] *Tri-Weekly Yeoman*, July 24, 1875; *Annual Cyclopaedia, 1873*, 400.

[3] *House Journal, 1875-76*, 6-35; *Courier-Journal* (weekly), January 17, 1876.

[4] *House Journal, 1875-76*, 46, 58. The surplus existed in part because a new method had raised property assessments by almost $27,000,000, resulting in over $121,000 more in receipts.

[5] The penitentiary—constructed to accommodate 684 inmates—now held 975 convicts.

[6] *House Journal, 1875-76*, 72, 50-52. McCreary reported that of 291,297 immigrants who arrived in America from Europe, only 800 went to Kentucky.

[7] *Ibid.*, 48-50. For the estimated 100,000 Negro children of school age this gave them the sum of 34.6 cents per child. Or, in a school of 60 children, the funding would be $20.76 for the school year.

[8] Clark, *History of Kentucky*, 415; *Daily Kentucky Yeoman*, March 23, 1876; *Courier-Journal* (weekly), January 20, 1876.

[9] *Kentucky Yeoman*, March 21, 1876.

[10] *Courier-Journal* (weekly), January 25, 1876; *Kentucky Yeoman*, March 21, 1876.

[11] *Kentucky Acts, 1875-76*, 139; *Annual Cyclopaedia, 1876*, 438; *Daily Kentucky Yeoman*, March 18, 1876.

[12] *Kentucky Yeoman*, March 23, 1876; *Courier-Journal* (weekly), January 25, 1876.

[13] *Commercial*, March 21, 1876.

[14] Quoted in Arthur Krock, *The Editorials of Henry Watterson* (New York: George H. Doran, 1923), 63.

[15] *Annual Cyclopaedia, 1876*, 439; *Cincinnati Daily Gazette*, May 19, 1876. See also Will D. Gilliam, Jr., "The Political Career of Benjamin Helm Bristow" (M. A. thesis, Indiana University, 1930), and Ross A. Webb, *Benjamin Helm Bristow: Border State Politician* (Lexington: University Press of Kentucky, 1969). Bristow broke with Harlan in 1877, in connection with the latter's Supreme Court appointment. See David G. Farrelly, "John Harlan's One Day Diary," *FCHQ*, XXIV (1950), 163-67.

[16] *Cincinnati Daily Gazette*, May 26, 1876; *Annual Cyclopaedia, 1876*, 440. While the Republican *Commercial*, March 21, 1876, suggested that most Kentucky Democrats favored inflated currency, the *Lexington Gazette* and the *Yeoman* retorted that the Democracy's devotion to specie was real and genuine. The Cincinnati paper reported (above) that the dominance of the Watterson-Breckinridge wing made the "hard money" plank a sincere one.

[17] *Courier-Journal*, April 25, 1876. The standard account of the 1876-77 events is C. Vann Woodward, *Reunion and Reaction* (Boston: Little, Brown, 1951).

[18] *Cincinnati Daily Gazette*, October 30, 1876.

[19] Henry Watterson, *"Marse Henry": An Autobiography* (2 vols., New York: George H. Doran, 1919), I, 294-300; Krock, *Watterson Editorials*, 53; Joseph F. Wall, *Henry Watterson: Reconstructed Rebel* (New York: Oxford University Press, 1956), 140.

[20] *Courier-Journal*, January 8, 1877. See also Woodward, *Reunion and Reaction*, 111.

[21] *Cincinnati Commercial*, January 18, 19, 1877.

[22] *Annual Cyclopaedia, 1877*, 440, 441; Woodward, *Reunion and Reaction*, 194-208; Wall, *Watterson*, 166.

[23] Krock, *Watterson's Editorials*, 56, 53.

[24] *Annual Cyclopaedia, 1877*, 420, 421; *House Journal, 1877-78*, 96.

[25] *House Journal, 1877-78*, 47-49.

[26] *Courier-Journal*, January 2, 1878; *Kentucky Acts, 1877-78*, I, 129-37.

[27] *Annual Cyclopaedia, 1877*, 419. Thomas C. McCreery's term would expire on March 4, 1879.

[28] *House Journal, 1877-78*, 19, 295.

[29] *Ibid.*, 36-39. The 532 Negro schools received $50,736 for their support, an average of about $95 per school.

[30] *Ibid.*, 50-53.

[31] *Kentucky Acts, 1877-78*, I, 2, 59, 25, 82.

[32] *Annual Cyclopaedia, 1878*, 471.

[33] *Courier-Journal*, April 13, 15, 11, 1878.

[34] *Ibid.*, April 11, 1879. With the passing of Harlan and Bristow from the Kentucky scene, Bradley assumed leadership of the Republican party in the state.

As a boy of fourteen, Bradley had run away from home twice to enlist in the Union army; his father brought him back each time. At eighteen, by special act of the legislature because of his age, he was granted a license to practice law.

Stockily built, five feet eight inches tall, weighing over 230 pounds, thick-chested, broad shouldered, Bradley possessed impressive physical attributes. His resonant voice gave "Billy O. B" (as his admirers called him) the reputation of a skilled campaign orator, surpassed by few if any. Bradley's keen sense of humor and love of debate served him well in his future campaigns. See Maurice H. Thatcher, *Stories and Speeches of William O. Bradley* (Lexington: Transylvania Printing Co., 1916).

[35] *Courier-Journal*, April 11, 1879; *Annual Cyclopaedia, 1879*, 541, 542.

[36] Lewis and Richard H. Collins, *History of Kentucky* (2 vols., Covington: Collins Publishing Co., 1874), I, 246; *Courier-Journal*, May 1, 1879.

[37] Ed. Porter Thompson, *History of the Orphan Brigade* (Louisville: Lewis N. Thompson, 1898), 530-33; *Courier-Journal*, May 3, 1879; See also *Commercial*, May 2, 1879, and Louisville *Evening Post and News*, May 2, 1879 (hereinafter *Evening Post*).

[39] Annual Cyclopaedia, 1879, 541; *Courier-Journal*, May 3, 5, 1879; *Kentucky Yeoman*, June 5, 1879.

[39] See letters of J. Stoddard Johnston and others to W. C. P. Breckinridge, 1879, Breckinridge MSS; *Kentucky Yeoman*, June 7, 19, 1879.

[40] William O. Bradley Personal Scrapbook, 1879-1896, University of Kentucky Library, has the speech. Strictly speaking, the Republican party had never been in power in Kentucky. Wartime leadership was Union and Governor Thomas E. Bramlette, for example, became a post-war Democrat.

[41] The treasurer's report of 1878 indicated that the treasury was empty. The state government had been using the Sinking Fund to help defray current expenses. *Kentucky Documents, 1878*, No. 5, 11, 13.

[42] The cost of operating public schools had, of course, greatly risen during that period.

[43] Bradley Scrapbook.

[44] Ellis P. Oberholtzer, *A History of the United States Since the Civil War* (5 vols., New York: Macmillan Company, 1928-37), IV, 37, 38; *Annual Cyclopaedia, 1879*, 542.

[45] *Cincinnati Commercial*, August 7, 9, 1879. See also Nancy D. Baird, "The Yellow Fever Plot," *Civil War Times Illustrated*, XIII (1974), 16-23.

[46] *Annual Cyclopaedia, 1879*, 542; Prichard, "Popular Political Movements in Kentucky, 1875-1900" (Senior thesis, Princeton University, 1935), 59, 60.

[47] *Commercial*, September 3, 4, 1879.

CHAPTER VIII

[1] The *Commercial*, September 3, 1879, suggested that Blackburn's free silver stance resulted from the influence of his secretary of state and kinsman, John Churchill. Whatever the source, Blackburn's views put him squarely in opposition to "sound money" Kentucky Democrats, including Watterson, Breckinridge, Buckner and others.

[2] *Ibid.*, September 3-5, 1879.

[3] *House Journal, 1879-80*, 35, 39, 40. See also William E. Connelley and E. Merton Coulter, *History of Kentucky*, edited by Charles Kerr (5 vols., Chicago: American Historical Society, 1922), II, 988.

[4] *House Journal, 1879-80*, 41, 42; *Annual Cyclopaedia, 1880*, 421, 422; *Kentucky Acts, 1883-84*, I, 151.

[5] *Kentucky Acts, 1879-80*, I, 83, 175, 194, 198, 172, 196; *Annual Cyclopaedia, 1880*, 422.

[6] *House Journal, 1879-80*, 42-46, 49-51.

[7] *Kentucky Acts, 1879-80*, I, 159, 165, 164. An act was passed prohibiting any person or corporation from employing convicts of other states within the limits of Kentucky.

[8] *Ibid.*, I, 159.

[9] *Ibid., 1881-83*, 35. Under increasingly heavy attack, Blackburn defended his pardon record. While admitting that he might have freed too many convicts, he declared that a prison sentence—no matter how brief—was equivalent to a death sentence, because of prison conditions. Young men convicted of minor offenses became "brutalized beasts, wrecked souls with all hope lost." Blackburn suggested that unscrupulous commonwealth attorneys "railroaded" these men to the penitentiary, in order to collect fees for their convictions. He therefore pardoned them.

[10] *Annual Cyclopaedia, 1882*, 451; *Daily Kentucky Yeoman*, February 6, 27, 1880.

[11] *House Journal, 1879-80*, I, 51, 52, 8; *Annual Cyclopaedia, 1880*, 424; *ibid., 1881*, 471.

[12] According to Judge Thomas H. Hines, Justice of the Court of Appeals, the Appellate Court in 1882 had 1333 undecided cases; since the court rendered approximately 400 judgements each year it was more than three years in arrears on its docket. See *Official Record of the Proceedings and Debates in the Constitutional Convention of Kentucky ... 1890* (4 vols., Frankfort: E. Polk Johnson, 1890), II, 3010-12.

[13] *Kentucky Acts, 1881-82*, I, 111-14; *Annual Cyclopaedia, 1882*, 453.

CHAPTER IX

[1] Quoted in Barksdale Hamlett, *History of Education in Kentucky* (Frankfort: Kentucky Department of Education, 1914), 171.

[2] Frederick A. Wallis and Hambleton Tapp, *A Sesqui-Centennial History of Kentucky* (4 vols., Louisville and Hopkinsville: Historical Record Association, 1945), II, 583; Hamlett, *History of Education*, 114-16.

[3] *Ninth Census: Population*, I, 396; *Twelfth Census: Population*, II, pt. 2, c, cciv; quoted in Hamlett, *History of Education*, 109.

[4] W. H. Perrin, J. H. Battle, and G. C. Kniffin, *Kentucky: A History of the State* (7th ed., Louisville: F. A. Battey and Co., 1887), 480; *Commercial*, September 22, 1884; Moses E. Ligon, *A History of Public Education in Kentucky* (Lexington: Bureau of School Service, 1942), 51, 43, 44; *Ninth Census: Population*, I, 454, 452.

[5] *Kentucky Documents, 1871*, II, No. 16, 105.

[6] *Ibid, 1874*, No. 1, 36.

[7] Ligon, *History of Public Education*, 135, 134, 131; Hamlett, *History of Education*, 135.

[8] Harvey C. Minnich, "William Holmes McGuffey," *Dictionary of American Biography*, XXII, 57, 58; John D. Philbrick, "Text Book Publications of John P. Morton and Company of Louisville, Kentucky, From 1867 through 1870," (M. A. thesis, University of Kentucky, 1948), 6, 14, 24, 33. Superintendent H. A. M. Henderson's multiple choice textbook list offered some variety of selection:
Text-Books —
Written Arithmetic — Towne's, Robinson's, Stoddard's, or Ray's.
Mental Arithmetic — Stoddard's or Towne's.
Geography — Monteiths and McNally's, Mitchell's, Cornell's, or Eclectic Series.
Readers — Goodrich's or McGuffey's.
Spellers — Butler's or DeWolf's.
Grammars — Butler's or Harvey's.
History of United States — Goodrich's, Venable's or Barnes'.
Penmanship — Payson, Dunton & Scribner's, or the Eclectic System of Penmanship.
Maps — Mitchell's New Outline Maps.
School Records — Published by John P. Morton & Co.
Bonnell's Composition.
Brown's Physiology and Hygiene.
William's Parser's Manual.
Smart's Manual of Free Gymnastics.
Object Lessons and Charts, Wilson's & Calkins'.
Nelson's Bookkeeping.
Bronson's Elocution.
Henderson's Text Speller.
Duncan's Examiner or Teachers' Aid.
From Hamlett, *History of Education*, 135, 136.

[9] *Louisville Municipal Reports . . . 1895* (Louisville: Courier-Journal Job Printing Co., 1896), 451-53; Hamlett, *History of Education*, 156, 157; Fred A. Shannon, *The Farmers Last Frontier: Agriculture, 1860-1897* (New York: Harper and Row, 1945), 375. There were 4,727 public schools, manned by 5,351 teachers (approximately two-thirds were men), and attended by 218,000 students. *Ninth Census: Population*, I, 452.

[10] Ligon, *History of Public Education*, 127-29; *Louisville Municipal Reports, 1895*, 437; *Annual Cyclopaedia, 1880*, 538.

[11] Ligon, *History of Public Education*, 120-23; *Annual Report of the Superintendent of Public Instruction, 1878*, 19.

[12] Hamlett, *History of Education*, 152, 153.

[13] *Courier-Journal*, April 30, 1883. Some Democratic leaders, notably Knott and Pickett, felt the state was supporting public education to the limit of its ability and thus centered their interest upon increased local support and control. Other Democrats, however, did favor federal aid and the state central educational committee of the party supported this stand in a resolution. Republicans generally championed centralized control of education. See *Annual Cyclopaedia, 1883*, 463.

[14] *Kentucky Acts, 1883-84*, I, 108-47.

[15] Material is from the *Tenth Census*, VII, 3, 12, 916-21.

[16] Dickey Diary, microfilm, University of Kentucky Library, May 27, June 3, October 17, November 1, December 18, 1883, July 4, 1886.

[17] *Ibid.*, March 24, 31, June 3, September 25, 29, 30, 1883, *passim* 1882, October 19, 1886, December 5, 1895. Another observer noted that in a mountain school he visited all the children were barefoot and the teacher but sixteen years old. S. S. MacClintock, "The Kentucky Mountains and Their Feuds." *American Journal of Sociology*, VII (1901), 18. Obviously, though, most of the counties of the state in the 1880s were not as poorly served as Breathitt, which was to know a better day.

[18] E. Merton Coulter, *The Civil War and Readjustment in Kentucky* (Chapel Hill: University of North Carolina Press, 1926), 254; Lewis and Richard H. Collins, *History of Kentucky* (2 vols., Covington: Collins and Co., 1874), I, 214; Ligon, *History of Public Education*, 285, 320.

[19] James F. Hopkins, *The University of Kentucky: Origins and Early Years* (Lexington: University of Kentucky Press, 1951), 74-76, 94-110; Frank L. McVey, *The Gates Open Slowly: A History of Education in Kentucky* (Lexington: University of Kentucky Press, 1949), 110-12.

[20] *House Journal, 1879-80*, 54; *Kentucky Acts, 1879-80*, I, 38, 45.

[21] Hopkins, *University of Kentucky*, 119; *Kentucky Acts, 1879-80*, I, 18, 19. Under the Morrill Act of 1862, Kentucky received the return on 330,000 acres of land, which amounted to $165,000. Designed to go to A & M College, by 1878 this fund had dwindled to approximately $10,000.

[22] Hopkins, *University of Kentucky*, 126, 136, 166-79. See chapter V for the growth of sports.

[23] Ligon, *History of Public Education*, 350, 351; Hopkins, *University of Kentucky*, 146.

[24] *Biennial Report of the Superintendent of Public Instruction . . . [1895-97]* (Louisville: George G. Fetter Printing Co., 1897), 751-93, 99; Edwin S. Bradley, *Union College, 1879-1954* (Barbourville: Union College, 1954), 18-41; Mrs. Frank P. Moore, "Western Kentucky State College—Past and Present," FCHQ, XXVIII (1954), 329; Thomas D. Clark, *A History of Kentucky* (rev. ed., Lexington: John Bradford Press, 1960), 368.

[25] Kentucky Writers Project, *A Centennial History of the University of Louisville* (Louisville: University of Louisville, 1939), 65, 79, 80, 84-86, 95-108; Hardin Craig, *Centre College of Kentucky* (Louisville: Gateway Press, 1967), 47, 48.

[26] W. A. Low, "The Freedmen's Bureau in the Border States," in Richard O. Curry, ed., *Radicalism, Racism and Party Alignment: The Border States During Reconstruction* (Baltimore: Johns Hopkins Press, 1969), 250-56; Coulter, *Civil War and Readjustment*, 355-57.

[27] *Ninth Census: Population*, I, 394; *Kentucky Documents, 1871*, I, No. 5, 21-24.

[28] Ligon, *History of Public Education*, 247-50. *Kentucky Acts, 1873-74*, 56-58.

[29] *Annual Cyclopaedia, 1875*, 418; Ligon, *History of Public Education*, 251.

[30] *Annual Cyclopaedia, 1879*, 539; Ligon, *History of Public Education*, 251-58; Collins, *History*, I, 246w.

[31] *Transcript*, March 30, 1886; *History of Daviess County* (Chicago: Inter-State Publishing Co., 1883), 367; *Twelfth Census: Population*, II, pt. 2, cv, xcv.

CHAPTER X

[1] *Cincinnati Commercial*, June 18, 1880; *Annual Cyclopaedia, 1880*, 426. The Ken-

tucky Republican delegation, led by W. O. Bradley, had been inclined to support Grant's third term bid. Bradley, in fact, seconded the nomination of Grant. That effective speech caused Roscoe Conkling to embrace the Kentuckian and declare, "In the North orators have to be made, but in the South they are born so." See Maurice H. Thatcher, *Stories and Speeches of William O. Bradley* (Lexington: Transylvania Printing Co., 1916), 21.

[2] *House Journal, 1881-82,* 3-6, 35, 91. All house members of the Greenback ticket came from economically depressed western Kentucky: J. R. Clark of Crittenden County, Richard Key of Hopkins County, Ben C. Keys of Calloway County and J. W. Lightfoot of McLean County. Charles W. Cook of Webster County received four votes as the Greenback candidate for senator against Beck.

[3] The Morgantown *Green River Courier* reported that "the remnant of the Greenback party in Butler County has been sold to the Republicans for a mess of pottage" (in the *Courier-Journal*, May 14, 1883). Be this as it may, the Greenback party's disaffection from the Democrats did not affect the party appreciably.

[4] *Courier-Journal*, April 27, 1883; *Weekly Kentucky Yeoman*, May 22, 1883; *Courier-Journal*, May 17, 1883.

[5] Born in Marion County, Kentucky, Knott moved to Missouri, studied law, won election tto the Missouri legislature, and became attorney general of that state in 1860. After his refusal to take the "test-oath" to support the Union—declaring that he took the oath upon being inducted into the office of attorney general—he lost his office and served some time in prison for his pro-southern sentiments. Knott returned to Kentucky and was selected to Congress from Lebanon for 1867 to 1871 and from 1875 to 1883. See Glenn Clift, *Governors of Kentucky 1792 to 1942* (Cynthiana, Ky.: Hobson Press, 1942), 93-95.

[6] George L. Willis, Sr., *Kentucky Democracy: A History of the Party and its Representative Members Past and Present* (3 vols., Louisville: Democratic Historical Society, 1935), I, 263.

[7] *Annual Cyclopaedia, 1883,* 461.

[8] A comparison of the Auditor's reports of 1866 and 1883 shows that the government's financial resources had shrunk from $7,105,000 to less than $300,000. See *Annual Cyclopaedia, 1866,* 433, and *Kentucky Documents, 1883,* No. 1, v.

[9] *Courier-Journal*, June 18, 1883.

[10] *Ibid.*, August 4, 1883.

[11] *Annual Cyclopaedia, 1883,* 461; *Commercial*, September 12, 1884.

[12] *Courier-Journal*, September 5, 1883.

[13] Z. F. Smith, *The History of Kentucky* (Louisville: Courier-Journal Job Printing Co., 1885), 818; *Annual Cyclopaedia, 1883,* 462; *House Journal, 1883-84,* 22, 23.

[14] *House Journal, 1885-86,* 21-25, 76.

[15] *Kentucky Acts, 1885-86,* I, 140-203.

[16] *House Journal, 1887-88,* 17, 20; *Annual Cyclopaedia, 1888,* 485.

[17] *House Journal, 1883-84,* 34; *ibid., 1885-86,* 36, 37.

[18] *Courier-Journal*, September 14, 1884; *Commercial*, September 14, 15, 1884. See also *Hartford Herald*, August 27, 1884.

[19] *Kentucky Acts, 1883-84,* 82-86.

[20] Blaine to Watterson, December 20, 1890, Papers of Henry Watterson, Manuscript Division, Library of Congress; *Courier-Journal*, September 16-18 and *passim* 1884.

[21] *Courier-Journal*, September 18, 1884.

[22] *Commercial*, September 2, 16, 1884. After a secret marriage in 1850 in Millersburg,

Kentucky—where Blaine taught at the Western Military Academy—the couple had an open ceremony performed in March 1851 in Pittsburgh.

[23] Letters dated September 24, 26, 27, 29, 30, October 2, 4-6, 1884 in Breckinridge MSS, vol. 336.

[24] *Cincinnati Weekly Times*, July 17, 1884.

[25] *Annual Cyclopaedia, 1884*, 424; *ibid., 1885*, 515.

[26] *Tri-Weekly Kentucky Yeoman*, August 6, 1885; *Annual Cyclopaedia, 1886*, 467.

[27] *Courier-Journal*, May 4, 1887. "Elder" Pickett, apparently fearful that he would not be re-nominated, wrote his kinsman W. C. P. Breckinridge, who had carried Pickett through an earlier convention. Threatened by a one-armed schoolteacher from Hopkins County, Pickett stated that the so-called "Armless Professor" had in fact lost his arm in feeding a "ground-hog threshing machine," not in Confederate service. Calling attention to his children's lot, "Cousin Issa" (Breckinridge's wife), and his Confederate background, Pickett asked that some "full-blooded Confederate" put his name in nomination. The letter ended: "Burn it after reading it." In Breckinridge MSS, vol. 373.

[28] Willis, *Kentucky Democracy*, I, 299; *Courier-Journal*, May 12, 1887. See also E. A. Jonas, *A History of the Republican Party in Kentucky* (Louisville: J. P. Morton Co., 1929), 19.

[29] *Annual Cyclopaedia, 1887*, 411; *Courier-Journal*, May 12, 1887.

[30] *Courier-Journal*, May 12, 1887.

[31] William E. Connelley and E. Merton Coulter, *History of Kentucky*, edited by Charles Kerr (5 vols., Chicago: American Historical Society, 1922), II, 1002.

[32] *Courier-Journal*, July 14, 1887; New York *Tribune*, May 8, 1892; A. M. Stickles, *Simon Bolivar Buckner: Borderland Knight* (Chapel Hill: University of North Carolina Press, 1940), 334-44.

[33] *Courier-Journal*, May 30, 2, 1887; *Louisville Republican*, August 6, 1887. See also New York *Tribune*, May 8, 1892.

[34] *Annual Cyclopaedia, 1887*, 411; *Commercial*, August 11, 8, 1887; *Annual Cyclopaedia, 1887*, 441.

[35] Stickles, *Buckner*, 344; *Commercial*, August 31, 1887.

[36] *Courier-Journal*, August 30, 31, 1887. See also Stickles, *Buckner*, 347.

CHAPTER XI

[1] *House Journal, 1887-88*, 17-28.

[2] George L. Willis, Sr., *Kentucky Democracy* (3 vols., Louisville: Democratic Historical Society, 1935), I, 300; A. M. Stickles, *Simon Boliver Buckner: Borderland Knight* (Chapel Hill: University of North Carolina Press, 1940), 365.

[3] Emmet V. Mitlebeeler, "The Great Kentucky Absconsion," *FCHQ*, XXVII (1953), 336-44, 350; Stickles, *Buckner*, 357, 358; Willis, *Kentucky Democracy*, I, 300.

[4] *Kentucky Documents, 1888*, II, 4, 13, 21. Mitlebeeler "Kentucky Absconsion," 345, notes that Tate's daughter received letters from her father throughout 1888. They were dated Tacoma, Washington, the Pacific Ocean abroad ship, Shanghai, China, and finally, San Francisco. A letter sent some time later by Tate to a friend, indicated that he was in Brazil. His later whereabouts are unknown.

[5] *Annual Cyclopaedia, 1888*, 463; Stickles, *Buckner*, 359; Willis, *Kentucky Democracy*, I, 300, 301.

[6] *Courier-Journal*, March 26, 1888.

[7] *Annual Cyclopaedia, 1888*, 462, 463; *Courier-Journal*, May 5, 1888.

[8] *Commercial*, May 4, 1888; *Courier-Journal*, May 5, 1888; John A. Lewis to W. C. P. Breckinridge, [1888], Breckinridge MSS, vol. 397.

[9] Henry Watterson, *"Marse Henry": An Autobiography* (2 vols., New York: George H. Doran, 1919), II, 140, 257.

[10] *Courier-Journal*, November 15, 1888; *Annual Cyclopaedia, 1888*, 463.

[11] *Annual Cyclopaedia, 1889*, 437, 438.

[12] *House Journal, 1889-90*, 18; *Annual Cyclopaedia, 1890*, 473; Willis, *Kentucky Democracy*, I, 306-15.

[13] *Annual Cyclopaedia, 1890*, 473; Stickles, *Buckner*, 378, 379.

[14] Stickles, *Buckner*, 380, 381; *Courier-Journal*, May 28, 1890.

[15] *Commercial*, May 26, 28, 1890.

CHAPTER XII

[1] George L. Willis, Sr., *Kentucky Democracy* (3 vols., Louisville: Democratic Historical Society, 1935), I, 326, 327.

[2] Rhea A. Taylor, "Conflicts in Kentucky as Shown by the Constitutional Convention of 1890-1891," (Dissertation, University of Chicago, 1948), 69, 78, 95-99. The initial spirit of cooperation was shown when a contested Washington County election between Democrat W. C. McChord and Republican John W. Lewis was decided in McChord's favor. That irregularities had occurred was clear. However, the delegates extended to Lewis, a prominent and able lawyer, the privileges of the floor.

[3] William E. Connelley and E. Merton Coulter, *History of Kentucky*, edited by Charles Kerr (5 vols., Chicago: American Historical Society, 1922), II, 1005; *Courier-Journal*, April 12, 1891.

[4] 92 Kentucky 589; 18 s. w. 522. (Miller vs. Johnson).

[5] Willis, *Kentucky Democracy*, I, 337-40; *Annual Cyclopaedia, 1891*, 405.

[6] *Annual Cyclopaedia, 1891*, 406, 407.

[7] *Courier-Journal*, April 11, 1891.

[8] Thomas D. Clark, *A History of Kentucky* (rev. ed., Lexington: John Bradford Press, 1960), 425.

[9] *Commercial*, May 1, 5, 1891; *Courier-Journal*, April 11, 1891; Willis, *Kentucky Democracy*, I, 341.

[10] Quoted in Willis, *Kentucky Democracy*, I, 343, 344.

CHAPTER XIII

[1] Hallam to Bettie Stevenson, March 7, 1875, Hallam Family Papers, University of Kentucky Library; John Means' Journal, Seaton Collection, University of Kentucky Library.

[2] The sketch of Allen is from C. Vann Woodward, *Origins of The New South, 1877-1913* (Baton Rouge: Louisiana State University Press, 1951), 432-34; Grant C. Knight, *James Lane Allen and the Genteel Tradition* (Chapel Hill: University of North Carolina Press, 1935); Francis B. Simkins and Charles P. Roland, *A History of the South* (4th ed., New York: Alfred A. Knopf, 1972), 424, 425; John W. Townsend, *Kentucky in American Letters, 1784-1912* (2 vols., Cedar Rapids: Torch Press, 1913), II, 4-9; William K. Bottorff, *James Lane Allen* (New York: Twayne Publishers, Inc., 1964); John W. Townsend, *James Lane Allen* (Louisville: Courier-Journal Job Printing Co., 1927) and

Clark's introduction to Sister Mary C. Browning, *Kentucky Authors: A History of Kentucky Literature* (Evansville: Keller-Crescent Co., 1968), x-xii.

[3] Townsend, *Kentucky in American Letters*, II, 174; Thomas D. Clark, *A History of Kentucky* (rev. ed., Lexington: John Bradford Press, 1960), 270, 271; Ish Richey, *Kentucky Literature, 1784-1963* (Tompkinsville: Monroe County Press, 1963), 70-74.

[4] Browning, *Kentucky Authors*, xii, 255; Richey, *Kentucky Literature*, 81; Townsend, *Kentucky in American Letters*, II, 165.

[5] J. Winston Coleman, Jr., *A Bibliography of Kentucky History* (Lexington: University of Kentucky Press, 1949), 427-31. The Collins, Shaler, Perrin, and others, and Smith volumes are cited elsewhere. See William B. Allen, *A History of Kentucky* (Louisville: Bradley & Gilbert, 1872), George W. Ranck, *History of Lexington, Kentucky* (Cincinnati: Robert Clarke & Co., 1872), and Elizabeth S. Kinkead, *A History of Kentucky* (New York, Cincinnati, and Chicago: American Book Co., 1896). George A. Hubbell, "Kentucky in the New Nation, 1865-1909," in Julia A. C. Chandler, ed., *History of the Southern States* (Richmond, Va.: Southern Historical Publication Society, 1909), I, 326, 327, noted a new historical consciousness in 1900 as a result of the new books.

[6] Mark Sullivan, *Our Times: The United States, 1900-1925* (6 vols., New York: Charles Scribner's Sons, 1928), I, 215; Cobb, *A Plea for Old Cap Collier* (New York, Charles H. Doran Co., 1920), 12-16.

[7] Browning, *Kentucky Authors*, 121, 134, 135; Clark, *History of Kentucky*, 273; Otto A. Rothert, *The Story of a Poet: Madison Cawein*, Filson Club Publication No. 30 (Louisville: John P. Morton and Co., 1921), 77-86, 183-87.

[8] Townsend, *Kentucky in American Letters*, I, 297, 298; II, 300; Frankfort *Capital*, April 28, 1891. Among Noe's later volumes, reflecting his nineteenth century memories, are *Tip Sams of Kentucky* (1926), *The Loom of Life* (1912), and *The Legend of the Silver Band* (1932).

[9] *American Newspaper Directory* (New York: George P. Rowell and Co., 1872), 63; *American Newspaper Annual* (Philadelphia: N. W. Ayer and Sons, 1897), 297, 303-05.

[10] Joseph F. Wall, *Reconstructed Rebel: Henry Watterson* (New York: Oxford University Press, 1956), 1-90 and *passim*; Clark, *History of Kentucky*, 246, 247.

[11] E. Polk Johnson, *A History of Kentucky and Kentuckians* (3 vols., Chicago and New York: Lewis Publishing Co., 1912), III, 1725; Clark, *History of Kentucky*, 247, 248; Ayer's *Newspaper Annual*, 299-309; Lexington *Herald*, July 27, 1902. Polk Johnson later returned to become managing editor of the *Courier-Journal*.

[12] James Lane Allen, *The Blue Grass Region of Kentucky* (New York: Macmillan, 1892), 205; J. Winston Coleman, Jr., *Three Kentucky Artists: Hart, Price, Troye* (Lexington: University Press of Kentucky, 1974), 1-23; Irving Sablosky, *American Music* (Chicago: University of Chicago Press, 1969), 94, 130; Sigmund Spaeth, *A History of Popular Music in America* (New York: Random House, 1948), 297. Ballads concerning late 19th century Kentucky events are in Jean Thomas, *Ballad Makin' in the Mountains of Kentucky* (New York: Henry Holt and Co., 1939), 1-27.

[13] Sullivan, *Our Times*, I, 257, 262, 266, 267; Sablosky, *American Music*, 103, 114, 123-38; Spaeth, *Popular Music*, 175-291.

[14] Clark, *History of Kentucky*, 261; Rexford Newcomb, *Architecture in Old Kentucky* (Urbana: University of Illinois Press, 1953), 157-62; Theodore M. Brown, *Introduction to Louisville Architecture* (Louisville: Free Public Library, 1960), 19-29; Arthur M. Schlesinger, *The Rise of the City, 1878-1898* (New York: Macmillan, 1933), 137; Allen, *Blue-Grass Region*, 225.

[15] Cale Young Rice, *Bridging the Years* (New York: D. Appleton-Century Co., 1939), 12; Coleman, *Three Kentucky Artists*, 27-77; Carol Sutton, "Frank Duveneck's Covington, Kentucky," *Courier-Journal*, February 24, 1974; Edgar P. Richardson, *Painting in America* (New York: Thomas Y. Cromwell Co., 1965), 274; H. Wayne Morgan, *Unity and Culture: The United States, 1877-1900* (Baltimore: Penguin Books, 1971), 89. See also William H. Downes, "Frank Duveneck," *Dictionary of American Biography*, V, 558-61.

[16] Justus Bier, "Carl C. Brenner: A German American Landscapist," *American-German Review*, XVII (1951), 20-24, 33; J. Stoddard Johnston, *Memorial History of Louisville* (2 vols., Chicago and New York: American Biographical Publishing Co., 1896), II, 512.

[17] Caroline W. Berry, "Kentucky Honors Robert Burns Wilson," *Register*, XV (1917), 57-59; J. Winston Coleman, Jr., *Robert Burns Wilson* (Lexington: Winburn Press, 1956), 5-15.

[18] John W. Townsend, "Paul Sawyier, Kentucky Artist: Some Recollections of Him," *FCHQ*, XXXIII (1959), 310-13. Discussions with Arthur F. Jones, who is preparing a biography of Sawyier, helped us better interpret his work.

[19] Allen, *Blue Grass Region*, 37.

CHAPTER XIV

[1] *Eighth Annual Report from the Bureau of Agriculture, Labor and Statistics ... 1889* (Frankfort: E. Polk Johnson, 1889), 23; *Ninth Census: Wealth and Industry*, III, 340, 341; *Abstract of the Twelfth Census* (3d ed., Washington, D. C.: Government Printing Office, 1904), 234. Fred A. Shannon, *The Farmer's Last Frontier: Agriculture, 1860-1897* (New York: Harper and Row, 1945) notes that tenancy statistics and others for this period are somewhat misleading. But they do hold generally truer for Kentucky than other southern states because of different prevailing farm patterns. The 1870 census is considered incomplete for the South.

[2] *Eighth Annual Report from the Bureau of Agriculture*, 53; *Twelfth Census: Agriculture*, V, pt. 1, cxxiii; Davie, *Kentucky: Its Resources and Present Condition* (Frankfort: Samuel Ire Monger Major, 1878), 33. Indiana's farm valuation in 1890 stood at $754,000,000 (*Eleventh Census: Agriculture*, 74, 75). See Appendix II.

[3] These figures are from *Twelfth Census: Agriculture*, V, pt. 1, lxix, lxxi, 8, xciii, cii, cx, cxxiii, cxlv, cxlvi; *Annual Cyclopaedia, 1896*, 375; *Eighth Annual Report from the Bureau of Agriculture*, 41; *Eleventh Biennial Report of the Bureau of Agriculture ... 1894* (Frankfort: Capital Printing Co., 1894), 248, 249; *Ninth Census: Wealth and Industry*, III, 82, 83, 159-65; and J. J. Hornback, "Economic Development in Kentucky Since 1860," (Dissertation, University of Michigan, 1932), 137.

[4] *Eleventh Report of the Bureau of Agriculture*, 196; *Annual Report of the Kentucky Bureau of Agriculture, Horticulture, and Statistics, 1880* (Frankfort: E. H. Porter, 1880), 56, 57.

[5] *Eleventh Report of the Bureau of Agriculture*, 197; Thomas D. Clark, *A History of Kentucky* (rev. ed., Lexington: John Bradford Press, 1960), 389; William E. Connelley and E. Merton Coulter, *History of Kentucky*, edited by Charles Kerr (5 vols., Chicago: American Historical Society, 1922), II, 1179, 1180.

[6] *Eighth Report of the Bureau of Agriculture*, 39; Edward F. Prichard, Jr., "Popular Political Movements in Kentucky, 1875-1900" (Senior thesis, Princeton University, 1935), 34.

[7] *Eleventh Report of the Bureau of Agriculture*, 215, 216; *Annual Cyclopaedia, 1894*, 395; Elizabeth R. Clotfelter, "The Agricultural History of Bourbon County, Kentucky Prior to 1900" (M. A. thesis, University of Kentucky, 1953), 119, 120; *Twelfth Census: Agriculture*, V, pt. 1, lxix-lxxi.

[8] James D. Bennett, "Some Notes on Christian County, Kentucky, Grange Activities," *Register*, LXIV (1966), 226; Lewis and Richard H. Collins, *History of Kentucky* (2 vols., Covington: Collins and Co., 1874), I, 246a, 246q, 246w; *South Kentuckian*, February 14, April 25, 1890; *Hazel Green Herald*, July 24, August 14, 1891; quoted in C. Vann Woodward, *Origins of the New South, 1877-1913* (Baton Rouge: Louisiana State University Press, 1951), 270. Collins reports the first organized Grange in Christian County in mid-September, 1873.

[9] Collins, *History*, I, 246m; Clark, *History of Kentucky*, 587, 588; quoted in Connelley and Coulter, *History of Kentucky*, II, 987.

[10] *Annual Cyclopaedia, 1887*, 410; *ibid., 1889*, 486; Prichard, "Popular Political Movements," 36; Collins, *History*, I, 211.

[11] Rhea A. Taylor, "Conflicts in Kentucky as Shown by the Constitutional Convention of 1890-1891," (Dissertation, University of Chicago, 1948), 36, 62, 63.

[12] *Kentucky Acts, 1879-80*, I, 92-95; *ibid., 1881-82*, I, 67-72.

[13] Stickles, *Simon Bolivar Buckner: Borderland Knight* (Chapel Hill: University of North Carolina Press, 1940), 362, 363.

[14] Julius H. Parmelee, "Albert Fink," *Dictionary of American Biography*, VI, 387, 388; *Second Report of the Railroad Commission* (Frankfort: S. I. M. Major, 1881), 116-18; *Twenty-First Annual Report of the Railroad Commission of Kentucky* (Louisville: George G. Fetter, 1900), 7; *Eleventh Report of the Railroad Commissioners* (Frankfort: E. Polk Johnson, 1891), 6, 13.

[15] Joseph G. Kerr, *Historical Development of the Louisville and Nashville Railroad System* (n. p., 1926?), 130n; Joseph L. Kerr, *The Story of a Southern Carrier: The Louisville and Nashville* (New York: Young and Ottley, Inc., 1933), 46, 47; Margaret Yent, "A History of the Chesapeake and Ohio Railway" (M. A. thesis, University of Kentucky, 1931), 15, 22-27; Prichard, "Popular Political Movements," 88. See also Mary K. Bonstell Tachau, "The Making of a Railroad President: Milton Hannibal Smith and the L & N," *FCHQ*, XLIII (1969).

[16] Thomas D. Clark, *Kentucky: Land of Contrast* (New York: Harper and Row, 1968), 199; Hornback, "Economic Development," 99.

[17] Hornback, "Economic Development," 98-100.

[18] Charles B. Roberts, "The Building of Middlesborough—A Notable Epoch in Eastern Kentucky History," *FCHQ*, VII (1933), 18-33; J. Stoddard Johnston, *Memorial History of Louisville*, (2 vols., Chicago and New York: American Biographical Publishing Co., 1897), I, 113.

[19] Allen, *Blue Grass Region of Kentucky* (New York: Macmillan, 1892), 266, 267; *Second Annual Report of the Inspector of Mines* (Frankfort: John D. Woods, 1885), 8-10, 14, 17-19.

[20] Hornback, "Economic Development," 139, 140. Less fortunate were the iron furnaces; from 22 in 1878 the number dropped to only 6 in 1890, due in part to transportation difficulties. See *ibid.*, 57, 58.

[21] *Ninth Census: Wealth and Industry*, III, 392; *Abstract of the Eleventh Census* (2d ed., Washington, D. C.: Government Printing Office, 1896), 141; *Abstract of Twelfth Census*, 332; Woodward, *Origins of New South*, 111.

²² James P. Sullivan, "Louisville and Her Southern Alliance, 1865-1890," (Dissertation, University of Kentucky, 1965), 36, 69-71, 46-50, 28, 34, 35, 80, 72, 266.

²³ *Ibid.*, 108-33, 273-77, 356; *History of the Ohio Falls Cities and Their Counties* (2 vols., Cleveland: L. A. Williams and Co., 1882), I, 330-56, and *passim.*

²⁴ Woodward, *Origins of New South*, 111, 140; *Abstract of Eleventh Census*, 141; *Abstract of Twelfth Census*, 332.

²⁵ *Courier-Journal*, July 25, 1887; *Annual Cyclopaedia, 1877*, 420; Bill L. Weaver, "Louisville's Labor Disturbance, July 1877," *FCHQ*, XLVIII (1974), 181-85.

²⁶ Herbert Finch, "Organized Labor in Louisville, Kentucky, 1880-1914" (Dissertation, University of Kentucky, 1965), 4-7, 27-29, 37, 148-53, 177, 240-43. See also Pier L. G. DePaela, "Management and Organized Labor Relations of the Louisville and Nashville Railroad During the Depression Year 1893," (M. A. thesis, University of Louisville, 1971).

²⁷ *Observer and Reporter*, July 27, 1870; Hickman *Courier*, January 14, 1871; Clotfelter, "Agricultural History of Bourbon County," 119, 120.

²⁸ Prichard, "Popular Political Movements," 35; Lowell H. Harrison, "Kentucky Agriculture, 1879: A British Report," *FCHQ*, XLIV (1970), 278; *Annual Report of the Bureau of Agriculture, 1880*, 16.

CHAPTER XV

¹ Thomas D. Clark, *A History of Kentucky* (rev. ed., Lexington: John Bradford Press, 1960), 418, 419; *Leader*, October 20, 1890; Edward F. Prichard, Jr., "Popular Political Movements in Kentucky, 1875-1900," (Senior thesis, Princeton University, 1935), 127.

² *Hazel Green Herald*, April 24, May 1, 29, 1891; Charles M. Meacham, *A History of Christian County, Kentucky* (Nashville: Marshall & Bruce Co., 1930), 219; *Leader*, October 20, 21, 1890.

³ Prichard, "Popular Movements," 128, 140; Clark, *History of Kentucky*, 420, 421; *Leader*, December 29, 1890.

⁴ M. R. Walter to Clay, December 8, 1890; H. W. Alexander to Clay, January 6, 1891; F. W. Spears [?] to Clay, January 16, [1891]; J. M. Benton to Clay, April 9, 1891; Cassius M. Clay Collection, University of Kentucky Library.

⁵ Jones to Clay, December 10, 1890. See also W. Carroll Chapman to Clay, February 20, 1891; Joseph B. Reed to Clay, January 17, 1891; Dudley Reynolds to Clay, January 19, 1891, J. M. Reid to Clay, January 12, 1891; Spears to Clay, January 16, [1891]', all in Clay Collection.

⁶ Bridgewater to Clay, December 22, 1890; John Goff to Clay, December 1, 1890, Clay Collection; John O. Hodges to W. C. P. Breckinridge, April 20, 1891, Breckinridge MSS, vol. 422; *Commercial*, April 4, 1891.

⁷ Winchester *Democrat*, May 20, 1891; Hickman *Courier*, May 22, 1891.

⁸ *Biographical Cyclopaedia of the Commonwealth of Kentucky* (Chicago and Philadelphia: John M. Gresham Co., 1896), 225, 226; George L. Willis, Sr., *Kentucky Democracy: A History of the Party and Its Representative Members Past and Present* (3 vols., Louisville: Democratic Historical Society, 1935), I, 303, 304.

⁹ *Annual Cyclopaedia, 1891*, 407, 408; Breckinridge to Breckinridge, May 21, 1891, Breckinridge MSS, vol. 422.

¹⁰ Willis, *Kentucky Democracy*, I, 341; *Annual Cyclopaedia, 1891*, 408.

¹¹ *Annual Cyclopaedia, 1891*, 408; *Courier-Journal*, May 21, 1891.

¹² *Annual Cyclopaedia, 1891*, 408.

[13] *Ibid.*; Clark, *History of Kentucky*, 421; *Official Manual . . . of the State of Kentucky* (Louisville: John P. Morton & Co., 1895), 122-25; Prichard "Popular Movements," 144, notes that 24 of the 31 counties where Populists received more than 15% of the vote were in the dark tobacco belt of western Kentucky.

[14] *Louisville Post*, September 1, 1891.

[15] *Biographical Encyclopaedia*, 193, 194; *Commercial*, September 2, 1891.

[16] *Courier-Journal*, September 1, 1891; *House Journal, 1891-92*, I, 6, 7, 18, 19, 23-30. See also Z. F. Smith, *History of Kentucky* (4th rev. ed., Louisville: Prentice Press, 1901), 805.

[17] *Courier-Journal*, August 10, 18, 1892.

[18] *Ibid.*, August 11, 1892; *Annual Cyclopaedia, 1892*, 372, 373. The revenue bill in its original form exempted not only railroads but also life and accident insurance companies and foreign building and loan associations from paying tax on their franchises.

[19] *House Journal, 1891-92*, I, 1053, 1054; *Annual Cyclopaedia, 1892*, 373. In the Senate where the Separate Coach Bill passed 18-10, Democrats Robert J. Breckinridge, Jr. and William Lindsay supported the measure, Goebel did not vote, and Judge James H. Mulligan opposed it. See *Senate Journal*, 621-23; Frankfort *Capital*, April 6, 1892.

[20] Watterson to Hill, November 21, 1890, Watterson Papers; Henry Watterson, "*Marse Henry*": *An Autobiography* (2 vols., New York: George H. Doran Co., 1919), II, 143-45; *Courier-Journal*, February 23, 1892; Joseph F. Wall, *Henry Watterson: Reconstructed Rebel* (New York: Oxford University Press, 1956), 204, 205.

[21] *Courier-Journal*, May 25, 26, 1892; *Annual Cyclopaedia, 1892*, 374.

[22] Wall, *Watterson*, 205-07.

[23] *Annual Cyclopaedia, 1892*, 374; *Official Manual, 1895*, 122-25.

[24] *Annual Cyclopaedia, 1893*, 425, 426.

[25] Born in Frankfort, an orphan at age twelve, Pettit had learned the printer's trade and purchased the Owensboro *Monitor* in 1864. He had his presses destroyed by Union soldiers and was sent South because of his sympathies, however. Returning in 1865, he entered the lumber business and aided in railroad construction. For a time Pettit served as reading clerk in the U. S. House of Representatives and had been conservative Governor McCreary's private secretary. A lifelong Democrat until the 1890s, he owned a large farm in Daviess County when he attracted state-wide attention as a Populist. See Thomas S. Pettit Papers, microfilm, University of Kentucky Library.

[26] *House Journal, 1894*, 6, 7.

[27] *Ibid.*, 25. The prison population had increased from 200 in 1865 to 1,607 in 1894.

[28] *Ibid,*, 21, 22, 29-32.

[29] *Ibid.*, 62, 1034; *Annual Cyclopaedia, 1894*, 393. See also Paul E. Fuller, *Laura Clay and The Woman's Rights Movement* (Lexington: University Press of Kentucky, 1975), 46, 47.

[30] *Annual Cyclopaedia, 1894*, 393; *Commercial*, March 15, 1894.

[31] James C. Klotter, "The Breckinridges of Kentucky: Two Centuries of Leadership" (Dissertation, University of Kentucky, 1975), 187-98. See also Breckinridge MSS, box marked "Pollard Affair" and vols. 480-82; *The Celebrated Trial: Madeline Pollard vs. Breckinridge* ([Cincinnati?]: American Printing Co., 1894); Fayette Lexington (pseud.), *The Celebrated Case of Col. W. C. P. Breckinridge and Madeline Pollard* (Chicago: Current Events Publishing Co., 1894), and Agnes Parker, *The Real Madeline Pollard* ([New York]: G. W. Dillingham, 1894). The trial was given front page newspaper

coverage throughout Kentucky and the nation.

[32] The *Commercial* and the *Evening Post* continually attacked the Whallen organization.

[33] *Commercial*, November 7, 1894.

[34] *Courier-Journal*, November 7-10, 1894. The somewhat suspicious nature of the shortage of ballots in some precincts can be seen in a few selected examples:

Precinct	Vote in Previous Election	Ballots Sent Out
Cane Run	21	275
Gilman's	41	350
Spring Garden	23	275
Jeffersontown	72	430.

[35] *Evening Post*, November 9, 1894; *Commercial*, November 8, 1894.

[36] *Commercial*, November 9, 1894. In the election for judge of the Appellate Court, Democrat Sterling B. Toney was declared elected by 25 votes. His opponent, St. John Boyle, contested the election. The State Board of Contest, consisting of five state officers, held in Toney's favor, but the governor and auditor supported Boyle. On February 21, 1895 Toney resigned and Governor Brown accepted the resignation. George B. Eastin, appointed to serve the remainder of the year, was succeeded by George Durell, a Republican elected in November, 1895. See *Annual Cyclopaedia, 1895*, 382.

[37] *Annual Cyclopaedia, 1894*, 396. The *Official Manual, 1895*, 126, offers slightly different figures, placing the 1894 Republican vote but 2,383 behind the Democratic.

[38] Quoted in *Commercial*, November 8, 1894.

[39] *Ibid.*, November 12, 1894.

CHAPTER XVI

[1] *Courier-Journal*, May 24, 26, 1895; *Annual Cyclopaedia, 1895*, 383; *Commercial*, June 27, 1895. The editor of the *Paducah Standard* had written, "The Democracy of Kentucky is divided on the silver question and neither side is in a humor to let the other side run over it roughshod in the convention. . . . If either side forces the other to the wall in the June convention, it's goodbye Democratic world and howd'ye do Republican hell." Quoted in *Commercial*, April 1, 1895. See also Z. F. Smith, *History of Kentucky* (4th rev. ed., Louisville: Prentice Press, 1901), 827.

[2] *Commercial*, June 27, 1895; E. A. Jonas, *A History of the Republican Party in Kentucky* (Louisville: J. P. Morton Co., 1929), 23; *Press-Transcript*, June 27, 1895; *Courier-Journal*, June 27, 1895.

[3] *Annual Cyclopaedia, 1895*, 383; Smith, *History of Kentucky* (rev. ed.), 827. The People's Party (Populist) convention, held in Louisville in July, nominated old leaders Pettit for governor and Blair for lieutenant governor. The rest of the ticket included M. R. Gardner of Hardin County for treasurer, C. H. Dean of Woodford for auditor, J. E. Quicksall of Wolfe for register of the land office, Silas M. Peyton of Hart for attorney general, Don Singletary of Hickman for secretary of state, H. H. Farmer of Henderson for superintendent of public instruction and W. L. Scott of Shelby for commissioner of agriculture. The platform called for free and unlimited coinage of silver at 16 to 1, a graduated income tax, and strict economy in government. See *ibid.* and Thomas D. Clark, *A History of Kentucky* (rev. ed., Lexington: John Bradford Press, 1960), 422.

[4] *Press-Transcript*, August 20, 1895. Bradley began his speech, in part, by appealing for an end to "bloody shirt" appeals: "Neither am I here to speak of the War—as my friend spoke of it. Thank God! The War has been over for many, many, long years; and I am one of those who believes that its animosities belong to oblivion, and that its glories are the heritage of all.... I am no 'carpetbagger.' I am not asking that I be permitted to fatten on the misfortunes of my state; but I am asking that you turn out of power the party that has fattened on her misfortunes." See Maurice H. Thatcher, *Stories and Speeches of William O. Bradley* (Lexington: Transylvania Printing Co., 1916), 170, 171.

[5] *Courier-Journal*, August 20, 1895; *Evening Post*, August 20, 1895; *Commercial*, August 31, 1895.

[6] The Populist candidate Pettit was an able campaigner and drew good crowds, especially in western Kentucky. Bradley further split the Democratic ranks by courting the vote of those sympathetic with the American Protective Association (APA), a secret fraternal organization opposed to Catholics and immigrants. While Bradley did not openly endorse its programs, a campaigner with the Republican noted that Bradley "was very anxious to get on the right side of the APA." Numbers of APA members, gold standard Democrats, and distressed farmers deserted the Democrats for either Bradley or Pettit. See "The Republican Campaign of Kentucky, 1895," MS in George D. Todd Papers, The Filson Club, Louisville (Todd was an organizer in the campaign); John E. Wiltz, "The 1895 Election: A Watershed in Kentucky Politics," FCHQ, XXXVII (1963), 131-34, and his "APA-ISM in Kentucky and Elsewhere," *Register*, LVI (1958), 143-55; John Higham, *Strangers in the Land: Patterns of American Nativism, 1860-1925* (2d ed., New York: Antheneum, 1955), 80-86.

[7] Dr. Godfrey Hunter had proposed at a top-level meeting a "plan" that "would guarantee the election of every man on the ticket." It would require $15,000 to carry out. After a week of haggling with the Republican candidates, some $4,000 in cash and $5,600 in personal notes were collected. Bradley, Taylor, Stone, and Long agreed to make up the shortage. With this fund, from their own pockets, the candidates waged their campaign.

They also had to fight splits in their party. The Executive Committee rebuffed Bradley's efforts to have two Negroes appointed to it. The Louisville *New South*, one of the largest black newspapers in the South, repudiated Bradley and Hardin as "demagogues and lightweights" and threw its support to Pettit. Blacks continued to vote Republican generally, however. See "Republican Campaign," Todd Papers; unidentified clipping, Pettit Papers.

[8] *Commercial*, August 31, 1895; *Press-Transcript*, November 4, 1895; *Official Manual ... of the State of Kentucky* (Louisville: John P. Morton & Co., 1895), 122-25; The Republican vote in Jefferson County rose from 7,937 in 1891 to 19,529 in 1895, while the Democratic vote gained but slightly, from 13,108 to 15,760. The statewide vote was Bradley 172,436, Hardin 163,524, Pettit 16,911, and W. B. Demaree, Prohibitionist, 4,186.

[9] While no published biography of Bradley exists, sketches of his life can be found in *Biographical Cyclopaedia of the Commonwealth of Kentucky* (Philadelphia: John M. Grisham Co., 1896); *Biographical Encyclopaedia of Kentucky* (Cincinnati: J. M. Armstrong Co., 1878); *Lawyers and Lawmakers of Kentucky* (Chicago: Lewis Publishing Co., 1897); Thatcher, *Stories and Speeches of Bradley*; E. Merton Coulter, "William O'Connell Bradley," *Dictionary of American Biography*, II, 576, 577; *Lexington Standard*, August 30, 1895; *Pineville News*, August 7, 1895.

[10] *Press-Transcript*, December 11, 1895. Watterson, who preferred Bradley to a silverite, declared his support for the governor's professed aims "that . . . public officers shall be held to a strict accountability as public servants, that our systems of education and taxation may be improved; that intelligent retrenchment and reform may be effected; and that the laws may be rigidly enforced. . . . So far as you fulfill the promises of your inauguration we are with you." *Courier-Journal*, December 11, 1895.

[11] Lexington *Herald*, January 3, 1896.

[12] The house was Republican, the senate Democratic. Only one of the Republican house members had served in the previous legislature and the "victory-happy" but "green" legislators had difficulty uniting on a program. This gave the Democratic minority in the house a decided advantage. See *Courier-Journal*, November 11, 1895.

[13] *House Journal, 1896*, 7-8; *Annual Cyclopaedia, 1896*, 375, 376; Lexington *Herald*, January 30, 1896.

[14] *Courier-Journal*, March 12-14, 1896.

[15] *Ibid.*, March 12, 1896.

[16] *Commercial*, March 17, 18, 1896.

[17] *Kentucky Acts, 1896; Commercial*, March 18, 1896.

[18] *Annual Cyclopaedia, 1896*, 377.

[19] Haldeman to Watterson, August 27, 1896, Watterson MSS; *Annual Cyclopaedia, 1896*, 378.

[20] Those in attendance included Carlisle, Breckinridge, Buckner, businessman John M. Atherton of Louisville, Judge T. H. Hinds of Frankfort, Judge J. Q. A. Ward of Paducah, former state official George M. Davie of Louisville, former Lt. Gov. Hindman, attorney John T. Shelby of Lexington, and W. H. Mackoy, Covington lawyer. Others were Wilburn Browder of Russellville, Rodney Haggard of Winchester, T. W. Bullitt of Louisville, W. K. Barnes of Hardinsburg, Judge J. C. Alcorn of Stanford, John A. Stewart of Madisonville, T. H. Dudley of Winchester, T. H. Hood of Cynthiana, James W. Johnson of Georgetown, J. C. Sims of Bowling Green, Judge H. D. Baker of Columbia, Cromwell Adair of Morganfield, H. R. French of Mt. Sterling, J. F. Ratliff of Louisa, John H. Mason of Catlettsburg, Nelson H. Trimble of Mt. Sterling, A. D. Hudson of Emminence, W. H. Morton of Catlettsburg, R. M. Wathen of Lebanon, state representative George Weissinger Smith of Louisville, Jerry Sullivan of Richmond, H. E. Pogue of Maysville, John I. and Anthony McElroy of Springfield, J. Whit Potter of Bowling Green, and W. W. Baldwin of Maysville.

[21] *Courier-Journal*, August 21, 1896, May 28, 1890, August 20, 1896; Joseph F. Wall, *Henry Watterson: Reconstructed Rebel* (New York: Oxford University Press, 1956), 225-32.

[22] Wall, *Watterson*, 232; Ellis P. Oberholtzer, *A History of the United States Since the Civil War* (5 vols., New York: Macmillan Co., 1928-37), V, 433; *Annual Cyclopaedia, 1896*, 378; *Official Manual . . . of the State of Kentucky* (Louisville: Geo.G. Fetter Printing Co., 1898), 88-91. Kentucky Republicans reversed the southern trend which saw the party's percentage of the vote fall from 40 percent in 1875 to less than 30 percent in 1896. See Vincent P. DeSantis, *Republicans Face the Southern Question* (Baltimore: Johns Hopkins Press, 1959), 262.

[23] William E. Connelley and E. Merton Coulter, *History of Kentucky*, edited by Charles Kerr (5 vols., Chicago: American Historical Society, 1922), II, 1007; *Annual Cyclopaedia, 1897*, 437.

[24] *Annual Cyclopaedia, 1897*, 437, 438; Wall, *Watterson*, 233, 234. The *Official*

Manual, 1898, 88-91 offers slightly different figures.

[25] Wall, *Watterson*, 235; James C. Klotter, "The Breckinridges of Kentucky: Two Centuries of Leadership" (Dissertation, University of Kentucky, 1975), 202, 203, 208.

[26] The Senate was 26 Democrats, 11 Republicans, and 1 Populist. The House was Democratic by a 75-25 margin. See *Official Manual, 1898*, 117-19 and *House Journal, 1898*, 7, 8.

[27] *House Journal, 1898*, 7, 8, 11; *Senate Journal, 1898*, 8, 12. The Goebel vote was 26-8.

[28] *House Journal, 1898*, 28-55; *Kentucky Acts, 1898*, 135-38.

[29] *Annual Cyclopaedia, 1898*, 357; William Lindsay, "Social Conditions in Kentucky," *International Monthly*, I (1900), 569.

[30] *Kentucky Acts, 1898*, 43-57; *Annual Cyclopaedia, 1898*, 356; Jonas, *History of Republican Party*, 29.

[31] Jonas, *History of Republican Party*, 28. Richard Knott's *Evening Post* bitterly noted: "After an illness of sixty days, the patient at times flighty and at others violent, the Kentucky Legislature is no more. Doctor Goebel, physician in charge, will be tried for malpractice, and it will be proven that his enormous doses of 'force bill' would kill any person or 'thing' taking it, not excepting the Kentucky Legislature." Then Knott reprinted editorial criticism of the bill from various papers, including the *Washington Post* and the Memphis *Commercial Appeal*. See *Evening Post*, March 15, 1898.

[32] *Courier-Journal*, February 25, 1898.

[33] *Evening Post*, March 15, 1898; *Annual Cyclopaedia, 1898*, 356; *Kentucky Acts, 1898*, 54, 55. The McChord Act, sponsored by the Democrats, sought to give the railroad commission the power to regulate and fix freight rates. Strongly opposed by the railroad interests, the Republicans, and many leading Democrats, including Breckinridge, the measure was vetoed by Governor Bradley.

[34] Temple Bodley and Samuel M. Wilson, *History of Kentucky* (4 vols., Chicago and Louisville: S. J. Clarke, 1928), II, 517-23; *Report of the Adjutant General . . . Kentucky Volunteers, War with Spain, 1898-99* (Louisville: Globe Printing Co., 1908), 1-223; Federal Writers Project of the Works Progress Administration, *Military History of Kentucky* (Frankfort: State Journal, 1939), 281-88; Graham A. Cosmas, *An Army for Empire: The United States Army in the Spanish-American War* (Columbia: University of Missouri Press, 1971), 271.

[35] An oft-repeated story, related in *History of Corporal Fess Whitaker* (Louisville: Standard Printing Co., 1918), 41, is, by the author's own words, incorrect. Whitaker states that "after the Battle of Santiago Teddy [Roosevelt], without a wound and I with a bullet wound in my left arm, took me by the hand and said: 'Fess we have gained a great battle for our country. You or I will be the next President of the United States, and if you get the nomination I am for you, and if I get the nomination I want you to be for me'." But Whitaker's narrative states that he served as a cook until 1899 with a Kentucky regiment that never saw Cuba. By 1899, he fails to note, the war was already over. The *Adjutant General's Report* confirms his service with the Kentucky regiment. He joined the Rough Riders only after the fighting ceased and months after Santiago. Whitaker told a good story but an inaccurate one.

CHAPTER XVII

[1] E. Merton Coulter, *The Civil War and Readjustment in Kentucky* (Chapel Hill: University of North Carolina Press, 1926), 361-63; Champ Clark, *My Quarter Century of*

American Politics (2 vols., New York: Harper and Brothers, 1920), I, 73; Charles G.
Mutzenberg, *Kentucky's Famous Feuds and Tragedies* (New York: R. F. Fenno & Co.,
1917), 25-27.

[2] *Annal Cyclopaedia, 1866*, 425, 426.

[3] *Ibid.*, 426.

[4] *Ibid., 1867*, 422; *Courier-Journal*, January 17, 1871.

[5] Coulter, *Civil War and Readjustment*, 364; *Courier-Journal*, March 24, 1871.

[6] Coulter, *Civil War and Readjustment*, 365. The act provided strong penalties for
persons convicted of sending threatening letters, and for those who "unlawfully confederate or band together" and then "go forth armed and disguised." The legislature
empowered the governor to offer up to a $500 reward for apprehension of offenders.
See *Annual Cyclopaedia, 1873*, 402.

[7] Coulter, *Civil War and Readjustment*, 365; Executive Journal, 1870-71, Kentucky
Historical Society, Frankfort.

[8] Executive Journal, 1870-71, entries of March 19, 21, June 14, 1870 and *passim*.

[9] Lewis and Richard H. Collins, *History of Kentucky* (2 vols., Covington: Collins and
Co., 1874), I, 208; *Annual Cyclopaedia, 1871*, 433, 434.

[10] *Annual Cyclopaedia, 1871*, 434.

[11] Collins, *History*, I, 234; *Courier-Journal*, October 23, 1872.

[12] Mutzenberg, *Feuds and Tragedies*, 267, 268; *Annual Cyclopaedia, 1878*, 473; *ibid.,
1879*, 541. Governor McCreary's report to the legislature somewhat exaggerated affairs
in eastern Kentucky. He stated that "no county is more ordered or peaceable than
Breathitt."

[13] *Cincinnati Commercial*, May 25, 1880; quoted in *Courier-Journal*, April 6, 1880.

[14] *Annual Cyclopaedia, 1882*, 453. See also *Courier-Journal*, April 3, 1883.

[15] Mutzenberg, *Feuds and Tragedies*, 119-23.

[16] *Ibid.*, 125; L. F. Johnson, *Famous Kentucky Tragedies and Trials*, (Cleveland:
Baldwin Law Book Co., 1916), 260; *Boone Logan's Letters to the Sentinel—Democrat
... Pertaining to the Rowan County Feud* (n. p., n. d.), 8, 14, 20-22.

[17] The *Majority and Minority Reports and Testimony Taken By the Rowan County
Investigating Committee* (Frankfort: John D. Woods, 1888), 5-7, 427, 228, stated in its
bitterly critical report that 20 people were killed between August 1884 and June 1887
and 16 more wounded. Not a single conviction was returned. Jurors, the report noted,
were "in the warmest sympathy with crime and criminals." Officials in the county were
"totally corrupt and depraved." A military investigation found the deputy sheriff
"almost daily drunk." According to one report, the county judge "can just write his
name."

[18] *Logan's Letters*, 9-11, 14, 23, 26; Mutzenberg, *Feuds and Tragedies*, 170.

[19] Johnson, *Tragedies and Trials*, 270; Report of Capt. Ernest McPherson, Louisville
Legion, to Adj. Gen. Sam E. Hill, in *Kentucky Documents, 1887*, No. 23; *Rowan
County Investigating Committee*, 233, 8.

[20] Virgil C. Jones, *The Hatfields and the McCoys* (Chapel Hill: University of North
Carolina Press, 1948), 18-53; Mutzenberg, *Feuds and Tragedies*, 43-47; L. D. Hatfield,
The True Story of the Hatfield and McCoy Feud (Charleston, W. Va.: Jarrett Printing
Co., 1944), 6, 7, 17-19.

[21] Jones, *Hatfields and McCoys*, 85, 121; *Kentucky Documents, 1888*, I, 2.

[22] Jones, *Hatfields and McCoys*, 93-107, 121, 122; Hatfield, *Hatfields and McCoy
Feud*, 28, 29; *Annual Cyclopaedia, 1888*, 464.

[23] Mutzenberg, *Feuds and Tragedies,* 92-109; Jones, *Hatfields and McCoys,* 176-80, 227, 240.

[24] Mutzenberg, *Feuds and Tragedies,* 189-92, 214-19; *Kentucky Documents, 1889,* IV, 55-65. Judge Lilly stated that these counties were "absolutely dominated and terrorized by savage and lawless men. All respect for justice . . . is not only set at defiance, but the most high-handed outrages are perpetrated in the presence of the court, and with the purpose and object of terrorizing and intimidating the officers of justice." *Annual Cyclopaedia, 1890,* 474.

[25] *Kentucky Documents, 1889,* No. 4, 46-48; *Annual Cyclopaedia, 1889,* 487.

[26] Mutzenberg, *Feuds and Tragedies,* 282-86; Thomas D. Clark, *Kentucky: Land of Contrast* (New York: Harper & Row, 1968), 209-13; Johnston, *Tragedies and Trials.* 322-27.

[27] Clark, *Kentucky: Land of Contrast,* 213, 217; Mutzenberg, *Feuds and Tragedies,* 306; R. L. McClure, "The Mazes of a Kentucky Feud," *The Independent,* September 17, 1903.

[28] Clark, *Kentucky: Land of Contrast,* 218-33; Johnson, *Tragedies and Trials,* 331-33; Mutzenberg, *Feuds and Tragedies,* 307-23.

[29] S. S. MacClintock, "The Kentucky Mountains and Their Feuds,"*American Journal of Sociology,* VII (1901), 171-75. See also Clark, *Kentucky: Land of Contrast,* 208.

[30] *The Nation,* November 23, 1882; *Courier-Journal,* June 14, 1887.

[31] Johnson, *Tragedies and Trials,* 205-21; *Annual Cyclopaedia, 1879,* 541.

[32] Johnson, *Tragedies and Trials,* 282-91; William H. Townsend, *The Lion of Whitehall* (Dunwoody, Ga.: Norman S. Berg, 1967), 30-33. See also Goodloe to Benjamin H. Bristow, July 8, 1875, Bristow MSS.

[33] *House Journal, 1889-90,* 27; J. Winston Coleman, Jr., *Stage-Coach Days in the Bluegrass* (Louisville: Standard Press, 1936), 238-44.

[34] Coleman, *Stage-Coach Days,* 245; *House Journal, 1898,* 24-27.

[35] Coleman, *Stage-Coach Days,* 245, 246.

[36] *Compendium of the Eleventh Census* (Washington: Government Printing Office, 1897), II, 10, 177, 196.

[37] *House Journal, 1889-90,* 34, 35, 19, 20.

[38] James G. Speed, "The Kentuckian," *Century Magazine,* LIX (1900), 946, 947.

CHAPTER XVIII

[1] Urey Woodson, *The First New Dealer: William Goebel* (Louisville: Standard Press, 1939), 229, 30; *Courier-Journal,* June 1, September 5, 1899; Irvin S. Cobb, *Exit Laughing* (Indianapolis and New York: Bobbs-Merrill, 1941), 201; William S. Lester, "The Goebel Affair," 2, 25, Unpublished MS, Kentucky Historical Society.

[2] Woodson, *First New Dealer,* 231-33; *Courier-Journal,* June 1, 28, 1899; William Goebel to Justus Goebel, June 30, 1886, Goebel Family Letters (microfilm), University of Kentucky Library; George G. Perkins, *A Kentucky Judge* (Washington, D. C.: W. F. Roberts, 1931), 230; Richard W. Knott, "History of Goebelism," 34-39, unpublished MS, Temple Bodley Collection, The Filson Club, Louisville; Cobb, *Exit Laughing,* 199-201.

[3] Lester, "Goebel Affair," 2; Woodson, *First New Dealer,* 241; Goebel to C. M. Clay, August 2, 1890, Cassius M. Clay Collection, University of Kentucky Library. George Willis later recorded that, after the 206th ballot, he had asked Goebel to give Hallam the one-fourth vote he needed to receive the nomination for Congress. According to Willis.

Goebel, half-smiling, replied, "I'd rather cut his throat." See George L. Willis, Sr., *Kentucky Democracy: A History of The Party and Its Representative Members* (3 vols., Louisville: Democratic Historical Society, 1935), I, 321.

[4] Nicholas C. Burckel, "William Goebel and the Campaign for Railroad Regulation in Kentucky, 1888-1900," *FCHQ*, XLVIII (1974), 45-47; Thomas D. Clark, "The People, William Goebel and the Kentucky Railroads," *Journal of Southern History*, V (1939), 39, and Clark, "William Goebel—Southern Demagogue," *University of Kentucky Research Bulletin*, VII (1941), 7. Stock dividends of the L & N in 1880 had been 100%. See Lester, "Goebel Affair," 24.

[5] Robert E. Hughes, F. W. Schaefer and E. L. Williams, *That Kentucky Campaign, or the Law, the Ballot and the People in the Goebel-Taylor Contest* (Cincinnati: Robert Clarke Co., 1900), 2, 6-9. Considering its closeness to events, this work is an excellent source.

[6] *Kentucky Acts, 1898*, 43-57; Hughes and others, *That Kentucky Campaign*, 7-9.

[7] Lester, "Goebel Affair," 120.

[8] William Goebel to Justus Goebel, August 29, November 14, 1898, Goebel Family Letters.

[9] *Ibid.*, February 26, March 3, 1899.

[10] *Glasgow Times*, April 3, 1899. The preceding two paragraphs are based on the various newspapers noted in this chapter.

[11] Lester, "Goebel Affair," 177; *Louisville Dispatch*, June 1, 1899 (hereinafter *Dispatch*); *Glasgow Times*, June 8, April 13, 1899.

[12] *Glasgow Times*, June 19, 1899. The reference is to treasurer "Honest Dick" Tate's flight with over $247,000.

[13] *Dispatch*, June 13, 14, 18, 1899; Lexington *Herald*, June 19, 1899.

[14] *Courier-Journal*, June 19-21, 1899; *Dispatch*, June 20, 21, 1899; Woodson, *First New Dealer*, 145, 146.

[15] *Courier-Journal*, June 21, 22, 1899; Lester, "Goebel Affair," 125; Hughes and others, *Kentucky Campaign*, 18; *Dispatch*, June 22, 1899. P. P. Johnston to John H. Whallen, February 5, 1897, Preston-Johnston Papers, University of Kentucky Library; Goebel to Sweeney, November 28, 1897, Bodley Collection; Z. F. Smith, *History of Kentucky* (4th rev. ed., Louisville: Prentice Press, 1901), 872. A different vote is given in the *Commercial*, June 22, 1899.

Goebel told a brother that Redwine "is an old friend of mine." They had served in the legislature together a decade earlier. An opening of a Court of Appeals seat in Redwine's district was mentioned. Goebel to Justus Goebel, July 6, 1899, Goebel Family Papers.

[16] Hughes and others, *Kentucky Campaign*, 21; *Dispatch*, June 22, 1899; *Courier-Journal*, June 23, 1899.

[17] *Dispatch*, June 24, 1899 and *Courier-Journal*, June 24-25, 1899, give the two arguments, each blaming the other side.

[18] *Courier-Journal*, June 24, 25, 1899; Hughes and others, *Kentucky Campaign*, 28-29.

[19] *Dispatch*, June 25, 1899; *Courier-Journal*, June 25, 1899; Woodson, *New Dealer*, 155. The Lexington *Herald*, June 25, 1899 gave a slightly different first ballot vote: Stone 397; Hardin 360; Goebel 331.

[20] *Dispatch*, June 27, 1899; Jacob H. Haager to Woodson, January 7, 1938, in Woodson, *First New Dealer*, 153, 154; *Courier-Journal*, June 27, 1899.

[21] *Dispatch*, June 27, 28, 1899; *Courier-Journal*, June 28, 1899; Lexington *Herald*, June 28, 1899. Again, the *Commercial*, June 28, 1899, gives a different count.

[22] Woodson, *First New Dealer*, 157; Paducah *Sun*, July 20, 1899; Hughes and others, *Kentucky Campaign*, 41, 42.

[23] *Courier-Journal*, June 28, July 1, 1899. Privately Watterson "as your personal friend" warned August Belmont in a June 30, 1899 letter that the Democrats would win—"under the operation of the Goebel law the result is not left to chance"—and the L & N should abandon their opposition to Goebel. In Arthur Younger Ford Papers, The Filson Club, Louisville.

[24] *Dispatch*, June 28, 1899; *Hazel Green Herald*, June 29, 1899.

[25] Lexington *Herald*. See August 18, October 30, July 30, August 22, 19, October 28, March 9, 1899. See also James C. Klotter, "The Breckinridges of Kentucky: Two Centuries of Leadership" (Dissertation, University of Kentucky, 1975), 204-06.

[26] *Courier-Journal*, July 12-14, 1899; Roberts to McKinley, William McKinley Papers, Manuscript Division, Library of Congress; London *Mountain Echo*, July 21, 1899.

[27] *Courier-Journal*, July 14, 1899; Bardstown *Nelson County Record*, July 14, 1899; Cobb, *Exit Laughing*, 203.

[28] London *Mountain Echo*, August 4, 1899.

[29] *Courier-Journal*, August 3, 17, 1899; Hughes and others, *That Kentucky Campaign*, 69; *Evening Post*, August 22, 1899.

[30] *Courier-Journal*, August 5, 1899; *Glasgow Times*, July 31, 1899; Paducah *Sun*, August 8, 1899.

[31] William Goebel to Justus Goebel, July 6, 1899, Goebel Family Papers.

[32] *Courier-Journal*, July 11, August 5, October 20, 1899; Woodson, *First New Dealer*, xv. Two studies of Goebel's speeches classify him as a demagogue. See Clark, "Goebel—Demagogue," 5 and Joseph G. Green, "William Goebel: Demagogue or Democrat?" *Southern Speech Journal*, XXVII (1961), 143, 148-50.

[33] In a later speech, recorded in the *Courier-Journal*, August 27, 1899, Goebel read a letter to him from August Belmont, dated August 18, 1899:

> *If, in order to gain adherents to your political ambition in the state, you endeavor to create a prejudice of the people against the L. and N. railroad, and try to excite animosity and legislation destructive to its interests, the L. and N. railroad is driven to take the best means within the law and its right to meet such attacks, and this it is now doing by bringing before the public the arguments which are at its command to counteract the evil influence of your unjustified hostility.*

[34] *Courier-Journal*, August 13, 1899; William Goebel to Justus Goebel, July 6, 1899, Goebel Family Papers.

[35] London *Mountain Echo*, September 1, 29, 1899; *Courier-Journal*, August 23, 1899; *Evening Post*, August 22, 1899.

[36] *Dispatch*, August 27, 1899.

[37] Lexington *Herald*, August 20, 1899; Cobb, *Exit Laughing*, 206-08. Theodore F. Hallam to Bettie Stevenson, March 31, 1875, March 17, 1876, Hallam Family Papers, University of Kentucky Library. Speakers for Goebel included Evan E. Settle, Ollie James, Charles K. Wheeler, Thomas S. Pettit, W. A. Helm, J. Campbell Cantrill, South Trimble, Harry V. McChesney, J. B. White and Charles C. McChord. See *Courier-Journal*, September 6, 1899.

[38] *Courier-Journal*, August 29, 1899.

[39] Lexington *Herald*, August 30, 1899; Klotter, "Breckinridges of Kentucky," 206.

[40] *Dispatch*, August 27, 1899; London *Mountain Echo*, August 4, 1899. See also Lucien Beckner Letters, Kentucky Historical Society, London *Mountain Echo*, July 7, 1899, and Stephen L. Blakely, "A Kentucky Tragedy," *Papers of the Christopher Gist Historical Society*, II (1950-51), 54.

[41] *Dispatch*, August 27, 1899; L. F. Johnson, *Famous Kentucky Tragedies and Trials*, (Cleveland: Baldwin Law Book Co., 1916), 277.

[42] *Dispatch*, September 5, October 26, 1899.

[43] Hughes and others, *That Kentucky Campaign*, 50; *Dispatch*, August 25, 1899; *Courier-Journal*, September 8, 17, October 27, November 3, 17, 1899.

[44] *Courier-Journal*, August 24, September 9, 19, 1899; London *Mountain Echo*, October 6, 1899. See also *Glasgow Times*, September 28, 1899.

[45] Quoted in *Dispatch*, November 23, 1899; *Courier-Journal*, October 3, 1899.

[46] *Courier-Journal*, July 28, September 6, 1899; Pettit to Goebel, July 8, 1899, Pettit Papers. The other nominees were: W. R. Browder (Logan County) for lieutenant governor, Samuel Graham (Marshall) for auditor, former Greenback state representative Ben C. Keyes (Callaway) for secretary of state, former Union Labor gubernatorial candidate A. H. Cardin (Crittenden) for treasurer, John T. Bashaw (Louisville) for attorney general, and John C. Southerland (Anderson) for superintendent of public instruction.

[47] Woodson, *First New Dealer*, 187; *Courier-Journal*, October 17-19, 1899.

[48] *Courier-Journal*, October 20, 25, 1899; Hughes and others, *That Kentucky Campaign*, 98. See also London *Mountain Echo*, October 27, 1899 and Paducah *Sun*, October 30, 1899.

[49] *Courier-Journal*, November 2, 3, 1899; Hughes and others, *That Kentucky Campaign*, 111; William Lindsay to W. H. Mackoy, August 5, 1899, Mackoy Family Correspondence, University of Kentucky Library. Peter Lee Atherton of Louisville told Lindsay that sound money Democrats there had either gone to the Democrats or Republicans, rather than accept Brown's free-silver stance. Lindsay Papers, University of Kentucky Library.

[50] *Courier-Journal*, October 26, 27, 1899.

[51] *Glasgow Times*, October 27, 1899.

[52] *Courier-Journal*, November 6, 7, 1899; January 29, 1900; Paducah *Sun*, November 6, 1899; *Dispatch*, November 6, 7, 1899; Henry L. Nelson, "The Kentucky 'Boss's' Desperate Campaign," *Harper's Weekly*, October 28, 1899.

[53] *Courier-Journal* November 8-10, 1899; London *Mountain Echo*, November 10, 1899; Smith, *History of Kentucky* (rev. ed.), 884; Knott, "History of Goebelism," 3d section, 17. Professor Clark, "The People, Goebel and Railroads," 44, argues that Louisville polling disputes were "hot and furious."

[54] *Dispatch*, November 10, 1899; *Courier-Journal*, November 10-18, 23, December 20, 1899; *Hazel Green Herald*, November 30, 1899. A "tissue ballot," in the Ford Papers, on examination is not tissue-thin, but parts of it are visible when folded.

[55] Bradley to McKinley, November 21, 1899, McKinley Papers.

[56] Paducah *Sun*, November 25, 1899; Hughes and others, *That Kentucky Campaign*, 84; *Courier-Journal*, December 3, 5, 1899; *Evening Post*, October 2, 1899.

[57] Quoted in Lester, "Goebel Affair," 258, 259; Taylor Interrogation, June 21, 1909 in William S. Taylor Papers (microfilm), University of Kentucky Library.

[58] *Courier-Journal*, December 7-9, 13, 1899. The certification of his election is in the

Taylor Papers, as is the original of his inaugural speech.

[59] *Ibid.*, December 15, 1899; William Goebel to Justus Goebel, December 20, 1899, Goebel Family Papers.

[60] *Courier-Journal*, January 2, 3, 10, 1900.

[61] *Ibid.*, January 5, 1900. George L. Willis, Sr., in his *Kentucky Democracy*, I, 384, offers this: "The writer has been told by the official who claims he manipulated the drawing in the House, exactly how he accomplished what he seemed then and seems yet to think was a justified fraud."

[62] *Courier-Journal*, January 2, 4, 5, 9, 16, 28, 1900; Smith, *History of Kentucky* (rev. ed.), 898.

[63] *Ibid.*, January 16, 1900; *Dispatch*, January 17, 1900.

[64] *Courier-Journal*, January 26, 27, 1900; Lexington *Herald*, January 26, 1900; *Dispatch*, January 26, 1900. Later, in a trial involving Caleb Powers, an unreliable witness, Wharton Golden, gave the following testimony: Powers told him to bring "regular mountain feudists" armed with "good Colts Forty Five" to Frankfort. Without adequate supplies for all, the Secretary of State ordered all but a select few to return home. Those remaining, according to Golden, were "to go into the legislative hall . . . and clean out them fellows [Democrats]." Golden admitted under cross-examination that Powers' stated purpose had been to collect men to serve as witnesses. See transcript of the examining trial of Caleb Powers, March 1900, 119-42, 196-99, Goebel Papers, Kentucky Historical Society.

Powers in his *My Own Story* (Indianapolis: Bobbs-Merrill Co., 1905), 121, 122, argued that the leaders agreed to bring prominent Republicans to Frankfort to protest. He was assigned the mountains and brought 1200. But he found no other sections had sent the expected numbers, so he told the men to return.

[65] *Courier-Journal*, January 29, 30, 1900. Eventually four Republicans lost their seats. Woodson, *First New Dealer*, 208.

[66] Lillard Testimony at the examining trial of Caleb Powers, 4-22, 66-68; Lillard and Chinn testimony in The Commonwealth of Kentucky vs. Caleb Powers, July 1900, 257-63, both in Goebel Papers.

[67] Testimony of T. R. Welsh, Dr. E. E. Hume, Dr. James R. Ely and Dr. John South, Ky. vs. Powers, 83, 103, 104, Goebel Papers. The bullet entered the body one-half inch above the right nipple, three inches to the right and exited three inches to the left of the spine.

[68] Hughes and others, *That Kentucky Campaign*, 201-10; *Dispatch*, January 31, February 1, 2, 1900. The constitution provides that legislative sessions be held at the seat of government, "except in case of war, insurrection or pestilence."

[69] Cobb, *Exit Laughing*, 205.

[70] *Courier-Journal*, February 5, 1900. Robert Burns Wilson eulogized Goebel in his poem "In Memory":

> . . . He was not one
> To weakly hedge along the path of life
> Afraid to be himself—His soul was strong—
> His mind like a bent bow, he never hid
> the target where his purposes were aimed,
> Like well drawn arrows, speeding straight and swift.
> He spoke his own words—rash at times—but his,
> Himself he lived and like himself he died.

Wilson concluded:
   And shall they not write, proudly, on his tomb;
   "Here sleeps a fearless champion of the poor."
Scrapbook in Beckham Collection, Kentucky Historical Society.

[71] Cobb, *Exit Laughing*, 215, 216; W. C. P. Breckinridge to Sophonisba Breckinridge, February 11, 1900, Breckinridge MSS, Vol. 506. Goebel's interment did not take place until March 13.

[72] Lester, "Goebel Affair," 446-54, 284; Hughes and others, *That Kentucky Campaign*, 259-66, 286, 294; *Courier-Journal*, December 23, 24, 27, 29, 1899, January 17, 1900. Attorney General Pratt fought his case through the courts alone and finally served out his term. Robert J. Breckinridge, Jr. was the only one of the Goebel slate not seated. Though the Louisville vote was declared void, none of the legislators from Louisville were unseated.

[73] Woodson, *First New Dealer*, 68. The story of the trials belongs elsewhere. A good source is Francis X. Busch, *They Escaped the Hangman* (Indianapolis and New York: Bobbs-Merrill Company, 1953), 13-100.

BIBLIOGRAPHICAL ESSAY

MANUSCRIPTS

Collections for this period of Kentucky history are not as numerous as historians might wish. The manuscripts in Special Collections, Margaret I. King Library, University of Kentucky, proved the most useful. On the political side, valuable items for Democratic politics appeared in the Cassius M. Clay, Jr. Collection, the Lindsay Family Papers, the Preston-Johnston Papers, the Hallam Family Papers, the Mackoy Family—all later gold Democrats—and the Goebel Family Letters. The W. O. Bradley Scrapbooks and the William S. Taylor Papers tell the Republican side in less detail, whereas the papers of the Populist Thomas S. Pettit furnish more background information than political items.

In the same library several collections offered insights into the social, cultural, and economic life of the times, in particular the Laura Clay Papers, John J. Dickey Diary, Joseph U. Milward Diary, Fox Family Papers, Edwin Green Bedford Diaries, William Moody Pratt Diaries, Grundy Family Papers, Seaton Collection, Evans Papers, and the G. C. Swetman Country Store Records.

The Filson Club, Louisville, provided additional manuscripts in both political and non-political areas. In the latter, the German Club Record Book, Guardian Angel Society Minute Book, Halsey Collection, and Cassius M. Clay Collection stand out. Some very interesting information on Republican politics in the 1890s is in the George D. Todd Papers; the Temple Bodley Papers and Arthur Younger Ford Papers contain some political material. The Knott Collection, Kentucky Library, Western Kentucky University, reveals the literary side of Proctor Knott better than the political. In the Kentucky Historical Society, Frankfort, trial transcripts of the Goebel cases are in the Goebel Papers. Other collections of interest are the scrapbooks of the Beckham Collection, the Executive Journals, and the Lucien Beckner Letters.

In the Library of Congress, Manuscripts Division, the best source on Kentucky political life remains the unwieldy and massive Breckinridge Family Papers, which are filled with patronage requests as well as major political

507

correspondence. While a few welcome items appear, the Henry Watterson Papers are, in the main, disappointing. Other collections include the Benjamin H. Bristow Papers, the William McKinley Papers, the Thomas J. Clay Papers, and the Joseph Holt Papers. For additional references in this and related areas see the footnotes in various chapters.

NEWSPAPERS

Henry Watterson's Louisville *Courier-Journal* garnered a large state and national audience almost from its birth in 1868. Views expressed in the paper were widely reprinted and its weekly edition went to a sizeable number of Kentucky households. For these reasons, of the more than forty papers examined, it proved the single most valuable newspaper used in the 1868-1900 period. Another excellent paper, the *Louisville Commercial*, gave readers the Republican viewpoint on affairs throughout most of the era. Richard Knott's *Evening Post* followed its editor's independent cause while the Louisville *Dispatch* during the 1899-1900 period was widely distributed by anti-Goebel forces.

J. Stoddard Johnston and others made the Frankfort *Kentucky Yeoman* the chief philosophical rival to Watterson's brand of Democracy. In its various editions—depending on the legislative sessions—it gave a detailed account of Bourbon politics and was used from 1865 to 1885. The Republican rival in the capital city, the *Commonwealth*, died in the early 1870s.

In Lexington the *Observer and Reporter* for the early decades of this study, the daily and weekly *Transcript* and the *Daily Press* for the middle ones, and the *Press-Transcript* and *Morning Herald* for the latter 1890s give a detailed account of Bluegrass life, seen through Democratic eyes. Samuel J. Roberts' *Kentucky Leader* defended the Republicans.

Weeklies, for the most part, dominated the smaller city presses, echoed the urban dailies' views, and provided less detailed information. But each portrayed its section's unique ways. In the West the Hickman *Courier*, Paducah *Sun*, and Hopkinsville *South Kentuckian* supplied material; in the east the Middlesboro *Weekly Herald*, the Alliance-backed *Hazel Green Herald*, and the London *Mountain Echo* did the same. Northern Kentuckians often read their news in Ohio papers; the Cincinnati *Gazette* for the 1860s and 1870s, the Cincinnati *Commercial* for the same period, and the Cincinnati *Weekly Times* for 1884 gave Kentucky news a prominent place in their columns. On the Kentucky side of the river the *Weekly Maysville Eagle* noticed regional affairs. No files of any black or Populist newspapers have been located.

Information was also gathered from these papers: the New York *Tribune*, the Winchester *Democrat*, the Frankfort *Capital*, the *Lexington Standard*, the *Nelson County Record*, the *Pineville News*, the *Glasgow Times*, the *Hartford*

Herald, the Stanford *Interior Journal*, the Paris *Kentuckian*, the *Woodford Weekly*, the Midway *Blue-Grass Clipper*, and the *Louisville Republican*. Also see Chapter XIII.

PUBLIC DOCUMENTS

While the Kentucky House and Senate *Journals*, 1865-1900, do not usually include a verbatim account of legislative debates, they do provide the material necessary to follow voting patterns, parliamentary maneuvering, and other developments. The *Acts of the General Assembly*, 1865-1900, show the results of some of the legislative battles.

In many ways more valuable, especially in non-political affairs, *Kentucky Documents*, 1865-1900, offers reports of various state agencies, including the superintendent of public instruction, the various asylums, the auditor, the treasurer, the railroad commission (after 1880), the inspector of mines (following 1884), the agricultural bureau, and others. In many cases these reports were separately printed as well.

On the national level the ninth through the twelfth censuses have a vast amount of raw data on a large number of subjects, including population changes, education, manufacturing, mortality rates, and agricultural patterns. The 1870 census should be used with care. At the local level muncipal reports and ordinances contain information on police and fire departments and other urban activities. The struggle with the 1890 constitution can be followed in the huge and often dreary *Official Record of the Proceedings and Debates in the Constitutional Convention of Kentucky . . . 1890* (4 vols. Frankfort: E. Polk Johnson, 1890).

AUTOBIOGRAPHIES AND REMINISCENCES

Henry Watterson's *"Marse Henry": An Autobiography* (2 vols., New York: George H. Doran, 1919) tells less than it might and has little chronology. Still, the diligent reader finds hints on political life and character sketches there. Somewhat less useful are Champ Clark, *My Quarter Century of American Politics* (2 vols., New York: Harper and Brothers, 1920), Basil W. Duke's *Reminiscences* (Garden City, N. Y.: Doubleday, Page and Co., 1911), and George G. Perkins, *A Kentucky Judge* (Washington, D. C.: W. F. Roberts, 1931).

Life in smaller towns remains difficult to portray but useful material on this matter is in Arthur Krock, *Myself When Young: Growing Up in the 1890's* (Boston: Little-Brown and Co., 1973), Pattie French Witherspoon, *Through Two Administrations: Character Sketches of Kentucky* (Chicago: T. B. Arnold, 1897), Gordon Wilson, *Fidelity Folks: A Visit to a Self-Suffi-*

cient Kentucky Village (Cynthiana: Hobson Book Press, 1946), Kent Eubank, *Horse and Buggy Days* (Kansas City, Mo.: Burton Publishing Co., 1927), Caleb Powers, *My Own Story* (Indianapolis: Bobbs-Merrill Co., 1905), *History of Corporal Fess Whitaker* (Louisville: Standard Printing Co., 1918), and Gabriel C. Banks, *Back to the Mountains* (n. p., 1964).

The titles describe the subject covered in William A. Pusey, *A Doctor of the 1870's and 80's* (Baltimore: Charles C. Thomas, 1932), Abby M. Roach, "Then-Girlhood in Louisville in the Nineties," *Filson Club History Quarterly,* XXXVII (1963); and Sam Johnson, "Life in the Kentucky Mountains," *Independent,* LXV (1908). Abraham Flexner, *I Remember* (New York: Simon and Shuster, 1940) concerns his childhood in Louisville, while *The Autobiography of Nathaniel Southgate Shaler* (Boston and New York: Houghton Mifflin Co., 1909) chiefly deals with antebellum life but does include Shaler's letters of a later time. See also *The Life of Cassius Marcellus Clay. Memoirs, Writings and Speeches* (Cincinnati: J. Fletcher Brennan & Co., 1886). A useful travel account is Charles D. Warner, *Studies in the South and West* (New York: Harper & Brothers, 1889).

REFERENCE WORKS

A surprising amount of information can be gathered from *Appleton's Annual Cyclopaedia and Register of Important Events,* 1865-1900, which gives a yearly summary of events in the state. Material concerning locally prominent leaders in Kentucky life is found in the *Biographical Encyclopaedia of Kentucky* (2 vols., Cincinnati: J. M. Armstrong and Co., 1878), H. Levin, comp., *The Lawyers and Lawmakers of Kentucky* (Chicago: Lewis Publishing Co., 1897), and *Biographical Cyclopedia of the Commonwealth of Kentucky* (Chicago: John M. Gresham Co., 1896).

Leaders prominent on a national level are usually included in *The Dictionary of American Biography,* Allen Johnson and Dumas Malone, eds. (20 vols., New York: Charles Scribner's Sons, 1928-36). G. Glenn Clift, *Governors of Kentucky, 1792 to 1942* (Cynthiana: Hobson Press, 1942) gives a brief account of each man's life.

The *Kentucky Gazetteer and Business Directory, 1887-8* (Detroit: R. L. Polk and Co., 1887), and in other years, describes each town, its businesses and some characteristics. Kentucky newspapers and their circulation can be located in *American Newspaper Directory* (New York: George P. Rowell and Co., 1872) and *American Newspaper Annual* (Philadelphia: N. W. Ayers and Sons, 1897).

BIOGRAPHIES

While historians have available some very good biographies of Kentucky leaders, overall there is a surprising paucity of studies. The closest detailed examination of a politician on the state level is Arndt M. Stickles' friendly *Simon Bolivar Buckner: Borderland Knight* (Chapel Hill: University of North Carolina Press, 1940) and Urey Woodson's equally warm *The First New Dealer: William Goebel* (Louisville: Standard Press, 1939). All the other governors await their biographer, with Maurice H. Thatcher, *Stories and Speeches of William O. Bradley* (Lexington: Transylvania Printing Co., 1916) offering some hope. William C. Davis' *Breckinridge: Statesman, Soldier, Symbol* (Baton Rouge: Louisiana State University Press, 1974) studies John C. Breckinridge's Kentucky career from 1868 until his death in 1875. Similarly, Paul E. Fuller, *Laura Clay and the Woman's Rights Movement* (Lexington: University Press of Kentucky, 1975) does an excellent job of scrutinizing Clay's career in this period, but her chief work came after 1900. Three top-notch biographies focus mainly on their subjects' national careers—to the exclusion of the state—and prove useful in that regard: James A. Barnes, *John G. Carlisle: Financial Statesman* (New York: Dodd, Mead and Co., 1931) is the oldest and least critical; Joseph F. Wall, *Henry Watterson: Reconstructed Rebel* (New York: Oxford University Press, 1956) has the best subject with which to work and handles "Marse Henry" well, but is brief in some spots; and Ross A. Webb, *Benjamin Helm Bristow: Border State Politician* (Lexington: University Press of Kentucky, 1969) displays a good grasp of both the local and national setting. Arthur Krock's *The Editorials of Henry Watterson* (New York: George H. Doran, 1923) is still valuable.

Away from politics, James Lane Allen has attracted several writers. Grant C. Knight's *James Lane Allen and the Genteel Tradition* (Chapel Hill: University of North Carolina Press, 1935) continues to be the best study of the complicated Allen. John W. Townsend's *James Lane Allen* (Louisville: Courier-Journal Printing Co., 1927) offers generally sympathetic ideas about Allen by one close to him. A briefer survey is William K. Bottorff, *James Lane Allen* (New York: Twayne Publishing, Inc., 1964). *Robert Burns Wilson*, by J. Winston Coleman, Jr. (Lexington: Winburn Press, 1956) studies that poet-artist in a short, sound sketch. Otto A. Rothert, *The Story of a Poet: Madison Cawein*, Filson Club Publications, No. 30 (Louisville: J. P. Morton and Co., 1921) includes a collection of letters and interpretations by one who knew Cawein well.

Articles dealing with the artists include the well-researched work by Justus Bier, "Carl C. Brenner: A German American Landscapist," *American-German Review*, XVII (1951); John W. Townsend, "Paul Sawyier, Kentucky Artist: Some Recollections of Him," *Filson Club History Quarterly*, XXXIII (1959); and Caroline W. Berry, "Kentucky Honors Robert Burns Wilson," *The Regis-*

ter of the Kentucky Historical Society, XV (1917). Studies of two politicians not known for their consistency are Hambleton Tapp, "Incidents in the Life of Frank Wolford," *Filson Club History Quarterly*, X (1936), Louis Hartz, "John M. Harlan in Kentucky, 1855-1877," *ibid.*, XIV (1940), and David G. Farrelly, "John Harlan's One Day Diary," *ibid.*, XXIV (1950).

OTHER BOOKS AND ARTICLES

Standard one-volume studies of Kentucky are Thomas D. Clark's *A History of Kentucky* (rev. ed., Lexington: John Bradford Press, 1960) and his *Kentucky: Land of Contrast* (New York: Harper and Row, 1968). The second volume of William E. Connelley and E. Merton Coulter, *History of Kentucky* ed. by Charles Kerr (5 vols., Chicago: American Historical Society, 1922) considers the 1865-1900 period. Other multi-volumed works used are Frederick A. Wallis and Hambleton Tapp, *A Sesqui-Centennial History of Kentucky* (4 vols., Louisville and Hopkinsville: Historical Record Association, 1945) and E. Polk Johnson, *A History of Kentucky and Kentuckians* (3 vols., Chicago: Lewis Publishing Co., 1912). Histories published before 1900 are discussed in Chapter XIII.

Francis B. Simkins and Charles P. Roland, *A History of the South* (4th ed., New York: Alfred A. Knopf, 1972) and C. Vann Woodward, *Origins of the New South, 1877-1913* (Baton Rouge: Louisiana State University Press, 1951) delightfully furnish the regional setting for Kentucky. The national, non-political atmosphere can be reviewed in Arthur M. Schlesinger, *The Rise of the City, 1878-1898* (New York: Macmillan, 1933), Fred A. Shannon, *The Farmer's Last Frontier: Agriculture, 1860-1897* (New York: Harper and Row, 1945), and H. Wayne Morgan, *Unity and Culture: The United States, 1877-1900* (Baltimore: Penguin Books, 1971). George L. Willis, Sr., *Kentucky Democracy* (3 vols., Louisville Democratic Historical Society, 1935) and the briefer E. A. Jonas, *A History of the Republican Party in Kentucky* (Louisville: J. P. Morton Co., 1929) display a political bias by two men intimately connected with political affairs in the era.

Many of the numerous county and city histories of Kentucky give the post-Civil War era only a passing reference. Among the most useful ones for this study were Robert Peter, *History of Fayette County, Kentucky, with an Outline Sketch of the Blue Grass Region*, edited by William H. Perrin (Chicago: O. L. Baskin and Co., 1882); J. Stoddard Johnston, *Memorial History of Louisville* (2 vols., Chicago: American Biographical Publishing Co., 1896); Otto A. Rothert, *A History of Muhlenburg County* (Louisville: J. P. Morton and Co., 1913); Charles M. Meacham, *A History of Christian County, Kentucky* (Nashville: Marshall and Bruce Co., 1930); and Kentucky Writers

Project, *Union County: Past and Present* (Louisville: Schulmann Publishing Co., 1941).

The older, standard work on the Civil War in the state, Coulter's *The Civil War and Readjustment in Kentucky* (Chapel Hill: University of North Carolina Press, 1926), offers some interpretations that have been challenged by Lowell Harrison, *The Civil War in Kentucky* (Lexington: University Press of Kentucky, 1975) and Ross A. Webb, "Kentucky: 'Pariah Among the Elect,' " in Richard O. Curry, ed., *Radicalism, Racism and Party Alignment: The Border States During Reconstruction* (Baltimore: Johns Hopkins Press, 1969). In trying to balance the pro-Confederate history of his era, Thomas Speed's *The Union Cause in Kentucky, 1860-1865* (New York: G. P. Putnam's Sons, 1907) went too far toward the other extreme.

The decade following the war requires further investigation. Studies making a start in this direction include Thomas L. Connelley, "Neo Confederatism or Power Vacuum: Post War Kentucky Politics Reappraised," *The Register of the Kentucky Historical Society*, LXIV (1966); Victor B. Howard, "The Kentucky Press and the Negro Testimony Controversy, 1866-1872," *ibid.*, LXXI (1973); Howard, "The Kentucky Press and the Black Suffrage Controversy, 1865-1872," *Filson Club History Quarterly*, XLVII (1973); James D. Bennett, "Some Notes on Christian County Grange Activities," *The Register of the Kentucky Historical Society*, LXIV (1966); and W. A. Low, "The Freedmen's Bureau in the Border States," in Curry, ed., *Radicalism, Racism and Party Alignment*.

Political events of the last five years of the nineteenth century have attracted a considerable amount of attention, but the period prior to that has not. Emmett V. Mittlebeeler, "The Great Kentucky Absconsion," *Filson Club History Quarterly*, XXVII (1953), on the Tate scandal, and Stickles' *Buckner*, previously cited, give some insights. On the election of 1895 see John E. Wiltz, "The 1895 Election: A Watershed in Kentucky Politics," *Filson Club History Quarterly*, XXXVII (1963), and his "APA-ISM in Kentucky and Elsewhere," *The Register of the Kentucky Historical Society*, LVI (1958).

While writings on Goebel and 1899-1900 events have regularly appeared, nothing definitive has yet emerged. Woodson, *First New Dealer* and Robert E. Hughes and others, *That Kentucky Campaign, or the Law, the Ballot, and the People in the Goebel-Taylor Contest* (Cincinnati: Robert Clarke Co., 1900) have been supplemented by numerous articles including Thomas D. Clark, "The People, William Goebel, and the Kentucky Railroads," *Journal of Southern History*, V (1939), Clark, "William Goebel-Southern Demagogue," *University of Kentucky Research Club Bulletin*, VII (1941), Joseph G. Green, "William Goebel: Demagogue or Democrat?," *Southern Speech Journal*,

XXVII (1961), Nicholas C. Burckel, "William Goebel and the Campaign for Railroad Regulation in Kentucky, 1888-1900," *Filson Club History Quarterly*, XLVIII (1974), and Stephen L. Blakely, "A Kentucky Tragedy," *Papers of the Christopher Gist Historical Society*, II (1950-51).

Goebel's assassination was only part of the violence that plagued the state in the period. Older studies, based in part on personal knowledge and interviews, still yield valuable information: L. F. Johnston, *Famous Kentucky Tragedies and Trials* (Cleveland: Baldwin Law Book Co., 1916), and Charles G. Mutzenberg, *Kentucky's Famous Feuds and Tragedies* (New York: R. F. Ferris and Co., 1917). A highly readable account is Virgil C. Jones, *The Hatfields and the McCoys* (Chapel Hill: University of North Carolina Press, 1948). Other feuds, and the mountain area in general, attracted attention, resulting in articles by S. S. MacClintock, "The Kentucky Mountains and Their Feuds," *American Journal of Sociology*, VII (1901); R. L. McClure, "The Maze of a Kentucky Feud," *The Independent*, September 17, 1903; and C. T. Revere, "Beyond the Gap: The Breeding Ground of Feuds," *Outing Magazine*, February 1907. William H. Harney gave his fellow eastern Kentuckians a sympathetic hearing in *The Mountain People of Kentucky* (Cincinnati: Roessler, 1906).

Lack of education contributed to the violence; the attempts to improve the state's educational status can be followed in Barksdale Hamlett, *History of Education in Kentucky* (Frankfort: Department of Education, 1914), which includes extracts from the official reports; Moses E. Ligon, *A History of Public Education in Kentucky* (Lexington: Bureau of School Service, 1942); and Frank L. McVey, *The Gates Open Slowly: A History of Education in Kentucky* (Lexington: University of Kentucky Press, 1949). Kentucky colleges have been favored with good histories; one of the best is James F. Hopkins, *The University of Kentucky: Origins and Early Years* (Lexington: University of Kentucky Press, 1951). Others abound.

The reading public found Kentucky authors rising to prominence in the period. Their story is presented in the form of brief sketches and then excerpts from their works in John W. Townsend, *Kentucky in American Letters, 1784-1912* (2 vols., Cedar Rapids, Iowa: Torch Press, 1913). Works depending heavily on Townsend, but updating his analysis are Sister Mary C. Browning, *Kentucky Authors: A History of Kentucky Literature* (Evansville: Keller-Crescent Co., 1968) and Ish Richey, *Kentucky Literature, 1784-1963* (Tompkinsville: Monroe County Press, 1963). Irving Sablosky, *American Music* (Chicago: University of Chicago Press, 1969) chiefly focuses on the more classical forms, as opposed to Sigmund Spaeth's *A History of Popular Music in America* (New York: Random House, 1948). Rexford Newcomb,

Architecture in Old Kentucky (Urbana: University of Illinois, 1953) briefly touches on post-war trends.

The commercial side of Kentucky life comes alive in the case of railroads in Leonard P. Curry's *Rail Routes South: Louisville's Fight for the Southern Market* (Lexington: University of Kentucky Press, 1969); in the case of general stores, in Thomas D. Clark's delightful *Pills, Petticoats and Plows: The Southern Country Store* (Norman: University of Oklahoma Press, 1944); and in the case of labor, Bill L. Weaver's "Louisville's Labor Disturbance, July 1877," *Filson Club History Quarterly*, XLVIII (1974). Good studies of two generally neglected peoples are Thomas D. Clark, "Southern Common Folk After the Civil War," *South Atlantic Quarterly*, XLIV (1945) and Herbert A. Thomas, "Victims of Circumstance: Negroes in a Southern Town [Lexington], 1865-1880," *The Register of the Kentucky Historical Society*, LXXI (1973). Contemporary studies of horseracing appeared in "The Running Turf in America," *Harper's Monthly Magazine*, XLI (1870) and William H. Bishop, "Among the Blue-Grass Trotters," *Harpers Magazine*, LXVII (1883). James G. Speed inspected the Kentucky spirit in his "The Kentuckian," *Century Magazine*, LIX (1900).

Works produced by the various projects of the Works Progress Administration vary in quality, but furnish needed information in neglected areas. See *Fairs and Fair Makers in Kentucky* (2 vols., Frankfort: Kentucky Department of Agriculture, 1942), *Medicine and Its Development in Kentucky* (Louisville: Standard Printing Co., 1940), and *The Military History of Kentucky* (Frankfort: State Journal, 1939).

OTHER UNPUBLISHED MATERIAL

The relative scarcity of published monographic material in this period forces the historian to turn to theses, dissertations, and other scholarly sources as yet unpublished. The result is often pleasing.

In the field of politics, Edward F. Prichard, Jr.'s excellent senior thesis at Princeton University (1935), "Popular Political Movements in Kentucky, 1875-1900," is based on careful reading of a good cross-section of Kentucky newspapers. The eventual effect of these earlier movements is examined briefly in William S. Lester's long manuscript in the Kentucky Historical Society, Frankfort. His "The Goebel Affair" surveys standard printed sources from a mildly anti-Goebel viewpoint. Richard W. Knott's "History of Goebelism," an unpublished paper in The Filson Club, Louisville, is even more critical of Goebel, written as it was by a bitter opponent of his. Rhea A. Taylor, "Conflicts in Kentucky as Shown by the Constitutional Convention of 1890-1891" (Dissertation, University of Chicago, 1948) and James T.

Wills, "Louisville Politics, 1891-1897" (M. A. thesis, University of Louisville, 1966) give some insights into their particular areas of study. Two good M. A. theses scan the careers of prominent politicians: Will D. Gilliam, Jr., "The Political Career of Benjamin Helm Bristow" (Indiana University, 1930) and T. Ross Moore, "The Congressional Career of James B. Beck, 1867-1875" (University of Kentucky, 1950). A chapter in James C. Klotter's "The Breckinridges of Kentucky: Two Centuries of Leadership" (Dissertation, University of Kentucky, 1975) examines the career of W. C. P. Breckinridge.

In more specialized areas, some well-researched dissertations are available for study, including Herbert Finch, "Organized Labor in Louisville, Kentucky, 1880-1914" (University of Kentucky, 1965); James P. Sullivan, "Louisville and Her Southern Alliance, 1865-1890" (University of Kentucky, 1965); and an older, more biased study, J. J. Hornback, "Economic Development in Kentucky Since 1860" (University of Michigan, 1932). Offering information on such varied topics as sports, agriculture, and commerce are the briefer University of Kentucky M. A. theses of Elizabeth R. Clotfelter, "The Agricultural History of Bourbon County, Kentucky, Prior to 1900" (1953); John D. Philbrick, "Text Book Publications of John P. Morton and Company of Louisville, Kentucky, From 1867 through 1870" (1948); Margaret Yent, "A History of the Chesapeake and Ohio Railway" (1931); Milton D. Feinstein, "History and Development of Football at the University of Kentucky, 1877-1920" (1941); and William B. Strother, "Negro Culture in Lexington, Kentucky" (1939). Pier L. G. DePaela studies labor in his 1971 University of Louisville M. A. thesis, "Management and Organized Labor Relations of the Louisville and Nashville Railroad During the Depression Year 1893."

INDEX

A & M College: *See* Agricultural and Mechanical College

Adams, Silas: contender for U.S. Senate, 252; defeated for speaker of General Assembly, 326; defeated for U.S. House, 337

Aftermath: See James Lane Allen

Agricultural and Mechanical College: becomes coeducational, 90; early football games, 112-113; becomes independent, 159; independence requested by Blackburn, 199; effect of 1873 Depression, 199; reorganized, 200; located in Lexington, 200; dedicatory address by Watterson, 200; referred to as state college, 200; student regulations, 200; typical student schedule, 200-202; student pranks, 202; extracurricular activities, 202; curriculum, 202; tuition, 203; Morrill-Nelson Act accepted by General Assembly, 331; size of football players (1890's), 479 n.26; endowment for, 486 n.21, *See also* Colleges

agriculture: decline of, 148; development of, 294-299; size of farms, 294; land prices, 294; soundness and diversity of economy, 294-295; production (1870-1900), 295; livestock production, 295; farm mortgages, 297-298; reliability of statistics on, 491 n.1; value of farms (Indiana, 1890), 491 n.2

Ainsle, George: Louisville social and economic leader, 308

Alford, Mitchell Cary: Democratic nominee for lieutenant governor, 317

Allen, James Lane: on Negro inferiority, 92; on Bluegrass elite, 95; on horseracing, 103; on court day, 110; career of, 269-270; dualism in, 270; evaluation of, 270; on postwar architecture, 285. *Works: Flute and Violin and Other Kentucky Tales*, 270; *The Blue Grass Region of Kentucky*, 270; *A Kentucky Cardinal* 270; *The Choir In-*

visible 270; *Summers in Arcady*, 270; *Reign of Law*, 270

Allen, William B.: *History of Kentucky* published, 272

Alliance: *See* Farmers' Alliance

Almshouse (Louisville): services described, 131

American Protective Association: role in 1895 election, 496 n.6

American Woman Suffrage Association, 87-88

Amis-Strong feud, 385-386. *See also* feuds; lawlessness

amnesty. *See* pardons

Anderson County: against Toll Gate War, 407

Anthony, Susan B.: speaking tours, 87

Anti-Republican politics, Kentucky's postwar switch to, 4

architecture, postwar: Italian villa style, 283; common people's architecture, 284-285; stylistic excess, 284; eclectic style, 284; Ky. architects, 284; first skyscraper in Louisville, 284; mountain styles, 285; James Lane Allen on, 285

art in Kentucky: evaluation of, 292-293

artists: 285-293; Samuel Woodson Price, 285; Edward Troye, 285; Paul Sawyier, 285, 289-292; Robert Burns Wilson, 285, 289; Carl Brenner, 285-289; Frank Duvenek, 285-286

Asbury College: enrollment, 203; tuition, 203

Asbury, Reverend J. W.: nominee for register of land office, 215

Ashland Baseball Club: organized, 111. *See also* baseball

Ashland Coal and Iron Railway Company. *See* mining, origins of.

"Assassination". *See* Judge John Milton Elliott; William Goebel. *See also* feuds, lawlessness

Atherton, John M.: reaction to Contest Committee Hearings, 446. *See also* election of 1899

INDEX

paign smears against, 169-170; elected governor, 170; inaugurated governor, 172; appeal for reform, 173; on fiscal reform, 173, 175; on court fraud, 175-176; on circuit courts, 176; on lunatic asylums, 176; on property valuation, 176; on budget deficits, 176; on prison reforms, 178, 182; calls for new penitentiery, 178; on prison conditions, 178; pardons by, 180; pardons opposed, 180; appeal to General Assembly (1882), 181; on federal grant for river improvements, 182-183; on river improvements, 182; advocates local school tax, 193; requests A & M College's independence, 199; Democratic leaders displeased with, 211-213; unpopular with Democratic Convention (1883), 213-215; passage of Railroad Commission Act, 301; additional Railroad Act passed, 301; and Carter County Regulators, 386; sketch of, 461-462; free silver issue, 484 n. 1; defense of pardon record, 484 n.9

blacks. See Negroes
Blaine-Cleveland Race: 223-228; state Republican party active in, 223-224; state Democratic party active in, 223; campaign abuses, 224. See also Election of 1884 (presidential)

Blaine, E. R.: candidate for clerk of Court of Appeals, 320
Blaine, James G.: criticized by Watterson (1884), 224; secret marriage of, 487, 488 n.22

Blair, Frank P. Jr.: advocate of Liberal Republican movement, 118, 119; family of, 479 n.2
Blair, John G.: elected president of Farmers' Alliance, 314; organized Kentucky Populists, 315; Populist nominee for Clerk of Court of Appeals, 320; Populist nominee for governor, 436
Blanford, Charles: Republican nominee for auditor, 319, 320; elected speaker of General Assembly (1896), 356
"Bloody Shirt": in Democratic campaign (1876), 150; Bradley on, 496 n.4

Bloom, Nathan: Louisville economic leader, 308

Blooms of the Berry. See Madison Cawein
Bluegrass Chautauqua: description of, 108
Blue Grass Region of Kentucky, The: See James Lane Allen

Blue Grass Temperance Convention: agitation of, 129. See also Prohibition party; temperance movement
Blue, Rep. James B.: bill for Kentucky River locks and dams proposed and defeated, 146; poem bill about, 146; Kentucky River improvement popularized, 154

"Board of Equalization": See taxes, property

Bolling, Richard R.: leader of "Conservative" party (1886), 16
Booth, Edwin: performances in Louisville, 97

Bourbon Democrats: centered in Bluegrass, 33; principles of, 33, 35; suspicions of reform, 35; different from Deep South Bourbons, 35-36; opposed Freedmen's Bureau, 35; opposes industrialization, 36; uniqueness of, 36; reaction to Liberal Republican movement, 121; favors independent Democratic ticket, 122; angered by Leslie, 128; threatened by Panic of 1873, 142; opposes reforms in General Assembly (1876), 145; strength at Convention (1887), 228

Bowden, James H.: selected Superior Court Judge, 184; selected Chief Justice of Superior Court, 184
Bowles, Samuel: advocate of Liberal Republican movement, 118, 119
Bowman, John B.: president of A & M College, 199
Boyd County: Regulators in, 386
Boyd, John R.: opposes Goebel, 434
Boyd, Robert: nominee for lieutenant governor, 134; nominee for U.S. Senate, 157
Boyle, St. John: candidate for Court of Appeals, 337; Republican nominee for U.S. Senate, 365

519

INDEX

Bradley, Solomon: in Martin-Tolliver feud, 388
Bradley, Gov. William O'Connell ("Billy O.B."): opposes social equality for races, 92; defeated for U. S. Congress, 123; chairman of Republican state convention (1879), 161; candidate for attorney general, 162; declines attorney general nomination, 162; in campaign (1879), 166-169; criticized by Watterson, 218; nominated by Republicans for governor (1887), 231; acceptance speech for governor's nomination, 231-232; debate with Buckner, 232-234; defeated for U.S. Senate, 245; Republican nominee for governor (1895), 349; debate with Hardin, 351; elected governor, 353-355; inauguration of, 355; inaugural address, 355; address to General Assembly (1896), 355-356; calls out State Guard, 359; opposed by Silverites, 359-360; calls special session (1897), 365; veto of Goebel Bill overridden, 371; evaluation of administration, 376; calls for end to Toll Gate War, 407; boycotts Republican convention (1899), 425; campaigns for Taylor, 437-439; appeals to blacks (election of 1899), 437-439; orders State Guard to Louisville, 440; requests Federal troops (election of 1899), 443; defeated for U.S. Senate, 444; in Contest Committee hearings (election of 1899), 446; appeals to Contest Committee, 449; sketch of, 463, 483 n.34; in Republican National Convention (1880), 487 n.1; on "Bloody Shirt" appeals, 496 n.4; and the APA, 496 n.6; Watterson on, 497 n.10
Brakeman's Union, 311
Bramlette, Gov. Thomas Elliott: thirteenth amendment, 2; pardons policy, 9; leads opposition to Burbridge (1864), 12; favors repeal of expatriation acts, 13; leader of "Conservative" Party, 16; Union Democrat leader, 20; on lawlessness, 379-380; sketch of, 460; party of, 483 n.40

Branch Penitentiary (Eddyville): site purchase authorized, 223. See also prisons
Breathitt County: violence in, 385-387; Hargis-Cockrell-Marcum-Callahan feud, 395-400; State Guard sent to, 398; Gov. McCreary's report to the legislature, 499 n.12. See also feuds, lawlessness
Breckinridge, Desha: editor of Lexington Morning Herald, 279; in Spanish-American War, 376
Breckinridge, Maj. Gen. Joseph Cabell: in Spanish-American War, 374; at Camp Thomas, 376
Breckinridge, Judge Robert J.: law lecturer at Centre College, 204; on bitterness in Democratic State Convention (1891), 319; Democratic nominee for attorney general (1899), 423; Separate Coach Bill vote, 494 n.19; not seated (election 1899), 505 n.72
Breckinridge, Sophonisba: first woman lawyer, 90
Breckinridge, William Campbell Preston: opposes social equality for races, 92; at Democratic Convention (1871), 38; attends a "hunt," 103; nominates "Elder" Joseph Desha Pickett for superintendent of public instruction, 164; in campaign (1879), 166; advocate for public education, 193; in presidential election of 1884, 226; editor of Lexington Morning Herald, 279; Madeline Pollard affair, 337; defeated for U.S. Congress (1894), 337; in Democratic National Convention (1896), 362-363; in Elliott assassination trail, 402; opposes Goebel after nomination, 424; joins Brown Democrats, 428; criticizes Goebel, 433; on Republican victory, 411; in Contest Committee hearings (election of 1899), 446; appeals to Contest Committee, 449; on Taylor after Goebel's death, 451; Madeline Pollard trail, 494 n.31
Brenner, Carl, 285; early life, 286; at Philadelphia Exposition, 286-289; at Louisville Industrial Exposition, 286; friendship with Gov. Knott, 289; in-

520

Buford, Thomas: in assassination of Judge John Milton Elliott, 401

Bunch, Judge John T.: contender for Democratic gubernatorial nominee (1871), 37

Burbridge, Maj. Gen. Stephen Gano: retaliations for guerillas, 7; executions of CSA prisoners; 7; interference in election of 1864, 12; issue in 1865 election, 13; General Assembly attempts to try, 22; public resentment of, 24; evaluation of, 469 n.12

Burke, John W.: Republican nominee for superintendent of public instruction, 426

burlesque: See theatre, burlesque

burley, white: origins of 296-297; effect on agriculture, 297

Burnam, A. Rollins: elected Appellate Court judge, 364

Burnam, Curtis E.: contender for gubernatorial nomination (1879), 161; temporary chairman of Republican State Convention (1887), 229; in Constitution Convention (1890-1891), 260

Burnett, County Judge John: in Amis-Strong feud, 385

Caldwell, Col. Isaac: opposes Cincinnati southern railroad, 55

Callahan, Sheriff Ed; in Hargis feud, 396-397, 400; killed, 400

Camp Collier (Lexington) 374

Camp George H. Thomas; 374

Cantrill, James E.: candidate for lieutenant governor, 163; swears in Goebel, 450; Contest Board Hearings, 453

Cardin, A. H.: Union Labor party nominee for governor, 232; in 1899, 503 n.46

Cardwell, Police Judge Jerry: in Hargis feud, 396-397

Carlisle, John G.: 1871 Democratic nominee for lieutenant governor, 37, 57; elected to U.S. Congress (1881), 211; presides at Democratic State Convention (1887), 228; re-elected to Congress (1888), 248-249; Speaker of U.S. House, 249; elected to U.S. Senate (1889), 251-252; recommended for

presidential nomination by Watterson, 329; appointed Secretary of Treasury, 331; anti-free silver, 348; contender for U.S. Senate nomination (1896), 356; Covington incident, 364

Carroll, A.J.: elected speaker of General Assembly (1894), 333; in General Assembly (1896), 356

Carroll, John D.: in Commission to conform statutes to 1891 Constitution, 268; appointed to Statutory Commission, 326

Carter County: Regulators in, 386-387

Caruth, Asher Graham: in Martin-Tolliver feud, 390

Castleman, Col. John Breckinridge: Louisville Legion sent to quell James-Walton disturbance, 359; in Sp. Am. War, 373

Catholics: numbers of in 1890, 71

Catt, Carrie Chapman: speaking tours, 87

Cawein, Madison: career of, 275; published works, 275; evaluation of, 275; *Works: Blooms of the Berry*, 275; *Myth and Romance*, 275

Cecil, J.G.: Dem. nominee for register of land office (1883), 215

Central Ky. Lunatic Asylum: established, 130; act improving 1874, 130; See also Eleemosynary Institutions

Central University: in football games, 113; curriculum, 202; medical enrollment, 203; department established, 204. See also colleges

Centre College: football games, 112; curriculum, 202; enrollment, 203; tuition, 203; law school lectures, 204; See also colleges

Cerulean Springs: description of, 108

Chant of the Woodland Spirit: See Robert Burns Wilson

Chautauqua: description of, 108-109

Chesapeake, Ohio and Southwestern Railroad: consolidation with L&N opposed, 334

Chinn, Col. Jack P.: witness to Goebel shooting, 447

Choir Invisible, The: See James Lane Allen

cholera: epidemic of 1877, 84

crime: Kentucky's relative standing (1890), 408

Crittenden, Gen. Thomas L.: leader of "Conservative" party (1866), 16

Culbertson, William W.: elected to U.S. Congress (1882), 211

Cumberland Gap: railroad effect on, 304-305

Cupin. *See* Negroes

Curtis, George M.: in Elliott assassination trial, 402

Cynthiana: post-war lynching, 8

Davie, Winston J.: on land prices, 294

Davis, U.S. Senator Garrett: Union Democrat nominee for senator (1867), 17; re-elected (1867), 18; opponent of Cincinnati Southern Railroad Bill, 57; in election of 1864, 469 n.17

Davis, Gen. Jefferson C.: investigates Lebanon lawlessness, 379

Davis, William J.: advocate for public education, 193; Republican nominee for superintendent of public instruction, 351

Dawson, James A.: Democratic nominee for register of land office, 19

Day, Walter R.: Republican nominee for treasurer, 426

Deboe, William J.: elected to U.S. Senate (1897), 365; in Republican Convention (1899), 425; at London rally for Taylor, 430-432; reaction to Contest Committee Hearings (1899), 446

Deming, O.S.: Republican candidate for lieutenant governor, 162

Democratic County Conventions (1883): sentiment of, 213

Democratic National Convention (1896): W.C.P. Breckinridge in, 362-363; William Lindsay in, 363; partial list of delegates, 497 n.20

Democratic Party: ex-Confederate leadership in, 11; 1866 reunification, 16; significance of 1866 victory, 16; opposition to ex-Confederates in, 17; candidates in 1867, 19; victory in 1867, 22; significance of factions in 1868, 24; factions refuse to reconcile in 1868,

24; dominance of ex-Confederates in, 26; post-war factions, 29; reaction to Leslie's victory (1871), 47; reaction to Horace Greeley, 122; majority in Constitutional Convention (1890), 259; problems after election of 1894, 345-346; on "Radical" Republicans, 468 n.8; in election (1867), 470 n.1; currency issue (1876), 482 n.16

Democratic State Convention: *1866*: controlled by pro-southerners, 15; resolutions, 15; beginning of postwar party, 15; *1867*: controlled by pro-Confederates, 19; platform of, 19-20; calls for pardons for ex-Confederates, 20; anti-congressional antagonism in, 470 n.1; *1871*: issues in, 36; proceedings of, 36; gubernatorial contenders, 37; platform of, 38-40; critical of Negro voting, 38; nominees, 38; nominates Leslie for governor and Carlisle for lieutenant governor, 57; resolution condemning lawlessness, 381; praised, 472 n.12; *1872*: Cincinnati Liberal Republican Convention endorsed, 122; platform of, 122; Duke resolution in, 470 n.1; *1875*: contenders for nomination, 132; nominees of, 132; platform of, 132; participants identified, 131-132; victory of, 138; *1876*: chaired by Gen. Lucius Desha, 149; platform of, 149-150; *1879*: 162-165; chaired by John W. Stevenson, 162; candidates nominated, 163; fight over superintendent of public instruction nomination, 164; *1880*: at Lexington Opera House, 210; unit rule defeated, 210; delegates at large selected, 210; Kentucky delegation supports Tilden, 210; Watterson at, 210; *1883*: held in Louisville's Liederkranz Hall, 213; balloting at, 213; Knott nominated, 213; Blackburn unpopular at, 213-215; ticket wins election, 218; disaffection of Greenback part, 487 n.3; *1887*: 228-229; at Liederkranz Hall, 228; presided over by Carlisle, 228; platform of, 229; "Elder" Pickett in, 488 n.27; *1888*: platform of, 249; *1891*: fails to endorse Constitution, 267; nominates John Young Brown for governor, 267; balloting, 317; nominees, 317; bitterness in, 319; *1892*: 329-330; platform of, 329-330; *1895*: 348-349; nominees, 348-349; free silver issue in, 349; platform of, 349; silver question, 495 n.1; *1896*: silverites at, 361; platform of, 361; *1899*: leaders in, 418. *See also* Music Hall Convention

Democrats: decisions within Constitutional Convention (1890), 259; Goebel declared Governor by, 449-450

Democrats, Conservative: favors restoration of Confederate rights, 13

Democrats, Southern Rights wing, 10

Democrats, Union: 3, 10; opposed secession, 3

Denny, George: reaction to Contest Committee Hearings (election of 1899), 446

Depression of 1893: effect on tabacco market, 297; effect on farmers, 298

Desha, Gen. Lucius: chairman of 1871 Democratic convention, 36; in Democratic State Convention of 1875, 131; chairman of 1876 Democratic State Convention, 149; in Liederkranz Hall Convention (1876), 153

Dickey, Rev. John J.: opposes social equality of races, 92-93; public school advocate, 197-198; organizes teachers' institute, 198

dime novels, 273-274

Disciples of Christ; numbers of (1890), 71

Dodge, L.V.: Republican nominee for supt. of public instruction, 320

Doherty, Matt O.: candidate for register of land office, 162

Droege, John C.: Brown Democrat nominee for treasurer, 428

drummers: work of, 307

"Dry": towns and counties, number of (1890's), 74; *See also* Prohibition Party; temperance movement

Duke, Gen. Basil W.: leader of opposition to Cincinnati Southern Railroad, 55; endorses Greeley for U.S. President (1872), 122; in Liederkranz Hall Convention (1876), 153; leader of railroad lobby, 414; criticizes Goebel, 433

"Duke of Buckingham." *See* John Whallen

Dulaney, W. H.: Louisville social and economic leader, 308; approves of militia use in James-Walton disturbance, 359

"Duluth Speech": J. Proctor Knott delivers, 215

Duncan, Henry T.: editor of Lexington *Press*, 279

Durham, Milton Jameson: elected to U.S. Congress (1872), 123; criticizes Democratic party (election of 1887), 234

Duvall, Appellate Court Judge Alvin: Democratic candidate (1864), 11-12; nominee for clerk of Court of Appeals, 15

Duveneck, Frank: 285-286; national reputation of, 286; "Munich style," 286; in Europe, 286; head of Cincinnati Art Academy, 286; contribution to art, 286

Eastern Insane Asylum. *See* eleemosynary institutions

Eastern Kentucky University: *See* Central University

economy: per capita wealth (1887), 308; industrial ranking (1880-90) 308-310; industrial production, 310

education: classrooms and curriculum, 188-190. *See also* colleges; public schools

Election Commission: *See* State Board of Election commissioners

election day: drinking and violence on, 128

elections: *1860* (presidential): Ky.'s vote for Bell, 5; *1864*: Democratic factions join together, 11; judge's race (Court of Appeals), 11-12; Judge Alvin Duvall withdraws, 11-12; Judge George Robertson elected, 12; Gen. Burbridge's interference, 12; Mortimer Murray Benton defeated, 12; Bramlette opposes interference, 12; opposition to interference, 12; former Whigs in, 469 n.17; vote totals in, 469 n.18; *1865*: Democrats win General Assembly,

Federal abuses: issue in 1865 election, 13

Federal troops: Ky. Negroes in 10th U.S. Cavalry, 376; accompany U.S. mail, 383

Feeble-Minded Institute: *See* eleemosynary institutions

Feland, John: Republican candidate for House speaker, 143

Ferguson, Edward A.: promotes Cincinnati Southern Railroad, 54

"Ferguson Bill." *See* Cincinnati Southern Railroad

feuds: effect of political campaigns on, 317; Amis-Strong feud, 385-386; Martin-Tolliver, 387-391; Hatfield-McCoy, 391-395; French-Eversole, 395; Howard-Turner, 395-396; Hargis-Cockrell-Marcum-Callahan, 396-400; characteristic of, 400

"Fiddlin' Mose." *See* James Thomas "Cotton" Noe

Field, Judge Emmet: rules in Beckham-Taylor suits, 451

Fifteenth Amendment: attacked by Gov. Stephenson, 26; favored by Watterson, 26, 30-31; rejected by General Assembly (1869), 26

Fink, Albert: career of, 303

Finley, Charles: in General Assembly (1894), 333; Republican nominee for Secretary of State, 351

Finley, Hugh F.: Republican nominee for U.S. Senator, 27; contender for gubernatorial nomination, 161-162

fiscal reform: need for, 173; Blackburn on, 173-175. *See also* state financial condition

Flute and Violin and Other Kentucky Tales: See James Lane Allen

football: early games, 112; in Kentucky colleges, 112-113; professionalism in, 113; early games described, 113

Foster, Hart: editor of Lexington *Press*, 279

Ford, R.C.: Democratic nominee for treasurer, 348

foreign-born citizens: percentage in urban population, 62

Fortress Monroe, Va.: Kentucky State Guard at (Spanish-American War), 374

Fourteenth Amendment: rejected by General Assembly, 17; reasons for rejection, 17; Republicans favor in (1867), 21; opposed by Union and Confederate Democrats (1867), 21; reaction to ratification of, 25; favored by Watterson, 30-31; opposed by Proctor Knott, 31

Fox, Fontaine Talbot: Prohibition party nominee for governor, 232

Fox, John Jr.: on isolation of eastern Kentucky, 80; on social position, 95; describes "ring" tournaments, 102; *A Knight of the Cumberland*, 102; describes rabbit hunt, 115; career, 270-272; evaluation of, 292. *Works: A Mountain Europa*, 272; "Hell for Sartain," 272; *The Little Shephard of Kingdom Come*, 272; *The Trail of the Lonesome Pine*, 272

Frankfort: shooting incidents, 8; postwar violence, 8; postwar murders, 9; lawless groups in (1871), 382-383

Freedmen's Bureau: opposed by Republicans (1865), 14; opposed by Bourbons, 35; opposition to schools, 204; schools established, 205

Free Silver issue: in Democratic Convention (1895), 348, 349. *See also* Democratic Convention (1895)

French-Eversole feud: 395. *See also* feuds; lawlessness

Friend, R.S.: Prohibition party nominee for clerk of court of appeals, 321

Fry, General Speed S.: Republican nominee for treasurer, 40; Republican nominee for lieutenant governor, 215; defeated for speaker of house, 239

Fulkerson, W. G.: Populist nominee for auditor, 320

fundamentalism: strength of, 73. *See also* religious life

Gaither, Col. Edward H.: leads Louisville Legion to quell James-Walton disturbance, 359; in Spanish-American War, 374

Gardner, Thomas T.: elected president of Farmers' Alliance, 315

Garrard, James H.: elected state treasurer, 469 n.18

Garrigus, Lewis C.: Republican nominee for attorney general, 215

Gay, William: Louisville social and economic leader, 308

General Assembly: *1865-1866*: issues in, 14; Bramlette appeals to, 379-380; *1869* (special session): tries to prevent Negro voting, 26; rejects 15th amendment, 26; passes railroad bonds, 54; *1871-1872*: leaders in house, 48; composition of house, 49; laws against organized violence, 50; fails to improve schools, 51; passes state bonds, 52; opposes additional taxes, 52; private acts, 58-59; care of mentally ill, 59; redistricting legislation, 59; evaluation of, 59; Johnston reports on lawlessness, 384; action on lawlessness, 384; *1873-1874*: acts passed, 129-130; measure against law-breakers passed, 381; act against lawlessness, 499 n.6; *1875-1876*: 142-148; election of speaker, 142-143; candidates for speaker, 143; farmers in, 143; parsimony of, 145; effect of economic program, 145; lack of leadership in, 145; reforms opposed by Bourbons, 145; interest reduction attempt by agrarians, 146; support for tax reduction, 146-147; improves conditions in asylums, 147; eases prison sentences, 147; evaluation of, 147-148; criticized by R. M. Kelly, 148; anti-railroad actions by agrarians, 301; *1877-1878*: 154-161; river improvements considered, 155; special tax bill for river improvements, 156; election of U.S. Senator, 156-157; speaker of house elected, 156-157; nominees for U.S. Senate, 157; Williams elected U.S. Senator, 157; call for constitutional convention, 158-159; state board of health established, 159; influence of Grange, 159; independence of Agricultural and Mechanical College, 159; bills passed,

159; assessment of railroad property, 159; considers "whipping post" law, 159-160; private contracting of prisoners, 160; private legislation, 160; public dissatisfaction with, 160; closing session, 161; *1879-1880*: 176-180; reforms acts, 176; tax reforms, 176; judicial reforms, 176-177; public executions abolished, 177; prison reforms, 180-181; grant A&M College independence, 199; Greenbackers elected to, 210; Railroad Commission Act, 301; prohibition of convict labor, 484 n.7; *1881-1882*: committee on prisons, 181-182; additional railroad act passed, 301; Greenbackers in, 487 n.3; *1883-1884*: tax assessment reforms recommended by Gov. Knott, 220; provides tax increase, 220; provides board of equalization, 220; *1885- 1886*: Knott appeals for tax reform, 220-221; tax reforms enacted, 221; provides for new prison site, 223; ends hiring of convict labor, 223; appointment of prison commissioners, 223; *1887-1888*: 239-241, 245-248; Johnson elected speaker of house, 239; creates state inspector and examiner office, 244; submits constitutional convention call to electorate, 245; acts passed, 245-246; Buckner vetoes private bills, 246; committee to investigate L & N lobby, 302; report of committee to investigage L & N lobby, 302; *1889-1890*: 250-257; speaker elected, 250; Buckner's message to, 251; U.S. Senate election, 251-252; passes property tax reduction, 252; overrides Buckner's veto of property tax reduction, 252; rebuked by Buckner for tax reduction, 255; defended by Watterson, 255-256; criticized by Kelly, 256-257; bill calling constitutional convention, 258; abuses of private legislation, 264; *1891-1892*: 325-329; absenteeism in, 327; extra session, 327; reason for calling extra session, 327-328; revenue legislation, 328; separate coach bill, 328, 494 n.19; exemptions in rev-

INDEX

enue bill, 494 n.18; *1893* (adjourned session): election of U.S. Senator, 331; question of moving state capitol, 331; accepts Morrill-Nelson Act, 331; bills passed, 331; *1894*: 333-336; Gov. Brown's address to, 333-334; railroad consolidation issue, 333-334; Judge Becker's bill on husband-wife property rights, 334; resolutions, 335; statutory reconciliation with constitution, 335; failure to correct constitution election law defects, 336; *1896*: reforms recommended by Bradley, 355-356; Goebel elected president pro tem, 356; Blanford elected speaker, 356; Populists in, 356; election of U.S. Senator, 356-360; ousting of Drs. James and Walton, 358; fails to pass revenue bill, 360; bills passed, 360; evaluation by Louisville *Commercial*, 360; adjournment, 360; Rep. disunity in, 497 n.12; *1897* (special session): 364-365; election of U.S. Senator, 365; state debt issue in, 365; *1898*: Goebel re-elected president pro tem, 366; Beckham elected speaker, 366; John Haswell in, 366; Bradley's reform message, 366-370; reaction to Bradley reform message, 370; attempt to recall Sen. Lindsay, 370; "Goebel Election Law," 370-373; Goebel Bill passes over veto, 371; Goebel Bill criticized, 498 n.31; provisions of McChord Act, 498 n.33; loss of Republican seats, 504 n.65; *1900*: selection of committee on governor's race, 444-445; investigation of Whallen bribery charges, 445; failure to resolve Whallen bribery investigation, 446; ordered to adjourn by Taylor, 449

general store: significance of, 66

Geological survey: recommended by Leslie, 52-53; origins of, 128; praised by McCreary, 144; extended (1876), 147; Brown critical of, 326; Proctor succeeds Shaler, 480 n.14

Georgetown College: football game, 113: curriculum, 202; enrollment, 203; tuition, 203

German immigrants: percentage of urban population, 62; colonies in Ky., 474 n.3. *See also* immigrants

Glasgow: barriers to racial equality, 93

Goddard, W. W.: Prohibition party candidate for auditor, 321

Godkin, E. L.: on Ky. violence, 400

"Goebel Election Law": provisions of, 370-371; passed over Governor's veto, 371; Watterson on, 371-372; Richard Knott on, 372-373; Taylor on, 373; provision for special board, 373; criticized by Richard Knott, 498 n.31. *See also* William Goebel; General Assembly (1898-1900); Music Hall Convention

Goebel, Gov. William: political enemy of L & N, 304; in Constitutional Convention, 346; elected president pro tem of senate (1896), 356; heads committee to investigate Bradley, 359; re-elected president pro tem of senate (1898), 366; "Goebel Election Law," 370-373; selects election commissioners, 371; Watterson on, 372; supported by Hargis, 398; personal background, 410; campaign style of, 410; early years, 412; early career, 412; personality of, 412; attention to railroads, 413-414; legislative years, 413-414; role in railroad legislation, 414; on political opposition, 415; on chances for nomination, 416; on "Tateism," 417, 501 n.12; rumors of Goebel-Stone deal, 417; importance of Sanford killing, 434; shooting of Goebel, 447-449; militia on scene following shooting, 449; sketch of, 464; Separate Coach Bill abstension, 494 n.19; denies congressional nomination to Hallam, 500-501 n.3; Watterson on prospects for election, 502, n.23; L & N opposes, 502 n.33; wound described, 504 n.67; poem eulogizing, 504-505 n.70; buried, 505 n.71; trials, 505 n.73

Goodan, S. B.: in Martin-Tolliver feud, 388

Goodloe, Judge William Cassius: 48; nominee for att. gen., 134; in Republican convention (1875), 134; at Lieder-

INDEX

Hewitt, Fayette: candidate for auditor, 163, 215; exonerated in Tate defalcation, 242

Hill, Judge R. Breck: Democratic nominee for secretary of state (1899), 424

Hindman, James R.: Democratic nominee for lieutenant governor, 215; in National Democratic convention (1896), 362

Hines, E. L.: Brown Democratic nominee for secretary of state, 428

Hines, Henry: in Music Hall Convention (1899), 418

History of Kentucky. See Elizabeth S. Kinkead

History of Kentucky. See William B. Allen

History of Kentucky. See Z. F. Smith

History of Lexington. See George W. Ranck

Hobson, (Gen.) Edward H.: "Conservative" candidate, clerk of the Court of Appeals, 16

Hodges, Albert G.: in Republican State Convention (1872), 480 n.8

Hoke, Judge William B.: linked with Whallen, 342

holiday celebrations; description of, 109

Holmes, J. M.: Prohibition party nominee for treasurer, 321

Holt, Chief Justice Joseph: in Miller v. Johnson (1884), 264

Holt, Judge William Henry: elected to Appellate Court, 227; contender for U.S. Senate nomination (1896), 356-357; in Martin-Tolliver feud, 388

Home Guard (Union): mission, 5-6; requirements, 6; lack of restraint, 6, injustice of, 7; in Civil War, 469 n.11

"Honest Dick" Tate. *See* James W. Tate

Honest Election League: organized by Whallen and Duke, 437; criticized by Goebel, 437

Hopkinsville: dances, 96; minstrel show in, 97

horse shows: description of, 103

horseracing: in Lexington, 103, 105

House of Refuge: 131

Howard-Turner feud: Judge Henry Clay Lilly in, 395; Gov. Buckner in,

395-396; Wilson Howard in, 395; Wilson Lewis in, 396; Kentucky State Guard in, 396. *See also* feuds; lawlessness

Humphrey, W. C. (Cook): in Martin-Tolliver feud, 388-390

hunt clubs: described, 115

Hunter, Dr. W. Godfrey: contender for gubernatorial nomination, 161; contender for U. S. Senate nomination, 356-357; naturalization questioned, 357; acquitted on bribery indictment, 357

"hunts": celebrities attending, 102-103; description of, 103. *See also* fairs and expositions

Huston, Henry E.: Republican nominee for lieutenant governor, 319

illiteracy rate: in 1876, 186; in Negroes, 207-208

immigrants: small percentage of, 61; concentrations of, 61; to Ky. (1875), 482 n.6. *See also* German immigrants

Independent Colored Voters League: supports Goebel, 435

Insane Asylums. *See* eleemosynary institutions

Institution for Deaf Mutes. *See* eleemosynary institutions

Institute for the Blind. *See* eleemosynary institutions

Institution for the Education and Training of Feeble-Minded Children. *See* eleemosynary institutions

interest rates: attempt to reduce, opposed by banks and newspapers, 146; attempt to reduce succeeds (1876), 146

Irish immigrants: percentage in urban population, 62. *See also* immigrants

Iroquois Hunt and Riding Club of the Bluegrass, 115

Jacobs, Mayor Charles D.: contender for Democratic gubernatorial nomination, 213; plagued by mob violence (1877), 310; reaction to L & N strike (1877), 311

Jacobs, Lt. Gov. Richard Taylor: Union Democratic leader (1867), 20

Brenner, 289; in Martin-Tolliver feud, 390; sketch of, 460, 487 n.5

Knott, Richard: editor of Louisville *Evening Post,* 279; ridicules Populism, 315; evaluation of Buckner, 324; critical of Buckingham gang, 342; on Democratic defeat (election 1894), 344-345; on Bradley's nomination, 349; on Hardin and Bradley debate, 353; approves State Guard use in James-Walton disturbance, 359; on "Goebel Election Law," 372-373; on Goebel, 412-413; joins Brown Democrats, 428; reaction to Contest Committee Hearings (election of 1899), 446; criticizes Goebel Bill, 498 n.31. *See also* Louisville *Evening Post*

Knox County: vote fraud charged (1899), 441

Krieger, William: in General Assembly, 333

Krippenstapel, William: Republican nominee for auditor, 40

Krock, Arthur: on race relations in Glasgow, 93-94; on Hayes-Tilden election deal, 154

Ku Klux Klan: depredations of, 8; postwar political connections of, 9; in immediate postwar period, 49; actions against, 50; political connections of, 377, 381; Watterson on, 381; opposed by Gov. Leslie, 381; attack on Negroes in Stamping Ground, 383; attack on Negroes in Watkinsville, 383. *See also* lawlessness

labor: 310-313; efforts to remedy shortages, 313

Laffoon, Polk: in Spanish-American War, 376

landscape artists: Paul Sawyier, 285; Robert Burns Wilson, 285; Carl Brenner, 285. *See also* artists

Langley, John W.: in General Assembly (1889-1890), 250

lawlessness: postwar, 58; political associations, 9; and Ku Klux Klan, 49; action against, 50; Gov. Leslie on, 124; "Commissioner of Inquiry," 124; election day, 128; effect of political campaigns, 317; during gubernatorial campaign (1895), 353; James-Walton disturbance, 357-359; background of, 377-378; in Bowling Green, 379; in Franklin, 379; in Frankfort, 382-383; Ku Klux Klan at Watkinsville and Stamping Ground, 383; State Guard to Frankfort, 383; North Benson attack on Negroes, 383; U.S. Mail interrupted, 383; investigation by Adj. Gen. Johnston, 384; action by General Assembly (1871), 384; lynching in Owingsville, 384; Amis-Strong feud, 385-386; in mountains, 385-387; in Breathitt County, 385-387; eastern Ky. Regulators, 386-387; in Rowan County, 387; Rowan County War, 387-391; Martin-Tolliver feud, 387-391; in Pike County, 391-396; French-Eversole feud, 395; Hatfield-McCoy feud, 391-395; Howard-Turner feud, 395-396; in Harlan County, 395-96; Hargis-Cockrell-Marcum-Callahan feud, 396-400; in Breathitt County, 396-400; in the Bluegrass, 400-408; E. L. Godkin on, 400; assassination of Elliott, 401-402; Watterson on, 401; Swope-Goodloe murder, 402-404; Buckner on, 408; Ky.'s reputation for, 409; Gen. Assembly 1873 Act against, 499 n. 6; McCreary's report to legislature, 499 n. 12; report on Rowan Co. violence, 499 n. 17. *See also* feuds; Toll Gate War

Lawrence County: Mutual Protective Society, 67

Lebanon lawlessness: 378-379; "Capt. Skaags" in, 378-379; violence against Negroes, 379; investigated by Davis, 379

Legal reform: recommended by Bradley, 369-370

legislature: *See* General Assembly

Leslie, Gov. Preston Hopkins: succeeds Stevenson as Governor (1871), 27; opposes 14th and 15th amendments, 31; Democratic gubernatorial nominee (1871), 37; background of, 37; opposed by New Departure Democrats,

Lyon, Gen. Hylan B.: appointed prison commissioner, 181

McBeath, K. C.: National party candidate for register of land office, 169

McChesney, Harry V.: Democratic nominee for superintendent of public instruction, 424

McChord, Charles C.: Railroad Commission Bill, 414; appointed to Railroad Commission, 325

McChord, William C.: on commission to conform statutes with 1891 Constitution, 268; appointed to statutory commission, 326

McClarty, Joseph K.: Republican nominee for register of land office, 40

McCoy, Randolph: in Hatfield-McCoy feud, 392

McCreary, Gov. James Bennett: member of House (1871), 48; elected speaker of the House (1871), 57; in Democratic state convention (1875), 132; in gubernatorial campaign (1875), 137; inaugurated governor, 139; inaugural address of, 139-140; message to General Assembly (1876), 143-144; reforms recommended to General Assembly (1876), 143-144; Geological survey praised, 144; on Negro education, 144-145; on state spending for Ky. River, 154-155; reasons for call on river improvements, 155; recommends spending for river improvements, 155; nominated for U. S. Senate (1877), 157; state of the commonwealth address (1878), 157; on state's financial condition (1878), 157; on "Ky. War Claim," 157; on public education, 157-158; on prison reform, 158; evaluation of administration, 170; evaluates his administration, 171; administration evaluated by Louisville *Commercial*, 171; contender in Senate race (1889), 251; reaction to L & N Railroad strike (1877), 311; contender for U. S. Senate nomination (1896), 356; sends State Guard in Amis-Strong feud, 385; in Music Hall Convention, 422; sup-

ports Goebel in campaign, 429; sketch of, 461; cautiousness of, 481 n.31

McCreery, Sen. Thomas C.: elected U. S. Senator (1868), 24; in U. S. Senate election (1869), 27

McDermott, Edward J.: on tariff reform, 224-225; in Democratic campaign (1884), 224-225; in Constitutional Convention (1890), 260; candidate for U. S. Congress (1894), 337

McGregor, Bradford: Prohibition party nominee for register of land office, 321

Machen, U. S. Sen. Willis B.: on Railroad commission, 302; appointed U. S. Senator, 302

McHenry, Henry Davis: in Constitutional Convention, 260

McIntyre, Malcolm: candidate for superintendent of public instruction, 162

McKee, Capt. R. W.: in Martin-Tolliver feud, 390

Mackoy, William H.: in Constitutional Convention, 260; joins Brown Democrats, 428

McManama, Judge O. D.: in Elliott assassination trial, 402

McQuown, Louis: in post-election controversy (1899), 443

Magoffin, Gov. Beriah: at Liederkranz Hall Convention (1876), 153

Male High School: curriculum of, 190. *See also* public schools

manufacturing: early growth, 306

Marion County: "Rowzee's band" lawlessness in, 380

Marcum, John B.: in Hargis-Cockrell-Marcum-Callahan feud, 396

Marcum, Thomas D.: nominee for register of land office, 132

"Marse Henry." *See* Henry Watterson

Marshall, Edward C.: in Liederkranz Hall Convention, 153

Marshall, John: Republican nominee for lieutenant governor, 426; reaction to Contest Committee hearings, 446

Martin, Henry L.: contender for U. S. Senate nomination, 365

Martin, John: in Martin-Tolliver feud, 388-89

intendent of public instruction, 164; Democratic candidate for superintendent of public instruction (1879), 165; advocate of public education, 193; advocates local school tax, 193; aids black education, 206-207; supports higher education for blacks, 207; Democratic nominee for superintendent of public instruction (1883), 215; in Dem. Convention (1887), 488 n.27

Pigman, Hiram M.: in Martin-Tolliver feud, 390

Pike County: violence in, 391-396. *See also* lawlessness; Hatfield-McCoy feud

Pikeville: State Guard at, 394

Pinkerton, Elder James P.: Republican nominee for superintendent of public instruction (1883), 215

plow, chilled iron: use of, 75. *See also* agriculture

poetry: 274-275. *See also* literature and the arts

Polk, E. J.: Prohibition party nominee for attorney general, 321

Pollard, Ott: in Hargis-Cockrell-Marcum-Callahan feud, 396

poll tax: for Negro schools, 205, *See also* Negroes

population: percentage of Negroes in, 61; homogeneity of, 62

Populism: Populist party organized by Blair, 315; nominees of Populist party (1891), 320; platform of party, 320-321; significance of Populist vote (1891), 321-324; Populist candidate Pettit defeated for speaker (1891-1892), 326; Weaver nominated for president (1892), 330; Gov. Brown and, 334; party nominates Pettit for governor (1895), 351; in General Assembly (1896), 356; fusion with silver Democrats (1896), 361; Watterson on, 363; nominates Blair for gov., 436; convention critical of Goebel, 436; strength in Western Ky., 494 n.13; 1895 Convention, 495 n.3; nominees in election (1899), 503 n.46

Potter College: merges with Ogden College, 203. *See also* Southern Normal College

Potter, Henry: National party candidate for auditor, 169

Powell, Gov. Lazarus W.: U.S. Senatorial nominee (1867), 17

Powers, Caleb: Republican nominee for sec. of state (1899), 426; at London rally for Taylor, 430-432; on mountaineers in Frankfort, 504 n.64; held for trial, 453

Poyntz, Charles B.: appointed to railroad commission, 325; appointed to State Election Commission, 414

Pratt, Att. Gen. Judge Clifton J.: in Republican convention (1899), 425; Republican nominee for Attorney General, 426; contest for office, 505 n.72

Pratt, Rev. William Moody: 46; on religion in Ky., 71

Prentice, George D.: hires Watterson, 278

Presbyterians: numbers of in 1890, 71. *See also* religious life

presidential elections. *See* elections of *1880, 1884, 1888, 1892, 1896*

Preston, Gen. William: in Liederkranz Hall Convention (1876), 153; selected as delegate-at-large in Democratic National Convention (1880), 210; in election (1864), 469 n.17

Price, Samuel Woodson: sporting prints artist, 285

prisons: conditions in, 127, 159-160, 178; contracting prisoners, 127; Blackburn calls for new prison, 178; easing of sentences, 147; private contracting of labor, 160; reform of 1880, 177-182; Blackburn on reform, 177-181; Blackburn on conditions in, 178; reforms enacted, 180; site chosen for new penitentiary, 181; commissioners appointed, 181; General Assembly (1881-1882) recommends reforms, 182; management of, in Bradley's Reform Message (1898), 368; population of (1875), 482 n.5

private academies: characteristics of, 187. *See also* public schools

INDEX

Proctor, John R.: training for geological survey, 480 n.14

professional schools: development of, 203-204

Prohibition Party: in election (1887), 232; nominees (1891), 321; platform of (1891), 321; Bidwell nominated for president (1892), 330. *See also* elections of *1887, 1891, 1892*

property tax reduction by General Assembly (1889-1890): vetoed by Buckner, 252

property valuation: Blackburn on, 176

Pryor, Chief Justice William Samuel: in Tate Defalcation, 245; re-elected to appellate court (1888), 249; in Bradley's inaugration, 355; appointed to state election commission, 371, 414; appointed to succeed Robertson, 473 n.25

public schools: financial conditions of (1867), 185; school tax ratified by electorate, 185; enrollment (1871), 186; school fund (1871), 186; illiteracy rates, 186; prejudice against common schools, 187; condition of schoolhouses, 188-189; Compulsory Attendance Law passed (1896), 189; elementary curriculum, 189-190; textbooks in, 190; qualifications of teachers, 191; low salaries of teachers, 191; qualifications of superintendent, 191-192; improvements by Henderson, 192; local support of, 193; provisions of Common School Law, 193-196; quality not uniform, 196; compared to neighboring states, 196-197; Negro enrollment, 205; characterized, 208-209; reforms recommended by Knott, 222; Buckner on status in 1887, 241; in Bradley's reform message (1898), 369; cost of, 483 n.42; textbook list, 485 n.8; teacher-pupil ratio (1870), 485 n.9; local versus federal financing, 485 n.13; conditions in mountain schools, 486 n.17. *See also* Sinking Fund

Pusey, Dr. Robert B.: charges for treatment, 84; calls by, 85

"Quadrilateral,": *See* Liberal Republican Movement

racial segregation: beginnings in Louisville, 90-91; not sudden development, 91; informal, 91. *See also* Negroes

"Radicals". *See* Republicans, radical

Railroad Commission: Buckner on, 241; provisions of Railroad Commission Act, 301; Railroad Commission Act passed, 301; first commissioners, 302; assessment of railroads by, 328; bill to establish, 414

railroads: passes issued to slaves, 3; bonds opposed by L & N, 54; Buckner on abuses, 240; Buckner on regulation reforms, 241; effect on rural lifestyle, 299-300; stock subscriptions, 300; mileage increases, 300; earnings in Ky., 300; companies chartered by legislature, 300; bonds floated, 300; farmers' antagonism toward, 300; political influence of, 301; Board of Equalization abolished, 301; provisions of additional railroad act, 301; rapid growth of, 304; effect of railroads in mountains, 304-305; strike against, 310; Goebel's attention to, 413-414; Goebel's role in legislation, 414; lobby led by Duke, 414; stock owned by state, 473 n.35

Ranck, George W.: published works, 273. *Work: History of Lexington*, 273

Randall, Judge William H.: contender for gubernatorial nomination, 161; in Amis-Strong feud, 385

Rardin, W. J. A.: Republican nominee for register of land office, 320

Ratliffe, Rodolphus B.: nominee for auditor, 134

recreation: early forms of, 113-115

redistricting: in General Assembly (1871-1872), 59

Redwine, Judge David B.: influenced by Hargis, 398; in Music Hall Convention (1899), 418-423; elected chairman at Music Hall Convention, 419, 501 n.15

Reed, William Murphy: contender for U. S. Senate nomination, 357

Regular Democrats: favored by Union Democrats, 11

Robinson, Dr. Stuart: opposes women's suffrage, 87

Rockcastle Springs: description of, 105-108

Rodman, John: Democratic nominee for attorney general (1867), 19, (1871), 38; in Elliott assassination trial, 402

Roland, George J.: and assassination of Judge John M. Elliott, 401

Rowan County War: 387-391; report on violence, 499 n.17. *See also* feuds; lawlessness

"Rowzee's band": lawlessness in Marion Co., 380. *See also* lawlessness

rural Kentucky: triumph of ethos, 65; provincial background of, 65; description of, 65-66; effect of railroad on lifestyle, 299-300. *See also* agriculture

Ryan, Charles, 1: in Whallen bribery investigation, 445

Sallee, I. G.: Populist candidate for treasurer, 320

Sanford, John: political opponent of Goebel, 413; shot by Goebel, 434

Sawyier, Paul: 285; early life, 289-292; art education of, 292; Frankfort influence on, 292; paintings by, 292; and Arthur F. Jones, 491 n.18

School reform. *See* Public schools

School tax. *See* Public schools

Schurz, Carl: advocate of Liberal Republican Movement, 118, 119

sculpture and music: 282-283

Sebree Springs: description of, 108

secession crisis: political parties, 10

Separate Coach Act: repeal recommended by Bradley, 369; issue in campaign (1899), 435; favored by Goebel, 435; in Lexington, 477 n.41

Settle, Evan Evans: contender in U. S. Senate race (1899), 251; candidate for U. S. Congress (1894), 337; in Elliott assassination trail, 402

Shackelford, Sam J.: in Music Hall Convention (1899), 418

Shadows of the Tree, The. See Robert Burns Wilson

Shaler, Nathaniel Southgate: on immigration, 61-62; on Ky. character, 94; appointed Geological survey head, 128; published works, 273; evaluation of, 273. *Work: Kentucky: A Pioneer Commonwealth*, 273

Sharp, Stephen G.: appointed state treasurer, 244; Democratic nominee for treasurer (1889), 249; elected treasurer, 250; background of, 480 n.14

Shelby County: postwar violence, 8-9

Sheldon, Ralph: candidate for register of land office, 163

Sheriffs: acts for relief of, 382

Silverites: opposed Bradley, 359-360

Sims, James H.: in commission for statutory conformity to 1891 Constitution, 268; appointed to statutory commission, 326

Sinking Fund: deficit, 51; state borrowing from, 124; misuse by state, 125; payments by Ky. River Navigation Co., 155; misuse of, 173; Watterson on misuse of, 217; abuse of, 473 n.32; abuse of, 483 n.41. *See also* public schools

Sizemore, Adam: in Martin-Tolliver feud, 388

Smith, D. Howard: Democratic nominee for auditor (1867), 19; Democratic nominee for auditor (1871), 38; nominee for re-election as auditor (1875), 132; on railroad commission, 302

Smith, Milton H.: president of L & N, 302, 303. *See also* Louisville and Nashville Railroad

Smith, Rev. S. E.: on Separate Coach Act, 435; supports Taylor, 435-436

Smith, S. F.: Populist nominee for lieutenant governor (1891), 320

Smith, Col. Thomas J.: in Spanish-American War, 374

Smith, Zachariah F.: Democratic nominee for superintendent of public instruction (1867), 19; educational program of, 185; on need for public education, 186-187; published works, 273. *Work: History of Kentucky*, 273

social activities: entertainments, 96; dances, 96; parties, 96; county court

Superior Court: establishment of, 183-184; justices selected, 184; eliminated, 184; need for, 484 n.12

Swango, Green Berry: Democratic nominee for register of land office (1895), 349

Sweeney, Rev. John S.: Republican nominee for auditor (1899), 426

Sweeney, William H. ("Roaring Bill"): in Music Hall Convention, 418-421; joins Brown Democrats, 428; in Contest Committee hearings, 446

Swope, Col. Armistead M.: in Swope-Goodloe murder, 402-404

Tanner, L. P.: Brown Democrat nominee for attorney general, 428

Tate defalcation episode: 242-245; investigation urged, 242; investigation delayed, 242; commission appointed, 242; Tate missing, 242; treasury shortage discovered, 242; suspicions surrounding, 242; Fayette Hewitt suspected and exonerated; 242; Murdock testimony in, 243; Tate impeached and expelled, 243; investigative commissioners in, 243; total embesseled, 243; total larceny, 244; Tate escapes, 244; Tate indicted, 244; Chief Justice Pryor in, 245; effect of, 245; effect on Constitutional Convention, 260

Tate, James W. "Honest Dick": Democratic nominee for treasurer (1867), 19; Democratic nominee for treasurer (1871), 38; nominee for re-election as treasurer (1875), 132; re-elected treasurer (1877), 156; candidate for treasurer (1879), 163; Democratic nominee for treasurer (1883), 215; re-elected treasurer (1885), 227; personality of, 242-243; impeached and expelled, 243; escapes, 244; indicted for embezzlement, 244; whereabouts after escape, 488 n.4. See also Tate defalcation episode

taxes: property, 124-125; reductions, 146-147; Knott on assessment, 176; reforms enacted, 176, 220-221. See also General Assembly

Taylor, Gov. William Sylvester: Republican nominee for attorney general (1895), 351; on Goebel Election Law, 373; contender for Republican governor nomination (1899), 425; opposed by Negro leaders, 425; nominated at Republican Convention, 425-426; personal background, 426; Irvin Cobb on, 426; London speech, 432; Clinton speech, 432; on Goebel bill, 432; opposed segregated railroad cars, 435; supported by blacks, 435-436; election as governor certified, 443-444; inaugurated gov., 444; reaction to Contest Committee hearings, 446; state of insurrection declared, 449; General Assembly ordered to adjourn, 449; following Goebel's death, 450-451; settlement proposal refuse, 451; fails to invalidate "Contest Board," 453; unseated as governor, 453; appeal to Supreme Court, 453; flees state, 453; sketch of, 463; election certification and inaugural speech, 503-504 n.58; declaration of insurrection, 504 n.68

"Telephone Girl": written by Gustave Kerber, 282

temperance movement: effect on whiskey production, 73; rise of local option, 73; chautauquas in, 74; number of dry counties (1890), 74; number of dry towns (1890), 74; failure of in eastern Ky., 74; Women's Christian Temperance Union in, 74; The Order of Good Templars in, 74; agitation of organizations (1873-1874), 129; Depression of 1893 and, 476 n.23; non-temperance at barbecue, 476 n.25

tenantry: increases in, 298; percentage of in farm population, 298; percentage of Black tenants in farm population, 298

Tennessee College: in football games, 113

tent shows: competition for theaters, 98; in Maysville, 98; types of, 100

theater: typical plays, 96-97; Edwin Booth performs, 97, 478, n.7; Macauley's theater founded, 97; Mary Anderson debuts, 97; audience preferences, 97; in rural Ky., 97; in Lexington, 98; vari-

INDEX

University of Kentucky. *See* Agricultural & Mechanical College

urban growth: threats to, 63-64

vagrancy laws: effect of an labor supply, 313

vigilantes: "Regulators," 7; hangings by, 9

violence. *See* lawlessness

Wadsworth, William Henry: contender for gubernatorial nomination, 162

"Wagoner Joe." *See* James Thomas "Cotton" Noe

Walton, Dr. J.: ousted from senate, 357-359

Walton, W. P.: editor of Stanford *Interior Journal,* 282

Ward, J. Q. A.: in National Democratic Convention, 362

Watkinsville: Negroes attacked by Ku Klux Klan, 383

Watterson, Henry: favors 15th amendment, 26; reasons for favoring 14th and 15th amendments, 29-31; leader of "New Departure" Democrats, 29; advocates postwar reconciliation, 31; advocates postwar industrial change, 31; favors natural resources development, 33; on Harlan as candidate, 42; committed to Democratic party, 44; reaction to Republican defeat in 1871, 47; reaction to Democratic victory (1871), 48; on significance of Leslie's victory, 48; on lawlessness, 49; leader of opposition to Cincinnati Southern Railroad, 55; opposes women's suffrage, 87; at the Bluegrass Chautauqua, 108; allies with Liberal Republican Movement, 119; supports Horace Greeley for president, 120; on Greeley's campaign for president, 120-121; endorses 1875 Democratic state ticket, 132; on defeat of 1875 Constitutional Convention, 139; on economy versus reform (1876), 145; opposes interest rate reduction (1876), 146; attacks Republican tariff, 148-149; supports Tilden for president, 150; serves in U. S. House, 151-152; calls for mass protests

(1876), 152; effect of call for protest in Ky., 152-153; effect of Hayes-Tilden deal on, 154; on inland waterways, 156; criticizes General Assembly (1877-1878), 160; predicts Democratic victory (1879), 165; on Blackburn, 165; gives A & M College address, 200; proposes unit rule at Democratic State Convention (1880), 210; selected as delegate to Democratic National Convention (1880), 210; editorializes for reform (1883), 213; supports Democratic ticket (1883), 217; on misuse of sinking fund, 217; critical of Bradley, 218; praises Hardin, 218; criticizes James G. Blaine, 224; on Democratic State Convention (1887), 228; evaluation of Knott's administration, 237; on Buckner's vetoes, 246; evaluates Buckner's administration, 247-248; displeased with Cleveland, 248; defends General Assembly (1889-1890), 255; opposes ratification of 1891 Constitution, 265; on Constitution of 1891, 265-266; managing editor of Louisville *Journal,* 278; hired by Prentice, 278; early life, 278; and New Departure, 279; editorial style of, 279; on Louisville's wealth, 307; on L & N strike (1887), 310-311; ridicules Populism, 315; on presidential election (1892), 329; advocates revenue tariff at Democratic National Convention (1892), 330; supports "Buckingham" ticket (1894), 342; on election of 1894, 343-344; anti-free silver, 348; on Hardin-Bradley debate, 353; contender for U. S. Senate nomination (1896), 356-357; on James-Walton disturbance, 358; on Populism, 363; on "Goebel Election Law," 371-372; on Goebel, 372; on lawlessness, 381; on lynching of Bascom (Owingsville), 384-385; supports Goebel, 424; eulogy of Goebel, 450; on presidential election (1872), 480 n.10; on Bradley, 497 n.10; on Goebel's prospects for election, 502 n.23. *See also* Louisville *Courier-Journal*

INDEX

LaVergne, TN USA
18 January 2011
212935LV00001B/41/P